DAVID J. GOLDBERG

JOHN D. RAYNER

THE JEWISH PEOPLE

THEIR HISTORY

AND THEIR RELIGION

VIKING

VIKING

Penguin Books Ltd, Harmondsworth, Middlesex, England
Viking Penguin Inc., 40 West 23rd Street, New York, New York 10010, U.S.A.
Penguin Books Australia Ltd, Ringwood, Victoria, Australia
Penguin Books Canada Limited, 2801 John Street, Markham, Ontario, Canada L3R 1B4
Penguin Books (N.Z.) Ltd, 182–190 Wairau Road, Auckland 10, New Zealand

First published 1987
Copyright © David J. Goldberg and John D. Rayner, 1987

Typeset in Monophoto Plantin
Printed in Great Britain by
Richard Clay Ltd, Bungay, Suffolk

British Library Cataloguing in Publication Data

Goldberg, David J.
　　The Jewish people: their history and their religion.
　　1. Jews – History
　　I. Title II. Rayner, John D.
　　909'.04924 DS117

ISBN 0-670-81219-6

CONTENTS

v

CONTENTS

ILLUSTRATIONS

Mosaic from the synagogue at Beit Alpha, Israel (*Wiener Library*)

An engraving of Joseph honoured by Pharoah (*Mary Evans Picture Library*)

Moses and Aaron and the Ten Commandments; an oil painting by Aaron de Chavez (d. 1705), the first Jewish painter to work in England (*BBC Hulton Picture Library*)

The building of Solomon's Temple; an engraving thought to be after Raphael (*BBC Hulton Picture Library*)

Anti-Semitic propaganda: the Jews of Cologne burnt alive, from a woodcut in the *Liber Chronicarum Mundi*, published in 1463 (*Mary Evans Picture Library*)

Baruch Spinoza (1632–77) (*BBC Hulton Picture Library*)

Moses Mendelssohn (1729–86); an engraving of 1772 after a painting by Anton Graffe (*Mary Evans Picture Library*)

The festival of Tabernacles, after an engraving by Picart, 1737 (*Mary Evans Picture Library*)

The search for leaven, after an engraving by Picart (*BBC Hulton Picture Library*)

The Jews expelled from eastern Rumelia, 1885 (*Mary Evans Picture Library*)

Emigration to America: Russians arriving at New York in 1892; a contemporary engraving from the *Illustrated London News* (*Mary Evans Picture Library*)

An anti-Dreyfus caricature, *c.* 1895, from a French magazine (*Jean-Loup Charmet*)

The disgrace of Captain Dreyfus: Dreyfus is reduced to the ranks, 1895; an illustration from a French magazine (*Jean-Loup Charmet*)

Zionists harvest their own grapes on an early commune in Palestine (*Historical Archives, Jerusalem*)

A Jewish book-seller in Whitechapel, 1952 (*BBC Hulton Picture Library*)

Theodor Herzl (1860–1904) (*Mary Evans Picture Library*)

A *cheder* in Slonim (now in the USSR), 1938 (*Roman Vishniac*)

A boy reading his bar-mitzvah portion (*Wiener Library*)

vii

ILLUSTRATIONS

A girl deported from Czechoslovakia by the Nazis (*Wiener Library*)

On the way to his first day at a *cheder* in Mukachevo, a town in the Ukraine, 1938 (*Roman Vishniac*)

'Jew baiting' in Austria: a Nazi passes an optician's shop in Vienna that is daubed with the word 'Jew' and a swastika in red and black paint (*The Photo Source*)

The Western Wall, Jerusalem, at the turn of the century (*Wiener Library*)

The Western Wall, Jerusalem, after 1967, when it came back into Israeli hands (*The Photo Source*)

The woodcut illustrations on the title and half-title pages are reproduced from *Die Prager Hagada von 1526*, published by the Verlag für Jüdischer Kunst und Kultur Fritz Gurlitt, Berlin 1920. The Hebrew alphabet reproduced on the chapter openings was used in Christopher Plantin's *Biblia sacra* of 1569. Photos courtesy of Berthold Wolpe.

PREFACE

It is with great diffidence that one presumes to add yet another book to the enormous stockpile of literature which over the centuries has accreted around 'the people of the Book'. That Jews should be interested in themselves is understandable; but their experience in history has aroused almost as much interest and comment from outside observers. Their stubborn fidelity to the faith of their ancestors, their resilience in adversity and their knack of adapting their talents and energies to changed circumstances, have ensured their survival long after the Greek civilization, which treated them with condescension, and the Roman empire, which held them in contempt, have passed into oblivion.

The two great religions of Christianity and, to a lesser extent, Islam owe their being to Judaism. The complexities of coping with a rejected mother religion whose adherents refused to convert or disappear encouraged medieval Christianity to excesses of anti-Jewish persecution which led, ultimately and inexorably, to the horrors of Hitler's Holocaust; and even Islam, with a theology more respectful towards Abraham and his monotheistic descendants, has on occasion been guilty of savage hostility towards its Jewish subjects.

Small wonder, then, that this numerically insignificant people and their religion – located, by chance or providence, at the geographical and cultural crossroads of early western civilization – should have exerted such a perennial fascination. During the Age of Enlightenment the notion took root among those sympathetic to Judaism that the manner in which the state treated its Jewish minority was a barometer of its civilization. The appalling evidence of the concentration camps prompted a surge of guilty sympathy from western countries towards the survivors of Belsen and Auschwitz, but since the establishment of the State of Israel – a state which has revived biblical language and place-names but

ix

behaves, on occasion, like any other modern practitioner of *realpolitik* –the Jew once again is at the centre of attention, and ultra-sensitive to the notion that his critics may be motivated not by political considerations – anti-Zionism – but by something more banefully persistent – anti-Semitism.

To say this is not to transfer all the guilt to the outside world. It is only now, nearly half a century after the event, that we Jews feel capable of the most tentative exploration of the trauma inflicted upon the collective Jewish psyche by Hitler's attempted genocide. That the loss of one-third of our people is a gaping wound is self-evident. To what extent it has healed, or whether any people can survive such a blow without permanent damage to the ideological assumptions which have traditionally underpinned their sense of historic vocation, is something only time will tell.

For the present, there is a need to update and evaluate Judaism – the entwined history of a people and their religious culture – for the contemporary reader. This historical and religious survey is offered as a modest attempt to do that. It tries to be comprehensive, but cannot claim to be exhaustive. It is a general synopsis which will serve as an introduction for the interested layman, or new student, to Judaism. Unlike most books on the subject, it seeks to present within a single volume both a chronological account of the history and literature, and a thematic analysis of the teachings and practices of Judaism. The select bibliography suggests further reading in the major areas of a national and religious history which is now nearly 4,000 years old.

Although we are both Progressive rabbis – and, as such, representative of the non-Orthodox section within Jewry – we have been conscious, when dealing with theology or ritual, of our duty to present primarily the *normative* Jewish response as it has evolved over the centuries. Where Progressive Judaism differs significantly from tradition we say so, but we try to refrain from making value judgements. Our aim has been to write a text which *all* Jews, whatever their synagogue affiliation, can read as an honest, factual survey of the history and religious culture we share, and which will be a useful guide to the rich variety of the Jewish heritage for non-Jews.

As close colleagues, and even closer friends, for many years, we accept joint accountability for the book's merits and defects, but the reader may care to know that David Goldberg was primarily responsible for the history section and a measure of overall synthesis, and John Rayner for the sections on literature, theory and practice.

Ministering to one of the largest Progressive Jewish communities in Europe leaves little time for the concerted study and thought involved in producing a book such as this. However, we would like to thank those congregants and study groups on whom we 'tried out' sections of the book during its gestation period. It was Felicity Bryan, the sweetest, steeliest of literary agents, who bullied us into completing the manuscript, and David Goldberg's secretary, Valerie Asher, who deciphered much of his handwriting and typed the final copy. Stephen Davies has been our sensitive, perceptive editor at Penguin Books. David Goldberg is pleased to record his personal thanks to two dear friends, Carole and Ash Lawrence, who loaned him their lovely cottage in Ravensdale, Derbyshire, which provided the ideal ambience in which to walk, think and write.

Finally, but most important of all, our respective spouses, Carole-Ann Goldberg and Jane Rayner, have been staunch, long-suffering partners whose worth is far above the price of rubies. We gratefully acknowledge our debt to them.

David J. Goldberg
John D. Rayner
London, 1987

INTRODUCTORY NOTE

Judaism is the religion – and, in a broader sense, the culture – of a unique people which, in the course of its history of nearly four thousand years, has been variously known as Hebrews, Israelites and Jews.

'Hebrews' refers primarily to their earliest ancestors, Abraham, Isaac and Jacob. Jacob was also called Israel, and 'children of Israel' or 'Israelites' refers to his descendants, who comprised twelve tribes. The tribe that claimed descent from Jacob's fourth son, Judah, gave its name to a kingdom whose capital was Jerusalem, and later, under Persian, Greek and Roman rule, to the province of Judea. 'Jews' comes from 'Judeans' and refers to their descendants as well as those who have joined them as converts.

For the last two thousand years Jews have lived scattered in many lands, but have always retained a presence in their ancient homeland on the eastern seaboard of the Mediterranean, where the present State of Israel was established in 1948. At the time of writing it is estimated that, in very rough figures, the Jews number fourteen million, including three million in the State of Israel. The Jewish communities of the rest of the world, collectively known as the Diaspora ('dispersion'), account for the remaining eleven million and include 5.8 million in the United States of America and something under 400,000 in Great Britain.

The ancient Jews spoke a Semitic language, Hebrew, written from right to left in a pictographic script which, however, was ultimately abandoned in favour of the alphabetic script of another Semitic language, Aramaic. In the Diaspora, Jews have retained Hebrew chiefly as a language of prayer and study; in Israel it is again the language of daily speech.

The Hebrew alphabet comprises twenty-two letters, all consonants. It was not until the early Middle Ages that a system of diacritic signs, consisting of dots and dashes, was devised to represent the vowels. These are used when necessary, but for most purposes Hebrew is still written and printed without vowels.

The twenty-two consonants serve as numerals as well as letters, the first ten representing the numbers one to ten; the next eight, twenty to ninety; the last four, one hundred to four hundred.

There is a large vocabulary of Hebrew terms for Jewish religious concepts and customs, institutions and functionaries, sacred books and ritual objects, with which one needs to become familiar if one wishes to understand Judaism at a more than superficial level. Accordingly, we shall introduce as many of them as seems appropriate in a work of this kind.

This poses a problem of transliteration. We shall use a system which is not scientific but designed to help the reader who is not a Hebraist to pronounce the words with some ease and with a modicum of accuracy. For this purpose he needs to know that the vowels are to be pronounced according to the values they have in European languages such as German and Italian; that 'ch' is meant to indicate the guttural in Scottish *loch* or German *Bach*; and that the apostrophe denotes a glottal stop.

Plurals are usually formed in Hebrew by the masculine suffix *im* or the feminine suffix *ot*. For example, the plural of *kibbutz* is *kibbutzim* and the plural of *mitzvah* is *mitzvot*. Sometimes, however, nouns and adjectives undergo internal changes when they are lengthened by a suffix.

Although Jews have written books in many languages, the classic texts of Jewish religious literature – Bible, Mishnah, Talmud, Midrash – as well as the Zohar and most of the codes, commentaries and responsa, were written in Hebrew or Aramaic or a mixture of the two. With the exception of the Bible, our translations of quotations from these works are our own, though frequently influenced, consciously or unconsciously, by published translations in so far as they exist, particularly H. Danby's translation of the Mishnah, and the Talmud and Midrash translations of the Soncino Press under the general editorship of Rabbi Dr I. Epstein, and of Rabbi Dr H. Freedman and Maurice Simon, respectively.

In the case of the Bible we decided to use the Revised Standard Version as a good compromise between old and new styles, and likely to be familiar to many readers. However, we have taken the liberty of capitalizing He, His and Him when the reference is to God, in conformity with our practice throughout the book; and in a few instances we have modified the translation of a verse so as to bring out the sense in which it was understood by the Rabbis for exegetical purposes.

The Revised Standard Version, however, stems from the Christian tradition, which goes back to the ancient Greek and Latin Bible translations, whereas the Jewish tradition bases itself on the standard Hebrew (Masoretic) text, and sometimes there is a discrepancy between the two in the division of the chapters and the numbering of the verses. In such cases we shall give the chapter and verse first according to Jewish tradition and then indicate the variant of the Christian tradition.

So far as dates are concerned, we shall refer throughout to the standard reckoning of the years, but, as is the Jewish custom, use the notations BCE (for 'Before the Common Era') and CE (for 'of the Common Era') instead of BC and AD, with their Christian connotations.

The Jewish calendar is a lunar one, adapted to the solar year, which will be explained in part IV, chapter 4. A table of the Jewish months, with the festivals falling in them, will be found on page 365. We should also like to draw the reader's attention to the Glossary on pages 383–4.

Finally, a list of what we have above called the classic texts of Jewish religious literature, and the notations we have employed in citing them, will be found on pages 385–6, as part of the Bibliography.

PART I

THE HISTORY OF
THE JEWISH PEOPLE

CHAPTER ONE   IN THE BEGINNING

The history of the Jewish people begins with Abraham, the history of the Jewish religion with Moses. That, in essence, is what the Bible says, and the vast majority of modern scholars agree, placing Abraham some time between the twentieth and early sixteenth centuries before the Common Era (2000–1550 BCE), and the Exodus from Egypt in the late Bronze Age (c. 1550–1200 BCE). It is tempting – and many have succumbed to temptation – to be more specific, now that dozens of sites of ancient cities have been excavated in the Middle East, and tens of thousands of documents contemporaneous with the period of Israel's origins have been analysed. By any objective criterion, though, it is still impossible to write a proper history of the period, because the evidence both from archaeology and from the Bible itself is too limited. The book of Genesis, for example, which narrates the stories of Abraham, Isaac and Jacob and the descent into Egypt, depicts its heroes moving through their world almost as though they were alone in it. We could not guess from this account that highly sophisticated cultures had long been in existence. The great empires of the day are barely mentioned; if the pharaohs of Egypt are introduced, it is not by name. In all the Genesis narrative no single figure is named whose identity has, as yet, been established by historical sources. For this reason alone it is impossible to say, within centuries, when Abraham, Isaac and Jacob actually lived.

Equally misinformed, though, is the reaction which concludes that because corroborating evidence is only partial, the biblical accounts of Israel's origins should therefore be dismissed. There is no scholarly reason to doubt that Abraham did emerge from Mesopotamia, that he and his descendants with their semi-nomadic clans journeyed through Palestine and then spent many years in Egypt, whence they returned to the land which they regarded as promised to their ancestors. Most of the literature of the ancient world – its epic tales, its traditions, its legal and liturgical material – was handed down orally from generation to generation. This was markedly true of the Israelites, with their strong feeling for clan and cult. Folk-memories of their ancestors, tenaciously retold by father to son, survived for centuries, and eventually were written down, to become the early chapters of the Bible.

Using both the Bible and modern knowledge, then, we can reconstruct a plausible background, from which the shadowy figure of Abraham emerges over a distance of nearly four thousand years. The first sobering realization is how little the world has changed. Then as now, rival powers vied for supremacy and individuals were prompted by the same needs, impulses and economic considerations that still motivate human behaviour. Then as now, there was a strong sense that the best had been, that the present compared unfavourably with a glorious past. The essentials of Mesopotamian civilization – essentials that would characterize it for thousands of years to come – had been established by the end of the fourth millennium. Agriculture nourished a growing population, an elaborate system of dykes and drainage-ditches irrigated the land, city-states had been founded.

The years between c. 3300–2800 witnessed in Mesopotamia a burst of progress rarely seen in world history. The land was intensively cultivated, new cities sprang up, mud-brick temples were built on platforms above the level of the flood-waters. The wheel, and ovens for firing pottery, were in widespread use, and a process for pounding and then pouring copper was developed.

Most significant of all was the invention of writing. The threshold of literacy had been crossed some fifteen centuries before the birth of Abraham, and the people who can claim credit for it are the Sumerians. It was they who gave shape to a brilliant culture that survived for over fifteen hundred years, reached its zenith between 2800–2360 and decayed long before the time of the Patriarchs. In its heyday the Sumerian empire extended from the Tigris to the Persian Gulf and from Lebanon to Susa. Its capital city, Ur, had half a million inhabitants engaged in agriculture, manufacture and commerce; but after a last, late cultural

flowering, the Third Dynasty of Ur came to an end around 1950
BCE, when the King of Elam sacked and destroyed the city. A
period of tension and instability followed, while erstwhile dependencies of Ur – notably Mari, Assyria and Babylon – emerged
as ambitious new powers, and jostled for supremacy.

In sharp contrast Egypt, at the other end of the biblical world,
was then preparing to enter possibly the most stable and prosperous period of her history. The earliest known cultures in Egypt
date from around 4000 BCE. Shut off from Asia by deserts and
seas, internally divided by the winding Nile, early Egyptian
civilization contrasts poorly with that of Mesopotamia. By 3000
BCE, though, there is evidence of a lively cultural interchange
between the two lands, much to Egypt's benefit. She borrowed
heavily from the arts of the Sumerian empire; pottery, architecture and quite possibly even her hieroglyphic script developed
under Mesopotamian influence. How these contacts were
transmitted and maintained is unknown, but it is logical to assume
that a major exchange route passed through Palestine and Syria.
With the rise of the Third Dynasty around 2600 BCE, all the
significant features of Egyptian culture had assumed forms which
one normally associates with them. The pyramids were built,
those astonishing examples of technical skill, with over two and a
quarter million blocks of hewn stone in the Great Pyramid alone,
each an average weight of two and a half tons, reared precisely
into place by sheer muscle-power, without benefit of machinery.
The copper mines of Sinai were worked, and Byblos was maintained as a vital colonial outlet for transporting the hardwoods of
Lebanon into an almost treeless country.

A period of decline followed in the twenty-second and twenty-
first centuries, when rival pharaohs claimed the throne, central
authority collapsed and provincial administrators virtually ruled
as local despots. Trade languished, Asiatic nomads infiltrated the
delta, famine was widespread. Eventually a Theban family – the
Eleventh Dynasty – reunited the land and restored order.

As the second millennium began, so did the reign of the Twelfth
Dynasty, headed by rulers who were, in many respects, the ablest
that Egypt ever had. The capital was moved from Thebes to
Memphis. Six kings enjoyed reigns of, on average, thirty years
apiece. Trade flourished, ambitious engineering projects were

undertaken, medicine, mathematics and literature reached new heights of development. When contrasted with the tension and turmoil of Mesopotamia, Egypt's prosperous stability must have beckoned as temptingly as did America for Europe's poor in the nineteenth century.

What, at this time, of the territory that lay between Mesopotamia and Egypt, the land of Palestine? All that we know about it suggests a rugged, barren, inhospitable country, sparsely populated by wandering clans. Palestine never was a naturally rich terrain. Even its more favoured and fertile areas, such as the maritime plain, the valley of Jezreel and the oases of the Jordan valley, are at the whim of brief winter rains and long, dry summers. The scrubby hill country offers scanty pasture and watering for flocks. Biblical praises of a land flowing abundantly with 'milk and honey' are poetic evocations rather than literal descriptions.

Ancient Palestine had no distinctive culture, no single group of peoples nor ruling dynasty to impose a lasting character upon its civilization. Its earliest population was predominantly Canaanite, their language an ancestor of biblical Hebrew. Many of the towns later mentioned in the Bible – Jericho, Megiddo, Shechem, Gezer, Lachish – were already in existence, but they scarcely compared with the cities of Mesopotamia and Egypt. Between the twenty-third and the twentieth century there is abundant evidence that life in Palestine was severely disrupted by the incursions of semi-nomadic invaders. Towns were destroyed and abandoned east and west of the Jordan, sedentary occupations virtually ceased; indeed, southern Transjordan remained nomads' country for eight centuries afterwards.

These semi-nomadic invaders were loosely and generally referred to as Amorites ('Westerners'), a people of northwest Semitic stock. The Arameans, and later the Hebrews, came of Amorite lineage. Since late in the third millennium, the Amorites had been pressing into all parts of the Fertile Crescent, perhaps even as far as Egypt. After the fall of Ur, Amorite dynasties took over nearly every Mesopotamian state. The impetus of their advance soon spilled over into Palestine. The most significant feature of the Amorite conquest was the Amorites' ability to adapt to, and if need be to change, existing cultures. Adaptability is the crucial characteristic of the patriarchal way of life; without being fanciful we can assert that this quality above all others has determined Jewish survival until the present day.

It would be ridiculous, on the basis of a tenuous character trait, to try and forge some link between the Abraham of the biblical narratives and the modern Jew living in Jerusalem, New York or London. The reasons for regarding Abraham as the ancestor of the Jewish people are fundamental, and will be outlined in the next section. For the present, having described the world in which Abraham would have led his life and fulfilled his destiny, let us content ourselves with the assumption that it was either as part, or in the wake, of the Amorite advance into Palestine, that Abraham and his clan journeyed from Mesopotamia some time between 2000 and 1550 BCE.

THE PATRIARCHS AND THE DESCENT INTO EGYPT

We have sketched in the historical background against which the patriarchal narratives of Genesis 12–50 take place. These chapters knit together several ancient traditions of diverse origin. According to Genesis, Abraham left his father's land at the command of the one true God. The Covenant he made with this God was faithfully upheld by his son Isaac and his grandson Jacob – later called Israel – who roamed the land of Canaan sustained by God's promise that one day it would belong to their seed, a progeny as numerous as the stars in the sky and the sand of the seashore. After Jacob's son Joseph rose to a high position at the pharaoh's court, Jacob and his eleven other sons – the progenitors of the twelve tribes of Israel – settled in the fertile land of Goshen, basking in Joseph's reflected glory. Yet when Jacob was about to die at a ripe old age, his last, urgent request was not to be buried in Egypt, but back in the land of his forefathers. The funeral cortège that accompanied Jacob's body was but a rehearsal for the momentous Exodus which would take place many years later, when *all* the children of Israel would return to the land which their God had originally promised to Abraham.

Any telling of history means, in a sense, imposing the orderly, causal logic of hindsight on events that at the time seemed disorderly, arbitrary and haphazard. There could have been no tidy pattern of progress whereby Abraham's Covenant with God reached its predestined fulfilment under Moses and Joshua several centuries later – unless, and this condition is crucial to a proper and sympathetic appreciation of the Bible – unless one recognizes the basic premise of every known and unknown biblical author, which is, quite simply, that a special relationship exists between God and His chosen people, Israel; that God supports, guides, exhorts and occasionally even intervenes in the history of this people; and that no matter how rebellious, stiff-necked or deservedly punished the chosen people are, God will never ultimately desert them, nor they Him.

Such a momentous premise will inevitably allow history to be interpreted in a particular – some would say distorted – way. This premise will give a point and purpose to the roles of individuals and the affairs of nations; people fulfil their destiny at divine behest, whether aware of it or not. The lives of men and women, the rise and fall of empires, are part of a divine master-plan – at times but dimly understood – which will culminate in nothing less than the establishment of God's kingdom on earth, through the special agency of His people, Israel.

It is essential to emphasize this sense of Israel's destiny and mission if one is to understand properly the history of the Jewish people and the Jewish religion, not only as it happened but as the Jews themselves *interpreted it as happening*. Without such a resolute faith in their own significance, this tiny, persecuted, exiled people would long since have disappeared; would never have maintained their distinctive cultural identity; would never have given birth to the two other monotheistic religions of western civilization. The reader may, or may not, accept the religious assumptions of the Bible; that is a matter of belief. What he can confidently accept, supported by most authoritative modern scholarship, is the presumptive veracity of the biblical narratives. Not surprisingly, the narratives draw from every incident a conclusion which validates the special relationship between God and His chosen people. Yet by and large the background details, locales and circumstances of each incident – even the earliest historical ones – are at least plausible, and at best (as in I and II Kings, for example) independently confirmed by other sources.

Bearing this in mind then, let us start with Abraham, complementing the biblical narrative, where possible, with the impartial evidence of archaeology and research. The Bible mentions Haran, in upper Mesopotamia, as the starting point for Abraham's journey. His father, Terah, had migrated to Haran from Ur. The religion in Mesopotamia at this time (as in Egypt) was a highly developed polytheism, with the gods ranged in a complex pantheon. Abraham's forebears had worshipped these gods. Bidden by the voice of his 'new' God, Abraham set out with his clan and flocks – as part of that semi-nomadic migration which brought a new population to Palestine in the early centuries of the second millennium – towards the unknown land which his God would show him. His journey was in that sense an act of faith. We cannot, though, properly talk of Abraham as the first monotheist. Abraham – and Isaac and Jacob after him – undertook by free and personal choice to worship their God, to whom they thereafter entrusted themselves and their families. The patriarchal religion was thus a clan religion, in which the patron God was worshipped above, but not necessarily to the exclusion of, all other gods.

It was a religion of simple piety, its ceremonies performed wherever the clan happened to be, by the Patriarch himself. In that respect it differed significantly from the official polytheism of Mesopotamia with its organized clergy. It also differed from the fertility cults of Canaan, of whose orgies there is no trace in the Genesis narrative. The story of the attempted sacrifice of Isaac is an early protest against their practice of child sacrifice. As the Patriarchs moved into Palestine they came into contact with existing shrines. There they worshipped their own clan deity under his various names; El, El Shaddai, El Elyon, etc., titles which evoked a God who is most high, enduring in power, who watches over the affairs of His people.

The Patriarchs and their clans wandered in Transjordan, the central mountains of Palestine and the Negev desert. That some followers intermarried, assimilated, went their separate ways, yet still retained ties of kinship is attested by the stories of Lot, Ishmael and Esau. Above all, the Patriarchs maintained contact with their Aramean relatives in Mesopotamia, preferring their sons' wives to come from 'back home' rather than from among the local Canaanite population. The Bible depicts the Patriarchs as men of peace, anxious to coexist amicably with their neighbours, either because they were neither numerous nor strong enough to be able to afford the enmity of more powerful chiefs, or because – certainly this is the impression one receives from the portrait of Abraham in the Bible – they were of courteous, hospitable but retiring dispositions. On occasion, though, they resorted to arms, the classical example being in Genesis 14, where, in order to rescue Lot, Abraham and 318 retainers pursued the invading kings. It is here that the term 'Hebrew' is first used in order to describe the ancestors of the tribe of Israel. The word 'Hebrew' (*ivri*) is popularly derived either from Eber, the name of Israel's traditional progenitor (Genesis 11:14–17) or, more fancifully, from a word meaning 'the other side', since Abraham and his clan came from the other side of the Euphrates. More probably, though, it is similar etymologically to the names Khapiru, Apiru or Habiru, a designation abundantly used in Mesopotamian and Egyptian texts to describe a nomadic people found all over western Asia from *c.* 2000 BCE until about the eleventh century. These Khapiru were usually semi-nomads, without rank or citizenship in the existing social structure, at times living peacefully, at others hiring themselves out as mercenaries, occasionally settling in towns. When driven by need they would even sell themselves as slaves. If the term 'Khapiru' was used to describe an alien population as loosely and as generally as we give such blanket descriptions nowadays, then undoubtedly Abraham and his clan would have been classified among them.

It was Jacob, the most complex, passionate and 'driven' of the Patriarchs, who, after a mysterious spiritual struggle at Jabbok ford, was renamed Israel – 'the champion of El' – and thereby gave to the descendants of the Abrahamic family the name by which they were ultimately known. His favourite son, Joseph, rose to become viceroy of Egypt at a time when that country was under the domination of the Hyksos. The term 'Hyksos' means 'foreign chiefs' and was applied to Asiatic invaders by the pharaohs of the Middle Kingdom. Predominantly of north-west Semitic stock, the Hyksos worshipped Canaanite gods, especially Ba'al. Most of their rulers were Canaanite or Amorite princes from Palestine, and therefore they were closely akin to the

Hebrews. The Hyksos ruled Egypt from their newly founded capital of Avaris (later known as Tanis) from approximately 1690 to 1580. It is plausible to place Joseph's premiership, and as a consequence, the descent of his family into Egypt, some time during this period. They came in order to take advantage of his prestige and Egypt's prosperity, and the book of Genesis ends with Jacob's ever-increasing clan established, seemingly permanently, in the fertile land of Goshen, their generations of wandering over.

But it was not to be. As the second book of the Bible, Exodus, puts it, 'there arose a new king over Egypt, who did not know Joseph.' It was Amosis, the founder of the Eighteenth Dynasty, who repeatedly attacked the Hyksos, capturing their capital around 1550 and finally expelling them from Egypt. His reign ushered in the period of Egypt's empire, when she became indisputably the greatest power in the world of that day. Under Thutmosis III (c. 1490–1435) her boundaries extended northward to the upper reaches of the Euphrates, and southward to the fourth cataract of the Nile, in Nubia. This empire remained intact until the fourteenth century BCE, when a religious revolution threatened to destroy it. The young King Amenophis IV declared the sun god, Aten, to be the sole deity, changed his name to Akhenaten, and built himself a new capital in the god's honour. Less than a century before the probable dates of Moses and the Exodus, a religion of monotheistic character had emerged in Egypt.

The Aten cult was bitterly opposed by the established priesthood and the conservative masses. The repercussions of the controversy severely threatened Egypt's position abroad, as the Amarna letters reveal. Written by the pharaoh's vassals in Palestine, Phoenicia and as far afield as Babylon, these letters show an empire in uproar and rebellion. Frequently mentioned among the seditious troublemakers, brigands and disturbers of the peace are – the Khapiru.

Akhenaten died, possibly assassinated, and his successors removed all traces of his heresy. They also set out to recoup Egypt's losses in Asia, which made war with the powerful Hittite kingdom of Asia Minor inevitable. Sethos I (c. 1309–1290) regained control of Palestine. His successor Ramesses II (c. 1290–

1224) was involved for over a decade in a large-scale, indecisive war against the Hittites, until exhaustion forced both sides to a peace treaty.

The cessation of hostilities enabled Ramesses to embark on a vast building programme. Avaris, now once more the capital, was renamed 'The House of Ramesses'. According to Exodus 1:11, Hebrews were forced to labour at the building of the cities of Pithom, in northeastern Egypt, and Raamses. In the texts of this period, Khapiru are frequently mentioned as state slaves working on royal projects. The only reason for not asserting with total confidence that the Exodus from Egypt took place during the first three-quarters, probably the first half, of the thirteenth century, is because the Bible explicitly states (I Kings 6:1) that it was 480 years from the Exodus to the dedication of Solomon's Temple. This would place the Exodus earlier, in the fifteenth century, at the time of the upheaval and dissolution described in the Amarna letters. Since, however, forty is a popular biblical number for a generation (as in the forty years spent wandering in the wilderness), it is likely that this 480 years is itself a round number for twelve generations. The insistence of Exodus 12:40 that it was 430 years, to the day, for Israel's stay in Egypt, is not to be taken too seriously. It is contradicted by Genesis 15:13, which mentions 400 years for the sojourn, and by the Greek translation of the Bible, the Septuagint, which makes the 430 years cover the wanderings of the Patriarchs in Palestine as well; if we accepted the genealogy of Exodus 6:16–20, where Moses is said to have been a grandson of Kohath, son of Levi, who entered Egypt with Jacob, then the stay in Egypt would be reduced to three generations.

In addition, such archaeological evidence as we have requires us to date Joshua's conquest of the Promised Land late in the thirteenth century. Taking biblical narrative and historical record together, we can say with a fair degree of certainty that Sethos I was the pharaoh 'who did not know Joseph', and Ramesses II the pharaoh in whose reign the Exodus took place.

The successful escape of a party of slaves was an affair of little significance to the Egyptians, not meriting an entry in their records. To the Hebrews it was an event of cosmic importance, preceded by miraculous plagues and accelerated by the direct intervention of God Himself, who brought them from bondage to freedom, from darkness to light, from paganism to the worship of the one true God.

The architect of the Exodus, and the leader who patiently turned a rabble of debased fugitives into a cohesive, ethically refined, monotheistic people was one remarkable man, Moses.

CHAPTER TWO   EXODUS, COVENANT
AND CONQUEST

MOSES

The Exodus from Egypt, and the still more momentous giving of
the law at Mount Sinai which followed, are events which require
a great personality behind them; and a faith as unique as Israel's
demands a founder, as surely as did its daughter religions, Christianity and Islam. We know nothing about Moses except what the
Bible tells us. Yet there can be no doubt that he was, as the
Pentateuch portrays him, the leader, guide and mentor who
patiently moulded his people to worship and have respect for the
one God, Yahweh.

The religion which Moses founded is still tenaciously maintained over three thousand years after his death. One cannot even
begin to assess the magnitude of Moses's achievement unless one
supplements the biblical record with a liberal use of the imagination. This is not to plead for a flight of fancy, but to suggest that
the gift of inspired leadership, of charisma, cannot be defined
solely by the accounts of those present. Which is why, after all
the voluminous assessments of Moses by scholars, historians,
psychiatrists, believers and debunkers, it is a great novelist,
Thomas Mann, who, in his short story, 'The Two Tablets of the
Law', probably comes closest, with certain reservations, to catch-
ing both the essence of Moses's personality and the nature of his
mission.

According to the Bible, Moses was the adopted son of an
Egyptian princess. His name – from a verb meaning to beget –
is an element in such names as Thutmosis, Ramesses, etc., and

14

the prevalence of Egyptian names among the Hebrews, especially in the tribe of Levi, is objective support for the tradition of Israel's slavery in Egypt. No people would willingly *invent* for its origins such a story of debased servitude.

Of the Exodus itself we have no extra-biblical evidence. Just as the Israelites were unlikely to make central to their faith a story of degradation, unless it did indeed culminate in redemption, so too the Egyptians were unlikely to record a reverse in which they had been outwitted by runaway slaves. It is impossible to estimate how many slaves actually escaped. The Bible talks of 600,000 men bearing arms, as well as women and children, and an accompanying 'mixed multitude' – perhaps three million people in all. Far more likely is the alternative biblical tradition of Jacob's seventy followers who settled and multiplied in Egypt, their needs adequately cared for by only two midwives (Exodus 1:15–22), who escaped in a single night and cringed before the larger Egyptian army sent to pursue them; perhaps five or six thousand souls in all.

The exact location of the Exodus is uncertain, especially since the Hebrews crossed a sea (*yam suf*) which is usually but incorrectly translated as the Red Sea, when it is properly the Reed Sea. In all probability this was a body of water to the east of Avaris, and the crossing took place near to the present-day El Qantara on the Suez Canal. The fugitives, penned between the sea and the Egyptian cavalry, were saved when a wind drove the water back, allowing them to pass. Their heavily-armed pursuers were caught by the returning tide in the reedy, marshy waters, and many of them drowned.

In truth, though, a precise reconstruction of the Exodus is no more essential than is a 'naturalistic' interpretation of the alleged ten plagues which preceded it. What is evident and undeniable is the effect it had on the Hebrews themselves. Ever afterwards it was remembered as the supreme manifestation of God's power in the cause of His people. It marked their birth as a nation. Each festival of Passover, on the anniversary of the passing out of Egypt, the details are retold by parent to child as though they, too, had been present at the deliverance.

From the Bible itself we get a clear indication of the difficulty Moses had in convincing the children of Israel that they should make a bid for freedom. They would not listen to him because of 'impatience of spirit and hard bondage', suspicious, no doubt, of a liberator with royal connections. Certainly he moved in and out of the pharaoh's palace with a strange immunity, considering his outrageous demand: that the Hebrews be allowed to go free, in order to worship their God.

Who was this God? In His first 'call' to Moses, He is identified as 'The Lord, the God of your fathers, the God of Abraham, the God of Isaac, and the God of Jacob'. Pressed by Moses to communicate a name which would assure the Hebrew slaves that he was also *their* God, the enigmatic reply came back (Exodus 3:14), '*Ehyeh asher Ehyeh*' – usually translated as 'I am that I am'. There is copious discussion among scholars, and little agreement, as to the meaning of this name (see also pp. 245–6). In the course of time *Yahweh* or Jehovah became a name used by non-Jews for the Jewish God.

Whether or not Yahweh was worshipped before Moses – perhaps among the Midianite clans of the Sinai peninsula where Moses's father-in-law was a priest – is neither known nor is it important. What cannot be denied is that through Moses Yahwism was given a special content and meaning. Yahweh alone was God, brooking no rivals. He was the Creator of all things, without intermediary, assistance, pantheon, consort or progeny. Other gods might exist for other people, but for Israel Yahweh was the *only* God, it was His mighty acts that had created the world, His power that ruled the cosmos, His special concern that had forged a covenant with the Patriarchs. Whatever our modern-day philosophical or linguistic quibbles, there can be little argument that the religion which Moses impressed upon his people was monotheism. Furthermore, it was ethical monotheism; God, who was all-good, all-just, all-merciful, demanded goodness, justice and mercy of the Hebrews. He bade them never to forget that once they had been slaves in Egypt and knew, therefore, what it was to be a stranger and a slave.

The religious consequences of worshipping Yahweh came later, at Sinai. First Moses had to convince the Hebrews to trust in their God. This he did with the help of his brother, Aaron, a skilful orator. Together they demonstrated how Yahweh was the link between past and future, between the dimly remembered glory of the Patriarchs and the still-to-be-fulfilled promise of permanent settlement in the land of Israel. It was Yahweh, Moses reminded them, whom Abraham, Isaac and Jacob had worshipped, albeit under other names, and it was Yahweh who would keep faith with their downtrodden descendants. Slowly, patiently, citing, as signs of His power, here an epidemic of boils, there an outbreak of cattle disease, Moses instilled in the slaves confidence in Yahweh. Eventually the day came when, after preparations, which were ritual-like in their solemnity, they were ready to be led into the unknown by their God.

And so the Exodus took place. The brittleness of the Hebrews' faith quickly became apparent. No sooner were the Egyptian cavalry sighted than the people railed against Moses. They begged to be returned to a slavery which hadn't been so bad after all. That crisis negotiated, the wilderness wandering began. It was a motley army that Moses led. The 'mixed multitude' (Exodus 12:38; Numbers 11:4) that escaped with Jacob's descendants was presumably made up of other fugitive slaves, perhaps Khapiru, possibly even Egyptians (Leviticus 24:10). Moses's father-in-law Jethro and his Midianite clan joined Israel on the march. Other groups, certainly Edomite ones, would have attached themselves during the wilderness period and accepted the religious traditions, the ritual observances and the rigorous legal code which Moses imposed upon his followers. Working day and night, he was turning a rabble into a people; a people with its own distinctive faith.

THE REVELATION AT MOUNT SINAI

It was at Mount Sinai that Israel received the Covenant and the law which transformed her into a religious people. The location of Sinai, or Horeb as it is also called, is uncertain. Its traditonal site is at Jebel Musa, situated near the southern tip of the Sinai peninsula. Some scholars, however, believing that the language of Exodus 19:16–19 suggests a volcanic eruption, prefer a location east of the Gulf of Aqaba, where extinct volcanoes are to be found. Again, one is bound to ask the pedant if the exact spot really matters. The Bible narrates the circumstances in a manner so impressive that clearly a never-to-be-forgotten act of affirmation took place there.

According to the Bible, it was in the third month of their Exodus from Egypt that the children of Israel came into the wilderness of Sinai. There, after three days of preparing themselves, on a morning of thunder and lightning and thick cloud, the people gathered at the foot of Mount Sinai. The mountain itself was covered in smoke because the Lord descended upon it in fire. God came down to Mount Sinai and spoke to Moses. When Moses returned to the people, God proclaimed the Ten Commandments. And the children of Israel, watching the thunder and lightning and the smoking mountain from afar, were frightened and begged Moses to stop God speaking to them, for fear they would die: but Moses reassured them.

That is how Exodus 19–20 tells the story of the revelation at Mount Sinai. And ever after it was regarded quite simply as the greatest event in the history of the people. The giving of the Torah – usually translated as law, but more accurately, teaching – was proof of God's special Covenant with Israel and confirmation of the original promise He made to Abraham. It was an event of such crucial significance that even the biblical description of it was deemed inadequate. A later commentary described it thus: 'When God revealed the Torah, no bird chirped, no fowl beat its wings, no ox bellowed, the angels did not sing, the sea did not stir, no creature uttered a sound; the world was silent and still and the Divine Voice spoke' (Midrash, Exodus Rabbah, 29:9). The Torah was God's greatest gift to Israel, and the proper vocation for a Jew was to turn it over and over, for everything was contained in it. Not only those who stood at Sinai, but generations yet unborn were irrevocably bound by the divine exhortation, 'You shall be to Me a kingdom of priests and a holy nation.' Israel's chosenness and Israel's mission were authenticated by that revelation in the third month after the departure from Egypt.

For centuries, no Jew would have dared to question the biblical account of the giving of the Law. It was in the Bible, the Bible was the word of God, therefore it must be true. God's role in history and Israel's role as God's witness were dependent upon it. To query it was to deny God. As a consequence of the Sinaitic Revelation the Israelite religion developed, based on the Tabernacle (later to become the Temple), the priesthood and sacrifice. Later, the prophets were to stress a different aspect of the revelation, emphasizing its ethical demands above the requirements of ritual. In the first centuries CE a balance was sought between the spirit and the letter of the law, so that fulfilling the demands of the revelation became a way of daily life. The medieval philosophers justified Judaism on the basis of the theophany at Sinai. Spinoza queried it – and was excommunicated for his heretical views by the Amsterdam Jewish community. The early leaders of the nineteenth-century Reform movement were vilified for re-interpreting the revelation symbolically. As recently as 1963, Anglo-Jewry's outstanding scholar was denied the principalship of Jews' College because he did not accept literally the biblical account of *Torah min ha-shamayim* – the law given from heaven at Sinai by God Himself. What the dogma of the Resurrection is to Christianity, the dogma of the Revelation at Sinai is to Judaism. There is no practising Jew who would deny the momentous happening at Sinai: its details are shrouded in the mists of antiquity, its results are tangible. Where differences occur they are only differences in the degree to which the Sinaitic Torah is regarded as immutable and all-authoritative. The Jew who describes himself as Orthodox would claim that he has no right to add to or subtract one iota from the Mosaic law; he is willingly bound by the biblical account and by the chain of tradition which developed as a result of it. It is true that, as the great Orthodox scholar, Solomon Schechter, pointed out, the 613 commandments of the Torah are, for all practical purposes, now reduced to about one hundred, if we exclude 'conventional' prohibitions against murder, theft, adultery, etc., and those commandments specifically connected with the land of Palestine and the Temple. Yet for the fundamentalist Jew, laws of sacrifice or of the Jubilee year (described in Leviticus 25:8 ff.) are not abrogated, but merely in abeyance: he has no man-given right to reject divine commands. Moses Maimonides stressed the equal importance of *all* of the Pentateuch by stating that there is no difference between verses like 'The sons of Ham: Cush, Egypt, Put and Canaan' (Genesis 10:6) and the Ten Commandments. The non-fundamentalist Jew, on the other hand, is readier both to limit the scope of the Sinaitic revelation, and to extend it. He will differentiate between a sublime piece of time-less legislation such as the so-called 'holiness code' in Leviticus 19, and cruder injunctions about treatment of lepers or women suspected of adultery, which betray attitudes prevalent at the time of composition but which are no longer acceptable today. On the other hand, he will recognize as Torah not only the legislation of Moses but also the visions of the prophets, the commentaries of the rabbis, the insights of the mystics and all wise and noble guidance in the way of holiness. For him, the Torah has never ceased to grow.

The often bitter division of modern Judaism into Orthodox and Progressive factions stems from these contrasting attitudes to revelation. (For the divergent approaches to Judaism, see p. 144 ff.) Yet, though differing in the obedience they offer to the folk-memory of the revelation at Sinai, Orthodox and Progressive Jews are united in recognizing its unique importance. It gave to a group of recently freed slaves self-esteem and a sense of mission: to become a people of priests and a holy nation. The person responsible for working the transformation was Moses.

According to the Bible, the next stopping place for the Israelites after the great Covenant at Sinai was the oasis of Kadesh, fifty miles south of Beersheba. There they remained for some considerable time. We can surmise that at Kadesh Moses and the appointed elders, the 'men of truth, hating unjust gain', began to implement the law which had been accepted at Sinai. The similarities of Mosaic law to second millennium Mesopotamian law codes – especially the codification written by Hammurabi (1728–1686) – are well known and not surprising, given the cultural background from which the Hebrews came. What is distinctive and characteristic about Mosaic legislation is its insistence that human conduct must pass the test of divine approbation or displeasure. Stated apodictically (thou shalt/shalt not), a major category of Israelite law enumerates the ways in which a person should behave if he wishes to find favour not only among his fellows, but, more importantly, with Yahweh. Tradition would have it that Moses wrote all of the laws in the Pentateuch. Clearly this is not so; the ceremony of the first fruits, for example (Deuteronomy 26:1–10), or the proclamation of the Jubilee, are backward projections, from a later time when the land had long been settled. But the stress which all subsequent legislation placed upon the Covenant entered into at Sinai is in itself witness to the lasting influence of Moses the lawgiver.

He was, in the simile used by Thomas Mann to describe Moses's relationship with his people, like a sculptor hewing and chipping and moulding a refractory piece of marble, until one day he could eventually say of it that it had been fashioned into a form pleasing to God.

After further wandering in the wilderness, which cannot be clarified in detail (sometimes because the biblical place names cannot be attached to specific locations, sometimes because the accounts are impossible to harmonize), the Israelites made a great detour through Transjordan. An authentic enough picture emerges, though, from the welter of incidents described in the Bible. Israel's routes are those of nomads who cannot stray far from water, and who have to fight their way in hostile territory. Forty years is the round figure given for what must have been a lengthy and dangerous quest for the Promised Land. The detour through Transjordan accords well with known conditions in the thirteenth century, when the frontiers of Edom and Moab were secured by a line of fortresses and the arable land in the south was occupied by the Amalekites. Their entry barred from the south, the Israelities forced their way into Palestine by crossing the Jordan. They attacked and destroyed the kingdom of Heshbon (Numbers 21:21–32), which gave them control of most of the land between the Arnon and Jabbok rivers. The alarm occasioned by the advance of this tough and, by now, disciplined and highly motivated fighting force, is reflected in the Balaam stories and poems of chapters 22–24 in the book of Numbers. No doubt some inhabitants preferred to make alliances with the Israelites rather than fight them. After all, much of the population of Palestine was of the same stock as the Hebrews. This fact has caused copious but ultimately fruitless controversy among scholars as to which of the so-called twelve tribes originally descended into Egypt, which actually participated in the Exodus and the Sinaitic revelation and which afterwards joined the swelling army commanded by Moses and, after his death, by Joshua. All we can say with certainty is that the origins of what later became the people Israel are complex and diverse, that onto the nucleus who left Egypt some elements would have assimilated voluntarily, being of similar language and culture, while others were absorbed through conquest; but common to all was an acceptance of Exodus and Sinai as their crucial, formative events. In that sense the Bible is profoundly correct in stating that *all* Israel, even generations yet unborn, stood at Sinai to receive the law.

Somewhere east of the Jordan, and before the last great onslaught into Palestine, Moses died. It seems so unjust, so sad, that he should not live to see the realization of his dreams, that the Bible imputes to him a minor error for which this was his punishment. Fifteen centuries later the rabbis were still pondering the reasons for his death so near to the Promised Land, and devising all manner of ingenious explanations for it. The simple, prosaic answer could well be exhaustion and old age. Perhaps, too, there is in the death of this great religious figure a powerful and universal metaphor about the human condition. Our reach exceeds our grasp; we behold the Promised Land from afar, knowing we can never attain it. And yet, we must keep on trying. That is the nature of the religious life.

THE PROMISED LAND

The conquest of Palestine was, as depicted in the book of Joshua, a bloody and brutal business. It was the holy war of Yahweh, by which He gave to His people the land originally promised to the Patriarchs. Archaeological evidence abundantly testifies to widespread devastation visited upon southern Palestine in the latter half of the thirteenth century. Israel's victories caused whole clans to join her in solemn covenant. Among those thus absorbed were groups of Khapiru, the populace of various towns in central Palestine, some Galilean elements, and the Kenizites and Kenites in the south. Israel's tribal structure speedily filled out with the influx of these new adherents, and her history as a recognizable, corporate people, living in its own land, may be said to have begun.

Early Israel was not, though, either a racial or a national unity. She was a confederation of clans united under Yahweh. The usual name given to this confederation is 'amphictyony', from the Greek word for a sacral league. Certain amphictyonies, for example the Delphic league and the Etruscan league of Koltumna, are known to have had twelve members, just as the Israelite amphictyony was made up of twelve clans claiming descent from Jacob. Having twelve members was hardly coincidental, but rather was dictated by the requirement of a monthly turn at maintaining the central shrine. This was at Shiloh, where the ark of the Covenant was housed. The ark was the dwelling-place of the invisible Yahweh, originally constructed in the desert, where it had been referred to as the tent of meeting. The twelve tribes of the Israelite amphictyony had no central government, no capital city, no national administration; they remained autonomous, and organized their own systems of self-government. On certain great annual feast-days the tribesmen would present themselves before Yahweh and renew their allegiance to Him. This was done at the feast of unleavened bread (Passover), the feast of weeks, and the feast of the ingathering. These nature festivals, far older than Israel, were invested with religious significance and became occasions for celebrating the mighty acts Yahweh had performed to help His special people.

Above all else it was subservience to Yahweh and His law that held together this precarious tribal frederation for about two hundred years. During this time the newcomers to Palestine were involved in continual, if intermittent, fighting. Their territory was fragmented: although the mountainous areas of Palestine were largely under Israelite control, a people appeared on the scene, approximately a generation after Israel's own arrival, and settled on the coast; a people who would give their name to Palestine – the Philistines. They came nominally as vassals of the Pharaoh Ramesses III (c. 1175–1144), who, from the fifth year of his reign, was desperately engaged in trying to repel the invasion of the Peoples of the Sea who were swarming down the Mediterranean coast and spreading destruction from Ugarit in the north to Ashkelon in the south. The Philistines and the Israelites did not immediately come to blows. However, tension was inevitable, first because the Philistines adopted the religious culture of Canaan, which was obnoxious to the worshippers of Yahweh; second because the Philistines enjoyed a local monopoly on the manufacture of iron, which gave them a tremendous military advantage they were keen to exploit.

The amphictyony was not only threatened along the coast. The Galilean tribes were separated from each other by Canaanite enclaves in the plain of Esdraelon. Between eastern and western tribes lay the deep Jordan rift. Local interests naturally tended to take precedence over the common good and the existing Canaanite religion, with its fertility gods, must have beckoned enticingly. If not for the spiritual power of the Covenant tradition and the loyalty which the worship of Yahweh invoked, early Israel would scarcely have held together.

THE RULE OF THE JUDGES

That Israel did hold together, and, without the benefit of a centralized government, managed to beat off invaders, was due to a group of leaders known as the judges. The book of Judges is itself our major source of information about Israel's fluctuating fortunes in the years of settlement. From it we learn that in times of danger there would arise a judge, upon whom 'the spirit of the Lord came'. He would call the tribes out to repel the foe, and those who failed to respond were execrated, for the call to arms was the call to fight in Yahweh's holy war. The judge was in no sense a king. His authority was neither absolute nor hereditary, but depended rather upon personal qualities, which won the people's confidence, which said that here indeed was Yahweh's representative. In both character and personality the judges differed greatly. Gideon reluctantly accepted his role after a profound spiritual experience. Jephthah was a shrewd bandit, Samson a bawdy rogue, Deborah an implacably determined woman. Yet all of them had the ability, in times of crisis, to rally the tribes most seriously threatened by danger.

The amphictyony and the judges kept Israel intact from the end of the thirteenth century until approximately 1050 BCE. Although Israel probably held less territory in the eleventh century than when she first invaded Palestine, and although the attraction of pagan, Canaanite cults had in places eroded the spare purity of her Yahwist faith, she had successfully repelled military and cultural attack; specifically, she had resisted any movement to imitate the city-state pattern of Canaan or to institute a monarchy. Yahweh as king was the ultimate overlord of His people, and it was He who would save them.

So matters might have gone on indefinitely, had not the Philistine crisis intervened, confronting Israel with an emergency with which the amphictyony was inadequate to cope.

CHAPTER THREE   KINGS AND PROPHETS: FROM SAMUEL TO THE BABYLONIAN CAPTIVITY

The Philistines were originally of Aegean descent, but once settled in Palestine they readily assimilated with the existing Canaanite culture and religion. They were tough soldiers, well-armed, with iron weapons (as the description of Goliath's armour in I Samuel 17:5–7 testifies), skilful in the deployment of chariots. Their centre of power was vested in five cities, closely linked: Gaza, Ashkelon, Ashdod, Ekron and Gath. Each was ruled by a local tyrant who was, however, unlike the twelve tribes of the amphictyony, always willing to make common cause with his fellows. The collapse of Egypt's empire under its Twentieth and Twenty-first Dynasties tempted the Philistines to expand into territory which had recently belonged to the pharaohs. The ill-trained, ill-equipped Israelite tribal levies, reliant upon an inspirational judge, were no match for such a foe. Some time after 1050 BCE, near Aphek on the coastal plain, the Israelite army was routed and the ark of the Covenant captured. The shrine of the amphictyony at Shiloh was destroyed and the Philistines set up garrisons at strategic points throughout the land.

For these events and the history of the subsequent century, we have at our disposal sources that are detailed, vividly written and of undoubted authenticity (I and II Samuel, I Kings, chapters 1–11). Their eye-witness flavour is accepted by modern scholars, who date these biblical books as being contemporaneous, or nearly so, with the events described.

SAMUEL AND SAUL

One man guided Israel through the dark days at the beginning of this period: Samuel. Before his birth he had been dedicated to Yahweh by a Nazirite vow; he spent his youth at the central shrine of Shiloh as a protégé of the old priest Eli. When Shiloh fell he returned to his ancestral home at Ramah, where he enjoyed fame as a holy man and a seer. He was both a priest and a successor to the judges, moving in a regular circuit between certain important shrines, administering Covenant law among the tribes and keeping alive the amphictyonic tradition.

It was inevitable, given the Philistine occupation, the prestige Samuel enjoyed and perhaps his own personality, that he should become the first and best-known instance of a type that frequently appears throughout Israelite history: the religious leader who embroils himself in politics. Samuel must have realized, as did the people, that the only way to expel the Philistines was by uniting behind a strong military leader: a king perhaps. Yet monarchy was an institution totally foreign to Israel's tradition. The reluctance, doubt and divisiveness occasioned by such a radical innovation are reflected in the two parallel biblical accounts of Saul's election, one tacitly favourable to the monarchy, the other bitterly hostile.

We can be sure that Samuel's personal feelings were extremely complex. Certainly they remain enigmatic. The exigencies of the situation demanded a charismatic leader, but the emergence of such a leader would necessarily detract from Samuel's own authority. Perhaps that was why he either chose and anointed Saul himself (the first account, I Samuel 9:1 to 10:16), or grudgingly consented to popular demand and presided over Saul's election at Mizpah (the second account, I Samuel 10:17–27). Either way, he hoped to be able to manipulate the people's choice. Saul was handsome, charming, dashingly courageous, but, when all is said and done, still a country boy, from the small town of Gibeah in the territory of Benjamin; no match intellectually for the subtle and experienced priest. Saul's early career fulfilled all expectations. A great victory over the Ammonites was followed by a campaign against the Philistines which successfully drove them from the heartland of Israel. Initially Saul enjoyed a popularity

26

among the tribes and therefore received corresponding loyalty from them, greater than that achieved by any of the judges before him. He was the national, not merely a tribal, king.

Yet his trappings of royalty were exceedingly modest. Archaeology reveals his seat at Gibeah to have been of rustic simplicity; he had no magnificent court, no harem, only his cousin Abner to command the levies. Tribal autonomy and self-government were left intact. To begin with, certainly, Saul deferred to Samuel, but their uneasy rapport did not last. Inevitable tension between religious and temporal authority was the cause; first, an accusation that the king had usurped the function of the amphityonic priesthood, then that he had ignored the *cherem* – a feature of sacral law regarding the conduct of a holy war. Samuel publicly revoked Saul's designation.

It was the beginning of the end for Saul. Ultimately, he was a tragic figure: his whole reign was taken up with war. The incessant pressures of his position, the dichotomy between his royal authority and his simple upbringing were too much for a temperament that, at the best of times, was volatile. He became melancholic and withdrawn, giving way to fits of depression in which only music could soothe him. The advent of a popular new hero, young David, drove Saul to obsessive paranoia. He became convinced that everyone, even his own son, Jonathan, and his closest retainers, were plotting against him.

THE HOUSE OF DAVID

Later generations were to idealize David as a great folk hero, 'the sweet singer of Israel', from whose lineage the Messiah himself would come. Certainly, as we shall see, under his rule Israel achieved a unity, military strength and territorial size the like of which she would never know again. Yet the real David was far removed from, and more interesting than, his later legend. He was very much a man of flesh and blood, in whom sensuality mingled with spirituality, raw ambition with generous altruism, severity with indulgence.

His youth was one of golden promise. He early gained fame by some spectacular feat of arms, possibly by killing the Philistine hero, Goliath, in single combat (II Samuel 21:9 instead credits the feat to one Elhanan). His skill with the lyre brought him to the notice of Saul, for whom he would play when the king's black moods descended. He won the deep friendship of the king's son, Jonathan, and the hand of Saul's daughter, Michal, in marriage. Perhaps he did not mask his ambitions sufficiently well, or perhaps the king was by now no longer of balanced mind. Made insanely jealous by David's growing popularity, Saul tried to kill him. David was forced to flee. The priestly family of Shiloh who unwittingly aided him in his flight were butchered by the enraged king. By such a shocking act Saul alienated the old amphictyonic order and drove its priesthood into support of David. Back in his native Judah, David gathered around him an army of desperadoes and pursued a precarious bandit-like existence, striking at the Philistines when opportunity offered, continually dodging Saul's pursuit, exacting protection from wealthy citizens and finally offering his services as a mercenary to Achish, king of Gath, who was delighted to employ such a notable defector, accepting David as a vassal and giving him the town of Ziklag in the Negev as a feudal holding. Although naturally expected to make as much trouble for Israel as possible, David played a dangerous and devious game, feeding Achish false reports about his raids – which were, in reality, against the desert Amalekites – and distributing the plundered booty among the towns and clans of the Negev of Judah, to convince his people that he was still their loyal friend.

Shortly afterwards, the Philistines marshalled their forces for the decisive encounter with Saul. The armies met at Mount Gilboa. Why Saul allowed himself to be drawn into battle at a time and place so unsuitable to his own forces, is only explicable as the action of a desperate and doomed man – one for whom the medium of Endor had summoned up the ghost of the long-dead Samuel (I Samuel 28). The Israelite army was routed, three of Saul's sons were killed and the severely wounded king took his own life. The victorious Philistines cut off Saul's head and hung it, together with the bodies of his sons, on the walls of Beth Shan. David was spared a part in all this. The Philistine lords did not trust him and sent him home before the battle, which was fortunate: David did not have to take the field against his own people.

Once again, the Philistines had control over most of Israelite territory. From his stronghold deep in Transjordan, whither he had been taken by Abner after the débâcle, Saul's surviving son, Eshbaal, hollowly claimed kingship over all of Israel. In Hebron, on the other hand, David was publicly acclaimed king over Judah – undoubtedly with Philistine consent. His authority extended over a wider area than that occupied by the tribe of Judah and this area comprised a distinctive state.

Eshbaal was ineffectual, a weakling. After a two-year reign he was murdered by two of his officers, who brought his head to David in expectation of a reward. Instead, David had them executed, thus shrewdly clearing himself of complicity in what was for him a convenient assassination. With no one left to further the claims of the house of Saul, the people now flocked to David in Hebron, and there, by solemn covenant, acclaimed him king over all Israel, Yahweh's designated one. The people were clearly looking to David for charismatic leadership which would be capable of ridding them of the invader, and the Philistines, too, understood it that way. They immediately moved their forces against the new king. However, David inflicted upon them a series of stunning reverses which culminated in the Philistines being forced to pay tribute to David; indeed, contingents of Philistine professional soldiers subsequently appeared as mercenaries in the king's service.

Freed of external danger, David now consolidated his kingdom. After a few years' rule in Hebron, he captured the Jebusite city of Jerusalem, in about the year 1000 BCE, and made it his capital. It was a cunning choice. Located halfway between the northern and southern tribes, yet in the territory of neither, it was an ideal location from which to rule. By transferring the ark of the Covenant there, David made Jerusalem the religious, as well as the political, capital of his kingdom.

Securely established as king of a country which was more united than it ever had been – or would ever be again – David now embarked on a policy of military expansion which within a few years transformed Israel into the foremost power in Palestine and Syria. David's empire extended from Phoenicia in the west to the Arabian desert in the east, and from the river Orontes in the north to the head of the Gulf of Aqaba in the south. The

Canaanites of Palestine had been incorporated into the state, while the Philistines, together with the tribes of Moab, Edom and Ammon, yielded tribute.

The very extent of such conquests necessitated sweeping changes in the old order: Israel was no longer a tribal amphictyony led by a charismatic representative of Yahweh, but a complex empire organized under a crown. The Bible tells us little about David's administrative machinery, but it is enough to deduce that his bureaucracy was patterned on Egyptian models. His court, while nothing like as luxurious as Solomon's subsequently, was grand in comparison with Saul's. David's policy in religious matters was to legitimize the state, to have it accepted as the true successor of Israel's ancient order. To this end, he was a lavish patron of the new shrine in Jerusalem where the ark was housed, and the ark's two chief priests sat as members of his 'cabinet'.

David ruled for approximately forty years. Israel prospered. The national shrine in Jerusalem evoked loyalty from all the tribes and cemented, as did material and military success, a unity which previously had been brittle. Yet the strengths of autocratic leadership became, in time, weaknesses. This new Israel was so much David's own achievement, and so centred on his own person, that the question of the succession provoked bitter rivalries. David's last years were marked, as in classical tragedy, by faded grandeur, intrigue, filial rebellion, the severance of old loyalties and his own declining authority, mingled with remorse and uneasy memories. He went to his grave a feeble, querulous, much put-upon old man, to be succeeded by neither the oldest, nor the most popular, but certainly the most astute of his sons: Solomon.

Solomon, like David before him, ruled for approximately forty years, from c. 960 to 920. Although no warrior, he maintained David's empire almost intact, mainly by judicious alliances, many sealed by marriage. The most distinguished of Solomon's numerous foreign wives was a pharaoh's daughter, a union which illustrated both Israel's new prestige and the low estate to which the once-proud Egypt had sunk under its Twenty-first Dynasty. Solomon's true genius, however, lay in his instinct for industry and trade. He appreciated the economic significance of Israel's position, astride the major trade routes from Egypt and Arabia, and he developed her commercial possibilities to the full. A merchant fleet went on regular voyages from the Red Sea as far as Ophir – present-day Somaliland – and brought back gold and silver, rare woods, jewels, ivory; even, for his majesty's amusement, monkeys. Taxes and duties from the overland caravan-trade with Arabia flowed into the royal treasury. At Ezion Geber the largest refinery known to have existed in the ancient Orient was built, where copper was refined for domestic use, or worked into ingots for export. A lucrative monopoly in Cilician horses and Egyptian chariots (both the best of their kind) brought in further revenue.

The Bible accurately depicts Solomon's reign as one of unexampled prosperity. Israel enjoyed security and material plenty such as she was never to know again. The arts and sciences flourished; music and psalmody reached standards of excellence as high as any in the contemporary world; a literature developed, mainly historical in character (but also of the Wisdom genre) which retold the exploits of Israel's early heroes and, in the court history of David (II Samuel 9–20; I Kings 1–2), produced a narrative of superb lucidity, drama and psychological insight. Most important of all, it was probably in Solomon's reign that the Yahwist (so-called for want of a better name) selected from among Israel's epic traditions of Patriarchs, Exodus and conquests, the stories which he shaped into his great theological history of Yahweh's dealings with His people. This is the document that forms the basis of the pentateuchal narrative.

This climate of confident affluence was reflected in numerous building projects; apart from military and industrial constructions, Solomon erected, north of Jerusalem's old city wall, a lavish complex which included his magnificent palace, an armoury known as the 'House of the Forest of Lebanon' because of the massive cedar pillars that supported it, a Hall of Judgement, a palace for the pharaoh's daughter, and – the crowning glory – the Temple. The Temple was built by a Tyrian architect; it was with Hiram, King of Tyre, that Solomon had his closest commercial alliance. Wheat and olive-oil were exported from Palestine to Tyre in return for hardwood from Lebanon for Solomon's building schemes. The Temple took seven years to build: it was the invisible Yahweh's earthly house, whence He ruled His people, enthroned between two giant cherubim. In the holy of holies at the rear of the Temple reposed the ark, the symbol of the Covenant between Yahweh and Israel. The size and magnificence of the new national shrine demonstrated to strangers and natives alike that the God of Israel was powerful above all other gods. In the eleventh year of his reign, amid great pomp and ceremony, Solomon dedicated the Temple: a far cry indeed from the simple tent erected in the wilderness by the early Israelites.

Even Solomon, for all his wisdom, could be excused, at such a sweet moment of triumph, for failing to recognize that by building the Temple he had sown the seeds of his dynasty's downfall. But this was indeed the case: the Temple's work-force had only been provided by means of forced labour – and not only state slaves or Canaanite levies, but free-born Israelites, who worked in relays in Lebanon, felling timber. The hostility occasioned by this corvée was compounded by the increasingly heavy taxes Solomon laid on his subjects. The king's revenue, great as it was, was simply insufficient to maintain his sumptuous court, his large army, his growing bureaucracy and his grandiose building schemes. His methods of raising money became harsher, then desperate. He reorganized the land into twelve administrative districts, not always coinciding with old tribal boundaries, and obliged each district to maintain the court for one month. Solomon even began selling off his territory, ceding to the King of Tyre certain towns along the bay of Acre.

Such measures increased the tension between royal authority and tribal independence, between the old amphictyonic tradition and the new order. The monarchy was neither long-established nor totally accepted in Israel. The northern tribes, especially, rejected the claims of the Davidic dynasty to rule in perpetuity, and there were many who placed loyalty to Yahweh higher than loyalty to their earthly ruler. There was sullenness and resentment, but apart from a promptly squashed rebellion initiated by one Jeroboam late in his reign (I Kings 11:26–40), Solomon saw out his days without serious disturbance. It was his successor who reaped the whirlwind.

THE DISSOLUTION OF ISRAEL

When Solomon died in about 920 BCE, his son Rehoboam ascended the throne in Jerusalem (possibly Rehoboam and Jeroboam are both throne names; their meaning is virtually identical – 'may the people expand (or) multiply'). Rehoboam was accepted in the royal city without incident, as the descendant of the Davidic line. When he journeyed to Shechem, though, to be acclaimed King of Israel by the northern tribes, Rehoboam received a cool welcome. The tribal representatives demanded, as the price of their allegiance, that the burdens imposed by Solomon, especially the hated corvée, be lightened. Rehoboam was an arrogant and reckless young man. Instead of listening to the advice of the court elders, he heeded the young bloods of his entourage. When the representatives returned, Rehoboam promised them that in place of his father's whips, they would now be whipped with scorpions. Israel's representatives angrily announced their secession, lynched Rehoboam's chief of corvée, forced the king to flee ignominiously and elected in his stead Jeroboam, who had recently returned from exile in Egypt.

Thus did the united kingdom, and an extensive empire, patiently built by David and shrewdly maintained by Solomon, come to an end. Henceforth two separate, second-rate states existed, sometimes actively hostile, sometimes in uneasy alliance, side by side, until the northern kingdom of Israel was destroyed by the Assyrians in 722 and the southern kingdom of Judah disappeared under Babylonian attack almost 150 years later. The glory had been brief – about seventy years. From now on the historical pattern was set; a long, wearing struggle, in north and south, to maintain a tiny kingdom against rapacious neighbours.

Jeroboam's new kingdom of Israel, or Samaria, or, as it is sometimes called in the Bible, Ephraim, took in the ten northern tribes. Only Judah, and, after some hesitation, Benjamin – the hesitation arising because Benjamin was historically a northern tribe, the seat of Saul, but was geographically on the border of Jerusalem – remained loyal to Rehoboam. At first it seems surprising that the smaller, southern kingdom should have survived so much longer than its larger, wealthier neighbour. But the kingdom of Judah, as it now became, had two great advantages.

First, it was centred around Jerusalem, a natural defensive stronghold where the Temple evoked loyalty, yearning and religious fervour from all worshippers of Yahweh; and second, it was fortunate to have a Davidic line of moderately impressive rulers, who governed efficiently.

Israel, in the north, less compact, was vulnerable to both armed aggression and peaceful cultural infiltration, and suffered from unstable or corrupt leadership. It could offer no religious counter-attraction to Yahweh's Temple, and lapsed instead into a decadent syncretism of fertility worship, Canaanite idolatry and Ba'alism.

Jeroboam's ability, vigour and determination – especially when contrasted with the inadequacy of Rehoboam who allowed, in the fifth year of his reign, a devastating Egyptian invasion – imbued the foundation of the kingdom of Israel with illusory promise. The new state had neither capital, nor administration, nor army, nor official cult, all of which Jeroboam now organized. He established his capital in Shechem, which had ancient cultic associations. At Dan and Bethel, at opposite ends of his realm, he set up two official shrines whose priests claimed a separate lineage from that of the Temple clergy. Instead of the feast of the seventh month, in Jerusalem, Jeroboam instituted an annual eighth-month feast; and instead of the Temple's winged cherubim he built, at Dan and Bethel, two golden bulls.

The book of Kings, which reflects the viewpoint of the Jerusalemite tradition, accuses Jeroboam (I Kings 12:28) of having set up two golden idols. Probably that was not his intention, but such a fertility symbol was dangerously attractive to the many Israelites of Canaanite origin, who were willing to confuse Yahweh with Ba'al and to worship the One with the other's pagan rites. Certainly, prophetic circles in the north could not tolerate Jeroboam's religious policy, and his former patron, Ahijah of Shiloh, soon broke with him, rejecting him, as Samuel had Saul.

When Jeroboam died, his son Nadab and his entire house were assassinated by Baasha, who reigned for twenty-three years (900–877). In turn, Baasha's son Elah and his entire family were assassinated by Zimri, who within a week of the crime (I Kings 16:15–23) faced a revolt led by his general, Omri, whereupon he took his own life. The throne had, by violence, changed hands three times in fifty years.

In Judah, by contrast, one king, Asa, had ruled for almost that whole period (913–873). His son Jehoshaphat reigned for a further twenty-four years. It was a period of stability for the southern kingdom, and of prosperity too, since Judah still controlled the trade routes to the south, via the Gulf of Aqaba.

Omri, having seized power, reigned in Samaria for only seven years (876–869), but in that time he managed both to restore a measure of Israel's fortunes, and to establish a dynasty which survived for three generations. His strategy was based on internal prosperity, friendly relations with Judah and judicious alliances abroad, especially with Tyre, then at the peak of her colonial expansion. The King of Tyre's daughter, Jezebel, was given in marriage to Omri's son, Ahab, to seal a commercial treaty. Thus occurred one of the most notorious unions in history.

It was accepted practice for Jezebel to bring with her to her newly adopted country the worship of her native deities, Ba'al Melqart and Asherah; the foreign wives of Solomon had done the same (I Kings 11:1–8). What was unusual was the fervour with which Jezebel served Ba'al, her barely concealed contempt for culturally backward, religiously austere Israel and her strength of will, which made her the dominant partner in her marriage.

Before long, Ba'al, not Yahweh, had the larger following. The temptations of paganism had always been present in the country, especially since the mass absorption of the Canaanite population under David and Solomon. Now a fanatical queen was leading a crusade, her pliant husband barely demurring. Those loyal to Yahweh were persecuted, even put to death. The prophets of Ba'al and Asherah received official status, and the royal court was thoroughly paganized. Where their leaders went, the masses were ready to follow.

It was not only in religious affairs that Jezebel had her way. When Ahab coveted Naboth's vineyard, which Naboth refused to sell, Jezebel mocked her sulking husband and obtained the vineyard for him by having Naboth stoned on a trumped-up charge of blasphemy. Despite crop failure, famine and drought, she maintained an iron grip on the country. However hated she may have been, resistance and opposition had been silenced.

It was now that the Bible's most visionary, fearless and awe-inspiring personality appeared on the scene, to champion

Yahweh's cause – Elijah the prophet. He gave his name to no book, no prophecies are recorded in his name. The details of his career are sketched briefly in a few chapters of I and II Kings. Yet so wondrous was the memory Elijah left behind, that his deeds became legendary, and subsequent generations venerated him as the harbinger of the Messiah.

He was the quintessential prophet. A lonely, zealous man, single-minded in his fidelity to the God of the Sinaitic Covenant. He erupted from the desert wastes whenever Yahweh's battles had to be fought, clad only in the hair mantle of his calling. On Mount Carmel he faced the massed prophets of Ba'al in direct competition for the people's loyalty and won, putting the idolaters to the sword. He dared curse the king for his crime against Naboth. Forced to flee from Jezebel's wrath, he sought renewal at Horeb, the mountain of Israel's desert origins, and there had his faith revived by the 'still, small voice'. He returned to the fight against an apostate kingdom with its pagan deity, its corrupt king and queen the ultimate anathema to his God of Sinai, who brooked no rival, and exacted blood vengeance for crimes against Covenant law. Jezebel rightly recognized Elijah as her mortal enemy. He did not live to see her downfall. As abruptly as he had appeared, he vanished into the desert. His mantle fell upon his disciple, Elisha.

Soon after, Ahab died in battle against the Arameans. His eldest son, Ahaziah, reigned for only a few months before suffering a fatal accident (849 BCE). He was succeeded by his brother Jehoram (coincidentally, there was in Judah at this time another king Jehoram, who ruled for exactly the same number of years, 849–842). Jehoram of Israel tried to appease his citizens by removing the more objectionable pagan cult-objects. But he soon became entangled in two lengthy, inconclusive wars, first against Moab, then against Damascus. At home, the queen mother maintained her influence over a decadent and luxurious court. In the field, the army grew restive and resentful. Elisha fanned these flames of revolution. While Jehoram was away, convalescing from wounds, Elisha had Jehu, a general, anointed king. Jehu struck with viciousness and savagery. He murdered Jehoram and his kinsman, Ahaziah, the new King of Judah, who had been visiting him.

Jehu and his chariots then entered Jezreel. The queen mother, with a courage that elicits reluctant admiration, painted her eyes, attired herself and boldly confronted Jehu from a palace window. Tauntingly she called him 'Zimri'. Zimri, thirty-four years previously, had assassinated all of Baasha's family, only to be king for a single week. Two soldiers flung Jezebel from the window into the courtyard below, where she was trampled under the horses' hooves. The dogs then devoured her mangled body, as Elijah had prophesied.

A blood lust was now upon Jehu. He slaughtered Ahab's entire family and his court entourage, as well as a delegation from Jerusalem. He then invited the many worshippers of Ba'al into their temple, on the pretext of offering a sacrifice, and butchered every one of them. The temple itself was razed to the ground.

It had been a purge of wanton brutality, but the cult of Ba'al was extirpated, at any rate for the moment, even though Jehu still maintained the golden bulls at Dan and Bethel. He succeeded in keeping himself in power for twenty-seven years, and in founding a dynasty that survived for a century.

THE PROPHETS

Jehu's purge left a memory so vivid that the prophet Hosea made grim reference to it a century later (Hosea 1:4). Its excesses could not even be justified on the grounds of expediency. The cult of Ba'al Melqart had indeed been rooted out, but Jehu was no zealous Yahwist, and he allowed native varieties of paganism to proliferate unchecked.

Politically, his slaughter alienated Israel's two former allies, Tyre and Judah. Friendless and alone, Jehu could not withstand invasion from King Hazael of Aram, who annexed the whole of Transjordan, seized the Philistine territory on the coastal plain and refrained from marching into Judah only on payment of a huge tribute. Jehu's son and successor, Jehoahaz (815–801), was even further humiliated. He was only allowed a bodyguard of ten chariots and fifty horsemen, and his truncated kingdom was reduced to the status of an Aramean dependency.

The situation in Judah was almost as gloomy. Joash's long reign (837–800) was drawing to a close in an atmosphere of religious unrest, bitterness and failure. In the end, the king was assassinated, and succeeded by his son, Amaziah. The eighth century did not dawn propitiously for either Israel or Judah.

External events brought about a sudden change of fortune. For a brief period, both kingdoms were to enjoy power and prosperity unequalled since the days of David and Solomon. The cause was war between Assyria and Damascus. Taking advantage of this confrontation between the area's two major powers, Jehu's grandson, Jehoash (801–786), was able to recover most of Israel's lost territory. Under his successor, Jeroboam II (786–746), the northern kingdom reached new heights of wealth, as the luxurious buildings and costly ivories excavated at Samaria, not to mention the invectives of the prophet Amos, show. In Judah, too, under the equally able and long-reigning King Uzziah (783–742), the economy boomed, agriculture flourished and the citizens were better off than ever before. It was a time of optimism and affluence, as though Yahweh was giving material proof of His guardianship of His people.

It was also the time when the first two of that remarkable line of prophets, whose words are preserved in the Bible, took up their calling. Amos and Hosea saw through Samaria's glitter and luxury to the corruption beneath. They were not deceived by the ivory palaces of the wealthy, or by the throngs worshipping in the great shrines. For them, the obligations of the Covenant had become debased and perverted, and lavish support for the cult could not conceal a social system that was rotten.

Since our main historical sources for the period culminating in the Babylonian exile of 586 BCE are not only the books of Kings and Chronicles, but also the writings of the major prophets, it is appropriate at this point to say something about the prophets and their role. By now, they had a history going back some two hundred years. Bands of prophets (*b'nei ha-nevi'im*) roamed the country in the days of Samuel. They were 'professionals', paid soothsayers, who prophesied in groups, induced by music and by dance into an ecstatic frenzy. At times, their fervour caused people to look at them askance, to regard them as mad. They were, however, zealous patriots who would follow the army in the field, urging the king and his soldiers to holy war; and they were staunch in their fidelity to Yahweh's Covenant, feeling free to criticize any leader who did not uphold it, and if need be, to help to overthrow him.

It is impossible to construct a precise sociological outline of the prophetic calling, because our biblical data are incomplete, of varied sources, and tantalizingly sparse in many instances where the reader's knowledge is assumed. It is clear, though, that as in every profession, prophets came in a variety of shapes, sizes and quality. There were those who functioned as members of a group; those who walked alone. Some were attached to the court, as was Nathan, who rebuked David for his liaison with Bathsheba; others, Nahum for example, were cultic prophets. Certain prophets attracted disciples; others scorned the idea of prophetic orders and broke with them. The earliest prophets were ecstatically fired, acting out their prophecies mimetically; the later prophets delivered their messages in the form of sophisticated poetic oracles, often of the highest literary quality. These were delivered publicly, remembered, transmitted both orally and in written form, and then collected in the prophetic books as we know them.

Certain important differences distinguish Amos, Hosea and their successors from their largely anonymous predecessors. Amos and Hosea were the first representatives of a movement which was to continue for some three hundred years and to influence, colour and inspire Israel's religious development from that day to this. These new prophets came from every walk of life. They were not, as the earlier prophets had been, professional soothsayers. They were spokesmen of Yahweh, champions of the Covenant, preachers of righteousness, who came to their vocation under the compulsion of a call. They denounced social injustice, despised empty acts of ritual made to obtain divine favour, and inveighed against political and military pacts which would not avert the inevitable day of reckoning for those who repudiated Yahweh's Covenant and ignored His inexorable demands for justice and mercy.

In this respect the prophets were not, as they have often and mistakenly been made out to be, spiritual pioneers. On the contrary, they were religious reformers who reached back to a tradition that had originated in Israel's desert wanderings and the Sinaitic Covenant. They rejected the notion that Israel's relationship with Yahweh depended upon land, shrine or cult, or that Yahweh's special favour would survive unconditionally for all time. He would be Israel's God, and they would be His people, only if Israel discharged the imperatives of His law in every dealing with native and stranger alike, totally accepting Yahweh's overlordship and having no truck with other gods. If Israel departed from the Covenant obligations, punishment and exile would follow; if she obeyed them, redemption and a glorious return would be granted.

It was by the light of these standards that the prophets judged the kingdoms of Israel and Judah, and found them wanting. So exacting were their demands that probably no king, no secular government, could have met them, even partially. Politics is the art of the possible, whereas the prophets were impassioned idealists. They were obdurate, critical, insistent men, their presence an irritant and a rebuke to rulers who would not – could not – implement their lofty principles. At times, the ordinary people, too, dismissed them impatiently. Amos was laughed out of the royal shrine at Bethel when he delivered a stinging attack on the social evils of the day to a complacent, wealthy congregation. Yet, even when least heeded, the prophets were usually granted uneasy respect. The fervour of their allegiance to Yahweh's Covenant was their protection, although on occasion they were roughly treated; at the height of the bitter Babylonian siege of Jerusalem, Jeremiah was thrown into a prison pit for preaching what any reasonable man would construe as mutiny. But there is only one mention in the Bible of a prophet ever being put to death. Their religious commitment was total, their social concern all-embracing, their integrity inviolable, their role unique in the history of world religions.

Amos prophesied during the long, prosperous reign of Jeroboam II. Hosea was active in the chaotic years following his death. Israel had five kings between 746 and 736, three of them seizing power by violence, none with any legitimate claim to the throne. While Israel was collapsing in civil war and anarchy, and Hosea was proclaiming her impending doom, Assyria's new king, Tiglath-Pileser III, was laying the foundations of a great empire. He pushed westwards beyond the Euphrates; temporarily, he was bought off by the payment of a heavy tribute from

Israel. This caused bitter resentment among patriotic Israelites, the assassination of King Pekahiah (738–737), and the seizure of the throne by an army officer, Pekah ben Remaliah. His leadership of an anti-Assyrian coalition, which joined with Damascus and certain Philistine cities, hastened the inevitable destruction of Israel. Hosea paints a vivid picture of a country riven by plot and counter-plot, law and order having broken down, neither life nor property safe, and paganism, lechery and debauchery corroding the once-stern morality of the national religion. In the name of Yahweh, Hosea furiously catalogued Israel's crimes and foretold disaster. Yet, beyond that fearful punishment, he anticipated a sublime gesture of divine grace, a second Covenant, which would heal the breach between God and His people.

In Judah, a new king, Ahaz, had succeeded to the throne in 735. Judah would not join the anti-Assyrian coalition. The coalition could not tolerate a neutral, potentially hostile, neighbour, and invaded Judah from the north, aided in the south by an Edomite insurrection against Judean sovereignty. Ahaz, in desperation, appealed to Tiglath-Pileser, despite a stern warning from the prophet Isaiah not to take such a step, but to trust in Yahweh's promises to David. Dire emergency had no time for prophetic faith, and the Assyrian king was only too keen to help. His army fell upon the coalition and destroyed it utterly, occupying territory, deporting the resident population and razing cities. Pekah, whose policy had brought about the disaster, was murdered, and the new ruler, Hoshea ben Elah (732–724), averted further destruction by surrendering and paying tribute; but it was only a temporary respite.

The truncated kingdom of Israel, now reduced in size to an area no bigger than the old tribal holdings of Ephraim and western Manasseh, made one last attempt to throw off the yoke of Assyrian domination. When Tiglath-Pileser died, Hoshea made an alliance with an Egyptian princeling and withheld his tribute to the Assyrians. It was an opportunity for Assyria's new ruler, Shalmaneser V, to show his mettle. He invaded, occupied the land and took Hoshea prisoner. The city of Samaria defended itself for two years, and during this siege Shalmaneser died, to be succeeded by Sargon II. It was to him that the city fell in 721 BCE, and he who deported its citizens – over 27,000, according to his account.

Thus did the kingdom of Israel pass out of history. Her people were exiled to upper Mesopotamia and Medea, where in the course of time they merged with the local population and forgot their identity, becoming the 'ten lost tribes'. Henceforth, it is to the tiny country of Judah that we must look for the history and religion of the Jewish people.

THE DEMISE OF JUDAH

Judah escaped the disaster which befell Israel because her king, Ahaz (735–715), refused to join the anti-Assyrian coalition. The result, though – as the prophet Isaiah had predicted – was as dire as if she had been defeated in battle. Ahaz not only swore allegiance to Tiglath-Pileser; he also paid homage to the Assyrian gods and erected an altar for them in the Jerusalem Temple: Yahweh had been deposed in His sanctuary. Ahaz allowed all manner of pagan practices, cults and superstitions to flourish, even sacrificing his own son to the god Moloch. Religious corruption and social injustice were rife. Judah survived temporarily, but only by perverting the demands of Yahweh's Covenant; and to a prophet like Isaiah, her apostasy meant inexorable future punishment. The mighty nations of Egypt and Assyria, between which Judah wavered, were themselves merely the instruments of God's vengeance. To trust in Yahweh's eternal Covenant with David, and His choice of Zion for a dwelling-place, was Judah's only hope.

It seems that the stern warnings of the prophets Isaiah and Micah, and the vivid moral they drew from the destruction of neighbouring Israel, helped to create in Judah a popular demand for reform. Certainly, when Hezekiah succeeded his father on the throne, he undertook a cultic purge. Not only did he close down paganized local shrines and put a stop to the foreign practices which Ahaz had allowed; he tried to reverse his father's foreign policy, too. In 705 BCE, Sargon of Assyria met his death in battle, at a time when rebellion was threatening at both the eastern and western corners of his empire. Along with several other vassal states, Hezekiah decided that now was the time to try for independence. He formally refused to pay tribute to the new emperor, Sennacherib, and prepared the defences of Jerusalem, ensuring a water supply by digging the Siloam tunnel, which brought the waters of the spring of Gihon to a pool within the city walls. The gauntlet had been thrown down.

In 701, Sennacherib moved against his rebellious dependencies. He advanced down the Palestinian coast, conquering Tyre, and thus ending forever that kingdom's importance. Six frightened kings hastened to Sennacherib with tribute, leaving only Ashkelon, Ekron and Judah defiant. Ashkelon and Ekron were systematically destroyed. Sennacherib now turned against Judah. According to his records, he reduced forty-six of Judah's fortified cities to rubble, and deported their populations, shutting up Hezekiah, and the remnant of his army, in Jerusalem, 'like a bird in a cage'. Excavations at Lachish, which Sennacherib stormed, have revealed a huge pit, into which some 1,500 bodies had been dumped. Seeing his situation was hopeless, Hezekiah sued for peace. Sennacherib's terms were severe, obliging Hezekiah to strip the Temple and the royal treasury in order to raise tribute, and to send his own daughters as concubines to Nineveh.

Ten years later, another rebellion against Sennacherib broke out, led this time by Babylon, and supported by Egypt and Judah. Sennacherib subdued Babylon with great ferocity, then moved against Judah as he had done before. Once again his army blockaded Jerusalem. This time Hezekiah refused to surrender. He was supported by Isaiah, now an old man, who was convinced that God would not allow Jerusalem to be taken. Nor was it. A mysterious epidemic, perhaps bubonic plague, laid waste to Sennacherib's army, which, as Byron's poem puts it, 'melted like snow in the glance of the Lord!' Sennacherib limped away with the remnants of his army and the Judeans celebrated a remarkable deliverance. Zion, they came to believe, was inviolable. It was a dangerous article of faith and must have been ironic proof to Isaiah of the way words could be turned against themselves. He had never proclaimed that Zion and Judah would stand for all time, *as they were*. On the contrary; both he and his contemporary Micah foresaw the inevitable destruction of Judah because of its sinful people. Only a remnant would survive, returning to rebuild a new Jerusalem, to which all nations would look for light and guidance. A king of the Davidic line, excelling all others in goodness, would rule over this kingdom, and it would be a kingdom dedicated to righteousness and social justice, its society testifying to the blessings which flowed from worshipping God aright and following His path.

Hezekiah died in 687 BCE. One hundred years later Jerusalem was finally to fall. Our major historical sources for this period – II Kings 21–25; II Chronicles 33–36 – are supplemented by the writings of the prophets who functioned during that century, especially Jeremiah, Ezekiel, Zephaniah, Nahum and Habakkuk. Cuneiform sources, particularly the Babylonian Chronicle, supply further important information. Hezekiah was succeeded by his young son, Manasseh, who reigned for forty-five years, and throughout that time remained a loyal vassal to Assyria. His father's great rival, Sennacherib, had been murdered and succeeded by Esarhaddon (681–669), an extremely able ruler. It was his son and successor, Asshurbanapal (669–627), who finally captured Thebes in 663, thus terminating the Twenty-fifth Egyptian Dynasty. With the one power capable of orchestrating resistance to Assyria crushed, Manasseh had little option but to remain subservient.

But he went further than that. He annulled Hezekiah's religious reforms and restored pagan cults and practices, setting up altars to the Assyrian deities. Sacred prostitution and fertility rites took place within the Temple itself. Human sacrifices occurred: Manasseh was, in the biting verdict of the author of Kings, the worst king ever to sit on David's throne. His long reign came to an end in 642, but his policy of subservience to Assyria continued.

Perhaps it was as a protest that in 640 BCE certain palace officials assassinated his son and successor, Amon. If so, their gesture was unsuccessful, because 'the people of the land' – presumably an assembly of the landed gentry – speedily executed the murderers and placed Amon's eight-year-old son, Josiah, on the throne. Although there were now but fifty years before the destruction of the kingdom of Judah, Josiah was to prove her most important king, and his reign's events were of momentous significance to the future of the Jewish religion and people. During his early years, regents maintained a discreetly amenable policy towards Assyria. By the twelfth year of his reign (*c.* 629-8), the rule of Asshurbanapal in Nineveh was drawing to an unquiet close, with unrest at home and danger threatening from without, from the Medes and Babylonians. The time was ripe. Josiah struck a blow for independence. Assyria had divided the territory of northern Israel into provinces, and these Josiah occupied. Then he launched the most comprehensive religious reformation in Judah's history. We cannot be entirely sure in what order the reformation's various stages were carried out, but certainly they all involved a consistent purge of foreign cults and practices, the suppression of native pagan cults, the destruction of Samarian shrines (particularly Bethel) and the death of idolatrous priests and sacred prostitutes. The reform culminated in the eighteenth year of Josiah's reign (622 BCE) with the discovery, during the course of repairs to the Temple, of 'the book of the law' (II Kings 22:3 ff.). Having consulted Huldah the prophetess, Josiah summoned the elders to the Temple, read to them the words of the book, and entered with them into a solemn covenant, before Yahweh, to obey those words. As one of its commandments was the observance of the Passover, Josiah commemorated the Exodus from Egypt with a great Passover in Jerusalem – the first time, according to the author of Kings, that the Passover had been kept since the days of the Judges.

Most scholars now agree that the law-book found in the Temple was a version of the book of Deuteronomy (a view first put forward, as it happens, by Jerome and other Church Fathers). Its discovery was of enormous importance: at a time of national unease, of a painful past and an uncertain future, here, suddenly, was an urgent reminder of the Mosaic Covenant. Insistently, these ancient laws spelled out the statutes and commandments which the people had promised to obey, before Yahweh, at Sinai. They called the people back to their stark obligations, to ethical duties easily overlooked in the political needs of the moment, or in dreams of kingship and imperial grandeur.

Josiah's reaction, when he heard the law-book, was to rend his garments in dismay. So much had been forgotten, so much ignored! It was this sense of having betrayed the past that gave conviction and impetus to his reforms. The people responded willingly. Outlying sanctuaries were abolished and Jerusalem was firmly established as the one legitimate place of worship. The state, led by its king, was officially committed to observance of Covenant law. This adherence to the written law, its elevation to the status of the ultimate authority, was a first step in that process which was to regulate the Jewish religion – Judaism – for more than two thousand years after the Babylonian exile. Josiah's reign was crucial for the survival of a people through its religion.

He died in 609 BCE, killed in battle at the Megiddo pass, which he was trying to hold against a large mixture of Egyptians and Assyrians. His chariot was brought to Jerusalem amid great lamentation, and his son Jehoahaz made king in his place. But not for long: within three months he was summoned to Pharaoh Neco II's headquarters at Riblah, deposed and deported to Egypt. His brother Jehoiakim was placed on the throne as an Egyptian vassal and the land was put under heavy tribute. Judah's political independence – and religious renaissance – had lasted scarcely twenty years. Jehoiakim was a grandiose and irresponsible despot, who preferred building himself a new and finer palace with forced labour to maintaining his father's religious reforms. The prophet Jeremiah expressed scathing contempt for him (Jeremiah 22:13–19).

In 605, the balance of Middle-Eastern power was rudely upset. The Babylonian forces of Nebuchadnezzar fell upon the Egyptian army at Carchemish and routed it, dealing the fleeing remnants an even heavier blow, near Hamath. Babylon was indisputably master of the region and Judah became, yet again, an unwilling vassal to a Mesopotamian empire. Jehoiakim still looked to Egypt. At Neco's instigation, he rebelled in 601. It was a fatal error. Nebuchadnezzar had no intention of relinquishing Judah. He bided his time, and in December 598, his army marched. That very month, Jehoiakim died – probably assassinated – and his eighteen-year-old son, Jehoiachin, had to bear the brunt of the Babylonian assault. The hoped-for Egyptian help did not come, and in March 597 Jerusalem surrendered. Jehoiachin, the queen mother, the high priests and leading citizens, together with vast stores of booty, were taken to Babylon.

Zedekiah, an uncle of the king, was installed as ruler of the truncated country. Yet still Judah would not learn from her disastrous experiences. The ten years of Zedekiah's reign were marked by sedition, attempted rebellion, internal dissent and eventual tragedy. A death wish was on the people and the land, poignantly evoked and poetically expressed by Jeremiah, who was, however, unable to prevent it and was himself, in the tensions of the time, denounced as a traitor and nearly put to death. Zedekiah was well-intentioned but weak. Whatever authority he had was undermined by the fact that most people still regarded his nephew, Jehoiachin, as the true king. So did the Babylonians. Their texts show that Jehoiachin was a pensioner at Nebuchadnezzar's court, and they describe him as 'King of Judah'. (This is why the Gospel according to St Matthew, when tracing back the genealogy of Jesus, does it through Jehoiachin, the legitimate king.) Despite repeated warnings from Jeremiah, in 589 BCE Zedekiah allowed temporary unrest in Babylon, a patriotic ground-swell at home and vague assurances from Egypt and other neighbouring states, to push him into yet another rebellion. The Babylonian reaction was swift and brutal. A large army arrived by January 588 and began the systematic destruction of outlying strongholds, until only Jerusalem remained. Morale was briefly raised by the news of an advancing Egyptian army, but it was only a temporary respite. The siege lasted two years: Jerusalem's inhabitants held out with desperate bravery, heavily outnumbered, lacking food, torn between the propaganda of Zedekiah and his faction and the doom-laden prophecies of Jeremiah, who urged them to surrender since resistance was hopeless, Babylon's mastery having been determined by the will of God.

In July 586, the city's walls were breached. Zedekiah fled during the night, but was overtaken near Jericho. He was brought before Nebuchadnezzar and shown no mercy. Forced to witness the execution of his sons, he was then blinded and taken in chains to Babylon. A month later Jerusalem was put to the torch, its Temple fired and its walls razed. Certain religious, military and civil leaders were brought before Nebuchadnezzar at Riblah and executed, while others were deported to Babylon. Only peasant labourers were left behind, to tend the land.

The state of Judah had ceased to exist. Yet still it twitched, if only briefly. Gedaliah, who had been chief minister under Zedekiah, was appointed governor. He tried to restore some semblance of normalcy to the land, but was murdered by diehards who regarded him as a collaborator. As a reprisal, the Babylonians deported still more of the population in 582, while others – taking Jeremiah with them – fled to Egypt.

Captivity and exile; that was the fate of Judah and its people, as it had been of the northern kingdom a century and a half previously. Unlike the ten lost tribes, though, Judah's citizens were to survive, and were to spread their message of Judaism wherever they settled. They had lost their Temple, the dwelling place of their God; but they had His words enshrined in their written law, a law which was not dependent on any physical location.

CHAPTER FOUR   EXILE AND RESTORATION

THE BABYLONIAN DISPERSAL

By any reasonable expectation, the kingdom of Judah and its religion would now fade away to become a footnote on the pages of history. The aristocrats and ecclesiastics and civil servants had been deported to Babylon, leaving behind a destroyed religious shrine and a shattered social structure. Nebuchadnezzar's army had razed the major centres of population. Fields lay fallow and harvests rotted as the peasants fled. The Babylonians did not replace deported Jews with new colonists, as the Assyrians had done in Samaria; thus it has been estimated that Judah's population of 250,000 inhabitants in the eighth century had now dwindled to about 20,000.

Their country had been ravaged, their morale sapped by years of withstanding superior forces and their religious faith traumatized by the burning and desecration of Yahweh's Temple, but by all accounts the exiles received a sympathetic welcome in Babylon. They were placed in their own settlements and they resumed their regular occupations. It was during the half-century of exile that Babylonian names, the Babylonian calendar and the Aramaic language were adopted by the captives. What more natural than that the Judeans should be assimilated into the wealthy and powerful Babylonian culture and that their religion – until now never rigidly adhered to, anyway – should wither in a strange land, with no central shrine at which to offer their sacrifices, their belief in Yahweh's eternal choice of Zion brutally disproven by Nebuchadnezzar's battering-rams? Instead, a new community was formed out of the wreckage of the old, and a new faith, purified, refined, was forged out of adversity. It was in exile that Judaism was moulded and took the shape that it was to follow through the centuries to come.

What were the reasons for this astonishing refusal to go the way of other small, defeated nations? Why do we glimpse here the first large-scale example of that stubborn, tenacious fidelity to self that is one of the distinctive traits of Judaism, and is the cause of such mingled exasperation and admiration in others? We can only suggest explanations from the evidence that has survived, and on the basis of that evidence we must give priority to the teachings of three prophets: Jeremiah, Ezekiel and the unknown author who is usually referred to as the second Isaiah.

It was Jeremiah's insistence that opposition to Nebuch-adnezzar's besieging army was pointless, because the Babylonians were the instruments of divine retribution, that had made him probably the most hated man in Jerusalem. Yet, even as the city was in its dying agony and his prophecies were coming to pass, he visualized a consolatory future when the exiles would return and God would make a new covenant with His chastened and puri-fied people. As proof of his certitude, Jeremiah bought from a kinsman a tract of land then occupied by the invading army. He sent a message of comforting encouragement to the captives in Babylon, telling them to rebuild their lives there until they were gathered home by their God.

If the prophecies of Jeremiah and his predecessors were eagerly scanned by the captives as vindication of the deserved punishment that had befallen them, the urgent, topical teachings of Ezekiel gave them solace in the present. Ezekiel does not attract the modern reader. Apart from his famous metaphor of the dispersed Israel as a valley of dry bones into which God will breathe new life, he is a coarser, more prosaic prophet than his two great contemporaries, at times ecstatically convulsed or crudely obsessed with images of disease, never reaching their heights of exalted vision; but his combination of ritual scrupulosity and the unwavering assurance that each individual is punished or rewarded according to his own conduct, rather than that of an-other, gave the people a theology which was comforting and therapeutic. Heightened emphasis on ritual is frequently the response of those who feel guilty of religious dereliction, and it was during the years of exile that sabbath observance and circumcision became increasingly stressed as marks of a loyal Jew. We learn from the book of Ezekiel that the exiles assembled in the prophet's house for instruction and inspiration, probably on sabbaths and holy days, and it was possibly in such conventicles that the institution which eventually came to replace the Temple – the synagogue – had its origin.

It was also during the exile, though we cannot say precisely where or how, that the narrative and legal records of Israel's past were assembled and edited into something like the form they were finally to take in the Bible. (For a fuller discussion of biblical literature, see part II, chapter 1.)

Homesick for distant Zion, and adjusting to life as sojourners in a strange land, the exiles must nevertheless have been aware of the disruptive events taking place within the Babylonian empire. After Nebuchadnezzar's death in 562 BCE, the throne changed hands three times in seven years, and its third claimant, Nabonidus (556–539), was a religious recluse who transferred his residence to a desert oasis and left the affairs of state in the hands of his son Belshazzar. Poised on Babylon's borders stood Cyrus, King of Persia, who, in a series of brilliant campaigns, had carved out an empire that stretched from Egypt and the Aegean shore of Asia Minor to eastern Iran. It was only a matter of time before he was to invade Babylon itself. Watching this imminent clash of two mighty nations, perhaps from Judea, as one of the few Judeans left there, perhaps from Babylon, as one of the exiles, was the third prophet, probably the greatest of all who bore that title. Because we do not know his name, and because the redactor of the Bible tacked his prophecies on to the thirty-nine chapters of Isaiah the son of Amoz, who had preached during the reigns of Uzziah and Hezekiah, two hundred years before, our anonymous prophet is called the second Isaiah. It is he whose talent for vivid imagery, whose radiant ability to give comfort, and whose radical reinterpretation of Israel's theology, raised prophecy to its peak of poetic and religious expression. When we read the fifteen chapters usually attributed to Second Isaiah, we are astonished – as we are when we read *Hamlet* – at the number of quotes therein. He is perhaps the greatest religious poet of all time.

His most important contribution to Israel's faith is the reiteration of absolute monotheism. The God of Israel is not merely Yahweh, a local god among other deities, but He is the One God, creator and ruler of the world. God is ruler of the world, and He is also the master of history. Even the mighty Cyrus is an unwitting tool of Yahweh's purpose. This all-powerful and all-redeeming God had chosen His people Israel a long time before to be His witnesses: His witnesses and His suffering servants, whose mission it was not merely to restore the Davidic kingdom, but to labour unremittingly for the day when all nations would accept God's law. Second Isaiah affirms that this is their ultimate, universal destiny, and it is in this context that Israel's mission, and world history, must be viewed. Such soaring and unequivocal faith was soon to receive practical confirmation. In 538, after conquering Babylon, Cyrus issued a decree permitting the Judean exiles to return to Jerusalem and rebuild their Temple.

THE RETURN TO ZION

When the Lord brought back those who returned to Zion,
We were like those who dream.
Then our mouth was filled with laughter,
And our tongue with shouts of joy.

So wrote the psalmist about the return from Babylonian captivity, but the harsh reality was far removed from poetic imagery. The – in second Isaiah's phrase – 'remnant of the house of Israel', who took advantage of Cyrus's decree, came back to a wasted and devastated Palestine. They faced years of hardship and danger. A succession of poor seasons and crop failures greeted them. Neighbours, especially those in Samaria, were openly hostile after their initial overtures of help had been rebuffed. The native Judeans were wary of the returnees, and resentful of their assumption of being the true Israel; nor could they have been happy to give back land that they had come to regard as their own.

It is at this crucial stage of Jewish history, when the universal and recognizable religion of Judaism is beginning to break through the mould of its parochial antecedents, that our sources of information about the next two hundred years are distressingly meagre. What we have is, at best, fragmentary, uncertain or in-consistent. It is possible, though, by using the biblical records of Ezra and Nehemiah, and the post-exilic prophecies of Haggai, Zechariah, Obadiah and Malachi, as well as our knowledge about the Persian empire, to reconstruct plausibly the events of the period.

Thus we know that Cyrus's original permission for the Judean captives to return home was in keeping with the enlightened colonialism with which he ruled his territories. A large army, efficient posts and communications, and a complex bureaucracy, whose highest echelons were staffed by trusted Medes and Per-sians, enabled him to govern with a loose rein and to allow a fair degree of autonomy to his subject nations. It suited him to have an enclave of grateful Jews in Palestine, strategically close to the Egyptian frontier.

We cannot be sure how many thousands returned under the leadership of Sheshbazzar and his nephew Zerubbabel, both members of the royal dynasty. The generation who remembered Zion would have been elderly, and for their children it would be a difficult, lengthy journey with an uncertain outcome. The venture would only appeal to those brave enough, or idealistic enough, to give up their Babylonian security for the hazards of pioneering.

Work on restoring the Temple appears to have started im-mediately, and the priesthood resumed its functions under Joshua, son of Jehozadak, a man of Aaronide lineage. But the initial enthusiasm soon faded. Those old enough to remember the glory of the first Temple wept bitterly when they saw the modest dimensions of its replacement. Promises of aid from the Persian court did not materialize. Tension between the returning exiles and their native kinsmen was exacerbated by religious differences. Haggai and Zechariah give hints of an impoverished and dis-pirited community, in which Second Isaiah's vision of a great ingathering and the establishment of Yahweh's universal rule from Zion was fragmented because of selfishness, indifference and religious syncretism – the mixing of Israelite and pagan prac-tices. Both prophets urged the people to complete the rebuilding of the Temple speedily, as a precondition of the fulfilment of Yahweh's promise.

Finally, around 515 BCE, in the sixth year of the reign of Darius, the second Temple was finished, and joyfully dedicated. It neither testified to national glory, as had Solomon's, nor did it presage the re-establishment of the Davidic dynasty and the dawn of Yahweh's rule, as Haggai had elliptically intimated. It did, however, provide the returned exiles with a symbol to justify their faith and vindicate their decision to leave Babylon for Jerusalem.

We know little about their fortunes over the next seventy years. This is not surprising. The small nation, precariously existing in the few square miles around its rebuilt Temple, was a sub-district of the Persian empire, an extra on the stage of world history – the stage where the irresistible onward march of Darius was only halted at Marathon by the Athenians, where his successors Xerxes and Artaxerxes were to continue the war against the Greek states, and where men such as Pericles, Socrates, Sophocles and Aeschylus were about to make their marks on western civilization.

Presumably, groups of Jews, not only from Babylon, but also from lower Egypt – where Jeremiah and others had gone after the fall of Jerusalem – even a few, perhaps, from the settled and flourishing Jewish colony at Elephantine at the first cataract of the Nile, continued to drift back to the homeland during these years. Certainly, the population of Judah had doubled by the middle of the fifth century. Nevertheless, it was an unhappy community, under pressure from without, divided within. There was constant friction with provincial officials in Samaria, who sent back critical reports to the Persian government. Edomite tribesmen harassed their borders.

External difficulties increased internal disillusion. Malachi is as vehement as any of his predecessors in denouncing moral laxity, priestly corruption and the breakdown of ethical standards. The high rate of divorce was a public scandal, and the line separating Jews from pagans was blurring, through numerous intermarriages which threatened the community's integrity. It was at this time of imminent disintegration that two men appeared on the scene whose efforts saved the Jewish community and the Jewish religion.

NEHEMIAH AND EZRA

The first, Nehemiah, was cup-bearer to Artaxerxes. Distressed by the reports of a delegation from Jerusalem about the desperate situation there, he approached the king and was appointed governor of Judah, with permission to rebuild Jerusalem. Sometime between 444 and 440 BCE, he set out from the Persian capital of Susa. Three days after his arrival in Jerusalem he made a secret, nocturnal inspection of the city walls, to assess the extent of the task. Nehemiah set to work with energy and determination. He faced the obstructionist tactics of the resentful governors of Samaria and Ammon, the incursions of guerrilla bands, an assassination attempt and accusations of sedition. His personal bravery and resourcefulness overcame all challenges. The walls of Jerusalem were rebuilt and solemnly dedicated. With the same furious energy – and temper – Nehemiah undertook a series of sweeping social reforms. He forced greedy landowners to return confiscated property and cancel the debts of an impoverished peasantry. As a personal example, he forwent the usual prerequisites of governorship, and lived in a conspicuously modest fashion. Then he turned his attention to religious laxity. To stop business being transacted on the sabbath, he ordered the city gates to be shut all that day. Dishonest priests were replaced. When he discovered children of mixed marriages who could not speak Hebrew, his rage was fearsome, and he demanded of the populace an oath not to intermarry with foreigners in the future.

Nehemiah's first term as governor lasted twelve years. It was either during it, or during his second term of office – the biblical chronology is confusing – that his contemporary, Ezra, made the journey from Babylon to Jerusalem, at the head of a large entourage. Ezra's commission, signed by Artaxerxes, was to teach the law of Moses to Jews living in the satrapy of Abar-Nahara, and to set up an administrative system to implement it. Thus he came for a specific religious task, bringing with him a copy of the law, his authority derived not merely from royal decree, but from his own priestly descent and expertise in the law. We are not told details of this law, this Torah, that Ezra brought with him. It might have been the Pentateuch (the five books of Moses) in what must have been close to its final redaction; certainly it contained the so-called priestly code, which chiefly comprises the book of Leviticus and concerns the laws of sacrifice, priestly privileges and ritual purification.

Two months after his arrival in Jerusalem, from a wooden platform in a public square, Ezra read to the assembled people from the law. He read from daybreak until noon, and his assistants translated the Hebrew text into Aramaic, so that everyone should fully understand. The response of the crowds was immediate. They were moved to bitter tears as they realized how abjectly they had neglected their religious heritage. Ezra had to remind them repeatedly that mourning was inappropriate on such a day of rejoicing. The following day, after further instruction, the people went out to gather foliage in order to build the booths which are a symbol of the festival of Tabernacles. It was celebrated with great joy, as had not happened since the days of Joshua according to the book of Nehemiah (8:17), in an echo of Josiah's reading from the book of the law and reinstitution of Passover, nearly a century before.

Ezra now moved against more serious violations. Chief among them was the high rate of intermarriage. Cleverly, Ezra induced the conscience-stricken people to propose themselves that such marriages should be terminated. Three months later a commission appointed by Ezra completed its investigations and all mixed marriages were dissolved.

The people now gathered for a solemn fast of repentance, after which they ratified a formal covenant, that henceforth they would live according to the law. They bound themselves to abjure foreign marriages in future, to refrain from work on the sabbath, to let the land lie fallow and forgo the collection of debts every seventh year, to levy an annual tax for the maintenance of the sanctuary and to present tithes and first-born offerings as Mosaic law prescribed. Nehemiah's social programme had found its realization in Ezra's religious reforms. The law, accepted by the people in solemn covenant before Yahweh, became the constitution of the people. In future, the distinguishing characteristic of a Jew would be neither nationality, nor ethnic origin, nor even participation in the Temple cult; it would be acceptance of, and adherence to, the law of Moses.

The fusion of peoplehood and religion was achieved. Henceforth, whether its followers were gathered in one land or scattered over the globe, whether persecuted or tolerated, the survival of Judaism had been secured.

THE REDACTION OF THE BIBLE

Since Ezra was venerated by succeeding generations as second only to Moses, the original lawgiver, and since records of Judah's political history over the next century are scanty, until the irruption on the world scene of Alexander the Great, we might usefully pause here and consider the nature of the reforms that Ezra instituted. It must be remembered that the repopulated Judean state was in no sense a restored Davidic kingdom. It was a dependency of the Persian empire, granted that degree of religious and administrative autonomy characteristic of Persian rule; but it was impotent – unlike the pre-586 kingdom – to pursue its own foreign policy. If we think of modern Monaco or the republic of San Marino, we have a valid, and not disrespectful, comparison with the size and political influence of fifth-century Judah. True, its Temple had been rebuilt. But this was no triumphant expression of the might and potency of Israel's national God, as the first Temple had been. Although the High Priest was to exercise authority for some time to come, if the chain of tradition later claimed by the Rabbis is to be accepted, then it was Ezra who convened the so-called Great Assembly and thereby created a new class of lay interpreters – *Soferim* (scribes) – of the law. It was this law which now defined the Israelite, where territorial inhabitation or cultic adherence had done so previously. The Jews – *Yehudim*, that is, inhabitants of Judah – were scattered in communities throughout Mesopotamia and Egypt. Nostalgia for Jerusalem's Temple would be no more effective in maintaining their distinctive identity than would dim memories of former glory under the Davidic dynasty. It was common acceptance of the law, given by Yahweh to Moses and, through him, to Israel, which henceforth would unite Jews, wherever they lived, into a religious whole.

In that sense, the law which Ezra brought with him and promulgated in the homeland expanded Judaism, rather than circumscribed it. Everyone who accepted the Covenant law and its conditions, whether they were Israelite-born or gentiles who renounced their previous allegiances, would be classed as a Jew.

It could be objected that Ezra's edict against foreign wives was a piece of nastily particularistic legislation, contrary to the spirit of second Isaiah's noble universalism, whereby Yahweh would become the God of all peoples. No doubt Ezra would have retorted that the exigencies of the hour demanded a clear definition of Jewish status, and that for those who accepted Mosaic law, as well as remembered the words of the prophets, the moral was clear: defection from the paths of Torah had caused persecution and exile. Fidelity to its commandments would be rewarded by an ingathering of the dispersed and Yahweh's special providence.

The tension between particularism and universalism is a peculiarly Jewish problem of theology, and one that has been constant since Ezra's time until the present day. Before the Second World War, for example, the Progressive movement within Judaism was boldly universalistic in outlook, and second Isaiah was its favourite prophet. Since the Nazi genocide of six million Jews, and the constant danger under which the young State of Israel has lived, the Jewish people have tended to withdraw into themselves, and perceive survival as their first priority. It is significant that one response to the traumatic shock of the Yom Kippur War in 1973 was a resuscitation in Israel of the hoary 'Who is a Jew?' controversy, the religious authorities seeking to define Jewish status by formulas that Ezra would have recognized and approved of.

It should not be supposed that Ezra's reforms were accepted without demur in his own time. The consensus of Bible scholars is that the book of Ruth – a pastoral idyll set in a dim and distant past in which Ruth, a Moabite, becomes the ancestor of the revered King David – was written as a deliberate retort to Ezra's edict against foreign wives. Likewise, the post-exilic book of Jonah is about a prophet delivering his message to gentiles, not Jews, and the God of all peoples accepting their repentance. In the main, though, the generations succeeding Ezra submitted willingly to the discipline and limitations of the law. Even the Temple cult became secondary to the law, because the priestly hierarchy and the sacrificial rituals existed only in so far as the Torah demanded them. The priest – even the High Priest – became a functionary of the law, rather than its arbiter. That role passed to the class of scribes who devoted themselves to study of the law and its interpretation. It was the Scribes and their disciples, who functioned as Ezra's successors, and were known collectively by later Jewish tradition as 'the men of the Great Assembly', who in all probability were responsible for the canonization of the Pentateuch in about 400 BCE and thereafter of the prophetic canon, which was fixed some time before the second century.

In the century between Ezra and Alexander the Great, then, this tiny, reconstituted people – not worth a second glance in terms of political importance – was engaged in an astonishing explosion of religious activity and self-definition, as well as literary activity. The prophetic oracles of Joel, Zechariah and Malachi were composed shortly before Ezra's ministry; subsequently, the historical narratives of I and II Chronicles, the religious lyrics of the book of Psalms, the Wisdom literature of Proverbs, the profoundly questioning book of Job and the love poems of the Song of Songs, were all written, or received their final form, in the Persian period.

The canonizing of the law gave Judaism tangible and absolute norms. 'Turn it [the Torah] over and over,' said a later teacher of the law, 'for everything is contained in it,' and so it must have seemed. Personal conduct, ethical guidance, religious duty, right and wrong behaviour and the endless saga of Israel's sinfulness and God's forgiveness, were there for all to learn about in the Pentateuch and the prophetical books. Since Aramaic was the lingua franca of the Persian empire, and also the language of the ordinary Jew, its square characters replaced the Hebrew script of pre-exilic times. For those unable to read or understand, the Pentateuch was expounded in the towns of Judea, not only on the sabbath, but also on Mondays and Thursdays – the market days. It is worth noting, too, that at some time during this period, along with the renewed stress on sabbath observance, circumcision and the purificatory obligations which the law demanded of the professing Jew, the Day of Atonement acquired its significance as the most solemn day of the Jewish calendar. Its ritual of confession of sin and expiation held a keen meaning for the Jews of the return. The great judgement of exile and their present lowly estate were sharp reminders of the punishment for transgressing the law's commands.

Were it not for the magnificent works of literature composed then, or our reconstruction of the process whereby the scribes gave canonical status to the Torah and expounded its teachings, we would know next to nothing about the situation in Judah during this period. We do not even know the names of the high priests or governors. We can safely assume that relationships between Jews and Samaritans continued to worsen during this century, even though the northern neighbours accepted the Pentateuch as the law of Moses. They did not accord the same esteem to the prophetical writings, though, and could not have been pleased with the claim of the historian of Chronicles that the true Israel was to be found in the restored remnant of Judah. Late in the fourth century the Samaritans built their own sanctuary on Mount Gerizim, near Nablus, and the religious rupture was complete, although members of the two communities maintained contact for a long time afterwards.

The course of world history, which swept tiny Judah along in its wake, can be summarized briefly. In Persia, Artaxerxes died in 424 BCE, that is, shortly after the reforms of Ezra and Nehemiah. Although Egypt managed to rebel successfully in 401, Artaxerxes II Mnemon (404–358) otherwise maintained his empire intact, his implacable Greek foes having exhausted themselves in the Peloponnesian wars. The succession to the Persian throne was marred by an orgy of intrigue and assassination which dangerously weakened the empire just as Philip II of Macedon (reigned 359–336) was beginning to dominate Greece politically and militarily. Philip was murdered and his son Alexander (born 356 BCE) ascended the throne. In 334 Alexander crossed the Hellespont and dealt crushing defeats to the Persian armies, which destroyed the empire and opened the way for Alexander's conquest of Egypt and large areas of western India. Owing to the astonishing victories of a man who, when not yet thirty, wept, so legend has it, because there were no more worlds to conquer, Jews and Judaism came under the influence of Greek language, literature and civilization.

CHAPTER FIVE   THE GREEK PERIOD

According to the Jewish-Roman historian Josephus, in a story amplified in later talmudic writings, Alexander the Great made obeisance before the High Priest in Jerusalem. Since the identical story occurs in Samaritan sources, with Alexander making obeisance to *their* high priest, we can consign that legend alongside the others which immortalize the great conqueror, from Iceland to China, whose name is still invoked as the ancestor of Afghanistan tribesmen and the protector of Greek fishermen on stormy Aegean seas. Such was the glamour of the Macedonian who fell sick and died in Babylon in 323 BCE, leaving his generals to divide up his territories between them.

By destroying the Persian empire, and opening the countries of the Orient to the Greeks, Alexander had effectively abolished the frontiers between east and west. Peoples merged and blended with each other in a fusion of cultural and social patterns that became known as Hellenistic civilization. This was not the 'high' Hellenic culture of Herodotus and Thucydides, Sophocles and Euripides, Plato and Aristotle, in the period before Alexander. Its standard-bearers were not scholars, but merchants and peasants, soldiers, adventurers and traders, who poured into the lands of the Orient. They brought with them Greek architecture, Greek notions of citizenship, Greek deities, science, philosophy, theatre, art, dress, the *Gymnasion* in which to inculcate Greek ideals of education and physical grace, and most important of all, the Greek language, which speedily took over as the medium of diplomacy, commerce and social intercourse.

After two decades of war between Alexander's quarrelling

generals, three major Hellenistic states emerged: the Antigonid dynasty of Macedonia, the Ptolemies in Egypt and the Seleucids in northern Syria, Mesopotamia and Iran. After 301, Palestine fell under Ptolemy's rule, and remained so for over a century. Over thirty Greek cities had been established in Palestine, along the coast and in the region of Transjordan, but since the Ptolemies continued the policies inherited from the Persians, granting a large degree of political and religious autonomy to subject nations, we can assume that the Jews accepted passively their new overlords. The High Priest, who was personally responsible for yielding tribute to the crown, came to be regarded, during this period, as the titular representative of the community, and a priestly aristocracy developed in the shadow of his influence. The Jews remained submissive subjects and enjoyed relative peace. Their contact with their Hellenized neighbours, and the influence of Greek thought, is apparent in two literary works of the period: in the sceptical and pessimistic fatalism of Ecclesiastes – the least likely book to be included in the Bible – and the Wisdom teachings of ben Sira.

It was, though, the Jews living outside Palestine, far outnumbering their Judean co-religionists, who were most receptive to Hellenism. The Jewish population of Egypt was augmented by an influx of immigrants who turned the city of Alexandria into a Jewish metropolis. Although Hebrew continued to be understood by a minority, Jews in Egypt adopted Greek as their native tongue: Greek was spoken in the synagogues, in the communal assemblies and in daily life. It was for these Jews, no longer conversant with Hebrew, that a translation into Greek of the Pentateuch, then of the other biblical books, had to be made. This Greek translation of the Scriptures became known as the Septuagint, or 'translation of the seventy', so-named because, according to legend, seventy scholars, working independently, each produced a translation that tallied word for word with the other sixty-nine. Equally improbable is the account in the Letter of Aristeas which claims that the initiative for the translation came from Greek courtiers of Ptolemy II, who were anxious to learn the Jewish Scriptures. The important fact is that a Greek version of the Bible now existed. The intersection of Jewish religion and Greek thought was to have a profound influence on the future history of western theology and philosophy, through the Middle Ages and beyond.

In 198 BCE, the Seleucid king, Antiochus III, defeated the Egyptian army at Baniyas, near the headwaters of the river Jordan, and thereupon annexed Palestine. The Jews, who had suffered in the struggle between Egyptian and Seleucid dynasties, took up arms against Ptolemy's garrison in Jerusalem, welcoming the change. Antiochus, in turn, approached the community with conciliatory tact. He ordered the release of Jews who had been captured while fighting for Ptolemy. Jerusalem was spared taxes for three years, in order to recover economically. The privileges that Jews had enjoyed under Persian and Ptolemaic rule were guaranteed, including the right to live 'according to their ancestral laws'. As a sign of good faith, Antiochus undertook needed Temple repairs, promised state aid for the Temple cult and exempted all religious personnel from taxes. Seleucid rule had begun auspiciously.

The great mistake of Antiochus was to give sanctuary to the defeated Carthaginian general, Hannibal, thus bringing the wrath of Rome down on his head. A crushing military defeat was followed by a humiliating peace treaty, whose terms included the payment of a huge indemnity and a son of Antiochus (later to rule as Antiochus IV Epiphanes) as a hostage to Rome. While plundering a temple in Elam in order to raise money to pay the Romans, Antiochus was killed.

Dire financial need is an important motif in the reign of Antiochus IV, who succeeded an assassinated brother in 175. Mocked by satirists as Epimanes ('the madman'), rather than Epiphanes ('the God manifest'), it was Antiochus whose meddling in Jewish affairs drove the people to open rebellion and a brief, glorious, passage of arms.

Since Hellenism triumphed by progressive assimilation, scholars are curious as to why Antiochus – a convinced exponent of Greek culture – should have tried so crudely and insensitively to force his culture on the Jews. One reason lies in his personality. He had all the wilful impetuosity, dangerously childish immaturity and latent cruelty of a Nero or a Caligula. The second reason lay in his mistaken assumption that the outlook of the aristocratic and priestly faction mirrored the mood of Judean society as a whole. The upper classes deemed it 'chic' to imitate Greek ways, and had the instincts of the wealthy and powerful everywhere, and at every time, to ingratiate themselves with their overlords. The rest of the population, conservative and traditionalist, resented the blithe disregard of its religious heritage and had scores to settle with its rulers, both foreign and home-born. The third reason was money. Desperately low on funds to maintain his ramshackle empire, and pressured by the growing might of Rome, Antiochus, like his father before him, covetously eyed the wealth of the various temples within his domain. A power struggle for the office of High Priest in Jerusalem provided him with a likely opportunity. Antiochus made himself available to the highest bidder. The legitimate, and conservative, High Priest, Onias III, was deposed and banished. His brother Joshua (who preferred the Greek name Jason), paid his bribe, assumed office, and pushed forward a policy of Hellenization. Jerusalem was given the outward appearance of a Greek city. A gymnasium was built and even the young priests enrolled to compete in athletic games. They tried to hide their marks of circumcision in order to participate naked, as Greek athletes did.

Jason enjoyed his office for three years, until an even greater rogue, one Menelaus, bought the king's favour by selling off Temple vessels in order to raise the bribe money. He also engineered the murder of the lawful pontiff, Onias III, who lived in Antioch. In 169 BCE, while Antiochus was invading Egypt, Jason attempted a counter-coup, which induced Menelaus's patron to march into Jerusalem on his way home from Syria and loot the Temple treasures as a reprisal. Patriotic Jewish feelings were aroused. A year later, the crisis came. Antiochus invaded Egypt again, and was marching on Alexandria when the Romans intervened, ordering him to withdraw. Antiochus asked for time to consider but the Roman ambassador, Popillius Laenas, drew a circle round him in the sand and told him to make up his mind there and then.

The humiliated king vented his spleen on Jerusalem. An occupying army was dispatched there, the city was looted and partially destroyed and a Seleucid garrison was installed in a citadel called the Acra, which stood as a hateful symbol of Syrian domination. The Acra was not merely a military stronghold; it was a colony of Hellenized pagans and apostate Jews, with a constitution, territory and walls of its own – a Greek *polis* in the heart of Jerusalem.

Next, decrees were issued abolishing Temple worship and replacing it with pagan cults, and the practice of Judaism was forbidden on pain of death. Copies of the law were destroyed, and the circumcision of male children forbidden. Pagan altars were erected throughout Judea, and unclean animals sacrificed on them. In December 167 an altar to Zeus was set up in the Temple itself, and swine's flesh offered on it.

Initial Jewish resistance was neither unanimous nor effective. Those Jews who welcomed Hellenization accepted the decrees, and others complied out of fear. The small and scrupulously law-observing sect of *chasidim* (pious ones) was cut down because of their refusal to bear arms in self-defence on the sabbath.

The last of the biblical books, that of Daniel, was composed at this time as a response to Seleucid oppression. Highlighting the courage of Daniel and his companions, who faced up to the tyrant Nebuchadnezzar rather than eat unclean food, and, by trusting in God, emerged unscathed from the fiery furnace, its author is giving the message that those who remain loyal to the law ultimately will be redeemed. In a series of powerfully apocalyptic chapters the writer foresees the imminent triumph of divine purpose, when the godless powers will be overthrown and those 'saints of the Most High' who had died under Antiochus would be rewarded with everlasting life.

But a doctrine of passive resistance was not to the taste of Mattathias, an elderly priest in the village of Modi'in, near Lydda. Mattathias flatly refused to obey the royal officer's request that he be the first to offer pagan sacrifice, and when another Jew stepped forward to do so, the furious priest killed both his compatriot and the officer, and demolished the altar. Calling on all those who were zealous for the law to follow him, he fled to the hills with his five sons. They were joined by other resistance fighters, including those *chasidim* who had survived their original policy of not taking up arms on the sabbath, and a guerrilla war was launched against Antiochus. In 166 Mattathias died, and leadership of the revolt passed to his third son Judas, nick-named Maccabeus ('the hammer'), who won four comprehensive victories against Seleucid forces and marched triumphantly into Jerusalem. The Syrian garrison in the Acra was cut off, and could not prevent the restoration of Jewish worship in the Temple. All the vessels and utensils used in the cult of Zeus Olympius were destroyed, and a group of priests 'without blemish and devoted to the Torah' cleansed the sanctuary.

In December 164, three years to the month after its desecration, and on the day of the winter solstice, the temple was re-dedicated and the first feast of Chanukkah ('dedication') was celebrated with great rejoicing. The forces of Hellenism had been halted and the adherents of Judaism had been vindicated. It was a heady time. If religious freedom had been won, were there not possibilities of political independence too?

THE PHARISEES, SADDUCEES AND ESSENES

In retelling Jewish history from the time of the Maccabees to the dawn of the Christian era, three important but distinct facts have to be borne in mind. The first is that, fascinating though the political events of the time undoubtedly were, and ample though our sources are about them (primarily I Maccabees and *The Jewish Antiquities* of Josephus), it must not be forgotten that Judea, successively a province of the Babylonian, Persian and Hellenistic empires, was now to come under the sway of the greatest empire of them all, that of Rome. The perspective we should use, to keep events in proportion, is that of mighty Rome, not of modest Jerusalem.

Second, it should not be forgotten that the Jewish communities of the Diaspora (from a Greek word meaning 'dispersion', today often used to signify any country other than Israel) now greatly outnumbered the Jews of Palestine. In Alexandria alone there were probably as many Jews as in the whole of Judea, and large Jewish communities had settled in Antioch and Damascus, in the cities of Asia Minor, in mainland Greece, in the Balkans and on the shores of the Black Sea. The Jewish communities in the Diaspora were able to flourish as religious entities because the Septuagint provided them with the basis of a Jewish education. Through the Bible, the Jews, wherever scattered, retained a distinctive and common identity as a people covenanted to God and obliged to fulfil His commandments, whether of circumcision, the dietary laws, or rest on the sabbath. Indeed, the strictly monotheistic and rigorously moral teachings of Judaism held great appeal for many converts in the cosmopolitan and morally anarchic climate of Hellenistic and Roman times; besides full proselytes, who identified completely with the Jewish religion, there were others known as *sebomenoi* – 'God-fearers' – who worshipped the Jewish God and followed some Jewish observances, without fully merging into Israel. Judea remained the heartland of the Jewish people, but the Diaspora was where its numerical strength, and much of its intellectual activity, now lay.

The third fact is that, beneath the surface of political events in Jerusalem, a crucial religious struggle was being waged about which, alas, we have few direct details. We know little about the origins of Pharisees, Sadducees and Essenes (still less about early Christianity), and face tantalizing lacunae when trying to reconstruct the feverishly expectant atmosphere which gave rise, in the two centuries before Jesus, to apocalyptic and eschatological hopes; notions about the end of days and the coming of the Messiah were rife, and zealots, revolutionaries and mystics vied with each other in touting their beliefs, while conventional religious leaders tried desperately to maintain a middle ground. One scholar has aptly described the times as being like a canvas painted by a madman or a drug addict. But for all that, our sources about religious developments are scanty, and no period in the evolution of Judaism has given rise to such controversy and disagreement.

In contrast, the political history is known in some detail. The momentum of the Maccabean revolt could not be stilled. What had started as resistance to religious persecution developed into a struggle for independence. In 163 BCE Antiochus Epiphanes was killed while fighting against the Parthians in Babylonia. His successor, Demetrius Soter, tried to appease Jewish religious feelings by appointing a High Priest from among the old ruling families, but in 161 Judas Maccabeus gained his most spectacular victory against the Seleucid general, Nicanor, at Beth Horon. A month later the Syrians returned with a large army and Judas died in battle. The surviving brothers withdrew to the Judean desert where the eldest, John, was put to death by unfriendly tribesmen. Military command was assumed by the youngest brother, Jonathan, who controlled all of Judea, outside the capital, from his headquarters at Michmash, which became the centre of patriotic sentiment. A power struggle for the Seleucid throne worked to Jonathan's advantage. Both claimants sought the help of his tough army. Demetrius appointed Jonathan provincial governor; his rival retorted by recognizing him as High Priest. In 152 BCE, on the feast of Tabernacles, he officiated in the Temple for the first time. Although Jonathan was captured by guile and put to death in 142, the last surviving brother, Simon, automatically took command and forced the evacuation of that hated symbol of Seleucid rule, the Acra in Jerusalem. In the autumn of 140 his authority was ratified by an assembly of priests, elders and the masses, who confirmed him in the offices of High Priest, military commander and ethnarch. Thus did the Hasmonean dynasty (so-called from the name of one of the family's ancestors) come into being. A formal alliance with Rome, and the striking of the first coins ever issued by the Jewish state, were the immediate fruits of newly won independence.

War with the Seleucids continued intermittently. When Simon was assassinated in a palace intrigue in 135, his son, John Hyrcanus, became High Priest and ethnarch. Antiochus VII besieged Jerusalem and reasserted his suzerain rights, but when he died in battle in 129 the Seleucid empire disintegrated and Judea was able to resume its independent status. John Hyrcanus ruled until 104 BCE. He pushed the frontiers of the state outwards into Transjordan and Samaria, where he razed the Samaritan temple on Mount Gerizim, and southwards in Idumea, homeland of the biblical Edomites, whom he forcibly converted to Judaism.

His eldest son, Judas Aristobolus, succeeded him, but only for a year. In 103 Alexander Janneus, the third son, came to power, and under him the Judean state extended to something like its size in the golden days of David and Solomon. It was also during his reign (103–76) that simmering ideological rivalries could no longer be contained, and led to civil war. At issue was the struggle for popular support between two religiously, and socially, conflicting groups, the Pharisees and the Sadducees. It would seem that the Sadducees were mainly upper-class, Judean adherents of the Hasmonean family and the Temple priesthood, as their name, derived from Zadok, a priest of Jerusalem in the reigns of David and Solomon, implies. Their opponents, the Pharisees, took their name from the Hebrew word *parush* – 'separated', not because they separated themselves from the masses for the sake of holiness, but, as recent research has shown, because they were thus described by their enemies for having separated themselves from the Saducean interpretation of the Scriptures. Already during the reign of John Hyrcanus, the Pharisees had challenged his assumption of priestly and regal legitimacy, on behalf of those veterans of the Maccabean campaigns who resented the manner in which one family had taken upon itself royal trappings and all the outward signs of a typical Hellenistic court, including the use of Greek mercenary soldiers.

However, the crucial dispute between the two groups hinged not on class or on politics, but on theology. Josephus relates that they disagreed about immortality, divine providence and free will, the Pharisees believing in all three doctrines and the Sadducees rejecting them. Clearly, these divergences were manifestations of a still deeper split. At stake were two conflicting views about the authority of Jewish law and the nature of Judaism.

For the Sadducees, the Written Torah, with its emphasis on priestly leadership, was the sole authority. The Pharisees saw themselves as heirs of a second, broader tradition which, since the days of Ezra, had expounded, interpreted and applied the written Scriptures, through the teachings of scribes and sages drawn from all strata of society. Pharisaic authority was justified by the notion of a second, oral Torah, which had been handed down from ancient times as an elucidation of, and complement to, the written Torah. This Oral Torah was the key to unlocking pentateuchal legislation, and its custodians were men skilled in law and wisdom, but who did not necessarily come from the hereditary, priestly caste.

The struggle between Pharisees and Sadducees was for ultimate religious control of the state. Since Pharisaism eventually triumphed, and gave rise in turn to Rabbinic Judaism, which shaped and moulded the Jewish religion at least until the French Revolution, it is tempting, but not necessarily accurate, to accept wholesale the tradition of the early Rabbis, which said that an unbroken chain stretched from Ezra and the men of the Great

Assembly down to the schools of the last two outstanding Pharisaic teachers, Hillel and Shammai, at the end of the first century BCE, and that the Pharisees enjoyed widespread public support.

However, in contrast to this conventional Rabbinic view, there is one body of modern scholarly opinion which holds that Pharisaism was but one of several factions vying for religious leadership before 70 CE, and that far from being a popular movement, it was confined to a small group who were beginning to develop principles that only came to fruition later, under the Rabbis. A second scholarly position (cautiously favoured by the two authors), is that the Pharisees were a new type of scribal intellectual who rose to prominence in the wake of social unrest and declining priestly prestige during the Maccabean upheavals. They effected nothing less than an internal revolution in Jewish religious life by extending to *all* Jews the obligations that previously had been the prerogative only of priests, by the doctrine of the Oral Torah, which emphasized individual salvation through fidelity to the law, rather than priestly intervention. Given their concern for involving more of the populace within a religious system that was to be based on leadership through learning and interpretative skill, rather than on priestly caste, it is also plausible to allow the Pharisees the major credit for developing the role of synagogues and houses of study during this period.

While one should be circumspect about attempting any dogmatic summary of these religious controversies, because our sources for them are all prejudiced in favour of the Pharisees, it is clear that the Sadducean, or priestly, ruling-class faction was trying to maintain its authority against mounting pressure. A third group, the Essenes, also rejected the Temple priesthood; they had withdrawn to rural communes where their carefully selected members devoted themselves to manual labour and a rigorously disciplined regime of study and ritual purity. Possibly these Essenes were descended from the *chasidim* who suffered martyrdom under Antiochus Epiphanes. If the so-called Dead Sea Scrolls, discovered in 1947 at Qumran, are indeed the remains of an Essene library, then the writings describe a movement which considered itself the true heir of the Mosaic Covenant and regarded with implacable hostility the 'sons of darkness' who officiated in the Temple and whose overthrow would presage the ultimate victory of divine rule over the whole earth.

This was the theological background to the civil warfare which marred the last years of Alexander Jannaeus's reign. His opponents even sought help from the Syrian king, Demetrius II, and Jannaeus retaliated by crucifying hundreds of Pharisees and forcing thousands of Jews to flee the country. A reconciliation of sorts was arrived at during the reign of his widow, Salome Alexandra, whose brother was the Pharisaic leader Simeon ben Shetach, but the tranquillity was short-lived. When Salome died in 67 BCE, a struggle for the throne broke out between her two sons, Aristobulus II and Hyrcanus II. Their rivalry provided the Roman general Pompey with a pretext for direct intervention in Judea. He favoured the claims of Hyrcanus and in 63 he occupied the Temple after a three-month siege, banishing Aristobulus and his children to Rome and recognizing Hyrcanus as High Priest, but not as king. Judea was reduced to the status of a Roman vassal. The most powerful figure to emerge in the Jerusalem administration was the Idumean adviser, Antipater, whose forebears had been forcibly converted to Judaism by John Hyrcanus. Antipater adroitly changed sides when Julius Caesar defeated Pompey in 48 and was rewarded by Caesar's confirming him as administrator, with his nominal master, Hyrcanus, as High Priest, of Judea. A year after Caesar's assassination in 44, Antipater, too, fell, a victim of treachery, but his sons, Phasael and Herod, retained his rule over Judea.

The Hasmoneans made a last attempt to return to power. Antigonus, son of the banished Aristobulus II, invaded Judea, and briefly took control of the country. Phasael committed suicide, but Herod fled to Rome, where Octavian and Antony secured his nomination, by the Senate, as King of Judea. Returning with Roman legions, Herod reconquered the country, captured Jerusalem and put Antigonus to death. He married Mariamne, granddaughter of Hyrcanus II, in the hope of attracting some of the popularity that still lingered around the Hasmonean name. After Octavian, now surnamed Augustus, defeated Antony at Actium in 31 BCE and became first citizen of an empire that stretched from the Atlantic to the Parthian border, Herod's kingship was reconfirmed. He ruled until 4 BCE as 'an ally and friend of the Roman people', a client king maintained in power to preserve order and security in Judea, but hated by most of his subjects as an upstart Idumean convert and a lackey of Rome.

CHAPTER SIX   UNDER ROMAN RULE

The Jews of Palestine were about to enter their most terrible period of history. 'It were better to be such a man's swine than his son,' was the comment of the emperor Augustus on Herod's jealous paranoia, which caused him to execute his beloved wife Mariamne, his two sons and any relative whom he suspected of theatening his security; but although Herod is best remembered for these excesses he was, in fact, an able ruler with several positive achievements to his credit. He cannot be held solely to blame for the combination of tense and irreconcilable forces which gathered momentum before and after his death and led, in 66 CE, to open rebellion against Rome and to tragedy.

Given his background and the manner of his accession to the throne, it was inevitable that the majority of Jews would reject Herod. It could be that affronted pride motivated many of his actions, such as the murder of the popular young High Priest, Aristobolus, or his conspicuous reliance on Greek advisers, and the enthusiasm with which he endowed pagan temples, even erecting a hippodrome in Jerusalem for games and combat against wild animals. The Hellenization against which the Maccabees had fought was doubly resented when imposed by one who had usurped their rule.

On the other hand, Herod dug deeply into his own coffers to help relieve suffering during the famine years of 24–23 BCE, and his ambitious building projects, including the magnificent new seaport of Caesarea and a string of imposing fortresses, of which Masada was one, provided work for many thousands of the population. Most impressive of all was the rebuilding of the Temple and its courtyards. (The Western or 'Wailing' Wall, which still stands, was part of the vast complex he constructed.)

It was so imposing that, according to a proverbial saying of the day, 'He who has not seen Herod's Temple has not seen anything beautiful.'

His reign ended in an orgy of intrigue, assassination and repression. An attempt to remove a golden Roman eagle which had been mounted over the Temple gate was punished by the burning alive of forty-two of the perpetrators, including two Pharisaic teachers. Herod lingered on with a painful terminal illness, made bitter by the knowledge that public celebration would mark the news of his passing. The precarious stability he had imposed upon Judea for his Roman overlords did not long survive his death.

An incalculable new factor had emerged on the Judean scene. The Pharisees, we can assume, had steadily been gaining in religious ascendancy over the past hundred years, especially as the Sadducees would have been tainted by association with Herod's Hellenization policies and their most prized possession, the office of High Priest, had become a political gift, changeable at whim. The supreme legislative assembly of the people, the Sanhedrin, which met in the Temple, was the forum which Sadducean priests and Pharisaic sages competed to control, but its authority was limited by the Roman administration. The Essenes had withdrawn to their desert communities to await the end of days.

None of these three movements actively challenged Roman domination, unless their religious sensitivities were offended. It was a fourth group, loosely composed of revolutionaries, zealots and individual charismatics, which threatened imperial stability. They disagreed and occasionally fought among themselves, as revolutionaries tend to do. Some of their beliefs were shared with the Pharisees; others echoed Essene teachings. What they had in common was a fervent longing for the deliverance of Israel from foreign oppression under an ideal, anointed king of Davidic descent – the Messiah, from a Hebrew adjective meaning 'anointed (with holy oil)' – and an urgent conviction that the apocalypse, which would usher in God's kingdom on earth, was at hand. Their emotional, near-hysterical expectations were fuelled by religious writings which were not included in the Hebrew Bible, but which appear in the Apocrypha of the Septuagint, or were preserved by early Christian communities. These mostly pseudepigraphical (that is, 'falsely attributed' to some ancient biblical personality) books pose questions about suffering and evil, transcendence over death, resurrection and the last judgement and the imminent manifestation of God's purpose in human history. The first century of the common era was the great age of Jewish apocalyptic and eschatological yearning, as Roman domination continued to prevail, and only some longed-for, extraordinary deliverance seemed likely to lift it.

Not all the seers, visionaries and holy men who abounded were revolutionaries. For example, the message of John the Baptist, who emerged from the Judean desert in a conscious imitation of the prophet Elijah, was a pacific one, a message of repentance, because the kingdom of heaven was nigh. To the Romans, embroiled in a turbulent ideological atmosphere the likes of which they had never encountered in any other administered territory, it could not have been easy to distinguish between those who passively awaited God's miraculous intervention, those who would render unto Caesar the things that were Caesar's provided their religious integrity was respected, and those who wished to hasten the end of days by fire and sword. From this heady and dangerously confusing brew would result not only the Jewish revolt against Rome but also the Christian schism within Judaism.

According to the terms of Herod's will, his territories were divided between three of his sons. In 6 CE the Emperor Augustus deposed Archeleus, who had been designated Ethnarch of Judea, Idumea and Samaria, and instituted direct Roman rule through a procurator, who was responsible to the legate of Syria. A nationalist uprising led by Judas of Galilee was crushed, and large garrisons of Roman auxiliaries saw to the collection of taxes and the administration of criminal justice. Until the procuratorship of Pontius Pilate (26–36 CE), Roman rule was generally careful to respect Jewish religious feelings. Contrary to his benign portrait in the Gospel of St John, Pilate was one of the harshest, most corrupt, of the Roman colonial administrators. It was during his tenure that incidents involving the installation of pagan symbols in Jerusalem and the expropriation of Temple funds heightened the tension between ruler and ruled. It was also during his term of office that, around the year 30 CE, the crucifixion in Jerusalem, on Passover eve, of one Jesus of Nazareth was to prove to be, quite simply, the single most significant event in the history of western civilization. The few Jewish disciples of Jesus were the forerunners of a new and triumphant world religion. The majority of Jews, who did not accept his messiahship, unknowingly bequeathed to their descendants a legacy of opprobrium that would heap discrimination and persecution on the very people Jesus had ministered to.

JESUS OF NAZARETH

Here, however, our purpose is not to argue the issues of faith which separate Christianity from Judaism, but to present, as accurately as the sources permit, a summary of the career of Jesus. In trying to do so, we encounter difficulties as great as those which hamper our knowledge about the development of first-century Judaism. Details about Jesus in the New Testament, in Jewish, Greek and Roman writings, provide only the scantiest biography, and it must be remembered that our major sources of information, the four Gospels, were composed forty years or more after his death, when Christianity was in the process of disentangling itself from its mother religion. Understandably, therefore, they recount Jesus's teachings and actions in the light of a growing Christian tendency to deify him, and the description they give of the Judaism which rejected that belief is necessarily unflattering.

Jesus grew up in the rugged hill country of Galilee, whose inhabitants had a reputation for hardiness, independence and nationalist fervour. He acquired celebrity as a faith-healer, exorcist and itinerant preacher, who proclaimed the imminent coming of God's kingdom. His personal magnetism, the authority with which he spoke, and his radical teachings (even though he probably taught nothing that contradicted Pharisaic Judaism), may well have stirred some hostility towards him. Certainly the impression he gave of being the leader of a messianic movement would have aroused grave apprehension among those Jews, from the High Priest downwards, who owed their positions to Roman patronage and who depended for their political survival on collaborating with the Roman authorities. His action in entering

Jerusalem for the Passover pilgrim festival riding on an ass, as Zechariah had promised the king would come, must have confirmed their fears. Jesus's trial, hastily convened by the High Priest, paid scant attention to the requirements of Pharisaic law and was most probably only an expedient preliminary to delivering him to the Romans. That he was accused and convicted of the religious offence of blasphemy seems to many modern scholars highly improbable. What is certain is that the Romans crucified him as a would-be 'king of the Jews', that is, as a potentially dangerous revolutionary.

Unless fresh sources are discovered, we have no way of authoritatively answering the many questions posed by the trial and crucifixion of Jesus. We must content ourselves with saying that, for his immediate followers, Jesus had been the true Messiah, whose death and claimed resurrection would shortly usher in God's glorious kingdom. For the overwhelming number of Jews he was one more tragic, and fallibly human, victim of the struggle against Rome.

In 36 CE, Pontius Pilate was dismissed as procurator after growing criticism, but the new Roman emperor, who ascended to imperial power the following year, Gaius Caligula, was no more circumspect about Jewish religious sensitivities; he ordered a statue of himself to be placed in the Temple. The legate of Syria delayed implementing the command, and in 41 CE Caligula was, opportunely, assassinated. His successor, Claudius, was a personal friend of one of Herod's and Mariamne's grandsons, Agrippa, who had been brought up in Rome. This Agrippa was declared King of Judea and, in a short reign (41–44), aided by his friendship with the emperor, he proved to be a popular ruler, but it was only a brief interlude in direct Roman rule. After his suspiciously sudden death at Caesarea, Judea reverted to provincial status, and his young son, Agrippa II, was divested of any real authority.

A succession of corrupt and maladroit procurators, in combination with declining economic conditions, led to a steadily worsening situation over the next two decades. Law and order slowly broke down. Anti-Roman terrorists assassinated Jewish sympathizers of the regime. The bodyguards of wealthy Jewish families clashed in the streets, and the High Priest fell a victim of the dagger which was the favoured weapon for use in crowds.

Those prophesying the end of the world saw ample portents all around them.

In 64 CE, a new procurator, Florus, arrived in Judea. The seizure of gold from the Temple treasury incited a riot which his soldiers put down with pillaging and crucifixions. After Florus returned to the administrative headquarters at Caesarea, pro-Roman Jews and the small Roman garrison in Jerusalem were butchered by the Zealots. In Caesarea, where Jews and pagans had long been squabbling over their respective civic rights, the gentiles attacked the Jewish community. Riots flared throughout the country.

In October 66, the legate of Syria marched on Jerusalem to reassert imperial authority. Compelled to withdraw, he retreated towards the coast. As his legion marched through the mountain pass of Beth Horon, where the Maccabees had won their greatest victory over the Seleucid forces, it was cut to pieces by Jewish rebels.

Rome had to avenge such a humiliating reverse. Nero put Vespasian in charge of pacifying Judea. He was an experienced general who had made his reputation in Britain. He gathered his army in the north and advanced on Galilee. In command of Jewish forces in the area was a certain Joseph ben Mattathias, who had recently visited Rome. He retreated to the mountain fortress of Jotapata, where he held out for two months. When the Romans finally broke in they slaughtered most of its defenders but not Joseph ben Mattathias, who deserted to the enemy, assumed the name of Flavius Josephus and wrote a self-justifying, but absorbing, account, *The History of the Jewish War*, to which we are indebted for our detailed knowledge of its progress.

By the winter of 67, all of Galilee and northern Palestine were once more under Roman control. In Jerusalem, awaiting the inevitable assault, a reign of terror set in, as zealot extremists ousted the moderate government and purged those suspected of being 'soft' about pursuing the war to its bitter end. In the spring of 68 Vespasian marched southward, systematically isolating Jerusalem. He was poised to begin its siege when news arrived of Nero's suicide. In the confused aftermath of Nero's successor's assassination, the eastern legions proclaimed Vespasian emperor. Before leaving for Rome he put his son, Titus, in charge of the Judean campaign, at the head of a vast army.

A few days before Passover in April of 70 CE, Titus set up camp outside the walls of Jerusalem. The subjugation of the city took six months, as the defenders fought with great courage and only ceded each vantage point after heavy loss of life. By the end of July the Romans had occupied the citadel adjacent to the Temple, and daily sacrifices were suspended. On 28 August (the same date, according to a later tradition, on which Nebuchadnezzar had destroyed the first Temple over 650 years previously: 9 Av) the sanctuary was stormed and went up in flames. It took another month of fighting before the whole city was in Roman hands and resistance ceased. Titus then razed Jerusalem, except for the towers of Herod's palace. Many thousands of Jews were enslaved, and their property confiscated. In 71 Titus and Vespasian celebrated their victory with a triumphal procession in Rome. The commemorative arch of Titus, depicting the Temple *menorah* and other holy objects, stands to this day as a tourist attraction in the Roman Forum. Several pockets of resistance still held out in Judea. Masada, the Dead Sea fortress of Herod, was the last to fall. When the Romans finally breached its mountain-top wall in April 73, they discovered that the 960 defenders had committed suicide rather than be taken captive.

The hopeless struggle against the might of Rome had been a national conflict, sucking in every stratum of Jewish society, including the Nazarenes, or early Christian Jews, who still worshipped at the Temple and observed Jewish laws, Idumean and Galilean adherents, even the ruling family of the tiny kingdom of Adiabene in northern Mesopotamia, who had recently converted to Judaism and come to live in Jerusalem. All were caught up in the catastrophe, whether fanatical zealots, Hellenized aristocrats, or followers of Jesus, who saw in these events an apocalyptic presage of the second coming. One large and important group had hoped all along for a negotiated settlement with the Romans, and that was the Pharisees. It was the Pharisees who were to enable Judaism to survive this latest and greatest disaster.

FROM THE DESTRUCTION OF THE SECOND TEMPLE TO THE ABOLITION OF THE PATRIARCHATE

Devastating though the war against Rome had been, and poignant though the destruction of the Temple was, there were two crucial and salutary differences between the disasters of 586 BC and 70 CE. When Nebuchadnezzar destroyed the First Temple and carried away the captives to Babylon, he uprooted a people from their land and despoiled the cultic shrine which was central to their religion. When Titus destroyed the Second Temple and forced the Jewish captives to fight in gladiatorial contests, he burned a sanctuary of symbolic prestige but one that was already being rivalled in influence by the Pharisaic synagogues, and he did not harm the majority of Jews, who lived in the Diaspora. In so far as news of events in Judea reached them in their Mediterranean, Mesopotamian and Egyptian communities, they felt for their Palestinian co-religionists the same keen anxiety as Diaspora Jews today, who follow developments in the State of Israel. And, like Diaspora Jews today, each local community administered its own finances, established its own places for study, worship and burial, cared for the needy and set up its own courts to arbitrate in disputes concerning Jews. Within the confines of Torah law, each community developed its own synthesis between Jewish practice and local cultural environment, so that in first-century Alexandria, for example, the great Jewish mystic and theologian Philo – who in all probability did not speak Hebrew, and was in all respects an outstanding exemplar of the Hellenistic ideal – interpreted the God of Judaism and Mosaic law in Greek philosophical categories. Throughout the cities of the Roman empire Judaism was an officially recognized religion, its followers exempted from the state cult of emperor worship, and from appearing in court on sabbaths and holy days; they were also permitted to send annual contributions to the Temple in Jerusalem. Until 70 CE Jerusalem had been, and would in many ways remain, the spiritual centre of Judaism. But once the second Temple had fallen, the emphasis shifted and Jewish history effectively became a Diaspora history, although it was not until the fifth century, when Jewish life finally declined in its homeland, that the Jews became almost entirely a Diaspora people. We shall stay with events in Judea for the centuries following Titus's reconquest, because these events have great religious significance, not only for the Judean survivors but for all Jews everywhere.

According to Josephus, there had been about 6,000 Pharisees during Herod's reign. The war with Rome would destroy the

Zealots, reduce the Sadducees' influence until it was negligible and overwhelm the Essenes. Shortly afterwards, Christianity ceased to be a sect within Judaism and became an independent movement, consisting primarily of non-Jews in the Hellenistic Diaspora, owing largely to the missionary genius of Paul of Tarsus, a Diaspora Jew and self-styled but unlikely Pharisee, whose radical theology of 'faith' rather than 'works' converted gentiles without demanding of them circumcision or acceptance of Mosaic law. It was the Pharisaic legacy of synagogues and houses of study that survived this general break-up. Their pattern of a religious life based on worship and education became the Jewish norm. During the siege of Jerusalem an aged teacher, Yochanan ben Zakkai, slipped away from the city and obtained Roman permission to establish a Pharisaic academy at Yavneh, on the seacoast near Jaffa. Presumably the quid pro quo for this concession was acceptance of Roman rule; certainly, five decades of peace followed, during which economic reconstruction of the country took place and scholars at Yavneh came to be recognized by Rome as the official leaders of the Jewish people.

The Yavneh school's first great achievement was that it reassured the people that Judaism did not depend on the destroyed Temple and its sacrificial cult, but on the inner religious life of repentance and good deeds. Characteristic of the Yavneh attitude is the parable attributed by later sages to Yochanan, in which he comforts a colleague surveying the desolate Temple with a verse from Hosea 6: 'I desire steadfast love and not sacrifice, the knowledge of God, rather than burnt offerings.'

The Yavneh scholars then took practical action to implement a post-Temple, non-priestly form of Judaism. They summarized the legal teachings of their predecessors, Hillel and Shammai, and usually decided for the more flexible, less literal approach of Hillel's followers. Hillel had been revered as a warm, patient and humane interpreter of the law, and formal acknowledgement of the Hillelite tradition was bestowed on a descendant, Gamaliel II, who succeeded Yochanan as head of the academy. The title rabbi, 'my master', came into general use around this time to describe a sage recognized by his peers, and an ordination procedure for rabbis, *semichah*, was devised, conferring authority to teach and to decide matters of law. The Sanhedrin, which in

Temple times had been a priest-dominated assembly, now became a reconstituted and democratic forum, presided over by a *nasi* (the biblical term for a 'princely leader') who was called *rabban*, 'our master'. The rabbis who made up the Sanhedrin were drawn from all walks of life and relied upon a craft, trade or private income for their living. They owed their religious leadership to expertise in interpreting and adjudicating Torah, and they attracted circles of disciples who followed them, much as students had followed the Greek philosophers.

Around the year 100, the rabbis of Yavneh completed the canonization of the third section of the Bible, the Writings. They also formulated the daily liturgy, and felt confident enough to transfer to the synagogue certain observances that previously had been associated only with the Temple, such as pilgrim-festival rituals and the blowing of the ram's horn on New Year's Day. Most significant of all, Yom Kippur, the Day of Atonement, on which the High Priest, arrayed in splendour, had alone entered the Temple's innermost sanctuary, to make atonement for the entire people, now became a day for individual confession of sin and for repentance. The heirs of the Pharisees had set their religion on the path of personal responsibility, manifested through obedience to the law's demands. This is described as Rabbinic Judaism, and it was, for the next seventeen centuries, at least, to regulate, define and keep cohesive a people scattered east and west, far and wide. Rabbinic Judaism was to be one of the great success stories of any religion, and its foundations were laid in the bleak aftermath of total defeat.

Although tranquillity prevailed in Palestine, in the Diaspora an uprising against the Emperor Trajan was joined by Jewish communities aroused by messianic expectations. The revolt was harshly crushed and between the years 114 and 117 the Jewish populations of Alexandria, Cyrene and Cyprus were virtually destroyed. Trajan had extended his empire to the Persian Gulf, but his successor, Hadrian, could not maintain these conquests, with the important result, for Judaism, that the large Jewish community in Babylonia, approximately half a million people, remained free from Roman domination; under the tolerant rule of the Persian kings, this community was later to develop into the major centre of Rabbinic Judaism.

The ripples of unrest in the Roman empire did not die down, and by 133 had reached Judea, where a carefully planned revolt erupted under the leadership of Simon bar Kosiba. That hopes of independence and divine intervention still flickered are evident from Simon's change of name to bar Kochba, 'Son of the Star', a messianic allusion to Numbers 24:17. For three years the insurgents held out, their numbers swelled by the enthusiasm with which certain rabbis, including the outstanding scholar of his generation, Akiva, championed their cause. The Roman general, Julius Severus, was recalled from Britain to take charge of the Roman forces. According to the early-third-century historian, Dio Cassius, fifty fortresses and more than one thousand settlements were destroyed in the fighting, and hundreds of thousands of Jews were killed. When the last Jewish stronghold of Bethar finally fell in 135 CE, Hadrian ordered that a harrow was to be drawn over Jerusalem and a new city, Aelia Capitolina, built on its site, in which no Jew would be allowed to set foot. The population around Jerusalem had fled, or died in the fighting, and agriculture had been destroyed. Rabbi Akiva and other teachers who had supported bar Kochba were tortured and put to death by the Romans. The teaching of Judaism was prohibited on pain of death, and some scholars migrated as refugees to Babylonia. But thanks to the previous groundwork of the Yavneh academy, and the accession in 138 of a conciliatory Roman emperor, Antoninus Pius, Judaism was able to overcome even this disaster.

Antoninus Pius rescinded Hadrian's edicts against the teaching and practice of Judaism in the Holy Land. Jerusalem and its environs had been devastated by the three-year revolt, but in Galilee the population was still largely Jewish, and it was there, at Usha, that the Sanhedrin reassembled. Although the country was never again to achieve the level of prosperity that had been reached before the two great wars against Rome, a time of peaceful cooperation with the authorities now followed. The *nasi* of the Sanhedrin was recognized as patriarch of the Jews and was given the right to collect taxes for Jewish institutions, to appoint judges for the Jewish courts and to send official emissaries to the Diaspora communities, which supported his office as once they had supported the Temple. Under Yehudah ha-Nasi (170–217)

– venerated in rabbinic literature simply as 'Rabbi' – the patriarchate assumed great splendour and prestige. Judah was a wealthy and cultivated man, who spoke both Hebrew and Greek in his house, as the languages of civilized discourse, maintained cordial relations with Rome and enjoyed the respectful admiration of his colleagues for his outstanding scholarship. It was during his term of office that in 212 CE the emperor Caracalla extended Roman citizenship to Jews, and most other peoples of the empire, mainly as a method of raising revenue. Of infinitely greater importance for Judaism was the redaction, under Judah's auspices, of the first major codification of Jewish law, known as the Mishnah (from a Hebrew verb meaning 'to repeat'). The Mishnah is both law code and textbook, collecting together the orally transmitted teachings and legal traditions of scribes, Pharisees and scholars, from the Second Temple period down to Yehudah ha-Nasi's day. In the Mishnah, the rabbis claim a continuous chain of oral transmission, parallel with the transmission of the Written Torah, from Moses through the prophets to 'the men of the Great Assembly' and, via them, to Pharisaic scholars, culminating with Hillel and Shammai and thence to the post-70 Sanhedrin. With the Mishnah, Rabbinic Judaism set the seal on its own authority by issuing a standard code of ritual and legal practice which henceforth would be Judaism's basic handbook for leading a religious life. (See part II, chapter 3 for a description of the Mishnah and subsequent rabbinic literature.)

There had been illustrious scholars in the century before Yehudah ha-Nasi, such as Rabbi Ishmael, Rabbi Akiva – who not only produced his own systematization of the law according to subject matter, but also developed a method of biblical exegesis and interpretation which became standard for future generations – and his disciple Rabbi Meir, who compiled a preliminary canon of laws based on those collected by his teachers; and there would be illustrious scholars in the century after Yehudah ha-Nasi, such as Rabbi Yochanan the son of Nappacha, whose decisions were carefully studied both in Palestinian and Babylonian academies, and his brother-in-law Simeon son of Lakish, who in his youth found employment as a gladiator. There were also several Babylonian rabbis who settled and taught in the land of Israel as part of a fruitful cultural interchange between the two communities.

But never again would the material and intellectual peaks of Judah's patriarchate be scaled. With his death, the age of the *tannaim* – as the succession of teachers from Hillel and Shammai are called – comes to a close. Yehudah's seat of government had been at Beth She'arim, and then had moved to Sepphoris, when ill-health forced him to move to the mountain air. Subsequently, a succession of patriarchs assumed the office because of claimed descent from Hillel or, more fancifully still, Davidic lineage, and presided over the Sanhedrin from Tiberias. Their dubious scholarship led rabbis to set up their own independent academies in Galilee and even Judea, where the Mishnah was expounded and implemented in daily life. In addition, other old rabbinic teachings which had not been incorporated in the Mishnah, were gathered in a compilation known as the *Tosefta*, and also taught (see below, p. 215). The several rabbinic schools, headed by individual sages, engaged in keen discussions of these sources, linked contemporary laws to biblical precedent by an elaborate system of exegesis, and, through the dialectic of debate, sharpened the characteristic Jewish genius for interpreting and applying law. Eventually, the overflowing records of these debates in the schools of Tiberias, Caesarea and Sepphoris were edited, about the year 400 CE , and became known as the Palestinian (or more popularly, the Jerusalem) Talmud. A Babylonian version of even greater scope was produced about a century later. The Talmud is a lengthy commentary on, and supplement to, the Mishnah, and together these two works comprise the vast legal foundation of Judaism.

Just as the redaction of the Bible eight hundred years previously had been an astonishing intellectual compensation for national and economic insignificance, so, too, was the creative activity which produced the Talmud. Politically, Palestine was at the whim of the Roman empire's fortunes. Between 235 and 285 the empire was close to collapse, as the barbarians threatened from the north and the Persians from the east, and rival generals struggled for power. Heavy financial tribute was exacted from subject peoples, and grim conditions in Galilee induced many Jews to emigrate. By now, Christianity had won over a substantial portion of the empire's pagan population, and the repression suffered by the Church under Diocletian was lifted by Constantine the Great, who extended official toleration to the Christian religion, legalized the privileges of its clergy and, in 325, convened a worldwide church council at Nicea to resolve doctrinal differences. Shortly afterwards, he moved his government to the eastern capital of Byzantium, and renamed it Constantinople; Palestine came under the jurisdiction of this Eastern administration.

Apart from the brief, mysterious interlude of the apostate emperor Julian (361–363), who intimated to Jewish leaders that he would rebuild the Temple, the Christianization of the empire continued in east and west throughout the fourth century. As a consequence, there was a marked increase in anti-Jewish legislation, and Judaism was reduced to a position of permanent, legal inferiority. It became a capital offence to convert to Judaism, and intermarriage between Jews and Christians was likewise punishable by death. The Sanhedrin in Tiberias was prohibited from notifying Diaspora Jews about the dates of forthcoming holy days, with the result that in 359 the patriarch Hillel II had to make public the closely guarded mathematical rules for calculating the Jewish calendar. The diminution of the Sanhedrin's authority was accentuated in 399 when Honorius, emperor of the west, forbade the collection of the voluntary tax which hitherto had helped maintain the patriarchate.

Finally, when the patriarch Gamaliel VI died in 425 without leaving a male heir, Theodosius II refused to appoint a successor, and abolished the office. A Jewish life of sorts continued in the Galilee: an imitation Sanhedrin still met in Tiberias and academies still studied and redacted the rabbinical traditions. Ironically, the influx of Christians, who built churches, shrines and monasteries on sites associated with Jesus, brought a renewed prosperity to the country, which was reflected in synagogues of similar opulence, such as the one at Beth Alpha. It is likely that two ramifications of Jewish scholarship emerged during this period; a scrupulous system of vocalizing and punctuating the Bible compiled by the Masoretes (a name derived from the word for tradition), and the first compositions of liturgical poetry for use in synagogues.

It was, though, a melancholy, twilight existence eked out by a Jewish minority in what had been its own land. When the Persians invaded Palestine during the reign of Heraclius, the Jews rose up against their Christian overlords, but paid dearly for the attempt once Christianity re-established itself in 628. A new rule was shortly to commence, when Egypt, Syria and Palestine fell to Arab conquerors, but it made little appreciable difference to the remaining Jews. Their status had been steadily eroded since the abolition of the patriarchate. It is not to this downtrodden residue of those who had come back from Babylonian exile, nearly twelve hundred years previously, but to the Jews of the Diaspora, that we must turn for the continuation of Jewish history and Judaism.

CHAPTER SEVEN   THE GAONIC AGE

FROM THE BABYLONIAN TALMUD TO THE TRIUMPH OF ISLAM

In one of the front rows of Yehudah ha-Nasi's academy had sat a young Babylonian scholar named Abba. Recalling him in later years, a Palestinian sage was to say, 'I can remember sitting seventeen rows behind Abba at school, and when he engaged Rabbi Yehudah ha-Nasi in discussion, the words flew like sparks.' Given his intellectual gifts, Abba could have remained in Palestine and risen to eminence. Instead he chose to return home and found an academy at Sura in central Mesopotamia, where he became known as Rav, *the* rabbi (*rav* being the Babylonian synonym for rabbi). Rav's career is an apt metaphor for the waning of Palestinian Judaism and the transfer of religious supremacy to Babylonia.

Jews had lived in Babylonia from the time of Nebuchadnezzar's deportations in the sixth century BCE. They had become both stable and prosperous, flourishing under a succession of Persian, Hellenistic and Parthian dynasties which granted large measures of autonomy to ethnic and religious minorities. It is possible that political considerations motivated, at least in part, the tolerance accorded to the large Jewish community in Mesopotamia; the Parthian kings may have wished to counter Roman control over Jews west of their empire, just as Roman recognition of the Galilean patriarchate was perhaps a response to Persian benevolence. Be that as it may, by the second century CE, the exilarch (in Aramaic, *resh galuta*, 'head of the exile'), who claimed descent from the Judean kings taken into captivity by Nebuchadnezzar, was officially recognized as the leader of the Jewish community and was given wide-ranging powers to collect taxes, appoint Jewish judges and represent his people at the Persian court.

The publication of the Mishnah, as well as the regular cultural interchange between scholars of Palestine and Babylonia, were the crucial factors in spreading Rabbinic Judaism in the east. Now there was an authoritative text for study and discussion in the schools, and students flocked to hear teachers expound on the Bible and the Mishnah, especially in the spring and autumn months when agricultural work was less demanding. Rav's academy at Sura was matched by that of his distinguished contemporary Samuel at Nehardea. When the latter was razed by Palmyran forces in approximately 260, the academy transferred to Mahoza on the Tigris. In the meantime, a still more important school had opened a few miles from Sura, at Pumbedita. For the next eight centuries, Sura and Pumbedita were to be the Oxford and Cambridge of Jewish learning, and their memory is still evoked nostalgically as the golden age of Rabbinic Judaism.

In 226 CE the Parthian Arsacid dynasty was overthrown by the Sassanians, who championed a revived Zoroastrianism and its priesthood (the magi) as the state church of Persia. Although the religious freedom of the minority religions was confirmed, state law had to be obeyed on matters such as taxation and property ownership, with important implications for Jewish law. In Palestine, Roman authority had perforce to be accepted, without it being granted any legitimacy in Jewish law. In the Diaspora, where Jewish legal autonomy depended upon the goodwill of the rulers, a clarification needed to be made between the dictates of Jewish law and the requirements of the non-Jewish government. It was Samuel who formulated the principle *dina de-malchuta dina*, 'the law of the state is the law', whereby in all civil, non-religious matters the primacy of state law was acknowledged; Samuel's formula applies to this day. Its acuity lay in the fact that by recognizing Jewish minority status, and ceding civil authority to the government, it actually enabled Torah law to prevail in almost all religious situations.

Sassanian Persia was a broadminded, tolerant environment, in which several versions of Christianity, a Persian literary revival, astrology, and various manifestations of Hellenistic and Indian thought all flourished. Judaism responded to the stimulus and the challenge. Generations of Babylonian rabbis honed to a fine edge the Galilean tradition of dialectic based on perceptive questioning, precise disputation and logical thinking. Their legacy is the Babylonian Talmud, a multi-volume work four times the size of its Palestinian counterpart, running to two and a half million words, largely completed by 500 CE. Until the close of the mishnaic period, rabbinic teachers are called *tannaim* ('teachers'); until the close of the talmudic period, they are known as *amoraim* ('debaters'). Six generations of Babylonian *amoraim* bequeathed to Judaism the Talmud, which to this day is its chief textbook of higher study. It is a book of complex, intellectual brilliance which studies, amplifies and interprets the Mishnah, subjecting thirty-nine mishnaic tractates to exhaustive scrutiny in a series of questions and answers, objections and rejoinders, refutations and redefinitions, that bind into a consistent whole the debates of sages living in different centuries and countries. Not only is the Talmud a thorough commentary on Jewish law, it is also a repository of parables, maxims, legends, folktales and ethical and theological speculations. This twofold strand in rabbinic thought of law (*halachah*) and lore (*aggadah*) is dealt with in part II, chapter 3.

The Babylonian Talmud gives ample evidence of a stable and prosperous Jewish community, in which the rabbinic academies were lively and crowded centres of learning, and their teachers were admired not only as masters of law and ethics, but also for their secular attainments. The teachers and their students formed an identifiable religious estate, with distinctive modes of dress, speech and deportment. Jewish institutions in Palestine may have declined, but generations of illustrious Babylonian sages maintained the stability of the single most important centre of Judaism in the world until the early eleventh century.

It was, unusually, not Judaism but Christianity which suffered more at the hands of the magi and their followers. Rome was Persia's chief enemy, and once Christianity had become the empire's state religion, its adherents came under sustained persecution in the east. Only for a time, in the mid-fifth century, was Judaism under attack, when synagogues and academies were shut down, the exilarchate suspended and Jewish children seized by the Zoroastrian priesthood.

Stability and toleration returned in the early sixth century, so that Babylonian scholars were again able to devote themselves to their leisurely redaction of Talmud material – a process which, unlike its Palestinian counterpart, spread over almost 300 years and is proof that its compilers did not feel themselves under urgent political pressure to complete the work. Jewish life resumed its accustomed course of scholarship and social acceptance, with Jews fighting in the Persian army that occupied Syria and Palestine at the beginning of the seventh century. In 651, however, the last of the Sassanian kings fell in battle against Arab invaders. All of Mesopotamia came under the domination of Mohammed's followers. A new chapter of Jewish history was about to commence, under the rule of Islam.

In 622, Mohammed fled from his birthplace, Mecca, and settled in the town of Yathrib (subsequently Medina), nearly 300 miles to the north. There he won the allegiance of the local Arabs and many bedouin tribes on the peninsula. It was only the Jews who rebuffed him, despite the flattery implicit in the Prophet's and his followers' observance of Jewish practices, such as praying towards Jerusalem, fasting on Yom Kippur and the rite of circumcision.

Jews had lived on the Arabian peninsula long before Mohammed's time. Divided into tribes, like their Arab neighbours, they controlled several oases and cities. Yathrib itself had been founded by Jewish date-growers, and elsewhere they were goldsmiths and artisans, as well as poets. As a strict monotheist who denounced paganism, and as one who had from his youth been familiar with the biblical stories of Jewish preachers, Mohammed had every reason to hope that the Jews would recognize him as a true prophet and heir to Moses. Their rejection caused him to turn bitterly against the Jews (and the Christians) for having twisted the words of Allah. The Koran was superior to the Torah and Gospels – it was God's revelation in its fulfilled, perfect form – and Islam was superior to Judaism and Christianity because it restored the pure monotheism of the first Muslim, Abraham.

As sign of his anger, Mohammed expelled two Jewish tribes from Yathrib and destroyed a third. He spared the Jews of the oasis at Khaybar only on condition that they gave half their produce as tribute. Mohammed died in 632 and the caliphs, his successors, initially maintained the same harsh policy. Because of Islam's spectacular military triumphs, and because of the grudgingly acknowledged affinities between Islam and Judaism, this payment of tribute soon became impracticable. Just twelve years after Mohammed's death, Syria, Palestine, Egypt, Iraq and Persia had all been overrun by Muslim armies. Seventy years later, a mixed force of Arabs and North African Berbers conquered the Iberian peninsula; Muslim rule now stretched from Europe to Asia Minor. It had been an astonishingly swift transformation from anonymity to empire, but it was not achieved without internal conflict. In 750 CE the Ummayads were overthrown and replaced by the Abbasid dynasty of caliphs, who ruled from Baghdad. The efflorescence of Muslim jurisprudence and theology in the following century had as its model the Jewish system of exegesis and interpretation of Scripture. The Koran became for Muslims what the Bible was for Jews, and Islamic scholars and judges filled a similar function to rabbis. Furthermore, the Arab conquerors controlled a vast population of different religious faiths. A working relationship had to be established with them. The so-called Pact of Omar (*c.* 800 CE) regulated association between Muslims and Jewish and Christian communities. The *dhimmi* (the term in Muslim law for subservient peoples, i.e., Jews and Christians) were guaranteed religious toleration, judicial autonomy, exemption from military service and security of life and property. In return they had to acknowledge the supremacy of the Islamic state by such outward signs as not building new churches and synagogues, not living in houses higher than those of their Muslim neighbours, not seeking converts and not bearing arms or riding horses. In time, such measures came to be honoured more in the breach, and capable Jewish and Christian statesmen attained positions of authority, while merchants and traders participated fully in the expanding economic life of the Islamic territories. The essential tolerance of Islam towards another 'people of the Book' was a decisive factor in ensuring the survival of Judaism throughout the east.

Islamic hegemony had three important consequences for the Jewish people. First, the expansion of trade in a realm stretching from the Atlantic to India, allied to the prohibitive land-taxes imposed on *dhimmi* farmers and peasants, stimulated the urbanization of the Jews. They flocked to the commercial centres of the new empire and took employment in such crafts as tanning, dyeing, weaving, silk manufacture and metal-work. Jewish merchants and bankers established a network of contacts in Muslim cities, and for the first time a prosperous, economically significant Jewish middle class emerged. Secondly, Jews now felt confident enough to travel outside their usual centres of settlement, and even to go beyond the limits of Muslim territory. It was Jewish merchants who converted the king and nobility of the Khazar people of the Volga to Judaism, some time in the early eighth century. Such fluidity of movement had significant demographic results: gradually the Jews migrated westwards from Persia and Iraq, so that by the thirteenth century, for the first time in their history, the majority of Jews lived in Europe rather than in the Middle East. Thirdly, Arabic became the lingua franca of the conquered territories. It was not only the language of Islam's religious literature, but also of the secular disciplines of science and philosophy. This flourishing of Arabic stimulated a revival of the Hebrew language as well, which was undertaken with careful regard for grammar and philology.

Leadership of Diaspora Jewry in the first centuries of Islamic rule remained in the hands of the Babylonian exilarch, who was recognized by the caliphate as the representative of the Jews, and granted wide powers of internal jurisdiction. Second to him stood the heads of the two great academies of Sura and Pumbedita. The authoritative decisions of the academy president (known as the *gaon*, plural *geonim* – excellency – from the shortened form of the Hebrew phrase, *rosh yeshivat g'on Ya'akov*, 'head of the academy which is the pride of Jacob') on all matters of Jewish law and liturgy were sought by Diaspora communities elsewhere. It is to these gaonic responsa, in answer to questions from abroad, that we owe much of our information concerning the history of Judaism at the time; about the correct order of reciting prayers, for example, and the earliest written prayer books, or the transmission of rabbinic authority. In the spring and autumn months the academies would be crowded with scholars and laymen who had come to hear the gaon lecture on the law. The prestige and influence of the geonim came to rival, then supersede, that of the exilarch, so that by the eleventh century the secular leadership was largely honorific and the real power was exercised by the president of the Pumbedita academy.

Impressive though the religious authority of the geonim was, in time it came to suffer from the defects of any system which perpetuates itself through a small, fixed caste. Just as the exilarchate was limited to a dynasty claiming Davidic lineage, so, too, rabbinic leadership was confined to half a dozen distinguished Babylonian families. Their jealously guarded privileges provoked opposition from the rest of the community and led, in the second half of the eighth century, to a major schism which called into question the validity of rabbinic law.

Anan ben David was leader of a dissident group which rejected the Talmud and sought to observe, as literally as possible, biblical law alone. The weighty and centuries-old tradition of rabbinic interpretation of the Scriptures was discarded by the Ananites, who practised an ascetic and pietistic fidelity to biblical commands. Rabbinic enactments which permitted lights and fire on the sabbath, if kindled beforehand, and emphasized sabbath joy, were abrogated, rabbinic definitions of prohibited marriages were considerably tightened and recourse to physicians was denounced as showing a lack of faith. It was one of Anan's successors, Benjamin of Nahawend, who gave this schismatic group the name by which it is known, Karaites (from the Hebrew word *mikra*, Scriptures), to designate those who followed biblical law alone, unlike their opponents the Rabbinites, who adhered to rabbinic legislation.

Resentment at the closed circle of rabbinic leadership gave broadly based impetus to the new movement, which, by the tenth century, had established several centres throughout the Middle East, and had founded an academy in Jerusalem. Karaism's rejection of rabbinic authority and its emphasis on individual decision, its ascetic simplicity of observance and its condemnation of the hypocrisy of the established hierarchy, attracted to its ranks many disaffected intellectuals. They provided powerful justifications for *Karaite* beliefs, arguing cogently and rationally against rabbinic uniformity and in defence of their claim to be the true 'remnant of Israel', the only authentic form of Judaism. It is possible that Karaism might have become a majority movement within Jewry – especially as it subsequently dropped its more

austere features and permitted intermarriage with Rabbinites –
had it not been for the sustained polemic directed against it by
Egyptian-born Saadiah ben Joseph (882–942 CE), the greatest of
the geonim.

A tough, combative personality, Saadiah had been summoned
from Palestine to become president of the academy at Sura and
restore its fading glory. The first outsider to be appointed to such
a prestigious post, he soon fell out with the exilarch. Their rivalry
disrupted Babylonian Jewry until Saadiah's death, but it did not
deflect him from prolific writing in the fields of Hebrew philology, liturgy and *halachah*. He also translated most of the Bible
into Arabic, and wrote the first systematic treatise on rabbinic
theology, the *Book of Beliefs and Opinions*. The counter-offensive
led by Saadiah halted Karaism. Although in subsequent centuries
the Karaites founded new settlements in the Crimea, Poland
and Lithuania, and the Egyptian community maintained itself
until the 1950s, their support dwindled until they became a
fringe sect within Jewry, like the Sadducees of the second Temple,
with whom they sometimes compared themselves. Once again,
Rabbinic Judaism had prevailed, although its power base in the
academies of Babylonia was soon to decline, as the Islamic empire
broke up into a number of smaller states. The lengthy and distinguished leadership of the geonim survived until the eleventh century, and the office of exilarch maintained a nominal existence for
a further two hundred years. By then, religious and intellectual
eminence had passed to a new and dazzling setting for medieval
Jewish culture: Muslim Spain.

CHAPTER EIGHT   THE SHADOW OF

THE CROSS

THE GOLDEN AGE OF SPANISH JEWRY

Spain was not the only territory where Jewish life benefited from the break-up of the Islamic empire into smaller, independent states. In Palestine, after the Muslim conquest of Galilee, the scholars of Tiberias were engaged in establishing the standard for vocalizing and punctuating the Hebrew text of the Bible, known as *masorah*, the impetus for their work being provided by Arab scholars perfoming a similar function for the Koran. When the Tiberias academy moved to Jerusalem in the ninth century, supported by the Jews of Egypt, Yemen and Syria, it even felt strong enough to challenge the primacy of the Babylonian academies.

The ancient community of Egypt was rejuvenated under the Fatamid dynasty, with new synagogues and rabbinic academies being established in the major cities. By the tenth century the city of Kairouan, near ancient Carthage, had become an important centre of Jewish learning, its scholars and philosophers maintaining a correspondence with the Babylonian geonim, supported financially by prosperous merchant families. In what is modern Morocco, many distinguished talmudists settled in Fez; the greatest of their number, Isaac Alfasi (i.e., 'man of Fez'), left there in 1088 for Spain. His migration, like that of Rav from Palestine to Babylon nine hundred years earlier, typified the lure of what had become the most important and populous centre of Jewry.

Jews had settled in the Iberian peninsula during the late Roman empire. Harried and intermittently persecuted by the Visigoth kings and the Catholic hierarchy of the seventh century, their situation was ameliorated after the Arab-Berber conquest of 711. Their numbers were swelled over the next three centuries by immigrant traders, merchants, bankers, physicians and scholars from the Middle East and North Africa, who penetrated into northern, Christian Spain as well. These Sephardim, as they were called (from Obadiah 1:20), were to enjoy a level of material prosperity, social acceptance and intellectual creativity that thereafter was remembered nostalgically as the golden age of Spanish Jewry.

Spain became an independent Muslim state in the latter half of the eighth century. Its population was a heterogeneous mix of Arabs, Berbers, Christians, Jews and Visigoths. Toleration was a necessary part of any policy, and the Jews, enjoying it, as did other sections of the population, were considered to be a particularly useful and loyal element. Their links with their coreligionists in other parts of the world, and their knowledge of languages, fitted them particularly well for errands of diplomacy, but they also were prominent at court, as landowning farmers, in medicine and astronomy.

The career of Chasdai ibn Shaprut (c. 915–970) was the most spectacular example of Jewish influence. Employed first as court physician, then as customs administrator of Cordova and diplomatic adviser to two successive caliphs of the Ummayad dynasty, Chasdai was also the official head of the Jewish community and a patron of learning. Under his leadership, Cordova became a thriving centre of Jewish scholarship, with an important *yeshivah* (rabbinic academy) and a glittering, élite group of poets and intellectuals. Some forty years after Chasdai's death the Ummayad caliphate in Spain broke up under the pressure of a Berber invasion. The Jews of Cordova scattered among the small Muslim principalities which were established throughout the peninsula. Their talents were utilized by the new rulers: Samuel ibn Nagrela (c. 993–1056) served for thirty years as vizier (prime minister) of Granada. He was a many-sided personality, who combined the careers of soldier, poet, scholar and statesman, and earned the admiring soubriquet of *ha-nagid*, 'the prince', the first Jewish leader to be so designated in the Muslim world. Contemporaries of his served the courts of Seville, Saragossa, Cordova, Toledo and other cities, and in Lucena, Isaac Alfasi's rabbinic academy trained a generation of outstanding legal authorities. By the mid-eleventh century, Spanish Jewry had achieved a synthesis of general culture, scientific and philosophical enquiry, artistic creativity (especially in literature) and Jewish scholarship, which, up to that point, represented the apogee of Diaspora existence.

The secure times did not last. In 1086 the Almoravides, Berber fanatics from North Africa, poured into the peninsula to help their Muslim allies stem the advance of the northern, Christian kingdoms. After a decisive Muslim victory at Zalaca, the Almoravide rulers dismissed Jews from all positions of authority and imposed heavy fines on the wealthy community of Lucena in an attempt to force a mass conversion to Islam.

Although such reforming zeal soon waned, a taste of impending persecution had been given. The next generation of Andalusian Jewry produced some of the greatest Sephardi poets, philosophers, biblical commentators and talmudic scholars; a last, late blooming before the dark days came. The poet Moses ibn Ezra, Judah Halevi, the poet-philosopher, the biblical exegete Abraham ibn Ezra and the historian Abraham ibn Daud, were four outstanding talents whose creativity was stimulated by the tense times in which they lived.

In 1146 other Berber tribes, this time from the Atlas region of Morocco, crossed the straits in order to help stem the Christian advance. The Almohades were uncompromising fundamentalists who instituted a systematic persecution of Christians and Jews. Synagogues and schools were closed, and those who would not don the turban were either converted forcibly or expelled. Some converted publicly but continued to practise Judaism secretly; others took to the high roads leading north, where they were welcomed as valuable immigrants to Christian Spain, or they journeyed even further afield, into the Middle East.

By 1172 the Almohad dynasty had brought all of Muslim Spain under its rule. When they were forced out of the peninsula by an alliance of the five Christian princes of Spain, Navarre and Portugal, whose armies defeated them at the battle of Los Navas de Toloso in 1212, not a single professing Jew remained in the south of the country. Spanish Jewry was to maintain a precarious existence for another 280 years, but under the banner of Christendom.

The fate of Spanish Jewry dimly mirrors the history of other Jewish communities under Muslim rule in the twelfth and thirteenth centuries. Reactionary religious sentiments, allied to economic decline, turned the Muslim states into inhospitable, despotic places. Italian maritime cities now dominated the Mediterranean trade routes, to the detriment of the international mercantile class in Muslim countries. The Pact of Omar was revived in order to regulate the freedom of religious minorities. Apart from a few merchant families connected with the Saharan gold trade, the bulk of North African Jewry became steadily more impoverished under the Almohades.

The only exception to this general state of affairs was in Egypt, where Sephardi Jews settled to escape Almohade persecution. They were not molested because of their religious beliefs or their economic position, and the greatest medieval Jewish philosopher, Moses Maimonides (1135–1204), became the spiritual head of the Cairo community and the court physician. Elsewhere in the east, the picture was gloomy. The Palestinian community suffered from the Crusades. Iraqi Jewry continued to decline, and the region as a whole was devastated by the Mongol invasions of the mid-thirteenth century. Egypt, Syria and Palestine came under the control of the Mamelukes, a Turkish military caste hostile towards Judaism and Christianity. A Jewish life of sorts continued in Persia, Yemen, the Caucasus, Central Asia, even India (from the tenth century) and China, where Indian and Persian Jews settled in the city of Kaifeng some time after 1127, the community remaining in existence until the beginning of the twentieth century. But intellectual vigour was lacking, and not until the sixteenth century would eastern Jewry again play a significant role in Jewish thought. It was in Christian Europe that Judaism would demonstrate its physical resilience, its capacity for religious survival and its intellectual strength.

EUROPE AND THE CRUSADES

European Jewish history is regional history, depending upon where on the continent Jews settled. And because – unlike in the east, where conformity was determined by the decrees of the Babylonian academies – each regional community had its own distinctive character, its own liturgical rites and customs, and sometimes its own Jewish variant of the native language, the reader must be prepared to skip from one country to another in order to follow the fortunes of European Jewry from the Middle Ages to the present.

Broadly speaking, the major division of European Jewry was between the Sephardim of the Iberian peninsula on the one hand, and on the other, the Ashkenazim of Germany and northern France. Ashkenazi Jewry, so-named from Genesis 10:3, developed in the special environment of western European Christianity as Christianity reacted to the fall of the Roman empire.

It was the Emperor Charlemagne (742–814) who halted the decay of urban life and the breakdown of central government which had resulted from the barbarian invasions. As a matter of consistent policy, he and the Carolingian dynasty encouraged Jewish immigration. Jewish merchants received favoured treatment because of their trade connections with the Mediterranean and the east. In 797 Isaac the Jew was one of a delegation sent by Charlemagne to Caliph Harun-al-Rashid in Baghdad; it was Isaac who returned with the elephant which was the caliph's gift to the emperor. Other Jewish merchants, from their bases in France, set out on daunting missions across eastern Europe and over the Russian steppes to the Middle East, whence they continued to India and China. Jewish businessmen were on familiar terms with the kings and nobles of western Europe throughout the tenth and eleventh centuries, so much so that canonical restrictions imposed on Jews by successive church councils were blithely disregarded by their royal patrons, such was their economic value. As a result, Jewish settlers came to Troyes, Mainz, Worms, Speyer, Cologne and other developing cities.

The communities they founded were independent and self-governing. They had no equivalent of an exilarch or *nagid* to represent them officially. Each *kahal*, as the community was called, set up its own law court, enacted its own regulations, and effectively controlled the behaviour of its residents in much the same way local barons and warlords governed feudal Christian society. The direst penalty a *kahal* could impose was a ban of excommunication (*cherem*), which would cut off the accused from contact with fellow-Jews.

By the close of the eleventh century, Jewish settlement had reached out from northeastern France to the commercial centres along the Rhine and the valleys of the Danube and the Elbe. Jews from Normandy had followed their duke across the Channel and established themselves in London and the major provincial cities. The transition from east to west was complete. France, Germany and the neighbouring countries now housed Jewish communities which were as important, numerically, intellectually and economically, as those of the Iberian peninsula, and the two centres together far outnumbered the ancient communities of the Middle East. For better or for worse, Judaism was now predominantly a European religion, and Christianity, not Islam, its custodian.

Characteristically, the study of Jewish law was a major priority of Ashkenazi communities. Since the tenth century, copies of the Talmud had been available outside the Babylonian *yeshivot*, and this had facilitated the spread, and development, of rabbinic scholarship wherever Jews had settled. The Rhineland cities of Mainz and Worms, then Troyes and Sens in northern France, became well-known academic centres. Rabbi Gershom ben Judah (*c.* 965–1028), remembered for his attainments as 'the Light of the Exile', established an academy at Mainz. Little of Gershom's talmudic commentary has survived, but among his attributed legal enactments (*takkanot*) is the decree which, among Ashkenazim, officially prohibited the polygamy which they had long since abandoned in practice.

The most eminent student of the Mainz academy was Rabbi Solomon ben Isaac (1040–1105), known by his acronym, Rashi. At the age of twenty-five he returned to his birthplace of Troyes, in Champagne, and earned his livelihood by winemaking, while devoting most of his time to scholarship. His commentaries on the Bible and Talmud became basic texts of Ashkenazi education. Rashi's successors, including members of his own family, built on his scholarly framework to develop new subtleties of deductive analysis and elucidation. These *Tosafists*, as they were called (from *tosafot*, 'additions'), elaborated Rashi's commentary, explored in depth the legal issues raised by both the Talmudic text and the interpretations of their great predecessor, and focused the dialectic of rabbinic reasoning. Their schools proliferated throughout eastern France, Lorraine and the Rhineland, and they trained generations of rabbis.

As in Spain, so too in western Europe the Jew was destined to suffer because of the conflict between Christianity and Islam. This time, the cause was reports from pilgrims to Palestine about the desecration of the holy places. In November 1095, Pope Urban II preached a sermon at Clermont in which he called upon Christendom to recover the Holy Land and its shrines from the Infidel. Thus began the history of the Crusades. For Jews it ushered in two grim centuries of persecution, martyrdom and expulsion.

In the spring and summer months of 1096, gangs of would-be Crusaders roamed through the Rhineland, attacking one Jewish community after another. Mob violence left a trail of siege, pillage and massacre all the way from Metz to Jerusalem, where, in 1097, Godfrey de Bouillon's army fought its way into the city, herded all the Jews into a synagogue and set it on fire. Neither the Church nor secular rulers had sanctioned this carnage, although both had helped to inflame religious passions and hopes of material reward among those who undertook to fight the Turks. Where the local bishops responded firmly, as in Speyer, the Jews survived, and elsewhere, those who had submitted to baptism under duress were permitted to return to Judaism. In 1103, Emperor Henry IV extended to Jews living in his territory the same protection accorded to the clergy, with an attack on them being answerable to the sovereign.

Such measures highlighted the vulnerability of the Jewish communities, dependent as they were on the goodwill of individual rulers. The interplay of religious and economic factors was to govern the treatment of Jews throughout the later Middle Ages. A money economy was developing in western Europe at a time when the Church taught that usury was morally repugnant. The Jew, standing outside the legal jurisdiction of the Church, was not hindered from answering the great demand for loans; he had the liquid assets, amassed from his mercantile connections, and the growing monopoly of Christian merchant guilds was, anyway, forcing him out of trade and into money-lending. Although there were other groups of money-lenders sanctioned by the Church – for example, Lombard bankers, the Cahorsins from southern France and the Templars – Jews dominated the occupation, with the connivance of their noble protectors, who took a share of the profits. The stereotype of the Jewish money-lender gave an added twist to the religious hostility directed against him.

Official Church doctrine regarding the Jew was usually more ambivalent than the simple message which the masses chose to receive. For the masses, the Jew was a deicide and a non-believer who murdered Christian children at Passover to use their blood for baking unleavened bread. This 'blood libel' first appeared in Norwich in 1144 and was to crop up repeatedly in Europe up to the twentieth century. Another popular superstition was that Jews would steal the wafer of the host in order to enjoy torturing the body of Jesus. Medieval credulity accepted such preposterous allegations, and Jews suffered accordingly. The papacy never condoned these folktales, and from time to time it would anathematize them. In papal dominions, almost alone in Europe, a policy of formal toleration prevailed. The popes' quarrel with the Jews was of a different kind. It concerned the discrepancy between apparent Jewish prosperity and the lowly status which their rejection of Jesus merited. Just as Cain had been branded, to wander the earth, so too the Jews were marked for perpetual servitude. Therefore, not only should they be forbidden to employ Christian servants, but they should also wear distinguishing dress and have their money-lending activities curtailed, since the Church's own property was being pledged as collateral for Jewish loans.

The two Crusades of 1146 and 1189 marked a further deterioration in Jewish security. Anti-Jewish riots even infected England on the day Richard the Lionheart was being crowned at Westminster, and spread in the following spring of 1190 to Norwich, Dunstable, Stamford and York, where the Jews, led by their rabbi, committed suicide rather than fall prey to the mob. This readiness to die a martyr's death paralleled many similar instances among European Jewry, whose liturgies prescribed the benediction to be recited before dying, 'for the sanctification of the divine Name'.

POGROMS AND EXILE

Ashkenazi pietism was a Jewish response to the charged emotional climate which, in the Christian world, gave rise to the Franciscan order. One of the best-known Jewish ascetics, Judah the Pious of Regensburg, was a contemporary of Francis of Assisi. The *Chasidei Ashkenaz*, as these especially devout pietists were called, studied esoteric texts such as the *Sefer Yetzirah*, or the Divine Chariot literature on the first chapter of Ezekiel, which went back, in part, to talmudic times, and described the ecstatic ascent of the mystic to heaven and his apprehension of the divine presence. Based in the Rhineland and led by several generations of the Kalonymos family, the *Chasidei Ashkenaz* emphasized the value of selfless love of God, the supreme manifestation of which was martyrdom. This overwhelming love of God was allied to the concept of the *chasid*, 'the pious one', who lived by the most exacting moral and religious demands and renounced worldly things in order to achieve spiritual insight, if necessary fasting, mortifying the flesh and leaving home as atonement for the sins of all Israel. Such a regimen of religious devotion and physical flagellation clearly had its similarities to contemporary Christian penitential disciplines, but this led to no blurring of the differences between the two religions. Instead, it gave the *Chasidei Ashkenaz* the inner fortitude with which to face the humiliations, the obloquy and the mortal danger which were an ever-present reality for Jews in medieval Europe.

They needed whatever resources they could summon. In 1182 Philip Augustus, King of France, expelled all Jews from the royal domains, confiscated their property and cancelled all outstanding Christian debts to them, except for a fifth, which he kept for the royal treasury. The accession to the papacy of Innocent III, in 1198, brought further hardship. This most powerful of popes was ambitious to establish his authority over secular rulers, and to extirpate Christian heresy, especially in southern France. To that end he proclaimed a Crusade against the Albigensians and enacted restrictive legislation against the Jews, who were suspected of complicity. He also encouraged the formation of two new preaching orders, the Dominicans and the Franciscans. The Dominicans were especially active against Judaism, being responsible, in 1240, for the public burning of the Talmud in Paris, as a work deemed slanderous to Christianity. Twenty-four cartloads of precious Hebrew manuscripts were consigned to the flames. English kings of the thirteenth century taxed the Jews inordinately, to increase royal revenue. The arrival of Italian banking firms rendered the Jews superfluous, and in 1290 they were expelled from England, their dwellings and assets reverting to the king.

Most of them crossed to France, where the situation was almost as ominous. A ritual-murder trial had been held in Troyes in 1288 and, two years later, a host-desecration trial was held in Paris. In 1306 the inevitable happened. An edict of expulsion was issued, and the French treasury took over all debts owed to Jews. Only in the papal territories around Avignon were Jews able to remain.

The Jews of Germany were granted a reprieve of almost another hundred years. They were a valuable source of imperial revenue, and had established several new communities. Charters protecting their lives, property and freedom of movement were issued first in Austria, then in Bohemia, Hungary and other parts of central Europe. It was only towards the end of the thirteenth century that their situation became untenable. The leading rabbi of his generation, and the last of the *Tosafists*, Meir of Rothenburg (c. 1215–93), was imprisoned in 1286, when about to make a pilgrimage to the Holy Land. Rather than acquiesce in the imposition of a special tax, which implied that Jews were the emperor's property, he refused to be ransomed, and died in prison. Five years after his death, roving gangs plundered and destroyed some 140 Jewish communities in what became known as the Rindfleisch massacres, after the nobleman who instigated them. In 1336 there were further mob attacks. Most terrible of all was the reaction to the Black Death of 1348–9. Jews, probably because of their greater hygiene and their dietary laws, suffered less than their neighbours from the bubonic plague which carried off a third of Europe's population. The story was put about that they had poisoned the wells. Unprecedented butchery engulfed them, spreading from southern France through Switzerland to western Germany, then breaking out in Belgium, northern Germany and Bavaria. Christian flagellants, wandering from place to place and whipping each other in atonement for sin, incited the mobs, as did some local rulers who anticipated Jewish booty.

Those who survived the attacks did so by moving from town to town, or further afield, to Poland and Spain. No expulsion order was imposed on German Jewry, but only because the authority of the Roman emperor was too weak to implement it, and any one of the dozens of small principalities would always take Jews in, to make use of them as money-lenders and petty traders, their status that of *servi camerae nostri*, serfs of the royal exchequer, the emperor's property.

Jewish suffering in the late Middle Ages was a cameo of the plague, war, social breakdown, economic stagnation, religious violence and casual death which affected all of feudal European society. There were upright churchmen and firm rulers who protected their Jews. In general, though, the defenceless and economically exposed Jew had been saddled with a terrible image; blasphemer of Christian belief; grasping money-lender; child-slayer; water-poisoner – the devil's accomplice. Even in those countries which had thrust the Jews out, this malign image was to persist in folk mythology, with grievous consequences in the centuries to come.

THE DECLINE OF THE SPANISH COMMUNITIES

Spanish Jewry merits its own particular requiem, because its fall from high estate to exile has the melancholy inexorability of classical tragedy. At least 200,000 Jews lived in Castile, Aragon and Portugal, barely affected by the Christian reconquest of the peninsula and avoiding the waves of persecution visited on Jewish communities elsewhere in Europe. Christians, Jews and Muslims coexisted amicably under Christian kings for almost two centuries. As they had done under Muslim sovereignty, Jews rose to positions of importance in diplomacy and finance, and Jewish favourites were usually to be found at court. Samuel Abulafia (*c.* 1320–61) became treasurer to Pedro the Cruel of Castile, and during his stewardship several synagogues were built for the 300 communities of the realm, including the lovely Sinagoga del Transito in Toledo. Jews participated in all the professions and crafts, with their own craft-guilds and guild-halls in the larger cities; money-lending was a minority occupation.

The Spanish-Jewish communities were governed by charters

which guaranteed economic and religious rights. These *aljamas*, as the Sephardi communities were called, were sizeable organizations, existing alongside and within Christian cities. The various social classes vied for representation on the communal committees which looked after education, the legal system and charitable services, and the relationship between the *aljamas* and court Jews was often a contentious issue.

Both Muslim and Ashkenazi influences contributed to the intellectual milieu of Spanish Jewry. The natural sciences, astronomy, mathematics, medicine and philosophy were studied, as well as mystical theology; the basic text of *kabbalah*, the *Zohar* ('splendour'), received its literary form in thirteenth-century Spain. In addition, the ideas of the *Tosafists* of northern Europe were known to Spanish rabbis and several Ashkenazi talmudists sought a haven from persecution in Spain. Jacob ben Asher (*c.* 1270–1340), the son of one of Meir of Rothenburg's students who had fled Germany, wrote, in Toledo, one of the most important compilations of Jewish law, the *Arba'ah Turim* ('four rows', from Exodus 39:10), which codified the decisions of both Talmuds, the geonim and previous codes, responsa and commentators.

Until the latter half of the fourteenth century, the Jews of Spain were spared the violence which had marred Ashkenazi existence. They were even granted large tracts of land to develop, as the Spanish kings completed the reconquest of the Iberian peninsula. After the civil war between Pedro the Cruel and his half-brother, Henry of Trastanara, for the throne of Castile, the Jews paid for having supported the defeated Pedro. Henry's troops and their French allies sacked several *aljamas*, and the ecclesiastical authorities enforced the wearing of the Jewish badge. For the next few decades ill-feeling continued to rise, exacerbated by political instability and the sermons of church leaders. In 1391, anti-Jewish violence erupted in Seville and spread throughout Castile and Aragon. Thousands were slaughtered by the mobs, who were quelled only when they turned on Christians and their property as well.

The effect on Spanish Jewry was traumatic. Unlike northern Europe, where martyrdom 'for the sanctification of the divine Name' was almost sought by pious Jews, in Spain tens of thousands converted *en masse* to Christianity, led by the wealthiest and most prominent of the community. The mass defection of these *conversos* or 'New Christians', encouraged the church, Dominicans in the vanguard, to increase pressure on those Jews who stayed firm. In 1413, a public disputation was staged in Tortosa, at which Jewish leaders were forced to defend their doctrine of the Messiah. The pope himself presided at some of the sixty-nine sessions, spread over twenty-one months, and at the conclusion of the proceedings issued a Bull which forbade the study of Talmud and ordered Jews to attend conversionist sermons for their benefit at least three times a year. A fresh wave of apostasy followed, by the end of which *conversos* were almost as large a group as loyal Jews.

For a while, these 'new Christians' enjoyed privileged social status. They became bishops and church officials, and demonstrated their sincerity by attacking erstwhile co-religionists with particular zeal. They entered branches of the state administration which had previously been closed to them. They married into the nobility and even the royal family of Aragon. While Jews were attempting to reconstruct communities out of the debris of formerly great centres like Toledo and Barcelona, *conversos* were infiltrating the highest and most important positions in the country.

By the mid-fifteenth century their popularity had waned. Priests accused them of being Jews in disguise, who secretly practised Jewish ceremonies. An anti-*converso* riot occurred in Toledo in 1449, the first of many over the next thirty years. *Marrano*, 'swine', was the epithet applied to *conversos* by their enemies. They were under threat as their grandparents had been in 1391, but this time they could not escape by being baptized.

In 1479, the marriage of Ferdinand and Isabella united the kingdoms of Aragon and Castile. A year later they established the Spanish Inquisition, to investigate charges against heretics. The first *auto-da-fé* was held in early 1481, six men and women of Jewish extraction being burned alive. In the first twenty years of its existence the Inquisition confiscated the property of 30,000 secret Jews and burned at the stake those who did not repent satisfactorily. The first and most fearsome inquisitor-general, Fra Tomas de Torquemada, was of Jewish descent.

The persecution of allegedly secret Jews soon spread to openly avowing Jews. A fabricated blood-libel charge at Avila was the pretext. This persuaded Ferdinand and Isabella to issue, in 1492, from the newly captured Alhambra of Granada – the last Muslim stronghold on the Iberian peninsula – a decree expelling all Jews from their dominions. They were given four months to leave. Those in favour of the decree argued that it would protect *conversos* from the malign influence of their former religion. Don Isaac Abravanel (1437–1508), the outstanding Jewish statesman and financier of his time, who served the Spanish sovereigns, tried to have the decree rescinded, but in vain. Between 100,000 and 150,000 Jews left Spain in the summer of 1492. As they undertook their mass exodus from a territory which had been home to Jews for well over a thousand years, and where Jewish culture had achieved its most brilliant synthesis of secular learning and rabbinic scholarship, musicians played lively tunes, by order of the rabbis, to keep up the spirits of the refugees.

Some of the refugees went to North Africa and Ottoman Turkey. Others who joined their families in Sicily discovered that the edict of expulsion extended there too. The independent kingdom of Naples offered temporary refuge, until it came under the control of Aragon. Avignon, territory of the pope, attracted some to cross the Pyrenees. The great majority took the obvious route, over the border to Portugal. There they were callously exploited and victimized, until the accession of Emanuel I in 1495. At first he looked favourably on his new subjects, but a prospective marriage with Isabella, daughter of Ferdinand and Isabella, led him to banish them unless they converted to Christianity. In the spring of 1497, at the beginning of the festival of Passover, an order was issued for all Jewish children between the ages of four and fourteen to be presented for baptism the following Sunday. Almost the entire Jewish population submitted to conversion; its spirit had been broken. The *marranos* of Portugal became the last representatives of Iberian Jewry, suffering a massacre at Lisbon in 1506 which accounted for 2,000 lives, and in 1531 being forced to welcome the Inquisition. The greatest medieval centre of European Judaism had fallen. We now have to look to the eastern Mediterranean and eastern Europe for the continuation of Jewish history.

CHAPTER NINE   BETWEEN DARKNESS AND LIGHT

MESSIANIC DREAMERS, TALMUDISTS AND COURT JEWS

In 1453 the Ottoman Turks had captured Constantinople, bringing to an end the Byzantine empire. Muslim in religion, Turkish in language, the Ottoman state spread steadily throughout parts of Europe and the Middle East until, by the mid-sixteenth century, it controlled Arabia, most of North Africa and several Mediterranean islands. Ruled by a military caste happy to leave economic activity to the religious minorities – Greek Orthodox, Armenians, Jews – in return for taxes, it provided a beckoning haven for thousands of refugees from the Spanish expulsion. According to a Jewish tradition, Sultan Bayazid II observed on hearing of King Ferdinand's expulsion order, 'How can you consider him a wise ruler, when he has impoverished his own land and enriched ours?' The Sephardi immigrants came with their business contacts, their experience in the manufacture of cloth, weapons and gunpowder, their medical reputation readily appreciated at the Ottoman Court in renamed Istanbul, and their diplomatic expertise. Joseph Nasi, nephew and son-in-law of the wealthy Portuguese *marrano* Donna Gracia Mendes (1510–69), was adviser to two sultans and ennobled as Duke of Naxos, while his mother-in-law controlled a large business empire from her new home in Istanbul, where she was a leader of the Jewish community. It was Nasi's misconceived advice which led indirectly to the crushing Turkish naval defeat at the battle of Lepanto in 1571, and thus to the decline of his influence; but in his heyday he had, among other ventures, established a textile project in

Tiberias, to which he hoped to attract Italian refugees expelled from the papal states by the harsh legislation of the Counter-Reformation. Although the Tiberias scheme did not materialize, nearby Safed in upper Galilee was to become an important centre of rabbinic and kabbalistic study. The favourable conditions of sixteenth-century Turkish rule attracted Jews to the Balkans, to Greece – where half the population of Salonika was Jewish – to Istanbul – which claimed to have 50,000 Jewish residents – and to the cities of Cairo, Damascus, Aleppo and Izmir, as well as encouraging a substantial Jewish migration to Jerusalem. The economic and intellectual traditions of the Sephardim stimulated Jewish life in the Ottoman realms, and the customs of the Iberian peninsula were tenaciously maintained in prayer, in folk music, and even in the Judeo-Spanish dialect of Ladino, up to the twentieth century.

Especially significant for the survival and development of Judaism was the burgeoning of rabbinic scholarship which now occurred in newly established *yeshivot* in Istanbul, Salonika, Cairo and elsewhere. A large responsa literature was published, adjusting Jewish law to conditions in the east. It was the desire to harmonize conflicting practices and to summarize all the Jewish laws in contemporary use that led, in the 1520s, to the emergence of one of the least attractive, most important figures in the history of Rabbinic Judaism.

Joseph Caro's early life was typical of his generation. Born in Toledo, his family transferred to Portugal in 1492 and from there, after the forced expulsions of 1497, to the Balkans. A tense, quarrelsome, ascetic man, absorbed by *kabbalah*, Caro – like other mystics of the time – claimed that a heavenly messenger (in kabbalistic terms, a *maggid*) guided him; his *maggid* told him to move to Palestine, where he founded a *yeshivah* in Safed and became involved in a controversy about re-instituting traditional ordination for rabbis. He had also begun work on a vast commentary to Jacob ben Asher's *Arba'ah Turim*, entitled *Beit Yosef*, The House of Joseph. In it, Caro gathered together all the talmudic and post-talmudic opinions up to his own day, and gave definitive *halachic* rulings. In order to make this *magnum opus* more accessible, Caro then produced a précis of it. The *Shulchan Aruch*, or 'Prepared Table', as it is called, published in 1564, is the most authoritative and minutely detailed code of Jewish law. Regularly reprinted and distributed throughout the Diaspora, it aroused the opposition of some Ashkenazi scholars especially, who justifiably claimed that it was based on the precedents of Sephardi rabbis, and favoured the French and German traditions. One particular critic was a Polish talmudist, Moses Isserles, who wrote a *Mappah* ('Tablecloth') for Caro's *Prepared Table* which added and incorporated the rulings of Ashkenazi practice and paved the way for the *Shulchan Aruch*'s eventual acceptance as definitive in both east and west.

Among Caro's contemporaries in Safed, which had grown during the course of the sixteenth century from a handful of families to a community of more than 10,000 Jews, was Isaac Luria (1534–72), a mystic of imaginative and original personality. Born in Jerusalem and brought up in Egypt by a wealthy uncle, *Ha-Ari ha-Kadosh*, 'the holy lion' as he was admiringly known, gave up both the study of the Talmud and attempts at a business career in order to immerse himself in the *kabbalah*. His teachings were preserved and transmitted by a group of devoted disciples, after his early death from the plague. Central to the Lurianic interpretation of the *kabbalah* is the doctrine of exile and restoration. God himself is in exile, but by fulfilling the divine commandments with mystical devotion, Israel becomes a co-partner with God in hastening the time of messianic redemption. It is no coincidence that the speculative thought of Caro, Luria and lesser contemporaries, such as Solomon Alkabetz and Moses Cordovero, was suffused with messianic yearning, or that Safed should become the home of Jewish eschatology. The trauma of exile had marked the personality of the Sephardi refugees and sharpened their sense of divine alienation, for which the only antidote was intensified piety and observance. Asceticism, prayer and mystical speculation was the response of the pious, and to this day one still catches in Safed – in the environs of the Ari Synagogue, for example – a combination of mood, climate and atmosphere that is deeply spiritual.

Contemporary with these scholars, the less devout, and more gullible, fell prey to messianism of a different kind. Charlatans and adventurers took advantage of the redemptive longings of the Jewish masses. In 1524 a young man, claiming to be a brother of the king of the independent tribe of Reuben, arrived in Italy to obtain military assistance for the struggle against the Turks. David Reubeni was received in audience by Pope Clement VII, who gave him letters of introduction to the rulers of Europe. Lavishly supplied with money and gifts, not only from the credulous, but also from hardheaded bankers, he let it be known that the hour of the ingathering of the exiles was at hand. In Lisbon, a young *marrano* who fell under his spell had himself circumcised, took the name of Solomon Molcho and went to Salonika to study *kabbalah*, where he met, and impressed, Joseph Caro. Molcho, too, made the journey to Rome, sitting among the beggars and the maimed in fulfilment of an old legend about the Messiah, and gained the pope's favour, supposedly for accurately foretelling a flood of the Tiber. Reubeni and Molcho joined up in northern Italy, and the two pseudo-Messiahs, perhaps feeding each other's fantasies, approached the Holy Roman Emperor, Charles V, in Ratisbon, to persuade him to arm the Jews of Europe against the Turks. The response of that dry bigot was to have them put in chains. Molcho was burned at the stake in 1532, anticipating by eight years the date he had announced for the coming of the messianic kingdom, and Reubeni met a similar death in Spain three years after.

Less than a century later, at a time when the Thirty Years War was devastating Europe and the Catholic Counter-Reformation was enacting blatantly anti-Jewish legislation, there was born in Izmir the most astonishingly successful and banefully tragic of all the false Messiahs. Shabbetai Tzevi evoked a frenzied response from large segments of the Jewish people who felt, because of their humiliated and vulnerable status, even more keenly than their Christian neighbours the millenarian fervour which gripped Europe in the mid-seventeenth century. As a young man, Tzevi studied the *Zohar* and subjected himself to intense bouts of asceticism, which accentuated his temperamental instability. Two brief, unconsummated marriages ended in divorce. Between 1648 and 1655, one of the worst massacres in Jewish history took place in Poland and the Ukraine; survivors were ransomed in the slave markets of Istanbul and they told of the horrors they had endured. This was the impetus which moved Tzevi to proclaim himself the redeemer of Israel. Expelled by the scandalized rabbis of Izmir in

1654, he left for Salonika, where he declared his messiahship in a ceremony of marriage with the holy law. Welcomed by the masses wherever he travelled, Shabbetai, in Egypt, met and married Sarah, a beautiful but deranged survivor of the Polish massacre, who desired to marry the Messiah.

In April 1665, Tzevi went to Gaza, where he made the acquaintance of the twenty-year-old youth who was to become his chief prophet, fund-raiser, publicist and apologist. Nathan of Gaza persuaded Shabbetai, whenever his conviction wavered, that he was indeed the Messiah, and an announcement to that effect triggered off intense excitement in the Gaza synagogue. Returning to Turkey, after an inconclusive sojourn in Jerusalem, Tzevi was joyfully received and heaped with honours. In letters to the Diaspora announcing the glad tidings, Nathan exulted that his master would shortly depose the sultan, restore the lost biblical tribes and usher in the time of redemption. The fervour spread throughout the Jewish world, and rumours were rife about a Jewish army which would advance from the Arabian desert to conquer Palestine. Wherever Shabbetai went, mass hysteria greeted him; people fell into trances and experienced visions of him crowned king of Israel.

In 1666, he went to Istanbul to 'depose the Sultan', and was promptly arrested. Confined to the fortress of Gallipoli, he nevertheless held court there, regally greeting thousands of pilgrims who joined in acts of penance and messianic rituals. The fast of the Ninth of Av, his birthday, was turned into a feast day, and Nathan of Gaza published special liturgies for the hastening of redemption. Messianic expectation ran high throughout Europe, where credulous Jews gathered with their belongings at the seaports, awaiting the signal to leave for the Promised Land. Eventually the Turkish authorities took action, to quell the ferment among their Jewish subjects. Shabbetai Tzevi was brought before the sultan and given the choice of conversion to Islam or death. He decided quickly, and was rewarded for his apostasy with a Turkish name, a title and a government pension.

Although the scandal of his conversion disillusioned most Jews, there were still those who clung pathetically to their belief in his messiahship. The persistent Nathan and his followers elaborated a philosophy whereby Shabbetai's suffering and conversion were an atonement for Israel, in accord with the kabbalistic doctrine of descending to the husks in order to redeem the scattered sparks of divine light. Just as the heroine of the biblical book of Esther had appeared to hide her religion in order to become queen and save her people, so too the Messiah had appeared to convert, in order to triumph the more completely.

In 1672, the Turks grew tired of their supposed convert, who still adhered to Jewish rites, and banished him to Dulcigno in Albania. Shabbetai's behaviour grew increasingly erratic over the last four years of his life and he died in ignominy on the Day of Atonement 1676, although the preposterous Nathan insisted until his own death in 1680 that the Messiah had not really died but had merely concealed himself in the supernal world. Thus ended in sordid farce what was, essentially, a tragic interlude in Diaspora history. Shabbetai Tzevi's impact had been spectacular and far-reaching, thanks to the trade connections which Sephardim and *marranos* maintained between the Ottoman empire and European countries. To an extent unknown before, or until the advent of modern communications, the false Messiah had transcended regional geography and brought brief hope to Jewish communities as far apart as Turkey and Poland. A collective fantasy had gripped the Jewish masses, fuelled by kabbalistic motifs, apocalyptic beliefs and messianic yearnings. The combination was so combustible because it was built on a base of widespread suffering, persecution and sense of exile, more keenly and universally experienced by Jews than at any time since the destruction of the second Temple. Part sincere, part deluded, Shabbetai Tzevi ended up as much the victim as the manipulator of mass wish-fulfilment. One can better understand, for example, why there were still those who trusted in him even after his wretched apostasy, when one realizes that the metaphor of the Messiah taking on the guise of another religion that he did not believe in would have intense personal validity for all *marranos*.

Several small groups of adherents survived the deaths of Tzevi and his chief prophet. One, in Salonika, led by the family of Shabbetai's last wife, formed a sect known as the *Doenmeh* ('Apostates'), professing Islam in public but observing a heretical form of Judaism in private. Secret Shabbetean circles met in Italy, and missionaries travelled through eastern Europe, despite the opposition of heresy-hunting rabbis, who were anxious to stifle any repetition of the messianic fervour that had been so harmful. In Poland, a Shabbetean group formed round the person of Jacob Frank (1726–91), who had close relations with the *Doenmeh* and presented himself as the spiritual heir and reincarnation of Tzevi. Frank and several hundred followers converted to Catholicism in the 1750s, encouraged by Polish clerics, until it was discovered that the sect intended to continue its orgiastic rites and fidelity to Frank as the 'Messiah who had come'. Imprisoned, then released by the Russians in 1772, Frank was succeeded by his daughter Eve, who died in poverty in 1817, although many baptized Frankists became prominent members of the Polish nobility.

Despite such lingering manifestations, the messianic furore of 1665–6 died down, as intangible and fantastical as a dream. Jewry in the Ottoman realms had exhausted itself in the excitement, and never properly recovered. The Ottoman empire itself went into a long, slow decline, undermined by army revolts and widespread corruption. Demeaning aspects of Islamic *dhimmi* legislation were reimposed and the Jewish communities of Turkey, Syria, Egypt and Palestine entered a period of economic and spiritual stagnation that did not noticeably ameliorate until the nineteenth century.

The largest Diaspora community of the sixteenth century was to be found in Poland. Expelled from Spain and dispersed throughout the Ottoman realms, subjected in western and central Europe to the repressive legislation of the Counter-Reformation, the Jew fulfilled in economically backward Poland the same indispensable function as middleman and distributor as he had done during the medieval period. Whereas Pope Paul IV's notorious Bull of 1555, *Cum nimis absurdum*, had reiterated that Jews were to be strictly segregated in their own quarter (later known as the ghetto, in imitation of the Jewish district in Venice, located since 1516 in the *Ghetto Nuovo*, the new foundry), that they were to be barred from all occupations other than dealing in secondhand clothes, that they were forbidden to employ Christian servants or workmen, that all their real estate had to be sold off and a distinctive badge of shame worn on their clothing, four years previously, in Poland, Sigismund Augustus had confirmed three hundred years of tolerant legislation by recognizing the right of rabbinical authorities to exercise internal jurisdiction over their flocks.

From the ninth to the eleventh centuries Jews had been drawn to France and the Rhineland in order to fill an economic vacuum. From the thirteenth to the sixteenth centuries, Poland was a similar magnet to Jews (and Christians) from Germany. In 1264, in the wake of recent Tartar depredations, Boleslav the Pious issued a model charter of liberties and protection for the Jews, in return for immigration to sparsely populated territories. Between 1334 and 1367, King Casimir the Great amplified the inducements, and a few years later the grand duke of Lithuania followed suit, so that large numbers of Ashkenazim settled in eastern Europe, soon outranking in importance, and outnumbering, the indigenous Jews who had come originally from the Caucasus and the Crimea.

The newcomers took advantage of the economic opportunities, becoming intermediaries between the landed nobility and the peasants, acting as tax-collectors and landlords' agents, importing textiles and luxury goods, exporting furs and raw materials. They were distributors of merchandise and agricultural products and they played a prominent role in the great fairs around which Polish commercial life revolved. The vitality, acumen and all-pervasiveness of the immigrants was such that their language – Middle High German as spoken in the Rhineland – became the Jewish vernacular throughout the region; with the addition of some Hebrew and Slavic expressions it was later and better known as Yiddish.

Although Polish-Jewish life was punctuated by those outbursts of mob violence, economic jealousy and blood-libel accusations which were endemic in western Europe, the communities enjoyed two advantages over their co-religionists elsewhere. Firstly, their economic importance won them the favour of successive kings and the protection of the nobility, whose agents they were. Secondly, the rivalry between Catholicism and reform in Poland during a good part of the sixteenth century eased pressure on the Jews, and prevented discriminatory ecclesiastical legislation making much headway.

Thus Polish Jewry expanded rapidly, from between 10,000 and

15,000 at the beginning of the sixteenth century to 150,000 or more by 1648. They were pioneers in opening up huge tracts of the Ukraine, leasing estates from their absentee owners and collecting taxes and produce from the serfs. The more visionary noblemen even founded private cities where Jews were welcome, laying the basis for a middle-class, urban population which persisted throughout large parts of eastern Europe until economic decline set in at the beginning of the twentieth century and eroded the unique phenomenon of Jewish *shtetl* ('small town') life; before that, hundreds of such *shtetlech* spread out like pearls on a string through Poland, the Ukraine, Galicia and Bessarabia.

Protected by the nobility and expanding commercially, even in those older cities that could not exclude Jews when they resided there as business agents of their lords, Polish Jewry organized itself into the most effective, autonomous system of government that Diaspora Jewry was ever to know. Each local *kehillah*, or small community, elected a committee of trustees that maintained the basic educational and social requirements, and collected the government taxes. The larger communities employed paid officials, including the rabbi, who was appointed by the *kehillah* committee to serve as legal expert and head of the *yeshivah*, where talmudic and rabbinic texts were studied intensively.

From the sixteenth century onwards, Poland was to become one of the greatest centres of rabbinic scholarship in Jewish history. Needy pupils were supported from public funds, and so advanced was the level of talmudic knowledge that many scholars opposed the use of Joseph Caro's *Shulchan Aruch* as the main text, preferring instead to analyse exhaustively the original sources. The casuistry of talmudic disputation reached new nuances of refinement in the methods of *pilpul* (literally 'pepper', in the sense of a sharp, casuistical clarification) and *chilluk* ('dissection'), which became so ingenious that some of the greatest Polish authorities criticized the practice as a degeneration into mere sophistry.

This absorption in talmudic law had a practical as well as a scholarly rationale. Central government was weak, with the power of the nobility increasing at the expense of royal authority. A large measure of autonomy devolved upon the Jews, who organized themselves on the model of the regional and national parliaments of the Polish nobility. A national body, the Council of the Four Lands (*Vaad Arba Aratzot*), composed of the leading rabbinic and lay personalities of the four provinces of Great Poland, Little Poland, Podolia and Volhynia, would meet twice a year, usually at the spring fair of Lublin and the summer fair of Jaroslaw, to coordinate all matters of Jewish concern, from apportioning the tax burden to selecting the Jewish representatives (*shtadlanim*) for the Polish court and issuing ordinances for the guidance of local *kehillot*. The well-organized infrastructure of Polish-Lithuanian Jewry ensured that communal affairs functioned smoothly in times of tranquillity; and in the times of chaos which shortly were to submerge Poland, it enabled the community to survive a disaster which otherwise would surely have destroyed it.

In 1648, Bogdan Chmielnicki led a nationalist revolt of Ukrainian Cossacks, in alliance with the Crimean Tartars, against Polish sovereignty. The Ukraine was a dangerous religious and ethnic mix of Greek Orthodox peasantry, Roman Catholic landlords, urban Jews and Cossack warriors. For two terrible months in the summer of 1648 Chmielnicki's hordes moved from one city to another, indiscriminately slaughtering Jews, Poles, Catholic clergy and Greek Orthodox Uniates (who recognized papal authority).

Warfare continued for almost twenty years, sucking in the Russians, who invaded northeastern Poland and the Ukraine, and Charles X of Sweden, who advanced into western Poland. During the fighting, Jews were massacred by almost everyone. Cossacks and Ukrainians despised them as agents of the detested Polish nobility. The Russians, who did not permit Jews to settle in their territories, assisted the Cossacks. Polish partisans killed them on the pretext that they were aiding the Swedes. Epidemics and famine added to the death toll.

Jewish martyrology literature of the period memorializes scores of communities where the ultimate ideal of Ashkenazi pietism – death *al kiddush ha-Shem* ('for the sanctification of the divine Name') – was the fate of their inhabitants. At least a quarter of Polish Jewry, probably more, over 50,000 men, women and children, died. Those who could fled to Germany and Holland;

thousands were ransomed from the Tartars in the slave markets of Istanbul.

Eventually, the Treaty of Andrusovo in 1667 brought to an end this period of Polish history, known feelingly as 'the Deluge', but not before the Chmielnicki massacres had joined the memories of the first Crusade, the Black Death and the Spanish riots of 1391 in the annals of Jewish suffering and martyrdom. The work of reconstruction began immediately, even in the Ukraine. But that blend of prosperity, relative security and autonomous jurisdiction, that had encouraged a flowering of Polish rabbinic scholarship, was never to be restored.

Once again, as in the aftermath of the expulsion from Spain, the highways of Europe were thronged with fugitive Jews. Survivors of the 'deluge' wandered south, into Moravia, Bohemia, Austria and Hungary, some continuing on to Italy. There, the wealthy Jewish community of the free port of Livorno passed a resolution to spend a quarter of its income on the maintenance of Polish refugees. Westwards, by way of Danzig and the Vistula region, the refugees came to Holland, newly independent of Spain, with a significant *marrano* community already settled in Amsterdam. Three thousand Lithuanian Jews reached Texel in the Netherlands.

In the main, they fled no further than they had to, back to Germany, and to those free cities and small principalities which were ready to admit Jews. The communities of Germany and Austria gave what support they could to the fugitives. One side-effect was that the Jews of Jerusalem, accustomed to receiving European alms, were deprived of their regular charity, and suffered badly from famine as a result.

German Jewry of the mid-seventeenth century had enjoyed a lengthy period of relative serenity, despite the upheavals of the Thirty Years War. Its status had improved considerably in the century-and-a-half since Luther had posted his ninety-five theses on the door of the castle church at Wittenberg. Initially, Luther had been compassionate towards the Jews, hoping to win them over to his reformed church. Disappointed in this hope, his attitude changed to one of vituperative hostility. He urged his followers to close the synagogues, burn books, forbid worship and harry the Jews from Christian lands.

The electors of Saxony and Brandenburg dutifully expelled their Jews. In those Protestant areas where they were allowed to remain, it was only in restrictive ghetto conditions, wearing the yellow badge of shame. The threat of expulsion was constant and regularly imposed. On the other hand, treatment of the Jews was given a basis in law, so that in a long career as representative of the communities of lower Alsace, Joselman of Rosheim (1480–1554) was able to intercede with local authorities, and even the emperor, on behalf of his co-religionists, in order to ensure that they were dealt with legally, not arbitrarily. The major Jewish communities developed in Frankfurt, Worms, Vienna and Prague; the latter, with its highly-organized *Judenstadt*, formed an important economic and cultural link between the Jewish communities of the west and the east.

The erosion of imperial authority and the proliferation of petty states as a consequence of the Thirty Years War had, from the Jewish perspective, positive advantages. It meant that whereas they were still excluded from city-republics, such as Nuremberg and the principalities of Saxony and Brandenburg, lesser states recognized the economic gain to be had from admitting them. As a result, the area of Jewish settlement in Germany, which had contracted steadily since the period of the Black Death, now expanded once more. The influx of Polish refugees accelerated the process, and they brought with them their tradition of talmudic scholarship, and its exegetical methods, which they taught in the *yeshivot* of Frankfurt, Metz and other Rhenish cities by means of the Yiddish vernacular, now spoken universally by the Jews of central and eastern Europe.

Furthermore, every tiny court set up in exiguous imitation of Versailles required funding. A new type of Jewish entrepreneur, the court Jew (*Hofjude*), appeared on the scene, able to use his business connections with fellow-Jews in the north Atlantic ports, in Poland-Lithuania and along the Mediterranean, to the benefit of German princes, both Protestant and Catholic. A characteristic and highly lucrative calling became that of military contractor, in charge of the army commissariat. Samuel Oppenheimer (1630–1703), the court Jew of the Austrian Hapsburgs, was succeeded by Samson Wertheimer (1658–1724), who supervised the provisioning of the imperial armies during the War of the Spanish

Succession. Most spectacular of all was Joseph Oppenheimer (*c.* 1698–1738), known as 'Jew Süss', who enjoyed himself as a powerful nobleman at the court of Württemberg until his enemies plotted his downfall.

Such court Jews brought their families and retinues of retainers with them and lived privileged lives, inconceivable to the typical ghetto resident of Frankfurt or Worms. Their status as 'protected' subjects freed them from the humiliating restrictions imposed on most of their German co-religionists, such as the *Leibzoll*, a special poll-tax, collected from Jews, and from both Jews and non-Jews for their livestock when it was taken from one principality to another. When Jews moved into vicinities previously barred to them but where they were welcome as financial agents, they established the nucleus of future communities, as happened in Hanover (1650), Mannheim (1660), Berlin (1671) and Dresden (1700). They dressed à la mode, imitated the style of the nobility, and had their first contact with general European culture. This tentative rendezvous, in the decades of Descartes and Spinoza, with ideas and manners unknown in the tenaciously medieval ambience of the ghetto, was to have important repercussions a century later when Jews, too, wanted to play their part in the Age of Enlightenment.

Meanwhile, in the city of Spinoza, *marranos* from the Iberian peninsula revelled in the sense of personal freedom which living in independent Holland made possible. The Treaty of Westphalia had confirmed, after eighty years of struggle, the break from Spain. The Inquisition was still active in Spain and Portugal, sentencing *marranos* and other suspected heretics to death in the *autos-da-fé*. Descendants of Jews were excluded from trade and professional organizations, owing to obsessive concern for the principle of *limpieza de sangre* (purity of blood).

A stream of *marranos* left for the more congenial atmosphere of the Protestant ports of northern Europe. Early in the seventeenth century the government of Amsterdam allowed several Sephardi congregations to be established, whose members played a prominent role in developing the city into a great centre of world trade and finance. An Ashkenazi proletariat followed, establishing its own synagogues and participating in the vibrant economy of the most egalitarian country in Europe. By the end of the century there were about 10,000 Jews in Amsterdam – the largest community in western Europe. They were active in overseas trade with the East and West Indies, on the stock exchange, in diamonds. Enjoying an unparalleled level of personal and religious toleration, they quickly adapted to their secular environment in dress, speech and culture, despite the forebodings of concerned rabbis who were ready to excommunicate the most important philosopher since the Middle Ages, Baruch Spinoza (1632–77), for his rationalist views and textual criticism of the Bible.

It was a rabbi friend of Rembrandt, Manasseh ben Israel, who approached Oliver Cromwell in 1655 about the possibility of readmitting Jews to England. The Old Testament sympathies of the Puritans, allied to a revival of foreign trade and growing anti-Spanish feelings, suggested that now was a propitious time to seek official sanction for the furtive *marrano* community that had existed in London for over a century. Accordingly, Manasseh ben Israel came over to London as self-appointed spokesman for his people, confident in the knowledge that his writings in Latin and Spanish were favourably regarded by Christian theologians. The Lord Protector received him cordially, but a solid body of opposition criticized the proposal at a specially convened White-hall Conference of merchants, theologians and interested parties which met from December 1655 until January 1656. War with Spain that year prompted Cromwell to give *de facto* permission to the existing *marrano* community – which had thrown off its religious disguise and claimed refugee status – to continue undisturbed with its mode of worship. In this pragmatic way recognition of Jewish settlement was granted, and more formally confirmed by Charles II after the Restoration. The new community was subject to the same restrictions imposed upon other dissenters from the established Church; in practice, it was often an advantage to be Jewish, rather than Catholic. As a result, neither the ghetto nor special taxation were ever foisted on the Jews and the door of social acceptability was soon opened to those wealthy enough, or adaptable enough, to take advantage of that peculiarly English diffidence about religion which helps make it such a tolerant country. Ashkenazi settlers soon followed the Sephardi pioneers, and although London was always to have the dominant attraction as commercial capital of the world, a number of congregations were established in provincial trading-towns and seaports, where it was usually a group of silversmiths and pedlars who formed the nucleus of the community.

All along the Atlantic seaboard, in ports such as Bordeaux and Hamburg, *marrano* merchants were followed by other immigrants who recognized the commercial potential of the New World. Brazil between 1630 and 1654, when it was temporarily a Dutch colony, the east coast of America, the English, Dutch and French colonies in the Caribbean, all had their contingents of Sephardi traders.

Business hegemony had passed to Protestant Europe and, because of their entrepreneurial skills, the wealthy Jewish brokers, financiers, jewellers and wholesale importers (mainly Sephardim), were accorded a grudging toleration by states and cities which a century before would have excluded them. Significantly, in those countries whose economies were on the wane, Jews were subjected to the full rigour of Catholic reaction. In Italy they were forced to live in ghettos, to wear distinguishing badges, to submit to censorship of their books, to restrict their business activities if they were in competition with Christian traders. Only in cities like Venice or Ancona, which still maintained a Levantine trade, or in the free port of Livorno, was greater laxity granted to Jewish merchants. It is a melancholy fact that Italy, which for centuries had played tolerant host to Jewish communities – at the proprietorial ordinance of successive popes, and owing to the expansive humanist spirit of the Renaissance – when the rest of Europe was reacting to Jews with superstitious barbarism, should now be the most retrograde country in its treatment of them.

Although the fortunate few enjoyed the rewards of their economic leverage, the vast majority of European Jews constituted an urban proletariat of tailors, pedlars, secondhand dealers and old-clothes men. Poverty was endemic; in most countries at least one-third of the Jewish population depended on communal charity to exist. Overcrowded ghettos shut their gates against the incessant stream of importuning paupers, in some case calling on the secular authorities to exclude them. Inside the ghettos, cut off from contact with wider culture, Jewish learning had petrified. Rabbis and their students pored over talmudic arcana, while the masses took comfort in superstition and mysticism. The Age of

Enlightenment was about to dawn, but Jewish life was firmly stuck in the Middle Ages. As the eighteenth century began, and thoughtful Christian scholars started to investigate Judaism with nascent respect for its history and attainments, the Jews *en masse* were intellectually, economically and spiritually impoverished. Nowhere was their demoralization starker than in the east European areas of settlement.

CHAPTER TEN   FROM CHASIDISM TO THE FRENCH REVOLUTION

The century after the 'deluge' was a period of progressive deterioration for the Polish state. The economy disintegrated; governmental authority dwindled and corruption spread; social and religious oppression increased. Exhausted by civil and external warfare, the Polish kingdom was, between 1772 and 1795, slowly dismembered. The partition of the country between Russia, Austria and Prussia was to have fateful consequences for the one million Jews living there. As the economy collapsed and central government weakened, the Polish nobility assumed monopolistic control of the production, purchase and sale of the output of their large estates. The more their incomes decreased, the harsher their exploitation of their Jewish and non-Jewish, urban and rural, subjects. In the towns, the Catholic reaction forced out Jewish traders and craftsmen. In the country, it was difficult to eke out a living in the stagnant agricultural market.

Once again, Jews took to the roads. They returned to the Ukrainian sites of the Chmielnicki massacres. They were grateful to settle on nobles' estates, as serfs of the landlord. By the middle of the eighteenth century, one-third of Poland's Jewish population, some 250,000 people, was scattered across the countryside, in many places no more than two or three families per hamlet. They were engaged in a new, and uncharacteristic, occupation. Poland's principal industry was the manufacture and sale of beer and spirits, under licence from the nobility. Jewish lessees became landlords of taverns and wayside inns. Village taverns were a focal point of Poland's peasant, still feudal society, and the Jewish landlord, collecting the tax on alcohol for his nobleman, was

126

saddled with the image of profiteer in addition to the burden of religious antagonism stirred by the rural Catholic clergy. When Cossack bands known as *haidemaks* raided the Ukraine in the 1730s and 1740s to protest their exploitation by the Polish gentry, they robbed and killed their Jewish tenants. The large-scale massacre of Jews in the town of Uman in 1768 revived memories of 1648.

The diffusion of the Jewish population throughout the countryside affected both religious life and the organizational structure of the community. Isolated village families could not maintain synagogues or support teachers and rabbis. They were cut off from, and had no influence on, the regional and national *kehillah* assemblies which governed Jewry. Authority was concentrated in a few wealthy families, and accusations of unfair taxation and venality were widespread. The Jewish craft guilds, especially – organized on the model of their Christian counterparts to meet specific economic and social needs – resisted the tax demands of the *kehillah* leadership. Faced with mounting debts, the *kehillah* borrowed from Church and nobility and resorted to additional taxation of the community, which led to further protests. Its power disintegrating parallel to the disintegration of central government, and no longer able to fulfil its prime task – collecting taxes from Jewish subjects – the Council of the Four Lands was dissolved in 1764.

MYSTICISM FOR THE MASSES

At this bleak juncture in Polish-Jewish history, two major personalities, at opposite ends of the religious spectrum, had the strength and charisma to inspire followers and to revive talmudic learning on the one hand, and simple piety on the other. Neither figure was associated with the traditional institutions of Jewish community life; they were not salaried rabbis or appointed leaders, nor were they supported by any organization or institution. Precisely because of this, their influence on their own and on future generations was extraordinary.

What Rabbi Israel ben Eliezer (*c.* 1700–60) and Rabbi Elijah ben Solomon (1720–97) had in common was the temperament of mystics. Both were messianic visionaries, imbued with the doctrine of salvation, at a time when messianic expectation still lingered among the masses. (It should be remembered that Jacob Frank and his Shabbetean followers had only recently converted to Catholicism.) Both leaders attempted to migrate to Palestine, but, in the words of the saying, 'They were prevented by heaven because their generation was not worthy of it.'

Their generation was not so much unworthy as in the throes of a spiritual crisis. The central institution of Jewish autonomy had been dissolved. At the local level, people whose main qualification for leadership was that they were on good terms with Polish officialdom tried to cope with small budgets, heavy debts and the increasing alienation of the laity from the rabbinate. Again, it is significant that the Frankist movement was antinomian, rejecting in grotesque form the rabbinic emphasis on fasting, repentance and talmudic legislation. Frank particularly protested against Jewish book-learning, urging his followers instead to pursue military might, wealth and earthly pleasures. This, then, was the mood in the Ukrainian villages, especially in the province of Podolia, home of the Frankists, when Israel ben Eliezer first appeared there as an itinerant preacher and folk-healer. Known as the Baal Shem Tov (usually abbreviated as the acronym Besht) – the 'Master of the Good Name', because he issued amulets inscribed with the Divine Name, to ward off diseases and evil spirits – he had spent his young adulthood in the Carpathian mountains, meditating on the *kabbalah*, before settling in the town of Medzibozh, where he speedily won a reputation as a spiritualist and wonder-worker. By the 1740s he had a growing body of followers drawn from the Jewish proletariat, as well as *maggidim* (chasidic wandering preachers), ritual slaughterers and school-teachers. The *Chasidim* personified a new definition of piety; not a solitary, ascetic way of study, prayer and meditation, but a life-affirming enjoyment of the world, its appetites and its pleasures. These were invested with spiritual import and transformed into a means of serving God. Whoever wanted to walk this path was already a *chasid*, and thus the way of chasidism was open to anyone, no matter how poor or unlettered or disregarded by the established communal institutions.

Where chasidism differed crucially from Shabbeteanism, or, for that matter, from the non-conforming Christian sects in the surrounding environment, which had broken away from the Russian Orthodox Church, was in its adherence to normative Judaism. The revivalist fervour of chasidic worship, with its singing, dancing and twirling, and the devout intensity with which the *chasid* sought God in even mundane activities, was essentially an endorsement of the rabbinic principle of performing the Commandments with joy. No heresy, as with Shabbeteanism or Christian sectarianism, was at issue, nor did chasidic exuberance ever degenerate into the orgiastic excesses of the Frankists. The Jewish masses who embraced Chasidism were accepting the theology of the *kabbalah* not in its speculative and esoteric mode, but in an optimistic, joyful form which proclaimed that even evil could be alchemized into worship of God.

The Baal Shem Tov died in 1760. His only literary legacy was a few letters. About twenty years after his death his oral teachings began to appear in print, and in 1814 tales and legends about the Besht and his disciples were published under the title *Shivchei ha-Besht* (*Praises of the Baal Shem Tov*). Leadership of Chasidism passed to Dov Baer of Mezeritch (1710–72). Thousands of adherents in southern Poland, the Ukraine and Lithuania swelled the new movement. By now it had attracted the hostility of *kehillah* authorities, who accused the *Chasidim* of denigrating Torah study, ignoring the observance of the Commandments, behaving wildly in their rituals and praying with the Lurianic rather than the Ashkenazi liturgy. Opposition was particularly bitter from the Lithuanian community of Vilna. There, Elijah ben Solomon, known as the Vilna Gaon out of respect for his rabbinic brilliance, was the leading figure in the reaction of talmudic scholarship against mass pietism.

The Vilna Gaon was a man of prodigious learning, austere temperament and iron will. He received a stipend from the community in order that he might devote all his time to study and teaching. His writings were copious and extensive, covering the fields of Bible, Talmud, Midrash, codes and kabbalistic literature, although he had no sympathy for Maimonidean philosophy. His wide-ranging curiosity led him to investigate secular learning such as mathematics, geography, astronomy and Hebrew grammar as aids to elucidating talmudic disputations, although he never strayed beyond the world-view of medieval scholasticism which affirmed, rather than questioned, faith. The methodology whereby he applied his erudition had a decisive influence on the subsequent direction of rabbinic scholarship in Poland and Lithuania. The Vilna Gaon dismissed the fanciful flights of *pilpul* and *chilluk*, insisting on a rigorous interpretation of the common-sense meaning of the text. Logic, clarity and deductive analysis were the cornerstones of his system.

Revered by his disciples, a perpetual student by nature and by conviction, he came to regard Chasidism's mystical elevation of daily routine above study as a perversion of Jewish values and a threat to the totality of the law. Adversaries of Chasidism, known as *Mitnaggedim* ('opponents'), gathered around the Vilna Gaon, who became their spokesman. The last decade of his life passed in vicious controversy. *Chasidim* were excommunicated, their books burned and their leadership denounced to the Russian government.

Although social and political factors were involved (the leadership of the Vilna *kehillah*, for example, issued its first ban of excommunication against the *Chasidim* at a time when the community was seriously split internally), the conflict between chasidism and its opponents was primarily ideological. Not study, but prayer, was the first concern of the *Chasidim*. 'God wants the heart' was a central motif of the Besht's doctrine, according to his followers. Chasidic literature is replete with tales about ignorant men and children whose prayers, nevertheless, are better received by God than those of the most learned scholar, because they come from the heart and are offered with *kavvanah* ('intent'), and *devekut* ('cleaving').

Alongside this demotion of traditional learning went the derogation of the traditional rabbi and the elevation instead of the *tzaddik* – 'the completely righteous man'. The Chasidic *tzaddik*, affectionately called 'rebbe' by his followers rather than the more formal 'rov', was the intermediary with heaven and the counsellor on earth of his flock. His was a quasi-sacramental role, transmitting requests from the simple folk to their heavenly Father, involving himself in their daily cares and anxieties; by comparison, the salaried rabbi was a more distant, legalistic figure. The *chasidim* venerated their *tzaddik* with unquestioning devotion, investing a visit to his court with the same awe as a pilgrimage to

Jerusalem. As one of Dov Baer's devotees put it, 'I did not visit the preacher of Mezeritch to study the law with him, but to observe how he tied his shoelaces.' Every movement of the *tzaddik*, down to his way of breaking bread, was of great significance.

Each *tzaddik* had a personal following which developed its own customs, legends and melodies for worship. Among the village and *shtetl* Jews of the Ukraine and Polish Galicia the *tzaddik* was elevated to regal splendour, living in conspicuous luxury off the gifts of his infatuated retinue. Such idolatry was anathema to an ascetic like the Gaon of Vilna. The tendency of the *Chasidim* to create their own prayer houses (*shtiblech*) and their permissive attitude towards *halachah* on such issues as waiting for the right mood to pray rather than adhering to fixed times, was a matter of concern to the *Mitnaggedim*. The impulse of the Besht was to bring the divine presence down to earth; the theology of the Vilna Gaon was to raise man to heaven. The way of the Besht was to reject guilt and excessive penance and to place complete trust in God's omnipresence. The way of the Gaon was to call for a strengthening of the talmudic tradition. The yearning of the Chasidic *kabbalah* was for unification of the soul with the divine light. The conclusion drawn by the Gaon was that the people Israel and the holy law were inseparably united in exile, and on the journey to redemption and restoration. *Chasidim* and *Mitnaggedim* were passionately convinced that only their way was the right way to God.

In the early part of the nineteenth century a cautious *rapprochement* was achieved between the two adversaries, and each borrowed from the other's ideology. The determination of the Gaon and his followers to uphold the primacy of learning had its effect on Chasidism. In Lithuania the Lubavitch branch of the movement fused kabbalistic speculation with rabbinical learning in its *chabad* philosophy (see p. 226) and the *Chasidim* of central Poland stressed the importance of Talmud study. For their part, the *Mitnaggedim* acknowledged the validity of some of the criticisms directed against them and incorporated study of ethical literature (*musar*) into the *yeshivot* curricula, as well as widening participation in *kehillah* decision-making.

Chasidism did not spread beyond central and southern Poland, the Ukraine and parts of Lithuania. Within fifty years of the Besht's death it had lost its impetus and rigidified into a hierarchical system of individual dynasties in which authority passed from father to son. A high birth-rate has maintained their numbers into modern times, and large Chasidic sects can be found in New York, London and the State of Israel, where they try to stem the tide of secularism by calling for a return to traditional observance in a manner that would have gladdened the heart of their arch-opponent, the Vilna Gaon. Their folk literature has been rediscovered as a rich storehouse for writers and philosophers of religion, and many of the sayings of the *tzaddikim* contain profound insights into the nature of human existence and the mysteries of faith.

In their own time, the careers of Israel, Baal Shem Tov, and Elijah, Gaon of Vilna, exemplified two ardent responses to the degradation of exile and the yearning for redemption so keenly felt by the Jewish masses of eastern Europe. Before long, a third option would be set beside Chasidic piety or talmudic study: a Jewish Enlightenment – the *haskalah* – was beginning in the west.

ENLIGHTENMENT FOR THE FEW

The avidity with which Jews responded to the ideas and ideals of the European Enlightenment in the eighteenth century was so intense that it provoked an excitement within Judaism as profound and far-reaching as would be the effects of the French Revolution in the wider world. The Jew, for centuries the victim of Church-dominated societies, now became, for rationalist philosophers, the symbol of all that had been retrograde and superstitious about those societies. Espousing the cause of Jewish emancipation was the 'radical chic' of its day, a swipe at organized Christianity and its reactionary clerics, who were held responsible for many of the malaises of the *ancien régime*.

As the eighteenth century drew to its close, there were about two and a quarter million Jews in the world, of whom one and three-quarter million lived in Christian Europe. In Holland and England (where there were about 50,000 Jews in all), they suffered from no more than those disabilities which affected anyone who did not profess the state religion. The Jews of Poland, numbering well over one million, and by far the largest settlement anywhere, also enjoyed – because of weak central government, a large measure of communal autonomy and diffuse economic influence – relative freedom.

It was the 420,000 Jews of central Europe who were subjected to a series of restricting and humiliating laws, the legacy of the Reformation and the Catholic reaction, that decreed their residence in ghettos, limited their economic activities, circumscribed their travel, prohibited their employment of Christian domestics, controlled their freedom to marry and extorted special taxes in return for the privilege of domicile or passage from one city to another. Such discrimination was an affront to those liberal political theorists who upheld the rights of the individual against the powers of the state. Although Montesquieu, Diderot and the Encyclopedists were dismissive of all organized religion, and Voltaire was antipathetic to Jews, the logic of their arguments about individual freedom had to apply to the Jews as it did to all other subjects of the state.

It was in Frederick the Great's Prussia, and in particular in his capital of Berlin, that the new mood of religious sufferance among Europe's enlightened monarchs showed most clearly. Prussia had grown spectacularly, from a population of 750,000 in 1648 to five million by 1786, of whom 140,000 lived in Berlin. The Jewish quota had increased correspondingly. The fifty families of 1670 had become a community of four thousand a century later, by far the largest Jewish settlement in the Germanies. Jews had been involved in the developing industries of Prussia from 1728. The Seven Years War (1756–63) gave them an opportunity to display their business acumen in helping to fund a long and costly war, and, by the end of it, several Berlin Jews were very wealthy indeed.

The government wished to channel this newly amassed Jewish capital into various industrial enterprises. Against its own instincts and policies, which as recently as 1750 had been incorporated in a Jewish charter that reaffirmed all the traditional restraints, the government relaxed certain restrictions so that the leading Jewish merchants could travel, settle, buy and sell, on a par with their Christian counterparts.

Alongside this growing Jewish middle class, with its unaccustomed contacts in wider society, there arose a Jewish intelligentsia. It was the versatility, grace and charm of this intellectual élite that, more than any other cause, helped to bring about a change in Christian perceptions of the Jew. Christians and Jews mingled freely in the many literary and artistic salons of Berlin, where the latest scientific and philosophical notions of the Enlightenment were keenly discussed. Two of the most popular meeting places were the homes of the philosopher-physician Marcus Hertz and his beautiful wife Henriette (who infatuated Mirabeau during his secret mission to the Prussian court in 1786), and of Moses Mendelssohn, the most illustrious Jew of his time.

In 1749 the dramatist, literary critic and liberal humanist Gotthold Lessing had written a short play, *Die Juden*, which portrayed a Jew of noble character. The reaction of the Christian theologian Johann Michaelis was 'that a noble Jew was a poetic impossibility'. In Mendelssohn, who became his lifelong friend, Lessing had the ideal rebuttal to this calumny. Born in Dessau in 1729, the son of a poor Torah scribe, the fourteen-year-old Mendelssohn had followed his rabbi to Berlin, in order to continue his studies. Speaking only Yiddish, he soon acquired fluency in German and Hebrew, as well as a knowledge of French, Italian, English, Latin and Greek. His natural talents, and the encouragement of Lessing and other Christian sympathizers, who saw in him the embodiment of the Enlightenment ideal that non-Christian peoples, too, could produce figures of refinement and learning, speedily brought him fame as an essayist and philosopher – 'the Jewish Socrates'. Although physically stunted and looking like a deprived product of the ghetto, Mendelssohn charmed all those who made his acquaintance, with his combination of modesty, sparkling conversation and sharp intelligence.

In 1763, Mendelssohn won first prize from the Berlin Academy of Sciences for the best essay on a metaphysical subject, placed ahead of Thomas Abt, and Immanuel Kant himself. His reward from Frederick the Great was to be accorded the privileged status of *Schutz-Jude*, a protected Jew with security of residence; but it was symptomatic of the general prejudice of the age that he could not take his place as a member of the Academy, ostensibly because it might offend the sensitivities of another member, Catherine the Great, to mix with a Jew.

In 1779, Lessing wrote one of his best-known plays, *Nathan der Weise*, in which the Jewish hero, clearly based on his friend Mendelssohn, appears as the spokesman for brotherly love and universalism. Two years later, at Mendelssohn's instigation, the historian Wilhelm Christian Dohm produced a pamphlet entitled 'Concerning the Amelioration of the Civil Status of the Jews', in which he urged the case for Jewish emancipation, arguing that centuries of Christian prejudice were responsible for the lowly condition of the Jews, and that given the opportunity, they could contribute their talents to all reaches of society.

Dohm's essay created great interest and had an influence on the Hapsburg emperor, Joseph II, who issued a *Toleranzpatent* (decree of toleration) in 1782 that granted the Jews of Austria wide commercial and domiciliary freedoms, and annulled such hurtful regulations as those requiring married Jewish men to wear beards, forbidding Jews from leaving their homes before noon on Sundays and Christian holidays, and barring them from amusement parks. Henceforth business records were to be kept in German, not Yiddish, and Jewish children were to be encouraged to attend state schools. In 1787 Jewish recruits joined the Hapsburg army.

Mendelssohn, meanwhile, whose natural creative bent was in the field of metaphysics and aesthetics, had been drawn by his intellectual prominence into religious polemics. He became, against his inclination, a defender of Judaism and an activist in Jewish affairs. Involved in a long and distasteful theological dispute with Johann Caspar Lavater, a Zurich pastor, from which he emerged with his reputation unimpaired but at the cost of his health, Mendelssohn turned his energies to projects which would hasten, so he and his associates believed, the civil emancipation of the Jews. Foremost among these was a translation of the Pentateuch into German, with a Hebrew commentary, highlighting the literary and moral qualities of the Bible. News of its intended publication was denounced by traditional rabbis, who saw in it a threat to the primacy of talmudic study and a seductive *entrée* for its readers into the world of secular learning. So fierce was their opposition that Mendelssohn's chief collaborator, Solomon Dubno, was intimidated and withdrew. The *Biur* ('commentary') eventually appeared in 1783, to be banned in several communities but enthusiastically appropriated by successive generations of the young in their search for wider culture.

At the same time Mendelssohn had been one of the founders of the Freischule in Berlin, which offered a general curriculum as well as Jewish subjects, and in the decade 1781–91 graduated more than five hundred pupils educated in Enlightenment ideals. He had also used his good offices and personal prestige on behalf of the Jews of Switzerland and the Alsace, when they had been threatened with discriminatory legislation. Finally, in 1783, three years before his death, Mendelssohn published his most important work, *Jerusalem*, a plea for Jewish emancipation in the name of freedom of conscience and the concept of the secular state, and a powerful defence of the Jewish religion and its adherence to Mosaic legislation as the particular law of the Jewish people.

A self-confessed tyro about the patterns of history, and a philosopher whose attempts to reconcile rational theism with Jewish traditionalism found few adherents after his own lifetime, Moses Mendelssohn is more important as a symbol than as an original thinker. By his example he demonstrated that it was possible to make the transition from ghetto to cultured society without surrendering Jewish identity. He inspired a mini-renaissance of Jewish literature and culture, known as the *haskalah* ('enlightenment'), and its exponents, the *maskilim* ('enlighteners'), whose goal was the integration of well-educated, ethically aware, socially productive Jews, were his fervent disciples.

Some of the *maskilim* helped him on the translation and commentary of the Pentateuch. Many more contributed, as did Mendelssohn himself, anonymously, to the first modern Jewish periodical *Ha-Me'assef* ('The Gatherer'). First published in Königsberg in 1783, then transferred to Berlin, the editorial policy of *Ha-Me'assef* was to revive the classic Hebrew of the Bible, to disseminate secular knowledge and to create a new Jewish aesthetic of literature, morality and art. The magazine published poetry, biblical criticism, essays in praise of nature and country life, historical studies and information about current affairs of Jewish interest.

The journal, like Mendelssohn's philosophy, did not survive long, mainly because German, not Hebrew, soon became the dominant language of German Jewish thought and the *haskalah* moved south, into the Austrian empire and beyond; by the middle of the nineteenth century its most significant contributions were being made in Russia, where the *maskilim* were in the forefront of educational and social reforms.

But a more important reason was soon to render academic all of the *haskalah*'s debates about achieving Jewish emancipation. The French Revolution was about to break down the ghetto walls.

EMANCIPATION FOR ALL

'How much the greatest event it is that ever happened in the world! And how much the best!' So said Charles James Fox on hearing of the fall of the Bastille. The Jews of Europe were, for the most part, passive witnesses of the tumultuous events taking place in Paris, but were perforce catapulted by them into the modern world. The French Revolution marked a turning point in Jewish history as decisive as the Babylonian exile or the expulsion from Spain. A cornerstone of the centuries-old structure, built on the twin pillars of rabbinic legislation and ghetto existence, was irretrievably loosened. Until now, European Jewish life had been circumscribed, set apart, inward-looking; to many, it was a not-displeasing situation. It made for greater physical security, allowed a measure of autonomy in communal affairs and enabled the Jewish religion, as traditionally practised and interpreted, to retain the loyalty of its adherents. External hostility and internally enforced discipline between them gave cohesion and continuity to the collective struggle for survival. Talmudic scholarship and rigorously observant lifestyles were the palliative against oppression, and the wisdom of Jewish law and lore was not challenged by disquieting secular culture.

All that changed with the French Revolution. Henceforth Jewish life fragmented. Emancipation presented the Jew with options, from conversion and assimilation at one extreme to fervent nationalism at the other, with *haskalah*, religious reform, neo-traditionalism and radical socialism somewhere in between. In any of its ideological manifestations, Jewish history since 1789 has been a response to modernity and to the opportunities, pain and dilemmas of confronting society beyond the ghetto walls.

In August 1789 the National Assembly issued its Declaration of the Rights of Man, proclaiming that 'all men are born, and remain, free and equal in rights'. Did this resounding statement also include the Jews? The debates of the Assembly on that issue were among its longest and stormiest, causing Mirabeau to quip about the obstructive tactics of the dissenting clergy representatives that their behaviour was 'reminiscent of one's image of a synagogue!'

What the debate did illustrate, in copious testimony, was the unflattering stereotype of the Jews in the minds of even their keenest champions. There were some 3,500 Sephardi Jews living in Bordeaux and Bayonne, mainly in comfort and security as well-regarded international merchants. They were readily granted full rights of citizenship in January 1790. The 30,000 Ashkenazi Jews of northeastern France were for the most part engaged in petty trade or money-lending. They spoke Yiddish, were organized in the traditional communal structure of central European Jewry and lived in uneasy proximity to their Christian neighbours. Alsatian delegates to the Assembly opposed Jewish emancipation on the grounds that they exploited the peasantry. Others argued that the nature of the Jewish religion precluded Jews from being full citizens. The clerical faction reiterated that the Jews were a fallen nation governed by barbarous laws. Newspaper editorials asked whether the very Christian king of France also had to be king of the Jews, and warned Ashkenazi delegates to suspend their representations during Easter week, which was 'full of memories which are unfavourable to them'.

Advocates of Jewish emancipation accepted such type-casting but, in keeping with Enlightenment ideals, wanted to reform and regenerate the Jews. A speech by Robespierre neatly summed up the approach. 'The Jews' vices are born of the degradation you have plunged them into; they will be good when they have found some advantage in so being.' Equality would only be granted to Jews as individuals, not as a recognized corporate group. The Parisian deputy Clermont-Tonnerre expressed it in a famous formula: 'Everything for the Jews as citizens, nothing as a nation.'

Eventually, in September 1791, the Assembly voted almost unanimously for total Jewish emancipation, thus advancing the work of a revolution which had abolished the privileges of the nobility, the special obligations of the peasants and the immunities of the clergy, and was shortly to guillotine the king. It is an interesting psychological speculation whether the equality finally accorded to the contemned Jews was unconsciously spurred by a sense of affinity on the part of would-be regicides with a people historically held responsible for deicide, just as it may have been a factor in Cromwell's favourable reception of Manasseh ben Israel over a century earlier.

The scepticism with which French Jews greeted their emancipation appeared to be justified during the Reign of Terror, when all religions were proscribed, religious property was confiscated and anti-Jewish propaganda in the departments of the Alsace and the Rhine reached new levels of virulence. A similarly cautious response greeted the armies of the Republic which brought the revolutionary message to Holland in 1795. Well-established Sephardim of Amsterdam stood to gain little from the civic rights offered to them in the newly-created Batavian republic. However, when French armies occupied northern Italy they abolished the ghettos, and were enthusiastically welcomed by the Jews of the Rhineland. The influence of the new French gospel spread to distant Portugal, where *marranos* were prominent in the pro-French party.

In this way, France came to be regarded as the protector and emancipator of the Jews, and from 1800 Napoleon was the embodiment of France. His attitude to the Jews was a combination of theological prejudice and revolutionary high-mindedness, in which he stigmatized them as corrupt and objectionable, an accursed race beyond redemption, but also hoped to 'regenerate' them by dissolving their racial propensities through intermarriage and incorporation in the body politic. He ruled the Jews with firm efficiency and ensured that defeated Prussia and the puppet kingdom of Westphalia undertook major reforms which granted civic equality to Jews.

In 1806, complaints about usury from the Alsace led Napoleon to suspend for a year all debts owed to Jews in eastern France. Posing as the champion of the peasantry, and having already reorganized the Catholic and Protestant churches under state control, Napoleon, inspired opportunist that he was, saw an occasion both for regulating the Jewish question to internal satisfaction and at the same time enhancing his reputation as the defender of the Jewish people among the many Polish Jews in the newly con- stituted Duchy of Warsaw. He convened an Assembly of Jewish Notables in Paris that summer. They were presented with a series of twelve questions, designed to clarify Judaism's attitude to the state and its institutions. The notables answered truthfully about their patriotism, skilfully about the civilly binding but religiously invalid nature of mixed marriages and evasively about en- couraging assimilation; on the whole, they made a favourable impression on Napoleon's two commissioners. Because a means had to be found of getting the several Jewries of the empire to accept the answers of the notables, and because the commissioners were surprised to learn that no central government existed to which all Jews owed allegiance, the happy idea took root of convening a 'Great Sanhedrin' of seventy-one members, like the legislature of ancient Palestine, to confirm the assembly's deci- sions.

The Sanhedrin met in February 1807, with great ceremony, in the converted chapel of Saint-Jean, rue des Piliers, renamed for the occasion rue du Grand-Sanhedrin. It only held a few sessions before Napoleon dissolved it, a contributory factor being Christ- ian outrage at the associations which the title Sanhedrin had with the trial of Jesus. Having pledged eternal loyalty to the emperor and declared that Jewish tradition was no longer binding where it conflicted with the requirements of citizenship, the Sanhedrin was deemed to have fulfilled its purpose.

Napoleon involved himself on two further occasions in Jewish affairs. A decree promulgated from Madrid in early March 1808 arranged every department with more than 2,000 Jews into a consistory of lay and ecclesiastical members, controlled by a central committee in Paris. This system – organized with the symmetry and precision of the Code Napoléon – still governs French Jewry. Prevalent anti-Jewish prejudice, notwithstanding high-flown Revolutionary idealism and conspicuous Jewish sup- port for the emperor, lay behind his second, so-called *décret infâme*, the 'infamous decree' of 17 March 1808, which subjected the Jews to discriminatory legislation in certain departments other than those of the Seine and the southwest. Restricted in their movements and trading activities, Jews were hampered by these special laws until the government of Louis XVIII completed their emancipation by refraining from renewing the 'infamous decree' in 1818.

Thus Napoleon initially flattered the Jews of France with his radicalism, only to deceive them later with his conservatism. In the countries to which he sent his armies, though, and over which he exercised control, however briefly, his effect on the progress of emancipation was salutary. The Jews of central Europe had cause to be grateful to *le petit caporal*.

The aims of the Congress of Vienna were to restore the status quo ante, to reward the victors and to reaffirm the principle of dynastic legitimacy. France reverted to the Bourbon dynasty. The thirty-nine German states (reduced from over three hundred) were organized into the Germanic Confederation, on the dismembered remains of the Holy Roman Empire. German Jewry lobbied the embassies in Vienna in order to safeguard the rights it had acquired under Napoleon. The resolution regarding the civic status of Jews finally agreed on by the assembled diplomats crucially inserted the preposition *by* rather than *in* in the decisive sentence: 'Until then, however, the rights of the adherents of this creed already granted to them *by* the individual Confederated States shall be maintained.' This enabled states' governments to claim that they were not bound by the equality bestowed on Jews by the French, rather than themselves. Some of the most important cities rescinded recently granted privileges.

A conservative reaction permeated Germany. The universalism of Enlightenment thought was replaced by a Romantic stress on patriotism, Christianity and idealization of the Teutonic folk spirit. Its greatest exponent, Goethe, was opposed to Jewish emancipation, and academics argued that Jews were Asiatic aliens who could not participate in Germanic-Christian culture without converting. In 1819 the Hep Hep riots (so called from the rallying cry of the rioters) broke out against the Jews in many towns and were used by governments as an excuse to postpone full emancipation indefinitely. Disillusioned in their hopes, Jews converted in droves. Half the Berlin community had become Christian by 1823. Moses Mendelssohn's youngest son, and two of his daughters, whose lives read as romantically as a novel by Madame de Staël, converted. Another son, father of the composer Felix Mendelssohn-Bartholdy, had his children baptized because 'Christianity is the religion of the majority of civilized men.' Another illustrious German, Heinrich Heine, also converted, doing so to gain admission to the Bar (at which he never practised) and masking his decision in a famous flippancy: 'The baptismal font is the entrance ticket to European culture.' His friend Edward Gans converted to obtain a chair of philosophy at the University of Berlin, where one of his students was Karl Marx, himself baptized at the age of seven. Another contemporary, the essayist Ludwig Börne, was even more studiedly casual about his conversion, which took place so that he would be able to edit a newspaper: 'The three drops of water were not even worth the small amount of money they cost me.' Not all conversions were for such *gefallsucht* (desire to please) reasons. David Mendel (1789–1850), a grand-nephew of Mendelssohn, 'saw the light' at the age of seventeen and went on to become a renowned Protestant Church historian under the name of Johann Neander. A like sincerity motivated Julius Jolson, who made his reputation as the great Prussian conservative thinker Friedrich Julius Stahl (1802–61).

Jewish women were, in a sense, even more vulnerable than their menfolk. They entertained high society in their salons, could quote Goethe's 'elective affinities' in justification of their liaisons with Christians and knew that conversion might lead to an aristocratic marriage and residence in Vienna, Paris or London, where they could more easily forget their origins. Rahel Levin (1771–1832), the daughter of a jeweller, presided over Berlin's most select literary salon, frequented by princes, diplomats and distinguished foreigners. The central obsession of her life, and several love affairs, was to escape her Jewishness. She converted in 1814 and married the Prussian diplomat and man of letters August Varnhagen von Ense, fourteen years her junior. On her deathbed, after a happy marriage, she came to understand herself, and, in memorable last words stated the central dilemma of her life: 'I am here a refugee from Egypt and Palestine and find help, love and care with you ... What was to me for so long the greatest reproach, the bitterest suffering and misfortune, to be a Jewess, not for anything would I now like to give it up ...'

Conversion did not necessarily make for acceptance. Like the *marranos* before them, converts remained Jews socially, in the eyes of Christians, and their chameleon facility for assimilating was to arouse greater anti-Jewish prejudice than that directed against the easily identifiable ghetto Jews.

Although the rush to apostasy assumed epidemic proportions, the majority of German Jews did not convert or change their names. They were faced with a new dilemma, as once again a mood of political liberalism swept Europe in the 1830s and 1840s. To what extent, if at all, should they modify their traditional practices in order to gain recognition as patriotic Jewish citizens? Were the messianic and nationalist aspects of Jewish theology compatible with full civic emancipation? Could traditional Judaism retain the loyalty of its followers in an increasingly open society? It was in response to these questions that the Reform and Orthodox movements developed as distinct modern branches of an ancient religion.

CHAPTER ELEVEN   ADJUSTING TO EQUALITY

THE BEGINNING OF THE REFORM MOVEMENT: NINETEENTH-CENTURY JUDAISM

The *idée fixe* of European Jewry in the first half of the nineteenth century was to achieve and extend emancipation. Bitter disagreement broke out among practising Jews about the correct method of presenting Judaism, either to its adherents, who were assimilating in increasing numbers, or to sceptical Christian legislatures; but the exponents of arch-conservatism and radical reform all agreed that the main thing was to play down the *national* element in Judaism and insist that Jews everywhere should be accepted as citizens of their countries, distinctive only in their religious observances. Both the Reform and Orthodox movements, as well as those who adopted an intermediate position, were responding primarily to the challenge and opportunities of European liberalism.

In 1801, Israel Jacobson – financier, philanthropist and early Reform leader – founded a Jewish vocational school in the small town of Seesen in central Germany. Nine years later he erected the first Reform temple on an adjacent site. Dedicated in the presence of a mixed Jewish and Christian congregation, with the sermon and many of the prayers in German and an organ accompanying the choir, Jacobson optimistically believed that a new era of brotherhood between religions was about to dawn. With the defeat of Napoleon and the collapse of the short-lived kingdom of Westphalia, Jacobson moved to Berlin. There he established a private place of worship in his home, continuing the innovations he had introduced in Seesen and in addition discarding the ceremony of bar-mitzvah for thirteen-year-old boys in favour of a Lutheran-style confirmation for both boys and girls. At his son's confirmation he delivered the sermon himself, in German (which did not deter the boy from subsequently converting and becoming a Catholic priest).

A second reformed conventicle opened in the home of the wealthy banker Jacob Beer, father of the composer Meyerbeer. Scandalized traditionalists appealed directly to the Prussian king, who ordered the closure of the two synagogues and forbade any deviation in language, ceremony or liturgy from ancient Jewish custom. However, in 1818 a Reform temple opened in Hamburg, at the initiative of Eduard Kley, who had been a preacher of the Berlin Reform Group. In 1819 the congregation issued a new prayer book which drastically pruned the liturgy and reworded traditional prayers that called for the coming of the Messiah and the restoration of the Davidic kingdom. As in Seesen and Berlin, an organ accompanied the choir and German featured as extensively as Hebrew in the service.

Controversy immediately ensued. The rabbis of Hamburg and Altona denounced the new prayer book and ordered their flocks to shun the Reform temple. For their part, the Reformers marshalled authorities to demonstrate that prayer in the vernacular was permitted by the Talmud, defended their modifications on the ground that they made Judaism compatible with the aesthetic values of contemporary society, and argued that their reforms would retain the loyalty of future generations of Jews.

Their opponents, who since the beginning of the nineteenth century had been known as Orthodox, reiterated that the entire written and oral Torah, interpreted since ancient times by an unbroken chain of rabbinic tradition, was divinely revealed and therefore immutable. In particular, Joseph Caro's *Shulchan Aruch* (see pp. 111f.) and its subsequent commentaries, provided the standard for proper Jewish observance.

At about the same time that the Reform-Orthodox split was developing, a third movement, with links to both yet bound to neither, was making its appearance in Germany. In 1819 a small group of university-educated young men formed a Society for Culture and Academic Study of Judaism. Influenced by the ideas of the philosopher Hegel, this *Wissenschaft* ('scientific study') group proposed to study Judaism objectively and scientifically, neither according its past uncritical veneration as the Orthodox did, nor appearing to reject it, as did the Reformers. Although the society soon disintegrated – two of its founders, Heinrich Heine and Eduard Gans, converted to Christianity – its most significant achievement was to produce a periodical of Jewish historical scholarship edited by Leopold Zunz. The principles of *Wissenschaft*, with its attention to facts, systematic research and scientific methodology, would shape the writings and adopted positions of the second generation of Reform-Orthodox protagonists.

The two most implacable opponents in the debate, Abraham Geiger (1810–74) and Samson Raphael Hirsch (1808–88), had been friends at the University of Bonn. There they organized a Jewish debating society, perhaps with their future rabbinic careers in mind, but their paths subsequently diverged. Geiger came from a distinguished, traditional Frankfurt family, and received a formidable education in Jewish, classical and German literature. At Bonn he learned Arabic in order to prepare his doctoral dissertation: 'What Did Mohammed Take From Judaism?' In 1832 he was appointed rabbi of Wiesbaden, where he edited a journal that published essays on Jewish history and the need for religious reform.

In 1838 he was offered the post of second rabbi in Breslau. The city's senior rabbi, the aged Solomon Tiktin, opposed his appointment on the grounds that Geiger had criticized Orthodoxy and advocated reforms. He refused to cooperate with his junior colleague and in 1842 issued a pamphlet which asserted the inviolability of rabbinic tradition as formulated in the *Shulchan Aruch*. Geiger's supporters responded with their own pamphlet and almost every German rabbi was drawn into the controversy, on one side or the other.

At the same time the Hamburg temple published a revised edition of its prayer book which omitted references in the liturgy for the ingathering of Israel in Zion and replaced the traditional doctrine of bodily resurrection with a vague affirmation of spiritual immortality. Predictably, the prayer book and its use were denounced by the Orthodox.

But the momentum for reform was gathering pace. Lay groups in Frankfurt and Berlin issued calls for sweeping changes in Judaism. The Frankfurt Reform Society proclaimed 'the possibility of unlimited development in the Mosaic religion', while the Berlin Reform association demanded services almost entirely in German and the abolition of such customs as covering the head to pray or blowing the shofar on New Year's Day.

In response to this agitation it was decided to convene a rabbinic conference to establish a consensus for orderly change. Twenty-five rabbis met in Brunswick in June 1844, to discuss the feasibility of formulating a Jewish creed, easing the sabbath and dietary laws, and modernizing the liturgy. Despite the protest of 116 Orthodox rabbis that it was impermissible to abrogate any traditional law of Judaism, a second, larger conference took place in Frankfurt-on-Main a year later. The first question on the agenda was the role of Hebrew in Jewish worship. After three days of heated debate a vote was taken, and the motion that the retention of Hebrew was 'advisable' but not essential was carried, by eighteen to twelve.

A third synod met in July 1846 in Breslau. Attended only by committed Reform rabbis rather than interested observers or the general Jewish public, it discussed the question of sabbath work. The mood was less radical than at previous conferences, and the sanctity of the sabbath as a day of recreation and spiritual refreshment was reaffirmed, with only minor qualifications. However, the custom of adding a second day to the festivals in the Diaspora – originally introduced when the calendar depended each year on lunar observation – was abrogated. Topics not dealt with were postponed until the next conference, planned for Mannheim. But it was not destined to take place; the 1848 revolution intervened.

Geiger's role in all this impetus for reform was central. Since 1848, when Solomon Tiktin died, the Breslau community had been divided into Reform and Orthodox factions, with Geiger officiating over the Reform congregation. In addition to pastoral activities, he laid the groundwork for a rabbinical seminary, wrote extensively on such diverse topics as the Mishnah, medieval Jewish poetry and the Bible, and was a leading figure at the Reform conferences. His early radicalism was tempered over the years, and Geiger urged reform from within, as part of the totality of German Jewry, against the iconoclasm of colleagues like Samuel Holdheim (1806–60) who wished to abolish circumcision or transfer the sabbath to Sunday. His life-long conviction was that *Wissenschaft* would enable Judaism to reshape its theology on an orderly, scientific basis. Coupled with his analysis of Judaism's historical evolution through four major phases, Geiger had an almost mystical regard for the spirit of a liberal Germany in which his co-religionists would take their place as German citizens of the Jewish faith, with Judaism recognized alongside Christianity as an essential component of the German heritage.

Where Samson Raphael Hirsch would have agreed with Geiger was in defining the Jews as a religious, not a national, fellowship. Otherwise, their views were diametrically opposed. Hirsch was born in Hamburg, of a long-established family in which both a grandfather and an uncle had been followers of Moses Mendelssohn. He was given a well-rounded education, according to the tenets of the *haskalah*. After university, and at the tender age of twenty-two, Hirsch was appointed *landesrabbiner*, or regional rabbi, of the Duchy of Oldenburg. In 1836 he published *The Nineteen Letters on Judaism*, and a year later *Horeb: A Philosophy of Jewish Laws and Observances*. From 1851 until his death Hirsch ministered in Frankfurt-on-Main, where he established a modern Orthodox school, edited a Jewish monthly, wrote biblical commentaries, and strenuously resisted the encroachments of Reform Judaism in his large and important community.

Hirsch, who wrote in fluent German and had a keen appreciation of drama and poetry, exemplified the *haskalah* ideal of fidelity to Jewish tradition combined with receptiveness to secular culture. He himself coined the phrase *Jissroel-Mensch* (Israel-Man) to describe a Jew who was both loyal to tradition and at home in the contemporary world. The changes which Hirsch permitted in his synagogues were minor ones, such as choral singing, or sermons in the vernacular. His neo-Orthodoxy, as it is often called, took as its motto a rabbinic dictum: *Torah im derech eretz* – '(Excellent is) the study of Torah together with a secular livelihood.' In his two major works, Hirsch mounts a defence of traditional Judaism based on observance of the Torah, which is eternal, just as the laws of nature are – 'Just such a fact as the sky and the earth.' The Torah is an organic unity, and the true science of Judaism is to approach the divinely revealed ordinances as primary facts constituting an interconnected system, not, as the Reformers do, bringing to bear on them external perspectives, or seeking to diminish Judaism's responsibilities for the sake of greater convenience. For Hirsch, the Revelation at Sinai was an indisputable event which rendered the corpus of religious legislation, from the Bible to the *Shulchan Aruch*, inviolable. Strict fidelity to tradition would not jeopardize the Jewish quest for emancipation because Jews were united not nationally but spiritually, by the bond of obedience to divine law, and therefore they could happily become German citizens in Germany, French citizens in France, and so on.

Geiger and Hirsch represented two extremes of the ideological spectrum. Although Reform, and neo-Orthodoxy to a lesser extent, gained their adherents, it was a third school, gathered round the figure of Rabbi Zacharias Frankel (1805–75), which best expressed the *Zeitgeist* of German Jewry. Frankel was the first rabbi in Bohemia to have received a secular education. Dedicated to the principles of *Wissenschaft*, he was not opposed to pruning the liturgy or introducing a choir, but accused the Reformers of bartering Judaism for emancipation. He withdrew from the 1845 Frankfurt Conference in protest at the decision to deem Hebrew 'advisable' rather than obligatory for divine worship. Frankel defined his approach as 'Positive-Historical Judaism', in which the will of the people, as embodied in the mainstream of the Jewish heritage, was a continuation of the revelation at Sinai.

In 1854 Frankel became principal of the newly established Jewish Theological Seminary in Breslau, an institution conceived by Geiger, who found the funds to set it up. Frankel declined to have him on the faculty. Similarly, he refused to give an undertaking to Hirsch that the seminary would adopt the Orthodox position on divine revelation and the immutability of tradition. Staffed by eminent scholars such as Heinrich Graetz (1817–91), the outstanding Jewish historian, Breslau's middle-of-the-road stance came increasingly to represent the expectations and wishes of German Jewry.

Whatever the disagreements and differences of emphasis between Reform, neo-Orthodox and Positive-Historical Judaism, its leaders were optimistic that they were about to witness a rejuvenation of Judaism and a recognition among enlightened Europeans of its historical mission to guide people towards a better future. This faith in a progress leading to the full integration of Jews in society was to be jolted by events in the 1870s and 1880s.

Before detailing the rising hostility against Jews in the latter decades of the nineteenth century – and the Jewish responses to it – we should pause to survey the geographical and political disposition of Jewry, in Europe and elsewhere, in the century since the French Revolution.

As a result of the Congress of Vienna, most of Poland's 1.2 million Jews found themselves under Russian rule. Whereas the pressures for social change had altered other European states drastically, in Russia the tsar, a privileged nobility and the state church doggedly resisted all calls for reform. The serfs were not emancipated until 1861, and the Jews had to wait until the 1917 Revolution.

Official policy was to limit Jewish habitation to the western provinces, 'the Pale of Settlement'. Ethnically distinctive and traditionally pious, mainly speaking Yiddish, the Jewish masses (1.6 million in 1825, 2.35 million in 1850, four million by 1880) engaged in petty trade and crafts, leased distilleries and inns, or migrated to the bigger cities, where they became part of the working-class poor.

The reign of Tsar Alexander I (1801–25) began in liberalism and ended in reaction. Attempts to ameliorate the condition of the Jews by encouraging agriculture, establishing modern schools and allowing entry, in limited numbers, to municipal office, were dropped in favour of a new scheme; encouraging conversion to Christianity. The idea was suggested to the tsar and his minister for spiritual affairs and public education, Prince Golitsyn, by an English eccentric, Lewis Way, the founder of the London Society to Disseminate Christian Faith Among Jews, who had travelled across western Russia and judged the Jewish masses to be ripe for missionary activity. In 1817 a Society of Israelite Christians was formed, which offered financial and legal inducements to baptized Jews. There were few takers.

Alexander's successor, Nicholas I (reigned 1825–55), ascended his throne by crushing the Decembrist revolt and learned from it a lesson: he decided to seal his empire off from any taint of western liberalism. While on an educational tour of Russia in 1816 he had been unfavourably impressed by the Jews. 'They are everything here; merchants, artisans and contractors; they operate taverns, flour mills, ferries. They are genuine leeches . . .' During his reign alone, 600 legal enactments concerning the Jews were promulgated. In 1827 an edict extended conscription to them for the first time, for twenty-five-year terms, as was customary in the Russian army, but to be preceded, in the case of Jewish youth, by six additional years of training, from the age of twelve, in military schools ('cantons'). Jewish communal authorities were made responsible for filling the government's conscription quota. Kidnapping and bribery flourished as Jewish parents tried to save their children. Alexander Herzen, the Russian revolutionary, describes in his autobiography the harrowing sight of a group of terrified, fever-stricken Jewish cantonists, between eight to thirteen years old, lined up at the railway station. Once in the military schools, and then the army, they were beaten and deprived of sleep as an encouragement to convert, or mocked for their inability to speak Russian and refusal to eat non-kosher food. No Jew could rise above the rank of non-commissioned officer. It was the poor, with no guild-certificates to exempt them or influential communal dignitary to intercede on their behalf, who provided most of the conscript roster.

In 1827 the Jews were expelled from Kiev and its surrounding province, and in 1835 forbidden to live within fifty versts of the western frontier. A year later, censorship was imposed on all Jewish books. But in 1841, in that oscillation between reform and repression which characterized tsarist policy towards the Jews, the government invited a young German Jew, Dr Max Lilienthal, to set up a network of schools, on the *haskalah* model, to replace the traditional system of *chadarim* (parochial primary schools) and *yeshivot* and so reduce Jewish 'self-isolation'. Lilienthal was received with distrust by communities which suspected that the government's aim was to encourage baptism through education, and the new schools, staffed mainly by Christians, had few enrolments. When Lilienthal became aware that the authorities were indeed hoping to undermine the teaching of the Talmud, he resigned his post and left Russia for America.

Much of the government's Jewish legislation, such as the abolition of the *kehillah* system in 1844, the attempt to prohibit traditional Jewish dress and uncut side-curls (*pe'ot*) in 1850, or the major 1851 plan to categorize all Russian Jews according to their economic value to the state, foundered on a combination of bureaucratic ineptitude and necessary, but unforthcoming, Jewish cooperation.

Then came the Crimean War (1853–6). Russia's poor showing in it demonstrated how far behind other European powers she had fallen, both economically and industrially. Alexander II (reigned 1855–81) recognized the need for change. The freeing of the serfs was followed by the reformation of the judiciary and local government. Forced conscription of Jewish youths was abandoned. Favoured groups of Jews, such as merchants (1859), university graduates (1861), registered artisans (1865) and medical personnel (1879), were permitted to live outside the Pale of Settlement. Jewish communities were established for the first time in St Petersburg and Moscow. Disciples of the *haskalah* were found in literary and professional circles. The easing of restrictions and general mood of liberalization persuaded many Russian Jews that full emancipation could not be far away.

Elsewhere in Europe, that emancipation had been almost totally achieved. In France, Holland and Belgium, recognized religions, including Judaism, were aided financially by the state. The Austrian revolution of 1848 guaranteed freedom of religious conscience in its new constitution, and prominent Jewish support for Kossuth's uprising ensured the rights of Hungarian Jews even after Hapsburg control was reimposed in 1850. Jews were active during the various phases of the *Risorgimento* in Italy; Mazzini's Roman republic, the Venetian republic of Manin (himself of Jewish descent) and Garibaldi's spectacular exploits all being dependent upon Jewish assistance. Jewish emancipation, granted in 1848 by the liberal kingdom of Sardinia, gradually spread as other Italian territories were annexed by the house of Savoy, and when, in 1870, Rome became the capital of a united Italy, the ghetto of the oldest-established Jewish community in the western world was finally abolished. Even Switzerland, with a negligible Jewish population, could not hold out against the diplomatic pressure of England, France and America, and abrogated restrictions on Jewish residence in 1866 and granted full emancipation in the 1874 constitution.

In England, perhaps the world's most tolerant, least religious, country, Jewish emancipation followed that of Catholicism. By 1880 there were about 63,000 English Jews, in London (where over half of them lived), Manchester, Liverpool and other industrial centres. Socially and economically the Jews had integrated almost from the beginning of their Cromwellian readmission. The original Sephardi settlers had given way in numbers and organizational energy to Ashkenazim, mainly from eastern Europe. The office of Chief Rabbi – deliberately modelled on the ecclesiastical hierarchy of the Church of England – had its first Ashkenazi incumbent in 1845. Marcus Adler, a native of Hanover, was faced with a Reform secession which had established a synagogue near Marble Arch in 1840. His response was to issue a ban; but since the Reform and Orthodox communities regularly intermarried, and since the innovations of the West London Synagogue were limited to sermons in English, an organ accompaniment and a mildly pruned liturgy, mutual toleration rather than hostility soon came to be the pattern of their relationship.

A House of Commons Bill in favour of Jewish emancipation was passed in 1833, but regularly rejected by the House of Lords until 1858, when a typically English compromise allowed each House to administer its own form of oath for new members. Thus Baron Lionel de Rothschild took his seat in the Commons, to which he had been elected by the city of London since 1847, and twenty-seven years later – after Benjamin Disraeli, a baptized Jew, had become leader of the Tory party and prime minister – his son entered the Upper House as Lord Rothschild, the first professing Jew to be raised to the peerage.

In Germany, the spokesmen for religious reform and political emancipation used similar arguments. Both groups rejected the notion that the national element in Judaism was a hindrance to patriotism. Gabriel Riesser, a magnificent orator and leading Jewish advocate of civil rights, neatly turned the tables on those who required conversion to Christianity as a guarantee of Jewish fitness for emancipation, by asserting that such a requirement hardly showed respect for Christian conscience, let alone Jewish.

He was elected a vice-president of the National Assembly in Frankfurt, convened after the 1848 uprising to devise a constitution for the German people that specified civil and political equality for the adherents of all religious confessions. Although a conservative reaction followed, the principle of Jewish emancipation had been established. Baden in 1862, Saxony in 1868 and Bismarck's North German Federation in 1869, decreed full Jewish emancipation. When all of Germany, except for Austria, came under the German imperial constitution of 1871, after Prussia's victory over France, the last restrictions on Jewish residence, marriage, choice of profession, acquisition of property and right to vote, were abolished.

European Jewry's century-long struggle for emancipation had never been an issue in America, to which a quarter of a million Jews, mainly from Germany, Bohemia and Hungary, but also from Russia and Romania, had emigrated between 1840 and 1880. There the constitution stipulated that no religious test should be required in order to hold public office. Economic opportunity, as the continent opened up, was similarly egalitarian. The original eighteenth-century Sephardi settlers were overwhelmed by the stream of Ashkenazi immigrants who pushed south and westwards from their port of arrival in New York, which had a community of 60,000 Jews. Levi Strauss – following in the wake of the California gold rush and providing miners with their work-clothes, 'Levis' – was one of many examples of the itinerant Jewish pedlar transformed into a merchant prince in the land of opportunity. In the confident, expansionist atmosphere which followed the Civil War (in which about 10,000 Jews fought, on both sides), Reform Judaism took hold and expressed the optimism of American Jewry more successfully than any other branch of the religion. The radical antinomianism of reformers such as Samuel Holdheim was disseminated by several energetic European rabbis like Max Lilienthal, fresh from his experiences in Russia, David Einhorn, and Isaac Mayer Wise, and it was sympathetically received by the immigrants who had crossed the Atlantic to escape precisely that prejudice and degradation associated with traditional Judaism. The 1885 Pittsburgh Platform of the Reform movement asserted that Jews were a religious fellowship not a national community, and that Judaism was a rational religion whose moral law pointed the way to the age of universal brotherhood.

If America in the latter decades of the nineteenth century represented the high point of western Jewry's aspirations and achievements, even the forgotten Jews of the east had entered a period of relative amelioration. European governments were vying for influence in the provinces of the ramshackle Ottoman empire, and were able to exert pressure for the protection of their nationals, Jewish as well as Christian. First Greece (1820–9), then Egypt (1831–40), rebelled against Turkey, and Jewish communities, their *dhimmi* status protected under the Pact of Omar of the Islamic rulers (see chapter 7), were caught up in the turmoil. The 20,000 Jews of Palestine, in particular, were sufferers, as the armies of the Egyptian pasha Mohammed Ali, the Lebanese Druse and insurgent local fellahin swept across the country.

In 1840 the Damascus Affair erupted. A Capuchin monk disappeared and the Jewish community of some 20,000 people, including many eminent and wealthy families, was accused of using his blood to bake Passover *matzah*. Several Jews 'confessed' to the crime, after appalling torture. The European press, much engrossed in 'the eastern question', was full of the affair. Liberal opinion was outraged at this resurgence of the medieval blood libel at a time of supposed enlightenment. A Jewish delegation including Sir Moses Montefiore, the most eminent English Jew of his age, and Adolphe Crémieux, the French statesman, travelled east to intercede. Supported by the consuls of most European governments, they were able to achieve the release of the innocent prisoners, and returned home to universal Jewish rejoicing.

The Damascus Affair was significant beyond its immediate impact, in that it awoke the interest of western Jews in their eastern co-religionists, and demonstrated – admirably to some observers, in a sinister fashion to others – that instinctive Jewish solidarity whenever any part of the whole is in peril. Philanthropic and educational institutions were opened in Egypt, Palestine and North Africa by the organizations of European Jewry, notably the Alliance Israélite Universelle, founded by Adolphe Crémieux.

Similarly, Jewish political leaders dealing with the Ottoman empire were careful to link the treatment of Jews to that of non-Muslims in general. Thus, in 1854 Albert Kahn, a representative of the Parisian Rothschilds in Turkey, formulated for the sultan a solution to the status of Jews as, 'All the rights and privileges that have been granted – and those to be granted in the future – to Christians, are to apply also to Jews.' The sultan readily agreed, and the 150,000 Jews living in European Turkey enjoyed self-administered and wide-ranging autonomy in a country where political freedom was not yet known.

It was in Palestine that the environment and expectations of the Jewish population had changed least during the nineteenth century. A militantly Orthodox rabbinate obstructed all attempts to modernize schooling or let in the spirit of the *haskalah*. Efforts at agricultural colonization were likewise impeded; a farm and agricultural school established by the Alliance near Jaffa in 1870 had to attract its students from Galicia. Clustered in Jerusalem and the three holy cities of Safed, Tiberias and Hebron, the majority of Jews were pious hermits who had come to Zion to die.

French domination of Algeria, Tunisia and Morocco, and British hegemony in India and large areas of the Middle East, enabled the Jewries of those countries at least to feel reassured by the watchfulness of a great power and, in benign circumstances, as in Cairo and Alexandria, to expand commercially, civically and, sometimes, by participating in government. Even in Persia, where the Jews still lived under oppressive conditions, representations by the British parliament elicited from the shah a promise to consider their grievances.

In the capitalist, industrialized west, the status of the Jew had changed beyond recognition, and even in the less advanced east it had improved immeasurably by the last quarter of the nineteenth century. The speed and intensity of the transition from ghetto pariah to assimilated bourgeois, and the avidity with which Jews had seized the opportunities of emancipation, prompted in Europe a resurgence of Judeophobia that differed in kind from previous anti-Jewish religious persecution and was to lead, relentlessly, to one of the greatest crimes ever committed in the long annals of human suffering. Anti-Semitism was the newly coined term to lend respectability to prejudice against the Jews.

CHAPTER TWELVE   ANTI-SEMITISM:
FROM THE FRANCO-PRUSSIAN WAR
TO THE RISE OF HITLER

WESTERN EUROPE

In 1873 a major stock market collapse, as a result of over-specu-
lation in the wake of the Franco-Prussian war, seriously affected
Germany. Populist agitators and impoverished share-holders
blamed the collapse on the Jews. It was a wry compliment to the
astonishing progress of Jews in business and commerce in the
quarter of a century since full emancipation, that such a charge
could be made and sound plausible. The power of the house of
Rothschild on the European monetary exchange and in floating
large government loans, had long been recognized. Other Jewish
bankers were prominent in railway construction, wholesale trade
and new industries. In Russia, the upsurge in textile and tobacco
manufacture, timber and grain export, railways and shipping,
was dependent upon Jewish capital.

Along with this banking influence, Jews had, in great numbers,
infiltrated the retail trades, the medical and legal professions,
publishing and journalism. With the *embourgeoisement* of the
Jewish population, significant changes had occurred in its demography. Families streamed in from rural areas to expanding
urban localities. From former Polish territories they moved to
Leipzig, Cologne, Frankfurt and Berlin; from Alsace to Paris;
from Moravia and Galicia to Vienna; from White Russia to the
cities of the Ukraine. Whether as assimilated but still detectable
members of the middle classes, or as a distinctive grouping in the

urban proletariat, the Jews of western and central Europe had come to the fore so suddenly, so *noticeably*, that jealous competitors, status-conscious bureaucrats, feudal Junkers who despised the new money-aristocracy, and apprehensive intellectuals, could all point the finger at a scapegoat for their, and society's, disaffections.

Anti-Semitism – the term was coined by Wilhelm Marr, a scurrilous journalist, the baptized son of a Jewish actor, in a pamphlet entitled 'The Victory of Judaism over Germanism' which was printed twelve times between 1873 and 1879 – became a weapon of political, economic and scientific controversy. Bismarck, the imperial chancellor, gave tacit support to anti-Semitic propaganda as he fought off liberal-progressive opposition and press. Its overt proponent was Adolf Stöcker, court chaplain to the kaiser, who founded a Christian Social Party in 1878. From the pulpit and at public meetings he inveighed against the Jewish 'menace' to Christian principles, the corrupting influence of Jewish 'control' of the press and the sinister conspiracy of Jewish 'international capitalism'. His appeal was to those elements of the petty bourgeoisie who resented Jewish economic competition, and their votes elected him to the Reichstag in 1881. That same year the anti–Semites collected over a quarter of a million signatures for a petition asking the government to ban further Jewish immigration, mob violence against Jewish persons and property broke out and the first 'international' congress of anti-Semites was arranged for Dresden in September 1882, although in reality the three hundred delegates who came were from only two countries, Germany and Austria-Hungary, with several Russian guests attending.

The high-water mark of political anti-Semitism was in 1893, when the anti-Semitic parties elected sixteen deputies to the German Reichstag. In neighbouring Austria, Karl Lueger, a former democrat turned demagogue, was so successful in harnessing the anti-Jewish sentiment among the Catholic working classes that he was elected mayor of Vienna in 1895, despite the reluctance of Emperor Franz-Joseph – whose capital had a population of 125,000 Jews, with two million spread throughout his empire – to allow him to take office.

At the same time the Dreyfus Affair was convulsing French society. There, anti-Semitism, which had surfaced after the humiliation of the Franco-Prussian war, was manipulated by monarchists and clerics opposed to the Third Republic. Captain Alfred Dreyfus, the only Jew on the general staff of the French army, had been convicted, on the basis of forged evidence, of selling military secrets to Germany. He was sentenced to life imprisonment on Devil's Island, but as details came to light of the roles played by Major Esterhazy and Colonel Henry, French public opinion, and even families, split violently into Dreyfusard and anti-Dreyfusard camps. The Dreyfusards, with Émile Zola and Georges Clemenceau in the vanguard, were appalled at a miscarriage of justice which threatened the very fabric of French democracy. The anti-Dreyfusards, ready to sacrifice an individual in order to protect the army's honour, regarded Dreyfus as the hireling of a vast Jewish and masonic plot. Eventually he was vindicated, and restored to full military rank in 1906. The Dreyfus Affair was, probably, the last great, clear-cut, moral issue to exercise the conscience of modern Europe, with the added piquancy that Dreyfus himself, had he not been the victim, by temperament and code of values would undoubtedly have belonged to the anti-Dreyfusard faction.

Intrinsically fascinating as the Dreyfus Affair was, for the tensions it revealed between the French Church and state, and its uncovering of obdurate, right-wing anti-Semitism, its resonances were to prove even more significant. One of the journalists who covered the Dreyfus trial, and was indelibly marked by the experience, was Theodor Herzl, the founder of political Zionism. If anti-Semitism manifested itself politically and economically, it depended upon academic and pseudo-scientific support for its intellectual justification. Eugene Düring, a disappointed philosopher who blamed some of his Jewish colleagues for his lack of advancement at Berlin University, in 1881 published a book entitled *The Jewish Question, as a Question of Race, Morals and Culture*. His thesis was that the Jewish people constituted the worst branch of the Semitic race, greedy, exploitative, bent on world domination. Their religious and ethical outlook was so inferior to Hellenism and the German spirit that they should be expelled from all governmental and educational posts and even forbidden to intermarry, to avoid 'Judaization of the blood'. More formidable, because less morbidly fantastical, were the articles of

Heinrich von Treitschke, the official Prussian historian. For him, Jewry posed a threat to the German national ethos, pushing in through the eastern frontier, convinced of its 'chosen people' superiority, insensitive to Germany's Christian culture, derogatory about her greatest men, as the writings of Graetz and the irreverent journalism of Ludwig Börne demonstrated. 'The Jews,' observed Treitschke, in what was to become a malevolent catchphrase for later, more determined anti-Semites, 'are our misfortune.'

The new science of anthropology added its weight to anti-Semitism. Charles Darwin's theory of natural selection was adapted by Joseph Gobineau and other racists to divide humanity into 'Aryan' and 'Semitic' species. The Aryan mentality was life-affirming, heroic, imaginative, whereas its Semitic counterpart was egotistic, cowardly, materialistic. At the end of the century, Houston Stewart Chamberlain, an Englishman who became a naturalized German and Richard Wagner's son-in-law, published a lengthy, bombastic, widely read book, *The Foundations of the Nineteenth Century*, in which he reduced all of cultural history to a struggle between the Aryan and Semitic races. Having destroyed the ancient world, the contemporary Jew was corrupting Europe, and the pure German spirit would only triumph by casting out the foreign body in its midst.

EASTERN EUROPE

While this ugly recrudescence of Judeophobia was breaking out in western Europe, where it never received official government sanction and where, to their credit, liberal rulers like the short-lived Frederick III of Prussia – who described anti-Semitism as 'the disgrace of the country' – politicians like Heinrich Rickert, leader of the Reichstag opposition, and scholars like Theodor Mommsen, the historian of ancient Rome, were raising their voices to defend Jews, in Russia the government, as a deliberate policy, was about to extend discrimination against its Jewish population and encourage the peasantry in its traditional Jew-hatred. In 1881 Tsar Alexander II was assassinated by revolutionaries. His successor, Alexander III, was a zealous Greek Orthodox autocrat. Soon after his accession a wave of pogroms swept over more than a hundred communities in the Ukraine. In each instance the mob action was uniform, and the response of the authorities was uniformly delayed until the third day of the killing, destruction and looting. The Russian government explained away the carnage as an outburst of peasant anger against Jewish exploitation, and reassured concerned foreign powers – notably Gladstone's administration in Great Britain, where readers had been shocked by a series of graphic articles about the pogroms in *The Times*, and a protest meeting at the Mansion House had been addressed by Lord Shaftesbury, the Anglican Bishop of London and Cardinal Manning – that it was energetically prosecuting the instigators.

A few months later Count Ignatiev, minister of the interior, issued a series of regulations which curtailed Jewish residence in the Pale of Settlement and limited the purchase or leasing of property. Pogroms continued throughout 1883-4. In 1887 the ministry of education introduced a quota system for Jewish pupils, restricting them to ten per cent of the Christian enrolment in schools in the Pale of Settlement (where Jews constituted thirty to eighty per cent of the entire population), to five per cent beyond the Pale, and to three per cent in the major cities. Four years later, in preparation for the transfer of the tsar's residence from St Petersburg, 20,000 Jews were forcibly expelled from Moscow. The municipal ordinances of 1892 deprived Jews in the Pale of Settlement of the right to elect, and be elected to, city councils. Another law forbade Jews to assume names other than those on their birth certificates. In 1893, the Crimean resort of Yalta was officially withdrawn from inclusion in the Pale of Settlement, and hundreds of Jewish families were expelled: the tsar had a villa nearby. He died there in October 1894, and the train carrying his coffin to St Petersburg glided along the same tracks that were taking the last Jewish exiles from Yalta to the Pale.

Conditions worsened under his youthful successor, Nicholas II. Faced by workers' strikes and revolutionary terrorism, the government responded by the mass arrests of those suspected of implication, and diverted popular discontent by focusing on the Jews. In Kishinev, the capital of Bessarabia, a government-sanctioned pogrom broke out on the eve of Passover, 1903. While the police stood idly by, awaiting orders from the governor, forty-five Jews were murdered, nearly 600 injured and 1,500 homes were destroyed. Russian newspapers were censored, and gave no details, but foreign journalists reported the story. Western Jews started a huge relief fund, and the shocked response from the American and European press prompted Leo Tolstoy and Russian liberals to condemn the outrage. Chayyim Nachman Bialik of Odessa, the finest Hebrew poet since those of medieval Spain, was prompted to write a savage, haunting, vengeful lament which, because of the censorship laws, he could not publish under its original title, 'On the Slaughter', but changed to the less provocative 'The Saga of Nemirow'. But its message was not lost. When a mob attacked Jews in Gomel, a town in White Russia, five months later, they were met by Jewish self-defence groups and military protection was needed, after clashes which left twelve Jews and eight Russians dead.

In 1904, partly to distract the population with an appeal to patriotism, Russia went to war against Japan. The unexpected Japanese victories led the reactionary press to accuse the Jews of secretly aiding the enemy, to whom they were racially related. In the two years between the pogrom in Kishinev and the Russian defeat at Port Arthur, 125,000 Jews emigrated to America. Between 1905 and 1907, as revolutionary activity increased and the tsar reluctantly ceded political rights, gangs of tsarist supporters, known as the 'black hundreds', mounted attacks on dozens of Jewish communities, with tacit government encouragement. In Odessa alone, 300 Jews were killed. As a gruesome finale to the worst period in Russian-Jewish history since the raids of the *haidemaks*, the blood libel was resuscitated. In 1911, Mendel Beilis, a labourer from Kiev, was charged with having murdered a Christian child for ritual purposes. His trial dragged on for two years, rousing intense interest within and beyond Russia, until he was acquitted. The piqued attorney-general then accused the liberal press and Jewish lawyers of having provoked the people against the government. But by now it was the summer of 1914, and Europe was about to be engulfed in war.

One instinctive response of Russian Jewry to the grim situation between 1881 and 1914 was to emigrate, if possible. The authorities were keen to encourage an exodus. When asked by a delegation from Paris in 1898 what would become of Jews under a system of constant persecution, one of the tsar's closest aides replied candidly that one-third would die out, one-third would leave the country, and one-third would assimilate without trace. Baron Maurice de Hirsch, a Belgian philanthropist, had a grandiose scheme to take two-thirds of Russia's Jews out of the country within twenty-five years, and purchased tracts of land in Argentina to turn into agricultural settlements; but only about 6,000 emigrated there between 1892 and 1894, although 115,000 Jews eventually settled in Argentina. It was North, not South, America that beckoned.

After the pogroms of 1881 a mass movement of east European Jewry, greater than anything seen even during the expulsions from Spain, brought over two million Jews to the United States of America. In all, some 2,750,000 Jews left eastern Europe between 1881 and 1914. 200,000 came to England, crowding into London's East End and prompting the Aliens Immigration Act of 1905 in an attempt to stem the tide. The communities of France and Germany were swelled by tens of thousands, and were none too happy about it. British colonies were attractive – 40,000 Jews went to South Africa, 100,000 to Canada. About 300,000 simply resettled elsewhere in Europe, with dire consequences when boundaries were redrawn after the First World War.

SOCIALISM AND ZIONISM

In western Europe in the last decades of the nineteenth century, intellectual anti-Semitism flourished. In eastern Europe, where the masses of Jews still resided, despite large-scale emigration, pogroms and legislative repression were a tangible, physical manifestation of anti-Semitism. In response, a significant number of Jews were attracted either to the internationalism of socialist thought, or to the nationalist aspirations of Zionism, as a panacea for the 'Jewish problem'.

The Marxist dialectic, which foresaw a world-wide proletarian revolution overthrowing the inequalities of capitalist society, appealed especially to *haskalah*-educated, Russified Jews. They were prominent in all the radical movements which threatened the tsar's autocratic government during the early years of the twentieth century. At the same time, Jewish activists in the cities of the Pale were organizing embryonic trade unions and agitating for better working conditions. In 1897 (the same year, significantly, as the first Zionist Congress), a group of Jewish workers met in Vilna to form the General Union of Jewish Workers in Lithuania, Poland and Russia (the 'Bund'), with the aims of raising the level of Jewish political consciousness, creating groups to defend themselves against pogroms, and becoming allied with the Russian labour movement on the basis of partnership, not assimilation. The tensions of clarifying the nature of the Bund's relationship with the Social Democratic (or Marxist) party led to a Bund withdrawal in 1903 which left Lenin's faction in control – hence the name Bolshevik, which means majority in Russian. When the Bund rejoined the Social Democratic movement three years later, its major ideological preoccupation (until the 1917 Revolution) was to try to define its attitude towards the survival of a Jewish identity, given that in an ideal Marxist state Jewish separatism would disappear when the capitalist economic structure which accentuated it also disappeared.

Whereas socialists of the Bund condemned Zionism as a dangerous form of 'romantic bourgeois nationalism' which was diverting Jews from the revolutionary struggle, Zionists dismissed the socialist hope of full Jewish equality in an egalitarian society as an unrealizable chimera; only the attainment of a Jewish national homeland would solve the problem of anti-Semitism. Shortly after the Damascus Affair of 1840, the British consul in Syria had written to Sir Moses Montefiore and the Board of Deputies of British Jews, urging them to organize a large-scale Jewish colonization of Palestine under the slogan, 'Palestine is the national sanctuary of the Jewish people.' Sir Moses and his fellow notables were sceptical. In so far as they supported Palestinian Jewry, it was for philanthropic, not nationalist, motives. An anonymous German pamphlet of 1840, which called upon Jews to acquire vast tracts of Missouri, Arkansas and western parts of America, to establish autonomous Jewish states, received a similarly negative response. Emancipation, not self-determination, was the goal of German Jewry.

The first serious proponent of Jewish nationalism was the erratic Moses Hess (1812–75), a defector from Orthodoxy, a disciple of Hegel and a pioneer socialist, who was responsible for introducing Friedrich Engels to Karl Marx. He collaborated with them until political disagreements and Marx's withering sarcasm severed the relationship. Returning to his Jewish roots in later life, Hess, in 1862, published *Rome and Jerusalem*, in which he argued the value of national groupings, and envisioned a re-established Jewish state in Palestine, founded on the principles of socialism.

In eastern Europe a younger contemporary of Hess, Peretz Smolenskin (1842–85), was using the *haskalah*-imbued Hebrew journal *Ha-Shachar* ('The Dawn'), which he edited and printed, simultaneously to attack Reform Judaism as a weak imitation of Christianity, and to propagate a form of Diaspora nationalism in which spiritual values and Hebrew would ensure the survival of a Jewish ethnic identity even without a homeland. The pogroms of 1881–2 transformed Smolenskin into an ardent advocate of the necessity for Jewish colonization, specifically in Palestine. The shock waves from that year of pogroms stimulated, in the Pale villages, the formation of a network of *Chibbat Tziyyon* ('Love of Zion') societies, dedicated to a return to Zion. A group of Kharkov university students, known as the *Bilu* association (from the Hebrew initials of the verse in Isaiah (2:5) which was their motto – 'O House of Jacob, come, let us walk') set off for Palestine to become farmers. Other groups followed. In the summer of 1882 an eminent physician from Odessa, Judah Leob Pinsker (1821–91) – whose father had been an authority on the Karaite sect (see chapter 7) – published a pamphlet entitled 'Auto-Emancipation: A Warning to His Kinfolk by a Russian Jew'. Pinsker argued that anti-Semitism was a psychological disease, exacerbated by the Jews' alien status everywhere. Relying on self-help, rather than the nebulous good will of European rulers, the Jews had to emancipate themselves by establishing a homeland. The pamphlet was widely disseminated, and Pinsker became chairman of the *Chibbat Tziyyon* movement.

By the last years of the nineteenth century the concept of Zionism had spread to western Europe, where it was espoused by university-educated, seemingly acculturated, ostensibly successful Jews. The outstanding personality amongst them was Theodor Herzl (1860–1904). Born in Budapest of bourgeois, Reform parents, educated in Vienna, a popular playwright and man about society, with a commanding presence and striking good looks, Herzl became the Paris correspondent of Vienna's leading liberal newspaper, the *Neue Freie Presse*, and reported the Dreyfus trial. The virulence of the anti-Semitism aroused by the trial convinced him that Judeophobia was no passing aberration. Galvanized into action, in 1896 he produced a pamphlet entitled 'The Jewish State: An Attempt at a Modern Solution to the Jewish Question', established links with the *Chibbat Tziyyon* movement, tried unsuccessfully to interest Baron de Hirsch in his plans, confronted the resistance of the German rabbinic association, which opposed Zionism, and convened the first Zionist Congress in Basle on 29 August 1897. The essence of Herzl's thinking was contained in an essay he wrote for the London *Jewish Chronicle*.

There are two striking phenomena in our time: high civilization and low barbarism. By high civilization I mean the remarkable achievements of technology that have enabled us to conquer Nature; by low barbarism I mean anti-Semitism ... Everywhere, we Jews have honestly tried to assimilate into the nations around us, preserving only the religion of our fathers. We have not been permitted to ... We are a nation – the enemy has made us one without our desiring it ... We do have the strength to create a state and, moreover, a model state.

The Zionist delegates in Basle elected Herzl their chairman and issued a resolution for the creation of a Jewish national homeland in Palestine, guaranteed by international law. Shunned by the majority of Jews, the World Zionist Organization nevertheless set up branches in Europe and America, opened a Jewish national fund to purchase land in Palestine, and started a variety of educational and cultural projects.

In the meantime, Herzl was engaged in an intensive round of diplomatic activity. He met twice with Kaiser Wilhelm II, with the Turkish sultan, with the Russian minister of the interior, and, in 1903, with the British colonial secretary, Joseph Chamberlain, who offered him a tract of land for Jewish colonization in British East Africa – the Uganda project. When Herzl submitted the project for discussion at the sixth Zionist Congress, it provoked acrimonious debate and was decisively rejected. Skilful negotiator and tireless organizer though he was, Herzl had little knowledge of Jewish history or understanding of east European Jewry's tenacious yearning for Palestine. The bitterness of the argument which took place before he accepted that Palestine was the only possible territory for a Jewish national home undermined his health, and he died shortly afterwards.

Herzl's enduring achievement was to have constructed a working political framework for the eventual attainment of a Jewish national home in Palestine – 'a land without a people for a people without a land', in his poetic but inaccurate evocation, which has come back to haunt subsequent generations of Zionists in their relationships with the indigenous Arab population.

The first pioneers of the 1880s and 1890s established twenty agricultural settlements. They had to contend with malaria, an underdeveloped economy and the obstructiveness of the Turkish government. Many had to rely on the generosity, and well-meaning interference, of Baron Edmond de Rothschild and his agents. The second *aliyah* ('going up' – the word used to describe the 'ascent' to the land of Israel) of 1904–14 brought 40,000 newcomers to Palestine, mainly idealistic youths who saw no future for themselves in Russia. It was their generation which achieved a synthesis between nationalism and socialism in Labour Zionism; national and personal redemption would come through a return to Zion, if their ideas were based on the socialists' pride in manual work and cooperative endeavour. The first cooperative farm, Deganya, was founded in 1910 and became the model for the kibbutz ('group') movement. (Kibbutzim are farm collectives, in which all members are equal, and life is based on socialist principles.) The year before, in 1909, a new Jewish city, Tel-Aviv ('the Hill of Spring'), had been founded on the sand dunes outside Jaffa.

Despite worsening political conditions throughout the Ottoman empire in the aftermath of the Young Turk revolt, by 1914 there were 85,000 Jews in Palestine, out of a total population of 800,000; forty-three agricultural settlements; an armed watchman association to guard them; a school network in which Hebrew was the language of instruction; a variety of political parties; a Hebrew press; and keen intellectual debate, stimulated by the essays of Achad Ha-Am ('One of the People', the pen-name of Asher Ginsberg, 1856–1927). He propounded the theory of 'cultural'

Zionism with Palestine as the spiritual centre of modern Jewry, in a lucid, classic Hebrew prose. He was to become, when he finally settled in Tel-Aviv in 1922, the revered doyen of Zionist intellectuals.

During the Middle-Eastern campaigns of the First World War – T. E. Lawrence's 'sideshow of a sideshow' – Palestinian Jewish volunteers gained valuable military experience fighting in the British Army. In England, Chaim Weizmann, Professor of Biochemistry at Manchester University and a leading Zionist, had done crucial war work, by supplying acetone for naval guns. When, on 2 November 1917, the British foreign secretary, Arthur Balfour, addressed a historic letter to Lionel Walter Rothschild stating that 'His Majesty's Government views with favour the establishment in Palestine of a national home for the Jewish people . . . it being clearly understood that nothing shall be done which may prejudice the civil and religious rights of the existing non-Jewish communities in Palestine, or the rights and political status enjoyed by Jews in any other country', the foundation stones had already been laid for the first Jewish state since Roman times.

POST-WAR EUROPE: 1917–38

As a result of the peace treaties signed at the end of the First World War – in which tens of thousands of Jewish soldiers served on the battlefield, fighting fellow Jews on a scale never dreamed of before – the Jews of eastern Europe found themselves distributed over a number of newly independent nation-states. Hundreds of thousands of Jews, along with other civilians, had been wounded, killed or made homeless on the eastern front, which ran through the Pale of Settlement. The German and Austrian conquest of parts of Poland and Lithuania had forced the Russian government to admit streams of Jewish refugees into the provinces of Great Russia, giving rise to the bitter jest that the Pale of Settlement had finally been abolished, not by Tsar Nicholas II, but by Kaiser Wilhelm II.

In March 1917, the tsar was overthrown. One of the first acts of the provisional government was to repeal all legal discrimination against Jews. Emancipation had come at last; but in the civil war which followed the October Revolution, the Jewish communities of the Ukraine suffered appallingly at the hands of Petlura's Ukrainian battalions, Denikin's White Army and bands of peasant guerrillas. When the fighting finally ceased at the beginning of 1921, over 1,100 pogroms against 530 communities had killed approximately 60,000 Jews.

Of the states which emerged from the dismemberment of the Russian and Austro-Hungarian empires, Poland acquired the largest Jewish population: over three million Jews. Romania, which had always closely imitated tsarist Russia's anti-Jewish discrimination, gained the provinces of Bukovina, Transylvania and Bessarabia, and an enlarged Jewish population of almost one million. Defeated Hungary retained 445,000 Jews; newly created Czechoslovakia had 375,000. The 191,000 Jews of Austria were concentrated around Vienna. Latvia (95,000 Jews), Lithuania (115,000), Yugoslavia (70,000), Bulgaria (50,000) and Greece (75,000, most of them in Salonika) were the other significant centres of Jewish population. The Soviet Union had lost about half its Jews, but the 2.8 million who remained now enjoyed the same rights as any other citizen.

The Paris Peace Conference of 1919 had adopted the principle of equal rights for all religions and ethnic minorities in the newly created states. Despite such constitutional guarantees, the Jews were discriminated against almost everywhere, with the exception of Thomas Masaryk's Czechoslovakia, which conscientiously honoured its obligations. Economic stagnation in the aftermath of an enormously destructive war led governments to favour the interests of their own nationals at the expense of minorities. The Jew, especially in the Ashkenazi heartlands of Poland, Lithuania and Romania, was easily recognizable by dress, customs and religious practice, and suffered from bias in education, the professions and civil services, banking and state-controlled monopolies. Poverty was endemic in central and eastern Europe as Jews, traditionally fulfilling the roles of middlemen, were squeezed by the worsening, and worldwide, economic slump of the late 1920s and early 1930s.

Russia's Jews were discovering that Communist equality was as insidiously restrictive as the overt tsarist repression it had replaced. Although they could now enrol at institutes of higher learning, live in the major cities, utilize their talents in the state bureaucracy or colonize the specially designated Jewish region of Birobidzhan, they became victims of the regime's systematic campaign to root out competing ideologies, including all religions. All political, Zionist or religious institutions, especially *yeshivot*, were disbanded. Once Stalin had prevailed over Jewish-born Leon Trotsky in the power struggle which followed Lenin's death, he closed the last remaining Jewish organizations, including the Jewish section of the Communist party (the *Yevsektsiia*), and purged the Jewish intellectual leadership, along with millions of other suspected Soviet dissidents, in the Great Terror of 1934–8. By 1939, all Jews had been removed from the Communist party and government.

Ironically, in view of their treatment in the USSR, the fear of 'Jewish Bolshevism' was one of the reasons why post-war western governments imposed restrictive immigration quotas and reduced the entry of east European Jews. In Germany a rehashed satire from the reign of Napoleon III, *The Protocols of the Elders of Zion*, which alleged a plot between Zionism, Bolshevism and high finance in order to gain world control, ran through several printings and gained credence even in England and the United States. The Wall Street crash of 1929, and the resultant collapse of international trade and a drastic increase in unemployment, triggered off fresh waves of anti-Semitic feeling in several European countries. Yet despite this, Jews as a group had become increasingly middle-class and acclimatized to the west, and individuals had achieved great prominence and recognition in politics, the arts, science and the humanities: Walther Rathenau, the German foreign minister (assassinated by anti-Semites), Léon Blum, the French premier, Freud, Einstein, Mahler, Chagall, Wittgenstein, Kafka, Proust, to mention just a few. Many of these diversely gifted Jews came from Germany or Austria. Yet it was in those two countries, despite their history of Jewish identification and symbiosis, that anti-Semitism was to flourish most malignantly, with the rise to power of Adolf Hitler.

Born in Austria in 1889, Hitler was a rootless, drifting individual, a would-be artist, who associated with the anti-Semitic factions in Vienna. After demobilization in 1919, he returned to Munich, where he soon became the leader of the tiny National

Socialist German Workers' ('Nazi') Party. Its platform was a crudely simple one of fervent German nationalism and virulent anti-Semitism and anti-Communism. In a country which felt duped by the terms of the 1918 armistic agreements, in which the currency had plummeted and unemployment risen to six million by 1932, Nazism's message found ready listeners and growing support. In 1923, an attempted *coup d'état* by Hitler dissolved in abject failure. In 1928, with financial backing from German industrialists, who were fearful of a Communist take-over, Hitler's party polled 810,000 votes; two years later it had over six million, and by 1932, fourteen million, with 230 seats in the Reichstag. Field Marshal von Hindenburg, Germany's elderly president, appointed Hitler as chancellor in January 1933. In the elections two months later, with Nazi storm-troopers blatantly intimidating political opponents, Hitler polled 44 per cent of the popular vote.

Once in power, the Nazis quickly implemented their programme. All civil liberties were suspended, political parties disbanded, strikes outlawed and trade unions dissolved. Totalitarian state control was imposed. The S S (*Schutzstaffeln*, or guard troops), led by Heinrich Himmler, became the police arm of Nazi policy, running the concentration camps and controlling the secret police (the Gestapo). After Hindenburg's death in August 1934, Hitler was elevated to supreme Führer ('leader') of Germany, and was thus ready to impose his aim of removing all Jewish taint from the culture, institutions and economy of the Aryan state.

The Nazis proceeded by stages, not wishing to antagonize the Church, the army or the middle classes. They need not have worried. There was virtually no protest as, between April 1933 and September 1935, non-Aryans were removed from the civil service, the legal and medical professons and posts in education. In September 1935 the Nuremberg Laws were promulgated. These deprived Jews of the vote, forbade marriages or sexual relations between Jews and Aryans as a crime against 'German blood and honour', and defined a Jew on the racial basis of anyone who had a Jewish grandparent. All of this in the third decade of the twentieth century, in the country which regarded itself as the most civilized in Europe. And still the church leaders, the university professors, the professional organizations, stayed officially silent. The result was a mass exodus of German Jewry's intellectual, cultural and scientific élite. By the end of 1937, 118,000 Jews had fled, almost a third of them to Palestine, the rest to North and South America and other European countries.

In March 1938 Hitler marched into Austria. The Nuremberg Laws and all other anti-Jewish measures were immediately enforced with enthusiastic Austrian support. Mass arrests took place and prominent Jews, among them the head of the Rothschild family, were deported to concentration camps.

Reports of the plight of thousands of Jewish fugitives prompted the president of the United States to call an international conference on the refugee question at Evian-les-Bains on Lake Geneva in July 1938. Since the western democracies were unwilling to allow entry to more than a trickle of Jews, Hitler deduced that – as with his provocative foreign policy actions, such as re-entering the Ruhr, giving military support to Franco in the Spanish Civil War or annexing Austria – the response to his anti-Jewish measures would be limited to verbal protest.

In October 1938, 17,000 Jews of Polish origin were expelled from Germany. Five thousand were stranded in no-man's-land, in wretched conditions, on the eastern border. The seventeen-year-old son of one such couple, who lived in Paris, obtained a pistol and went to the German Embassy, where he fatally wounded an attaché. It was an ideal pretext for the Nazis. On the night of 9 November 1938, a pogrom was launched throughout Germany, led by the SS. Nearly six hundred synagogues were set alight, Jewish department stores looted, Jewish shop-windows smashed, homes wrecked, their inhabitants beaten and murdered, and some 30,000 people carried off to concentration camps during the violence of *Kristallnacht* ('night of broken glass'). Those shops and businesses which survived the devastation were expropriated, and the German Jewish community was fined one billion marks for Herschel Grünspan's act of vengeance in Paris.

No German Jew could now doubt Hitler's intentions. By 1939 he had driven away 300,000 people from a population which had numbered half a million when he became chancellor six years previously. Germany was not yet *judenrein* ('Jew-free'), but Hitler was embarking on greater schemes. In March 1939, contrary to the Munich agreement, he occupied Czechoslovakia. In August, he signed a non-aggression pact with Stalin, which secretly divided Poland between their two countries. On 1 September 1939, German troops invaded Poland, prompting a declaration of war from Britain and France.

World War II had begun, and with Germany's Panzer divisions soon conquering most of Europe, an undertaking of vast magnitude, complex planning, technological challenge and an audacity so breathtaking that it could only be referred to by euphemism, was within Hitler's grasp: a 'final solution' to the perennial problem of the Jews.

CHAPTER THIRTEEN

THE 'FINAL SOLUTION'

It is fortunate that copious testimony exists – in written eye-witness accounts, in official documents of Germany and the Allied powers, in photograph and on film – to the mass extermination of between five and six million European Jews during the years of the Nazi Holocaust. There are those today who, for reasons of their own, would seek to deny that the Holocaust happened, or dispute the scale of Hitler's genocide. The evidence refutes them, and the death camps now stand as tourist sights. Because it is still too painful for any Jew to attempt a dispassionate interpretation or objective analysis of the greatest tragedy ever to engulf the Jewish, or any other, people, a bald summary of facts and statistics will have to suffice.

Immediately after the speedy conquest of Poland in September 1939, the Jews were herded into ghettos (the largest of which was in Warsaw), forced to wear the yellow badge and put to work on the German war-effort. Denmark and Norway, the Netherlands, Belgium and France, all fell to the German armies during 1940. In the summer of 1941 Germany invaded the USSR. By October, Moscow and Leningrad were under threat and most of the Ukraine had fallen. Some three and a half million Jews were now under German control. It is generally agreed by historians of the Third Reich period that plans for the extermination of the Jews, to be carried out under SS supervision, had been finalized by Hitler and Himmler between December 1940 and February 1941, while they were preparing for the invasion of Russia. Armed, mobile SS 'action groups' (*Einsatzgruppen*), aided by Ukrainians, Lithuanians and Moldavians, would round up Jews, Soviet officials and gypsies in the occupied territories, march them outside the city limits to dig trenches or pits, strip them and then shoot them. In September 1941 more than 34,000 Jews were massacred at Babi Yar, a ravine outside Kiev. During 1941–2 at least one and a half million Russian Jews were killed by the *Einsatzgruppen* and their associates.

Another, more efficient, method of extermination was the death camps. Plans to deport all Jews from the occupied territories to eastern Europe were dropped in favour of a programme of biological annihilation, adopted at a secret conference (the minutes of which survived the war) in Berlin-Wannsee on 20 January 1942. Six camps were constructed on Polish territory. The first to be put into operation was at Chelmno, near Lodz. Between 150,000 and 340,000 Jews, some Soviet prisoners of war and gypsies were killed there in camouflaged gas vans. At Belzec, near Lublin, 600,000 Jews were liquidated by carbon-monoxide poisoning. Sobibor and Majdanek, both on the outskirts of Lublin, accounted for 400,000 east European Jews, as well as many prisoners of war. In the Treblinka camp, near Warsaw, an estimated 800,000 Jews were gassed in the fifteen months between July 1942 and October 1943.

The largest camp was at Auschwitz, a small town in Galicia. Sealed cattle-cars would arrive from all over Europe, filled with deportees for 'resettlement'. The fit were selected to be worked to death in nearby factories. The rest were stripped of their clothing and valuables, and taken naked to the 'shower rooms'. There, thanks to the scientific ingenuity of the pesticide firm Degesch, which manufactured Zyklon B gas, death was rapid. Visiting Nazi dignitaries would watch the process through peep-holes. Afterwards, gold fillings would be extracted from the corpses and women's hair cut off for industrial use. One to two million Jews were murdered in Auschwitz between 1942 and 1944. Hitler's propaganda minister Goebbels noted in his diary in 1943 that Jews were being exterminated by 'a rather barbarous procedure' but 'one must not allow sentimentality to prevail in these matters'.

Although most of the victims went passively and unbelievingly to their deaths, gulled by the official jargon of 'evacuation' and 'resettlement', there were instances of resistance and uprising, the most heroic of which took place in the Warsaw ghetto in April 1943. There, several thousand survivors of the half million Jews who had been confined to the ghetto refused to obey a deportation order. For six weeks they held out, in cellars and sewers, against SS artillery and tanks, until the attackers set fire to the ghetto and thus captured it.

By 1943 American intelligence agencies had corroborated details of the 'Final Solution' directly from Germany, but Allied military authorities refused to bomb the concentration camps, on the ground that it would divert the main war-effort. As the Russian advance drove the Germans from Poland, and eventual military defeat became inevitable, it is an insight into the perverse Nazi psychology that the extermination programme intensified at the concentration camps on German soil: in Dachau, Bergen-Belsen and Buchenwald. And even after the Normandy landings, large groups of Jews were being rounded up and sent on essential railway stock to the camps.

In the autumn of 1944, Himmler ordered a stop to the killings. It was not soon enough to hide the evidence. Skeletal survivors, too weak to greet the liberating armies, died in their thousands of starvation, typhus and other epidemics. Allied personnel saw the gas chambers and cremation ovens still standing. At the Nuremberg war crimes trials, evidence revealed that torture and medical experiments were carried out on prisoners by German doctors and camp guards, who killed thousands of men, women and children daily, and relaxed to Wagner's music in the evening.

It is not possible to determine precisely the total number of Jews gassed, murdered, starved or driven to suicide during the Holocaust, because those most closely implicated in the Final Solution tried to destroy the relevant documents. But independent studies have established that only 3.1 million Jews remained in Europe in 1945, out of a total Jewish population of about 9.2 million before the Second World War.

Whereas the nationals of many east European countries, notably Poland and the Ukraine, gave vent to their inherent anti-Semitism by actively participating in the work of extermination, it should be recorded that the governments of Finland, Bulgaria, Romania and Italy, although allied with Germany, did not surrender their native Jews to the SS. The Danes smuggled more than 6,000 Jews to neutral Sweden in October 1943. Thousands more survived because Christian friends and clergy, even in Germany itself, sheltered them at great personal risk. Nevertheless, when confronted with the awesome magnitude of the Holocaust, and the zealous, pedantic efficiency which a sizeable proportion of the German nation devoted to its execution (while the rest of the population could, at best, claim ignorance of what was going on); when one knows that accurate details of the Final Solution were in the possession of Allied leaders by the fourth year of the war, but were not made public, fearing that their citizens would not want to fight against Hitler on behalf of 'the Jews'; then one is bound to ask deeply agonizing questions, not only about civilization in Christian Europe, or the mentality of anti-Semites, but about human nature itself. In the words of the American literary critic, Lionel Trilling, in his essay, 'Art and Fortune', in *The Liberal Imagination*,

The simple eye of the camera shows us, at Belsen and Buchenwald, horrors that quite surpass Swift's powers – a vision of life turned back to its corrupted elements, more literal and fantastic than that which Montaigne ascribed to organized society. A characteristic activity of mind is therefore no longer needed. Indeed, before what we now know, the mind stops: the great psychological fact of our time, which we all observe with baffled wonder and shame, is that there is no possible way of responding to Belsen and Buchenwald. The activity of mind fails before the incommunicability of man's suffering.

CHAPTER FOURTEEN   STATEHOOD AND RECOVERY

As the full extent of the Nazis' Final Solution became known in the aftermath of World War II, western Jewry's determination to succour the survivors and to prevent the recurrence of the Holocaust by establishing a Jewish state in Palestine took on a messianic intensity. It is indicative of the strength of that determination, aided by the guilty good will of the victorious Allies, that within three years, on 14 May 1948, the State of Israel was officially proclaimed.

It had been a complex situation, an uphill struggle, since the Balfour Declaration of 1917. Between the two world wars the population of the *yishuv* ('settlement') in Palestine had grown to half a million Jews. About a quarter of them lived in over 200 agricultural settlements, with 150,000 in Tel-Aviv, 90,000 in Jerusalem and 60,000 in Haifa. The Hebrew University had been opened in Jerusalem in 1925. The Jewish Agency, the Histadrut (General Federation of Hebrew Workers), and the Hadassah Medical Organization developed social, industrial and health institutions on cooperative principles. These achievements had transformed Palestine into one of the most advanced areas of the Middle East, and established the infrastructure for an independent state.

But the colonial objectives of the British government, and the antagonism of the one million native Arab inhabitants, were major obstacles to the Zionist goal. The detachment of territory east of the Jordan – as a reward to the Hashemite family of Mecca for leading the Arab revolt during World War I – had left Palestine only 160 miles long and seventy miles wide. Tensions between

Mosaic from the synagogue at Beit Alpha, Israel

An engraving of Joseph honoured by Pharaoh

Moses and Aaron and the Ten Commandments; an oil painting by Aaron de Chavez

The building of Solomon's Temple; an engraving thought to be after Raphael

Anti-Semitic propaganda: the Jews of Cologne burnt alive,
from a woodcut in the *Liber Chronicarum Mundi*, published in 1463

Moses Mendelssohn (1729–86)

Baruch Spinoza (1632–77)

The festival of *sake* soba, after an engraving by Picart, 1722

The Jews expelled from eastern Rumelia, 1885

Emigration to America: Russians arriving at New York in 1892;
a contemporary engraving from the *Illustrated London News*

An anti-Dreyfus caricature, *c.* 1895

The disgrace of Captain Dreyfus: Dreyfus is reduced to the ranks, 1895;
an illustration from a French magazine

Zionists harvest their own grapes on an early commune in Palestine

A Jewish book-seller in Whitechapel, 1952

Theodore Herzl (1860–1904)

A *cheder* in Slonim (now in the USSR), 1938

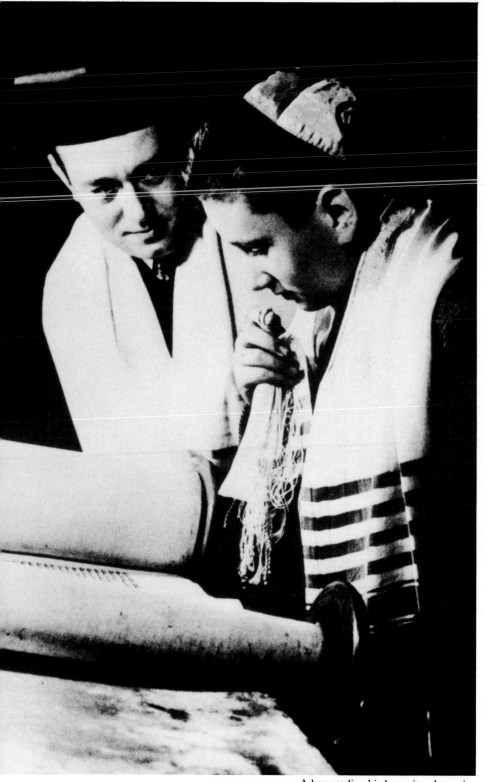

A boy reading his bar-mitzvah portion

A girl deported from Czechoslovakia by the Nazis

On the way to his first day at a *cheder* in Mukachevo, a town in the Ukraine, 1938

'Jew baiting' in Austria: a Nazi passes an optician's shop in Vienna
that is daubed with the word 'Jew' and a swastika in red and black paint

The Western Wall, Jerusalem, at the turn of the century

The Western Wall, Jerusalem, after 1967, when it came back into Israeli hands

Arabs and Jews easily ignited. Arab riots in 1929, after a dispute about Jewish access to the Western Wall of the Temple, led the British, empowered by League of Nations mandate to maintain law and order, to announce a curtailment of Jewish immigration and land purchase.

The situation deteriorated during the following decade. Arab attacks against Jewish individuals and settlements increased. The Zionist movement split between those who advocated a policy of *havlagah* (self-restraint) and those who preferred active retaliation against the Arabs; another point of dispute was between those who, like Chaim Weizmann (see above, p. 168), believed in working with the British authorities while opposing their policies, and those who insisted that compromise with the Arabs or the British was futile if a Jewish state was to be achieved. Finally, the Union of Zionist Revisionists, founded by Vladimir Jabotinsky, withdrew from the Zionist movement and formed its own organization and military cadres. Jabotinsky recognized the Arab attachment to the land, and believed that only by force – by an 'iron wall' – could the idea of a Jewish state become reality.

In 1936, an Arab general strike was followed by a guerrilla revolt. The Jews, the British and the moderate Arab leadership were its targets. At the height of the disturbances, in 1937, a British commission of enquiry (the Peel Commission) proposed that Palestine be partitioned into Jewish and Arab states, with a contiguous British zone. The official Zionist leadership, after some sharp debate, cautiously accepted the proposal, which the Arabs rejected, but the disagreement was academic. Another world war was looming, and Britain, anxious not to forfeit Arab sympathy, in 1939 published the last in a series of White Papers about Palestine. This one rejected the option of partition; anticipated an independent Palestine in ten years; and limited future Jewish immigration to an additional 75,000. Coming at a time when hundreds of thousands of Jewish refugees were desperately trying to escape from Europe, the White Paper succeeded in provoking almost total Jewish opposition.

Nevertheless, many Jews of the *yishuv* enlisted in the British army, and a Jewish Brigade fought in the European campaigns towards the war's end. The British general election of 1945 was

an overwhelming success for the Labour Party, up to then sympathetic to Zionism. But the foreign secretary, Ernest Bevin,
obdurately insisted upon implementing the 1939 White Paper,
even though some 250,000 Holocaust survivors were languishing
in European DP (displaced persons) camps. Those who tried to
enter Palestine illegally were sent back to Europe or interned on
Cyprus, behind barbed wire again.

Feelings in the *yishuv* ran high. The Revisionist movement
launched terrorist attacks against British personnel and instal-
lations, and the British responded by trying to curb the activities
of the official Zionist militia, the *Haganah* ('defence'). International sympathy sided with the *yishuv*'s struggle for independence, and the British government, in the face of an intractable
situation, turned the question of Palestine's future over to the
United Nations. On 29 November 1947 the General Assembly
voted by thirty-three votes to thirteen, with the United States
and the Soviet Union in accord, to partition Palestine between
the Arabs and the Jews.

As the British army prepared to evacuate Palestine, bands of
Arab guerrillas began to harass Jewish settlers and ambush
convoys. The *Haganah*, for its part, tried to keep the roads open
between settlements, especially the highway linking Jerusalem
with the coastal plain. Once the State of Israel had been officially
proclaimed, the forces of five neighbouring Arab countries
attacked. Despite being heavily outnumbered and poorly
equipped, the Israeli army displayed, in the fighting which
followed, the bravery, verve and morale which have become its
hallmarks. By the time a series of armistice agreements were
signed between Israel and the various Arab governments between
February and July 1949, the Israelis had established themselves
over 8,000 square miles of Palestine (in contrast to the 6,200
square miles allocated by the UN partition plan), but had not been
able to wrest back the Old City of Jerusalem, occupied by the
British-trained and -officered Arab legion, and then annexed,
along with the West Bank, by the kingdom of Jordan. A legacy of
Israel's War of Independence, far more serious than the persistent
refusal of the Arab countries to recognize the State of Israel, or
the temporary loss of old Jerusalem, was the moral and humanitarian problem of some half a million Palestinian refugees who

fled the battle areas, either in anticipation of a quick Arab success, or because they feared the outcome of a Jewish victory.

In May 1949, just a few days short of the first anniversary of her declaration of independence, Israel was admitted as the fifty-ninth member of the United Nations. An intensive period of state-building and expansion followed, remarkable by any standards, and astonishing in a people who had so recently suffered the crushing losses of the Holocaust. The 'ingathering of the exiles', as the traditional liturgy phrases it, was the first priority. Jews were brought in from the DP camps and from eastern Europe. Thousands of English-speaking immigrants, attracted by the idea of rebuilding the ancient Jewish homeland, came from the UK, South Africa and America. Most of all, the Jews in Arab lands, their safety now a matter of concern, arrived by special airlifts from Iraq, Libya and Yemen, to be followed within a few years by large contingents from Morocco, Tunisia and Egypt. At the beginning of 1948 there were 630,000 Jews in the *yishuv*; by 1952, Israel's Jewish population had doubled.

To absorb this increased population and find it employment in a tiny country, with limited natural resources, surrounded by hostile neighbours, would not have been possible without the educational and technological foundations already laid in the pre-state days, and without the 'melting-pot', vocational role of the army, which took in young conscripts from a hundred different countries and backgrounds, and moulded them into highly motivated Israeli citizens. Intensive agriculture and advanced scientific planning enabled Israel to make effective use of Diaspora fundraising, American government aid and German war reparations (negotiated amidst great controversy in 1952 by prime minister Ben-Gurion), in order to develop as a progressive, widely acclaimed parliamentary democracy – the only one in the Middle East.

Foreign policy success was more elusive. Arab intransigence utilized the plight of Palestinian refugees, lingering in United Nations-funded camps, as a *casus belli*. Persistent terrorist incursions from the Gaza Strip prompted Israel, in October 1956, to collude with France and Great Britain, who were both smarting from President Nasser's nationalization of the Suez Canal, in order to mount the Sinai campaign. American pressure forced

Israel to withdraw from her territorial gains. Until his death in 1970, it was Gamal Nasser's personality that dominated Middle-Eastern politics. During the sixties, Israel's euphoric rate of development inevitably slowed; disappointed western immigrants left the country in greater numbers than newcomers arrived, and the first social tensions surfaced between Ashkenazi Jews, whose predominance in politics, industry, the military and the bureaucracy derived from pre-state days, and the Sephardim, who were generally less well educated and less vocationally adaptable, but who by now constituted 50 per cent of the country's Jewish population. Nasser read the signs, came to the wrong conclusions, and in May 1967, having reached diplomatic and military agreements with Syria and Jordan, he closed the Gulf of Aqaba to Israeli shipping. Arab propaganda triumphantly predicted the imminent destruction of Zionism, while vain attempts were made by neutral countries to devise some negotiating formula to save Israel from what appeared to be inevitable catastrophe.

In the event, between 6 and 11 June 1967 – known as the Six Day War – Israel won one of the swiftest and most stunning victories in the history of warfare, which left her, before the Arabs sued for a cease-fire, within striking distance of both Cairo and Damascus; bridging the Suez Canal; and in control of Sinai, Gaza, the Golan Heights – from which Syrian artillery had regularly bombarded the kibbutzim below – and all of the West Bank. The retaking of the Old City of Jerusalem, and the return of the Western Wall of the Temple, especially stirred the imagination. They were heady days.

Unfortunately it can be said of Israel, as it was of Hannibal, that she knows how to win a victory but not how to utilize it. Convinced that her enemies would now sign comprehensive peace treaties – when, in fact, the Arab countries reiterated their non-recognition – Israel administered the newly acquired territories, internally debated formulas which weighed the return of the land against greater border security, was drawn into a costly war of attrition along the Suez Canal in 1969–70, and in the early hours of the Yom Kippur War of October 1973 might have succumbed to a surprise, but predictable, joint attack by Egypt and Syria. It required feats of great valour, and heavy casualties, before the battle was turned to Israel's military advantage, but not before the Egyptian army had salvaged some of its honour by recrossing the Suez Canal.

Diplomatic stalemate once again followed the cease-fire, but with the significant difference this time that Arab economic pressure on western countries, with oil as the weapon, had the effect of focusing more critical attention on Israel, in particular her response to emergent Palestinian nationalism. The appearance of PLO (Palestine Liberation Organization) chairman Yasser Arafat, with a gun in his belt, at the podium of the United Nations General Assembly in 1974, and the obsequious applause; and the UN resolution a year later equating Zionism with racism, represented, according to one's perspective, either the high moral concern of many of the member states for the plight of the Palestinians, or their craven capitulation before the threat of oil blackmail.

In 1977, with a solution to the future of the occupied territories no clearer, and its credibility weakened by a series of scandals, the Labour-dominated alignment, which had governed Israel from the beginning, was defeated in the general election by a Likud coalition led by Menachem Begin's Herut ('Freedom') party. Begin himself had an ambivalent reputation: first as a pre-state terrorist, shunned by the Zionist leadership, whose breakaway Irgun group had been responsible for the massacre of Arab civilians at the village of Deir Yassin during the War of Independence, but who had, since the formation of the state, conducted himself, in the long years of political opposition, with punctilious regard for parliamentary democracy. As the ideological heir to Jabotinsky's Revisionists, the Herut party made no secret of its wish to retain control of the West Bank, henceforth designated by the party by the biblical names of Judea and Samaria.

In November 1977, President Anwar Sadat of Egypt, with a boldness unique in Arab–Israeli relations, paid a historic visit to Jerusalem. It was the start of a negotiating process, supervised by the Americans, which culminated in March 1979, in the Camp David accords, when Sadat and Begin signed the first peace treaty between Israel and her most influential Arab neighbour. According to the terms, Egypt would receive back Sinai, and the future of the West Bank would be determined after a five-year period of progressive autonomy. It soon became apparent that prime minister Begin felt free to interpret the clauses dealing with the West Bank in such a way that eventual Palestinian self-determination would be impossible. Jewish settlers, many of them religious fundamentalists or supporters of the old Jabotinsky dream of a Jewish state in *all* of biblical Palestine, were attracted to new development towns by government loans and other inducements. Military rule over the Arab population became increasingly severe.

In spite of international criticism, as well as the anxieties voiced within Israel about the corrupting effects of a continued occupation and a deteriorating economy, Mr Begin's popularity with Sephardi voters ensured a second term of office for Likud. Colonization of the West Bank accelerated at a pace which fuelled hostility among the one million Arab inhabitants, whose sympathies were overwhelmingly with the PLO. Since being driven out of Jordan by King Hussein in 1970, the PLO had established itself in Lebanon as a state-within-a-state. From there it conducted its terrorist campaign against Israel, provoking ever heavier reprisals. Accepted by a growing number of governments as the official representative of the Palestinian people, the PLO refused to recognize Israel or to modify those articles of its charter which called for the destruction of the Zionist entity and its replacement by a binational state. Huge subventions from Arab countries enabled the PLO to acquire sophisticated weaponry from the Communist bloc, with which it harassed Israel's northern border until a cease-fire was negotiated in the summer of 1981.

In June 1982, using an assassination attempt on Israel's ambassador to London as the pretext (although it was a breakaway terrorist group which was responsible for that action), Israel invaded Lebanon, in order to destroy the military and political credibility of the PLO. The architect of the invasion was defence minister Arik Sharon, a flamboyant and controversial former general. Effectively utilizing its superior firepower and control of the skies, the Israeli army soon attained its stated objective of clearing a forty-kilometre zone from the northern border, and advanced on Lebanon's capital, Beirut. The residue of the PLO fighting force – about 7,000 guerrillas – was besieged in the Muslim sector of the city for three months.

During that time, intensely critical coverage of the siege by the international media, and growing doubts at home about the aims, scope and implementation of the original invasion plan, produced in Israel the unprecedented situation of public opposition being voiced even while her citizen army was engaged in fighting. Jewish Diaspora communities, usually instinctively supportive of Israel, were equally divided in their reactions.

In August, after a particularly heavy Israeli bombing of west Beirut, an agreement was reached whereby the disarmed Palestinian fighters were evacuated from the city by sea and by land. Soon afterwards Lebanon's new president, Bashir Gemayal – of the Christian Phalange movement, which had maintained ties with Israel since the Lebanese civil war began in 1975 – was assassinated at his headquarters. Phalangist troops then entered the Palestinian refugee camps of Sabra and Shatilla, under Israeli army supervision, purportedly to weed out any remaining PLO guerrillas, but in reality to exact vengeance. Between 800 and 1,000 Palestinian civilians were massacred before the Israelis belatedly intervened. The shock and revulsion which the massacre, over the Jewish New Year, prompted, led to a remarkable demonstration in Tel-Aviv against the war by an estimated 400,000 Israelis. As Israel was drawn ever deeper into the quagmire of Lebanese factional politics, a broken Mr Begin ignominiously resigned, and a rigorous commission of inquiry into the refugee camp massacres censured the defence minister, the chief of staff and other senior officers, for failures of command. Although the PLO had been damaged as a military and political force, Palestinian nationalism on the West Bank did not abate. It was no surprise that in the 1984 general election the Labour alignment, committed to the principle of territorial compromise in the search for peace, emerged with the largest number of parliamentary seats, although not enough for an overall majority.

At the time of writing, in the summer of 1985, the government of Mr Shimon Peres has honoured its election pledge to withdraw from Lebanon. Instead of the PLO, Israel is faced on her northern border by the chilling spectre of Shi'ite Moslem fanaticism, with volunteers happy to earn martyrdom in suicide attacks. Lebanon is subsiding into sectarian anarchy, with Syria still manipulating the reins of power, as she did before Israel's misconceived invasion. Despite the usual round of frantic Middle-

Eastern diplomatic activity, no Arab leaders have shown themselves ready to follow Egypt's example and engage in negotiations with Israel in order to reach a mutually acceptable solution to the perennial Palestinian problem.

It is one of history's painful ironies that the Jews, for centuries denied full self-expression or a state of their own, should be locked in conflict with another people equally and as sincerely attached to the land of Palestine. A resolution of that conflict would enable Israeli expertise to benefit the whole region, to everyone's advantage. Failure to resolve the conflict will leave Israel as an embattled outpost of western values in a hostile environment, and the Zionist enterprise, so bold in conception, so vigorous in execution, and such a source of pride to most Jews, will yet remain only partially fulfilled.

CONCLUSION

Having outlined the course of Jewish history from Abraham's time to the present, it only remains to draw the strands together, and to offer a few tentative, general observations about the Jewish people, their religion, and their expectations in the closing years of the twentieth century.

The state of Israel has been in existence for nearly forty years, but the Jews remain essentially a Diaspora people, as they have been since the sixth century BCE. Of the fourteen million Jews in the world, slightly more than one-fifth live in Israel; there are more Jews in New York than in all of the Jewish homeland, and with an estimated 5.8 million Jews, the United States has by far the largest single community in the world. Between them, the United States, Canada (305,000) and Latin America (an estimated 617,000) aggregate more than 65 per cent of world Jewry.

In Europe, by contrast, the mass migrations of the late nineteenth century followed by the Nazi genocide have led to the virtual disappearance of former centres of Jewish population in Poland, the Hapsburg empire and the east. Perhaps 80,000 Jews remain in Hungary and 60,000 in Romania. There are still over two millions Jews in the USSR, mainly residing in Moscow, Leningrad and Kiev, where tsarist legislation tried to prevent them from settling. Although the Soviet constitution guarantees freedom of belief and worship, Communist policy towards its Jewish citizens has displayed all the paradoxes of the tsarist regime, veering between attempts at assimilation and using the Jews as scapegoats for economic or political shortcomings. Joseph Stalin was quick to recognize the State of Israel, using it as a means of countering British influence in the Middle East, but the last years of his rule were marked by the executions of eminent Yiddish writers, the Slansky show-trial in Prague, which alleged a plot by international Jewish capitalists, Zionists and American intelligence agencies to subvert socialism, and the so-called 'Doctors' Plot' of 1953, in which Jewish physicians, supposedly bribed by the West, were said to have conspired to murder Soviet leaders; shortly after Stalin's death the plot was admitted to have been a fabrication.

Since 1967, Soviet courtship of the Arab world has led to a virulent anti-Zionist campaign which equated Israel with Nazism and Zionism with racism. One unlooked-for result of this propaganda has been to revive a sense of Jewish identity and nationalist sentiment in Soviet Jewry. Many thousands of Jews have risked imprisonment, loss of livelihood or banishment in order to apply for permission to emigrate to Israel, and the cause of these 'refuseniks' has been taken up by western Jewish communities and civil rights organizations. At the same time there has been an upsurge of interest in Jewish history and tradition, despite official antipathy to any kind of religious education. Clearly the authorities are concerned that such Jewish recidivism, after more than sixty years of Communist indoctrination, could have repercussions on other national and religious minorities within the Soviet Union; the sharp fluctuations in the number of Jews allowed to leave at any given time depends not only on the state of relations with the West, but also, perhaps, on whether the Soviet government is ready to lose some of its most qualified citizens as the price of siphoning off potentially troublesome dissidents.

The largest community in non-Communist Europe is in France, with 550,000 Jews. The majority are Sephardim from North Africa, who became French citizens during colonial rule there. In Great Britain Anglo-Jewry, optimistically numbered at half a million in the post-war years, is now more realistically assessed at between 350,000 and 400,000; it is, in common with other Ashkenazi communities of Europe, an elderly population, with a declining birth-rate. Jews have almost entirely vacated the Arab world, although significant residual communities remain in Turkey (30,000), Iran (75,000) and Morocco (30,000). The two other countries with noteworthy Jewish populations are the former British colonies of Australia (72,000) and South Africa (118,000).

The most striking feature about modern Jewish demography is

that few people today live where their grandparents did a century ago. The balance has shifted, probably for ever, away from the ancient Jewish centres in Europe and the east. And as the geographical location has changed, so too have the occupations traditionally undertaken by Jews. The Jewish proletariat has steadily diminished, and the majority of Diaspora Jews have become middle-class. Only in Israel can Jewish factory workers, farmers and artisans be found in large numbers. Elsewhere in the west they tend to be self-employed businessmen, white-collar workers, or in one of the professions, such as medicine, law, accountancy or teaching; journalism, the theatre, cinema and the performing arts have also been attractive, relatively open, careers for Jews in the last century.

The struggle for emancipation having been long since concluded – although sporadic manifestations of economic, social or professional anti-Semitism still occur in even the most enlightened countries – the Jew has steadily been acclimatized to the language and *mores* of his chosen environment. It is only the devoutly Orthodox who remain apart, in order to preserve their distinctive way of life. Yiddish, once the vernacular of the European masses, is fast disappearing, except for a few colloquialisms which have been taken into everyday speech. Owing to the influence of Israel, Hebrew has once again become the basic language of Jewish education, after the native tongue of Diaspora communities.

In the secular, modern world, where religion is a matter of personal choice rather than definition, Judaism is no longer the all-embracing amalgam of faith, practice and behaviour that it was for the vast majority of Jews until the French Revolution. The daily routine of observance has been reduced for almost all, except the ultra-Orthodox or *Chasidic* sects to, at best, a weekly acknowledgement of the sabbath and the celebration of the major festivals and folk-customs, such as bar-mitzvah. A detectable swing towards fundamentalism and Jewish assertiveness among sections of Jewish youth is probably due – like the growth of fringe sects and flirtations with eastern religions – to the attempt to give order and coherence to fragmented modern life.

Another result of successful integration is that previous restraints against intermarriage or assimilation have lost much of their force. It has been calculated that in America one in three marriages involving a Jew is with a partner of another religion, and the statistic is almost as high in Great Britain. Even in those cases where the non-Jewish partner converts, a Jewish birth-rate which is usually below the national average means that most Diaspora communities, even the most vigorous, are numerically static.

It has been said, in explanation of the decline in religious observance, that it is hard to have faith after Auschwitz. But the truth is that Judaism today is no more or less theologically credible and the problem of theodicy no greater, than they would have been at the time of the wars against Rome or during the Cossack massacres of 1648. In reality, since the eighteenth century Judaism has had to face the competing claims of science, atheism, humanism, political creeds and a world view that has become increasingly man-centred rather than God-centred, and her response to the challenge has been as varied, and as mixed in its success, as that of Christianity.

The spiritual vacuum has been filled, to a large extent, by the State of Israel. Almost all modern Jews support, identify with, and share vicariously in, the triumphs and tribulations of the Jewish state. Zionism has been a bond for Diaspora Jewry, and a source of pride, hope and self-respect – a symbol of the Jewish will to survive and the determination that, in a popular formula-tion, 'Hitler will not be granted a posthumous victory'. But commendable though the concept of Jewish survival may be, and mutually sustaining though the Israel-Diaspora relationship is, it has to be said that, in philosophical and theological terms, if survival is postulated as the ultimate goal, then it precludes any higher moral value, and that to give one's total loyalty to the idea of the state is not only an embarrassing nineteenth-century anachronism but also, by Judaism's ethical standards, a form of idolatry. The survival of the Jewish people, through its many vicissitudes over the centuries, has clearly owed more to fidelity to religious teachings than it has to attachment to a strip of land.

It would be tempting, looking at Judaism and Jewish society today, to concur with the historian Arnold Toynbee's judgement that it is a 'fossilized religion', and to conclude that it will inevit-ably be swallowed up by assimilation, as were the ten lost tribes

2,700 years ago. Such pessimism about the future has been a recurring motif in Jewish thought. The biblical prophets were convinced that they were addressing generations imminently doomed to dispersion and assimilation; the Mishnah was compiled because of the fear that Jewish law would otherwise disappear; Moses Maimonides undertook his *Mishneh Torah* with conviction that he represented the last generation of Jewish scholarship; the exiles from Spain lamented a lost golden age; the Chasidic leader Levi Yitzchak of Berdichev put God on trial for all the sufferings and persecution He had permitted to fall on the Jews.

Yet, in spite of everything, Judaism, that unique combination of religion and tribal unity, still continues to exist, and still makes its distinctive contribution to civilization. To the Jew of faith, that is a sure sign of divine guidance over the destiny of the 'chosen people'. To the neutral observer it is a remarkable saga of tenacity, resilience and loyalty to the ancient tradition which gave monotheism to the world. God, Torah and Israel – faith, law and people – have always been the entwined, three-fold components of Judaism. The emphasis may alter according to time and circumstances, but there is an underlying continuity. It is this ability to adapt while still retaining its essential identity which gives one cautious hope that Judaism – the history of a religious culture and a people more than thirty-two centuries old – will survive into the future for as long as humanity continues to acknowledge that man does not live by bread alone.

PART II

THE LITERATURE OF JUDAISM

CHAPTER ONE   THE JEWISH BIBLE

Judaism is a 'revealed religion', in the sense that it bases itself on a literature which it regards as divinely inspired. That literature is commonly called the Old Testament.

It is, however, important to recognize that 'Old Testament' is a Christian term, with implications foreign to Judaism. For, since 'testament' means 'covenant', it implies that God's Covenant with Israel was in some sense superseded by another with the Christian Church, which is the subject of the New Testament, so that the earlier collection of writings is related to the later as prelude to sequel, or preparation to fulfilment. This view tends to colour the Christian approach to the Old Testament in ways that are misleading for an understanding of the place it holds in Judaism.

From a Jewish point of view, the Old Testament needs to be interpreted and amplified (and much of the subsequent Jewish literature is such an interpretation and amplification), but it does not look beyond itself to another revelation, and the Covenant between God and Israel, which is its central theme, has never ceased. To Jews, therefore, it is simply the Bible or – to obviate confusion with the Christian use of that term – the Jewish Bible, or the Hebrew Bible, Hebrew being the language in which it is written, apart from a few chapters and verses in the related Semitic language of Aramaic.

The word 'Bible' comes from the Latin *biblia* ('little books'), and derives ultimately from the Greek name for an ancient Syrian city renowned for its papyrus industry: Byblos. This fact should remind us that when we speak of the Hebrew Bible we are not dealing with a single book, but with a whole library. Indeed, the Jewish Bible comprises virtually all that has survived of ancient

Hebrew literature down to about 150 BCE. (It is known that some writings failed to survive; these include the book of Jashar, mentioned in Joshua 10:13, and the book of Chronicles of the Kings of Israel, mentioned in I Kings 16:27.)

There was, however, a process of selection. Only those books were included which were believed to have been written by prophets under the guidance of the 'holy spirit', that is, under divine inspiration. Thus some books, extant at the end of the biblical period, were excluded on the ground that they failed to satisfy that condition – about these we shall have more to say in the next chapter. Only the selected books were officially declared sacred and so became part of the 'canon' (the root-meaning of this word is 'yardstick' or 'standard') of the Jewish Bible. According to Jewish tradition they number twenty-four; but some of these, such as the book of the twelve 'Minor Prophets', can be further sub-divided, yielding a total of thirty-nine.

The process of canonization seems to have occurred in three stages: first the Pentateuch, then the Prophets, then the Writings. This threefold division, obscured in the Christian arrangement of the books, is preserved in the Jewish arrangement and explains yet another name by which Jews commonly refer to their Bible: the *Tanach*. This is an abbreviation composed of the initial letters of the Hebrew words, *Torah* (Teaching), *Nevi'im* (Prophets) and *Ketuvim* (Writings).

TORAH

The word Torah originally referred to an individual teaching communicated to the people by a spokesman of God, such as a prophet or priest, but it came to be used collectively for the entire corpus of such teachings which, it was believed, God had revealed, through Moses, to the Israelites at Mount Sinai. Since these teachings consist largely of commandments, the word Torah is commonly, though somewhat misleadingly, translated as 'law'; and since these teachings constitute the core of the first division of the Bible, comprising the books of Genesis, Exodus, Leviticus, Numbers and Deuteronomy, the word Torah also serves to designate that unit, otherwise known as the Pentateuch (from the Greek for 'five scrolls') or the Five Books of Moses.

The latter name reflects the belief that these books were actually written by Moses. The Pentateuch itself does not make such a claim; it is an anonymous work, although many passages in it are introduced by such phrases as, 'The Lord spoke to Moses, saying'. Nevertheless, the belief in its Mosaic authorship is ancient. There are allusions to it in the later books of the Bible itself; the Rabbis took it for granted even when they did not assert it explicitly; it went virtually unquestioned (among Jews as well as Christians) until relatively recent times; and among Orthodox Jews it is still commonly believed as an article of faith.

However, modern biblical scholarship tells a more complex story. According to this, the Pentateuch is a composite work which did not attain its final form until some time after the Babylonian Exile. Although many details of this theory are still in dispute, it is generally agreed that at least four 'sources' can be broadly identified on the basis of differences in language, style and outlook, as well as tell-tale allusions to historical conditions. Of these sources, the two oldest are believed to date from approximately 1000–800 BCE; the third, comprising the book of Deuteronomy, from the reign of Josiah in the seventh century BCE (see above, p. 45); while the fourth, including most of the priestly legislation, has generally been regarded as post-exilic.

The dating of the written documents is, however, not as significant as it may seem, since the writers often made use of antecedent oral traditions of much greater antiquity. Some of the Genesis narratives, for example, are explicable only on the assumption that they rest on authentic traditions going back to the age of the Patriarchs. That being so, it is possible that some of the laws attributed to Moses may have originated in the wilderness period, although which of them, and how much change they underwent subsequently, is in most cases impossible to determine.

The book of Genesis opens with an account of the creation of the world and the beginnings of human life and civilization which, though in many respects reminiscent of ancient Mesopotamian mythology, has a grandeur all its own. The Patriarchal narratives follow, and occupy the rest of the book. They are human stories, of epic proportions and deep psychological insights, raised to suprahistorical significance by their underlying theme of God's Covenant with Abraham and his descendants, and the inexorable working out of the divine plan, which is often imperilled by human foibles, but never ultimately thwarted.

The book of Exodus moves rapidly from the enslavement of Jacob's descendants in Egypt to their liberation under the leadership of Moses and the theophany at Mount Sinai, where the Covenant is dramatically reaffirmed and re-enacted, and the entire people pledge themselves to obey its laws.

From this point onwards, through the rest of the Pentateuch, narration becomes sparser, and legislation increasingly takes its place. Certain episodes, such as the construction of the Tabernacle, the reconnaissance mission of the twelve spies and the Balaam story, are recounted in detail and at length; but the main emphasis is now on commandments. Some of these are general moral precepts. Some are intended to regulate social relationships and belong to what we would call civil and criminal law. Many concern the sacred calendar, the sacrificial cult and the laws of ritual purity and impurity. A major purpose of these laws is the attainment of 'holiness', that is, separation from anything that is spiritually or morally debasing; for the Israelites are to be 'a kingdom of priests, and a holy nation' (Exodus 19:6).

The book of Deuteronomy recapitulates the legislation, and to a minor extent the narratives, of the preceding books, in the framework of the farewell discourses of Moses, with whose death the book ends.

PROPHETS

The second division of the Jewish Bible, known as the Prophets, falls into two parts: the Former Prophets and the Latter Prophets. The first, comprising the books of Joshua, Judges, I and II Samuel, and I and II Kings, is a collection of historical narratives written in a prophetic spirit: they not only relate events and actions, but evaluate them according to the divine guidance they show and the moral lessons to be learned from them.

Like the Pentateuch, this series of books is anonymous. An old Jewish tradition attributes it to Joshua, Samuel and Jeremiah. Modern scholarship regards it as emanating from the same kind of sources as the Pentateuch, particularly the author of Deuteronomy, or a school of writers sharing his outlook; but it

also utilizes, especially in Samuel and Kings, otherwise un-
preserved court chronicles from the days of the monarchy.

The book of Joshua begins where the Pentateuch leaves off,
relating the Israelites' conquest of Canaan under the leadership
of Moses's successor, Joshua. The book of Judges recounts
episodes from the ensuing period, including the exploits of such
heroes as Deborah, Gideon and Samson. The books of Samuel
begin with the life story of the prophet Samuel and the institution
of the monarchy, towards which it records two opposing attitudes,
favourable and unfavourable, presumably emanating from different source materials or traditions. The books then chronicle the
royal careers of Saul and David, the conflict between them, and
David's friendship with Saul's son Jonathan. I and II Kings
continue in the same vein, relating the story of the reign of
Solomon and the building of the Temple, then tracing the histories of the Two Kingdoms down to the conquest of Samaria by
the Assyrians and that of Judah by the Babylonians.

The subdivision known as the Latter Prophets largely comprises
collections of prophetic speeches committed to writing either by
the prophets themselves or by their disciples. These 'writing
prophets' flourished from the eighth down to the fifth century
BCE. There are of course many individual differences between
them, but they also have much in common. They are all charismatic preachers, impelled by a conviction of having been personally commissioned to act as God's spokesmen, rather than
cultic functionaries, though some of them may have been, inci-
dentally, professional prophets in that sense. They are all interpreters of current events in the light of general religious and
moral principles. They are all, in varying degrees, critics of
contemporary society, fearless in delivering their message, however unpopular it may be. And they all employ powerful rhetoric,
often rising to the heights of poetry.

Frequently occurring themes are: God's unity and majesty, His
concern for all mankind, His special love for Israel, His exacting
moral demands; denunciations of idolatry, immorality, injustice,
empty ritualism, reliance on power politics; threats of impending
disaster by way of divine retribution; appeals for repentance
through renewed loyalty to the Covenant, compassion for the
weak, social justice; emphasis on Israel's special responsibility as

God's 'chosen people'; visions of a golden future when God's power will triumph, Israel will be loyal to Him and mankind will be redeemed by Him: an age of universal righteousness and peace.

This section of the Bible is further divided into the Major Prophets and the Minor Prophets, a distinction which refers not to their relative importance, but to the relative sizes of the books. The Major Prophets are three large books: Isaiah, Jeremiah and Ezekiel. The book of Isaiah contains in its first thirty-nine chapters the prophecies of Isaiah, son of Amoz, who flourished in Jerusalem in the second half of the eighth century, and in its remaining chapters, those of one or more later prophets, principally a nameless one who prophesied during the Babylonian Exile and who is commonly referred to as the Second Isaiah or Deutero-Isaiah. Jeremiah prophesied in Jerusalem from the reign of Josiah until the destruction of the Temple by the Babylonians. Ezekiel prophesied during the Babylonian Exile.

The Minor Prophets are a collection of twelve short books which include the prophecies of Amos, a Judean who preached in the northern kingdom of Israel in about the middle of the eighth century; Hosea, a citizen of the northern kingdom who prophesied a little later; Micah, who was active in Jerusalem towards the end of the eighth century; and the post-exilic prophets Haggai, Zechariah and Malachi. The book of Zechariah is regarded by modern scholars as a composite work, incorporating some apocalyptic passages from a later age. One book in this section, that of Jonah, differs from all the rest in that it is not a collection of prophecies but a short story, probably post-exilic, about a prophet who, after resisting and evading God's command to preach repentance to the pagan citizens of Nineveh, finally carries out his mission and thereby saves the city from destruction. The other books in this section – mostly of uncertain date – contain the prophecies of Joel, Obadiah, Nahum, Habakkuk and Zephaniah.

WRITINGS

The third division of the Jewish Bible, known as the Writings or Hagiographa ('holy writings'), is a miscellany. In it, the first place is occupied by the book of Psalms, a collection of 150 poems or songs, all or most of which were probably composed, or came to be used, for the purpose of liturgical recitation, especially in the Temple. They represent a great variety of moods and themes: individual and national; praise, thanksgiving and lament; celebrations of kingship; laudations of wisdom and Torah. Many of them are of great literary beauty and express a profound religious faith.

About half of them are superscribed 'A Psalm of David', which early led to the assumption, later extended to *all* the Psalms, that King David was their author. Modern scholars, without ruling out the possibility that the Psalms may include *some* composed by David, believe that they stem from various periods, ranging from remote antiquity to the post-exilic age.

The book of Proverbs, which follows, is largely an assemblage of religious, moralistic and prudential maxims, evidently intended for the instruction of the young, though it includes some longer passages in praise of, and even hypostatizing, wisdom. Its superscription, 'The Proverbs of Solomon the son of David, king of Israel', has traditionally been taken to indicate its authorship, but modern scholars tend to assign to the book either a very early date, even as early as the Monarchy, or a very late one, a key issue being whether it shows signs of Greek influence.

Next is the book of Job, which deals with the problem of theodicy, that is, how and whether the suffering of the innocent can be reconciled with God's justice. The hero of the book is a man of exemplary virtue who suffers impoverishment, bereavement and sickness, and the problem is explored in a series of poetic dialogues between him and his 'comforters'. These dialogues are set in the framework of a prose prologue and epilogue concerning a wager between God and Satan as to whether there is such a thing as disinterested righteousness. The book is remarkable for its philosophical profundity and for its boldness in challenging conventional beliefs. It is probably post-exilic but may contain earlier elements.

After it come the so-called Five Scrolls: the Song of Songs, Ruth, Lamentations, Ecclesiastes and Esther. The Song of Songs is a series of lyrical and erotic love poems which Jewish tradition has ascribed to King Solomon and, in order to justify its place in the canon, has seen as an allegory about the love between God and Israel. Modern scholars tend to place its final composition in the post-exilic period.

The book of Ruth is a short story, set in the period of the Judges, about a Moabitess who marries an Israelite and, on his death, insists on returning with her mother-in-law Naomi to Judah, where she becomes the wife of Naomi's kinsman Boaz and an ancestress of King David. Traditionally attributed to the prophet Samuel and regarded as historical, modern scholars are agreed that it is considerably later than the Monarchy, if not post-exilic, and tend to view it as fictional.

The book of Lamentations is a collection of poetic elegies bewailing the destruction of Jerusalem and calling for repentance so that its fortunes may be restored. Its traditional attribution to the prophet Jeremiah is considered improbable by modern scholars; but it may have been composed in part by eye-witnesses of the Babylonian conquest.

The book of Ecclesiastes is prefaced: 'The words of Kohelet, the son of David, king in Jerusalem.' Tradition identifies Kohelet with Solomon; modern scholarship regards the book as post-exilic but with older elements incorporated. It is a series of reflections, pessimistic in tone, about the seeming futility of life, but it ends, somewhat abruptly, with a reaffirmation of faith. Along with Proverbs and Job, it is the chief example of 'Wisdom literature' in the Bible.

The book of Esther is a short story, set in Persia, about a plot to exterminate the Jews of the empire, engineered by Haman, the chief minister, and foiled by a combination of lucky chance and the intervention of Esther, the emperor's Jewish wife, in collusion with her cousin and guardian, Mordecai. To celebrate and commemorate the deliverance, the feast of *Purim* is instituted. Traditionally taken as historical, modern scholars are inclined to regard the book as fictional (although remarkably apt – extravagant details apart – as a paradigm of the Jewish experience of persecution) and as possibly reflecting the intense nationalism of the Maccabean period.

The remaining books of the Hagiographa are Daniel, Ezra and Nehemiah, and I and II Chronicles. The book of Daniel begins with a short story, set in the court of King Nebuchadnezzar and his successors Belshazzar and Darius, which relates how Daniel and his companions, Judean exiles, are miraculously saved from death. This is followed by a series of apocalyptic visions about the rise and fall of the 'four world empires'. Jewish tradition attributes this book to 'the men of the Great Assembly'; modern scholarship assigns it to the Maccabean age, though the story part may be somewhat earlier.

The books of Ezra and Nehemiah are historical narratives, partly in the form of autobiographical memoirs, concerning the return from Babylon, the rebuilding of the Temple and (chiefly) the reconstruction of Jerusalem – both its walls and its religious life – under the leadership of Ezra and Nehemiah. These narratives raise many perplexing chronological problems and are therefore difficult to date; they were probably written fairly late in the Persian period, perhaps even completed early in the Greek period.

Written about the same time, I and II Chronicles – after some lengthy genealogical lists which begin with Adam – retell the history of the Jewish people from the reign of David to the end of the Babylonian Exile, but with significant differences from the Samuel–Kings account. There are some startling omissions and elaborate amplification, and the chronicler's approach is Priestly rather than Deuteronomic: he focuses on the Temple rather than the Monarchy (except that he idealizes David), and he virtually ignores the northern kingdom.

As this survey has shown, the Jewish Bible is rich and varied in content and style. Almost every literary genre is represented: mythology, folklore, epic, genealogy, history, autobiography, short story, legislation, prophecy, apocalypse, epigram, philosophy, dramatic dialogue and religious and secular poetry. In religious outlook, too, the Bible exhibits diversity, which is anything but surprising since it is the work of scores of writers and redactors, spanning a history of a thousand years – even longer, if the antecedent oral traditions are taken into account.

What nevertheless lends the Bible a kind of orchestral unity is the fact that it is dominated by a single theme, or group of themes; the one all-powerful, holy, righteous God, Creator of heaven and earth; His guiding and redeeming activity in the history of mankind in general and Israel in particular; and the way of life He demands from those who would worship Him and do His will.

Its grandeur, both as *religious* literature and simply as literature, has caused the Bible to be admired, revered and loved far beyond the confines of the people who produced it and of the Christian Church which adopted it. Already in ancient times it was translated into Greek, Aramaic, Syriac and Latin; in the Middle Ages it was translated into Arabic; and since the invention of printing it has been published in nearly a thousand other languages. But it is above all the Jews themselves who have preserved, cherished, pored over and interpreted it. It is the bedrock of Jewish education, thought and practice, and all subsequent Jewish literature is to a large extent a commentary on it.

THE BOOKS OF THE BIBLE ACCORDING TO THE
TRADITIONAL JEWISH ARRANGEMENT

PENTATEUCH			Genesis Exodus Leviticus Numbers Deuteronomy
PROPHETS	Former Prophets		Joshua Judges I & II Samuel I & II Kings
	Latter Prophets	*Major Prophets*	Isaiah Jeremiah Ezekiel
		Minor Prophets	Hosea Joel Amos Obadiah Jonah Micah Nahum Habakkuk Zephaniah Haggai Zechariah Malachi
WRITINGS			Psalms Proverbs Job
		Five Scrolls	Song of Songs Ruth Lamentations Ecclesiastes Esther
			Daniel Ezra & Nehemiah I & II Chronicles

CHAPTER TWO   NON-CANONICAL JEWISH LITERATURE OF THE GRAECO-ROMAN PERIOD

During the last centuries of the Second Temple period, and for some little time thereafter, a large number of books appeared, written by Jews in Hebrew, Aramaic or Greek, which were not admitted into the canon of the Jewish Bible, either because the canon was already closed or because they were not considered to possess the necessary credentials of divine inspiration.

Some of them did, however, gain canonical status in the Roman Catholic and Eastern Orthodox Churches, having been included among the books of the Old Testament in the Septuagint, a Greek translation of the Bible begun by the Jews of Alexandria about 250 BCE (see part I, chapter 5). They are known as the Apocrypha, which is Greek for 'hidden books'. Jewish tradition knows them as *Sefarim Chitzonim*, 'external books'. Although they exerted no direct influence on Rabbinic Judaism, and were preserved only by Christianity, they deserve some attention for their historical interest as well as for their literary and religious merit.

The most substantial of them, and the only one occasionally cited in Rabbinic Literature, is variously known as 'The Wisdom of Jesus Son of Sirach', 'Ben Sira' or Ecclesiasticus. It belongs to the genre of Wisdom literature and consists mainly of moralistic maxims in much the same spirit as the biblical book of Proverbs, but it also includes some hymns and historical narratives, and was written in Palestine shortly after 200 BCE. Similar in some ways, but more concerned with the philosophical interpretation of history and with life after death, is 'The Wisdom of Solomon', written in Alexandria, perhaps in the first century BCE.

History is represented in the Apocrypha by I and II Maccabees, which recount the events of the Maccabean Rebellion and the institution of the feast of Chanukkah. I Maccabees, which is the more soberly factual of the two books, begins its account with Alexander the Great and carries it down to the death of the Hasmonean ruler, Simeon. II Maccabees is more emotive and propagandistic. Both were written before 100 BCE, the former in Palestine, the latter in Egypt.

There are also some short stories, including Tobit and Judith, both probably dating from the Greek or, even earlier, the Persian period. The former is a travel-tale about a young man, Tobias, who, accompanied by his dog and a guide (who turns out to be the angel Raphael), discovers a cure for the blindness of his father Tobit, a Jewish exile in Nineveh. Judith, the heroine of the latter book, is a Jewish widow who saves her people by decapitating Holofernes, the commander of Nebuchadnezzar's invading army. In addition, the Apocrypha include some slighter short stories, as well as epistles, prayers, and imaginary amplifications of the biblical books of Esther and Ezra and, in one instance, apocalyptic visions.

Less well known, because not included in the Christian canon, is a collection of books known as the Pseudepigrapha because many of them were fictitiously attributed to ancient heroes. In general, the Pseudepigrapha are, compared with the Apocrypha, further removed from normative Judaism and show more extensively the influence of gnostic and sectarian movements, as well as traces of Christian editing.

Of the works included in this collection, perhaps the most appealing to the modern mind is *The Testaments of the Twelve Patriarchs*, which is an early example of the genre of Ethical Wills, and probably dates from somewhere between 150 BCE and 50 CE. It depicts the twelve sons of Jacob, one by one, as, in anticipation of their own deaths, they exhort their children concerning the sins they should avoid and the virtues they should practise. Of great interest for their eschatology, including the figure of the Messiah, are the books of *Enoch*, purporting to contain the apocalyptic visions of that ancestor of the human race who, according to Genesis 5:24, was believed to have ascended to heaven. I *Enoch* was preserved mainly in Ethiopic, as was the book of

Jubilees which, in the form of an angelic revelation to Moses, reviews the early history of mankind and of the Jewish people down to Moses, dating each event according to a precise chronology based on the jubilee cycle; it often differs from Pharisaic tradition in its interpretation of the Pentateuchal laws, including those appertaining to the sabbath and festivals.

The literature with which we are concerned in this chapter has been greatly enriched and illuminated by the discovery, since 1947, of a large quantity of ancient manuscripts in the Qumran caves northwest of the Dead Sea. It is now generally agreed among scholars that these Dead Sea Scrolls are the remnants of the library of a monastic sect which can probably be identified with the Essenes and which had its headquarters in that region from *c.* 130 BCE until 73 CE (see above, pp. 70 f.). Among them are two Isaiah scrolls and fragments of other biblical, apocryphal and pseudepigraphic books, some previously unknown.

They also include some of the writings of the community itself. Noteworthy among these are: a commentary on Habakkuk, which finds in that prophetic book cryptic hints by which contemporary events may be interpreted and future events predicted; a collection of *Thanksgiving Psalms*, which stress the certainty of the ultimate destruction of the ungodly; a *Manual of Discipline*, which states the ideals of the community, the rules its members must observe and the penalties for breaching them; and the *Scroll of the War of the Children of Light against the Children of Darkness*, known for short as the *War Scroll*, which derives from Daniel (11:40 ff.), the tactics of the forty-year war by which, in the eschatological age, the forces of evil will be finally defeated. These documents seem to be closely related to another, of which two fragmentary manuscripts were discovered by Solomon Schechter at the end of the nineteenth century in the *genizah* (store-room) of an ancient synagogue in Cairo. This document which has variously been called the *Zadokite Fragments* and the *Book of the Covenant of Damascus*, apparently emanated from a branch of the Qumran community which fled to Damascus during the reign of the Hasmonean ruler Yannai (103–76 BCE).

In addition to the literature thus far surveyed, two individual authors need to be mentioned. One is Philo, who flourished in Alexandria in the first half of the first century CE and wrote in

Greek. His writings are mainly philosophical and allegorical interpretations of the Pentateuch; through them he seeks to demonstrate the rationality and nobility of Judaism, by showing it to be in accord with the best in Greek, and especially Platonic, philosophy. Although he was therefore an apologist for Judaism, his attempted synthesis of Judaism and Hellenism did not appeal to subsequent tradition, which largely ignored his writings, whereas they exerted a strong influence on Christianity.

The other author is Flavius Josephus, a Palestinian Jew who, as commander of Galilee, played a prominent part in the Jewish war against the Romans but then defected and spent the rest of his life in Rome (see above, p. 78). There he wrote, mainly in Greek, two voluminous works which make him the outstanding Jewish historian of antiquity. One of these, *The Jewish War*, is a military history of the war in which he played such a large part. The other, entitled *The Jewish Antiquities*, is a massive history of the Jewish people which begins with the Creation and continues down to the writer's own time. Josephus also wrote an autobiography and a passionate defence of Judaism against its detractors, especially against an anti-Semitic orator in Alexandria named Apion: *Against Apion*.

The New Testament, although written partly by Jews, represents as a whole a viewpoint too diverse from Judaism, and in some respects hostile to it, to be included in our survey. It should be noted, however, that many of its ideas have roots in the literature which has been the subject of this chapter, especially the apocalyptic material in the Apocrypha and Pseudepigrapha, the Dead Sea Scrolls and the writings of Philo.

CHAPTER THREE   RABBINIC LITERATURE

Some time after the Babylonian Exile there began a new phase in the history of Judaism which ultimately burgeoned into Rabbinic Judaism. According to the traditional view, it was initiated by Ezra and carried on by the 'men of the Great Assembly' and thereafter by the *soferim* (Scribes). There is, however, little solid evidence to support this view, and some scholars doubt it. What cannot be doubted is that the new phase becomes clearly discernible in the second century BCE with the emergence of the Pharisees, whose teachers, known as *chachamim* (sages), engaged in a twofold activity: the interpretation of Scripture and the formulation of the Oral Law.

After the destruction of the Temple in 70 CE, Pharisaic Judaism became the norm for the great majority of Jews, both in Palestine and in the Diaspora. About the same time, its teachers became known as Rabbis. That is, what had previously been a mode of address now became a title, conferred by ordination on those who were judged to have acquired the necessary learning. From this time on, therefore, we may speak of Rabbinic Judaism. But in all essentials Rabbinic Judaism was a continuation of Pharisaic Judaism, and the term may therefore, with a little licence, be projected backwards to the second century BCE, if not earlier.

In particular, the Rabbis continued the same twofold activity. The interpretation of Scripture became known as Midrash, from a Hebrew verb meaning 'to search out'; the formulation of the Oral Law became known as Mishnah, from a verb meaning 'to repeat'. However, since the Oral Law was itself, to a large extent, deduced from the Bible, any particular ruling could, in principle, be taught by *either* method: as an interpretation of its proof-text, or as an independent tradition. Ultimately, the Mishnah method came to be preferred because it lent itself better to the task of *systematizing* the Oral Law, which became increasingly important as it grew more voluminous and complex.

In the course of time, each method produced its own genre of literature. But the writing process was long delayed on the ground that oral traditions should remain oral and therefore fluid; also in order that they should not be confused with the Holy Scriptures. It was only when the material became too massive to be memorized, and when political insecurity threatened the continuity of the oral transmission, that the principle was finally abandoned, but this was not until about 200 CE. Thus the *contents* of Rabbinic Literature are often generations, and even centuries, older than the documents.

Rabbinic Literature may be classified in various ways. First, according to its genre: whether it follows the Midrash method, interpreting Scripture verse by verse, or the Mishnah method, formulating the Oral Law topic by topic. Second, according to its subject matter: whether it is *Halachah* or *Aggadah*. *Halachah*, from a Hebrew verb meaning 'to walk', may be translated as 'law', but it covers a much wider range of topics than would be dealt with, say, in an English court. It includes everything that regulates human conduct and everything that is or can be expressed in the imperative, whether it is enforceable or not. *Aggadah*, meaning 'narration', is everything else: theology, history, legend and parable. *Halachah*, we might say, is prescriptive: *Aggadah* is descriptive.

While literature based on the Midrash method is generally aggadic, it may also be halachic, namely when the Scripture verse being interpreted is of the legislative kind; in the latter case it is called *Midrash Halachah*. Conversely, although literature based on the Mishnah method is primarily concerned with *Halachah*, it often digresses into aggadic topics.

In addition, Rabbinic Literature may be classified according to the chronological provenance of its contents, the major distinction being between (a) the age of the *tannaim* (70–200 CE) and their predecessors and (b) the age of the *amoraim* (200–500 CE). Tannaitic literature is generally Palestinian and written in Hebrew; amoraic literature may be Palestinian or Babylonian, and is characteristically written in Aramaic.

One way of interpreting Scripture is to translate it into another language, more familiar to the listener or reader. Every translation is also an interpretation. But therefore, too, it may be a *mis*-interpretation. To minimize this danger, it became customary in the ancient Palestinian synagogues to employ a competent interpreter, known as *meturgeman*, who translated the Scripture readings orally, one (in the case of the Torah) or three (in the case of the Prophets) verses at a time, into the Aramaic vernacular. This practice stimulated – and was ultimately superseded by – the publication of an approved Aramaic translation of the Pentateuch, which is known as *Targum Onkelos, targum* being Hebrew for 'translation' and Onkelos the name of its reputed author, whose identity is, however, uncertain. Probably dating from the second century CE, it acquired an authority second only to that of the Hebrew text itself, and its weekly reading was declared obligatory. Aramaic translations of the other sections of the Bible also appeared, but did not gain the same status.

MIDRASH

However, what is chiefly meant by the interpretation of Scripture is not translation but exposition: that is, Midrash. This varies in character according to the nature of the occasion, and therefore the purpose of the expositor: whether he is preaching to a congregation, instructing students or discussing the text with fellow scholars. Thus it may be terse or discursive, straightforward or fanciful, and more or less amply spiced with analogies, parables and legends.

From the tannaitic period, though they were edited somewhat later, we have midrashic works only on the Pentateuch, and particularly on its legislative portions. Therefore, though they contain much aggadic material, they are essentially halachic, testifying to a time when the Oral Torah was still being taught by the midrashic method. Some of these writings are said to stem from the school of Rabbi Akiva and his disciple Rabbi Simeon ben Yochai, who used a sophisticated system of interpretation; some from the school of Rabbi Ishmael, who favoured a more straightforward exegesis. These Midrashim are: the *Mechilta* (the name means 'rules of interpretation') on the book of Exodus; the *Sifra* (meaning 'the book') on Leviticus; and the *Sifrei* ('the books', short for 'the books of the rabbinic school') on Numbers and Deuteronomy.

The other midrashic works consist mainly of amoraic material, though they were compiled during the centuries following the amoraic period, some as late as the Middle Ages. There are two kinds. Some, like the tannaitic Midrashim, are in the form of running commentaries, proceeding verse by verse; these are known as 'exegetical Midrashim', and they originated mainly in the schools and academies. Others are essentially collections of sermons or anthologies of sermonic interpretations, arranged according to the sabbaths and festivals of the year for which they were intended; these are known as 'homiletical Midrashim', and they emanated mainly from the synagogues, especially those of Palestine, where Jewish preaching (partly in response to the challenge of Christianity) chiefly flourished. All of them are either wholly or largely aggadic in content.

The largest collection is called *Midrash Rabbah*, 'The Great Midrash', comprising works that were originally separate on the five books of the Pentateuch plus the Five Scrolls (the Song of Songs, Ruth, Lamentations, Ecclesiastes and Esther). The homiletical type of Midrash is best exemplified by the Pesikta collections, the word Pesikta referring to the 'sections' into which they are divided. They are the *Pesikta de-Rav Kahana*, named after a third-century rabbi whose interpretations it includes, and the *Pesikta Rabbati*, meaning 'The Great Pesikta'. Also homiletical is *Midrash Tanchuma*, named after the fourth-century rabbi whose sermons feature prominently in it. It is sometimes referred to as *Yelammedenu* ('Let him teach us') because many of its sections, though otherwise aggadic, begin with a halachic problem introduced by that word. There are many other midrashic and quasi-midrashic works, including *Yalkut Shim'oni* ('The Collection of Simeon') which is a comprehensive anthology, exegetically arranged and compiled in the Middle Ages by an author unknown except for his name.

MISHNAH

We now turn to the other type of literature, whose primary concern is not the verse-by-verse exposition of the Jewish Bible, but the topic-by-topic exposition of Jewish law. The first major work of this kind is the Mishnah. Originally, this word denoted an individual tradition of the Oral Law, memorized and taught independently of its scriptural derivation. Later it was applied collectively to a whole corpus of individual traditions. Such collections were made – mentally if not in writing – by several *tannaim*, including Rabbi Akiva and Rabbi Meir, and the process culminated in what became the most authoritative compilation, that of Rabbi Yehudah ha-Nasi which was committed to writing shortly after 200 CE (see above, p. 84).

Judah's Mishnah is thus the earliest published compendium of the Oral Law and the end-product of centuries of Pharisaic and tannaitic activity. It is written in a terse, post-biblical Hebrew, and is almost entirely halachic. However, it does contain some Midrash and *Aggadah*; it cites divergent opinions without always making it clear which of them is to be accepted as decisive; and it therefore falls short of being a *code* in the normal sense.

It is divided into six 'orders'; each order (in Hebrew, *seder*) is divided into a number of 'tractates' – the total number of tractates was originally sixty but, by a process of subdivision, it has become sixty-three; each tractate (*masechet*) is divided into a number of chapters; and each chapter (*perek*) is divided into a number of paragraphs, an individual paragraph being called a *mishnah* (in the original sense) or a *halachah*.

The first order is called *Zera'im*, 'Seeds', and deals mainly with agricultural laws; for instance, there is one that expounds the biblical law (Leviticus 19:9 f.) requiring the farmer to leave the corners of his field unharvested so that the poor may glean their produce. It begins, however, with a tractate on the subject of daily prayer; its placement here has been variously explained: because its relevance to the daily life of every Jew entitles it to first position; because the benedictions to be recited before and after the consumption of food, which it includes, give it a link with the topic of agriculture; and because it does not fit appropriately into any of the other orders.

The second order is called *Mo'ed*, 'Season', and concerns the sacred calendar. It includes, for instance, a tractate about the sabbath, one about the festival of Passover, one about the Day of Atonement, and so forth.

The third order is called *Nashim*, 'Women', and treats of matrimonial law. Its various tractates cover such subjects as betrothal, marriage contracts, levirate marriage and divorce.

The fourth order is entitled *Nezikin*, 'Damages', and contains the civil and criminal law. However, it includes a tractate known as 'Avot', 'Fathers', which differs from the rest of the Mishnah in that it is entirely aggadic, tracing the 'chain of tradition' from Moses down to Hillel and beyond, and citing the most characteristic teachings of the leading scholars, pre-pharisaic, pharisaic and tannaitic. These teachings are mainly ethical in content and epigrammatic in style. Why the tractate was included in this order, and whether it originally occupied a different position, are unsolved problems.

The fifth order is entitled *Kodashim*, 'Holy Things', and it spells out all the rules and regulations of the sacrificial cult, reflecting both the hope that one day the Temple would be rebuilt and the belief that meanwhile it was meritorious to study the relevant legislation, even though it could not be put into practice. However, the ritual slaughter of animals for food, which is the subject of one of its tractates, retained its practical relevance.

The sixth order has the title *Tohorot*, which means 'States of Purity', but this is a euphemism for 'States of Impurity', and it embodies all the complicated laws of ritual purity and impurity.

The Mishnah does not contain *all* the oral traditions known to the *tannaim*. Rabbi Judah included in it only those which he endorsed or thought worthy of mention. Therefore another compilation was made. It is known as the *Tosefta*, which means 'supplement'. While following the same arrangement, it is considerably larger than the Mishnah, including – along with many traditions that agree with the Mishnah – a large number which are more or less at variance with it or are altogether unmentioned in it. But it never gained the same authority.

Any tannaitic teaching of a halachic kind which Rabbi Judah did not include in his Mishnah is known as a *Baraita*, which is Aramaic for an 'external' Mishnah. Such teachings are to be found, not only in the *Tosefta*, but also in the halachic Midrashim (*Mechilta*, *Sifra* and *Sifrei*) and in the Talmud, to which we now turn.

TALMUD

Once available, the Mishnah became the obvious textbook for halachic study in the rabbinic academies. There was much to discuss and decide: which of the opinions stated in the Mishnah was correct; how it was, or might have been, derived from Scripture; how it was to be reconciled with seemingly contradictory opinions in the Mishnah itself or among the *Baraitot*; how exactly it was to be understood; how it was to be applied in circumstances which the Mishnah did not envisage, or which might have arisen since its time; these questions, and many more.

As generation succeeded generation, these investigations and debates produced a further body of traditions, supplementing the Mishnah and vastly exceeding it in volume; and once again, the effort required to remember them all, together with the desire to preserve them for posterity and the fear that some political upheaval might frustrate this desire, generated an urge to commit it to writing. The result was the Talmud, a Hebrew word which means both 'learning' and 'teaching', in two recensions: Palestinian and Babylonian.

The Palestinian Talmud, completed about 400 CE, is commonly referred to as the *Yerushalmi*, the Jerusalem Talmud, even though it emanated mainly from academies situated in northern Palestine. The Babylonian Talmud, known as the *Bavli*, was completed some time after 500 CE.

Neither of them covers all the sixty-three tractates of the Mishnah. The Palestinian Talmud covers thirty-nine, the Babylonian only thirty-six. Nevertheless, the Babylonian Talmud is many times larger than the Palestinian – an English translation of it, published by the Soncino Press, runs to over 15,000 pages. It also came to be regarded as the more authoritative. Indeed, it became the chief textbook of higher Jewish study throughout all the subsequent centuries, whereas the Palestinian Talmud was largely neglected until recent times. Therefore, whenever the Talmud is quoted or referred to without qualification, the Babylonian Talmud is meant.

The Talmud is organized in the same way as the Mishnah. Indeed, it is organized *around* the Mishnah, which it cites in its entirety, instalment by instalment. After each instalment, there follows what is known – to distinguish it from the Mishnah – as the *Gemara*, from a verb which in Hebrew means 'to complete' and in Aramaic 'to learn'. The *Gemara*, being amoraic, is largely in Aramaic – except when it quotes, as it frequently does, a scriptural verse or a Mishnah or a *Baraita*.

The *Gemara* which follows a particular instalment of the Mishnah may be short or long; often it runs to several pages before it 'exhausts itself' and the next instalment of the Mishnah is cited. Essentially, the *Gemara* examines the Mishnah text under a magnifying glass, phrase by phrase, in order to determine as precisely as possible what the law is, or what it should be. In the process, it often adduces real or imaginary arguments between two or more famous rabbis, arguments which sometimes become so complicated that it requires a strenuous intellectual effort to follow them. Moreover, the *Gemara* frequently digresses into topics, both halachic and aggadic, which are not directly relevant. The editor, it seems, put into it whatever he was reminded of, even by a remote association of ideas, lest he should subsequently forget it, or find no other place for it, with the result that it would be lost to posterity.

The Talmud, therefore, is not so much a book as a literature, and one that is unlike any other literature. It is vast and deep as the sea, to which it has often been likened. Though not a code – indeed it is less 'code-like' than the Mishnah – it contains all the material necessary for the construction (which was, in fact, accomplished subsequently) of a legal system of the utmost comprehensiveness and precision. It is a monument to the intellectual exertions of thousands of scholars during three long centuries, and an inexhaustible mine, not only of jurisprudence, but of history and theology and many other subjects.

CHAPTER FOUR   JEWISH LITERATURE
SINCE THE TALMUD

The literature Judaism has produced since the Talmud is so vast, amounting to tens of thousands of volumes, that all we can try to do in this chapter is to classify it, and to single out from the various categories, a few of the most influential authors and works.

BIBLE TEXTS

The sanctity ascribed to the Bible demanded that the utmost care be taken to transmit the text accurately. To this end, a stringent scribal discipline developed. It was known as the *masorah*, probably from a verb meaning 'to bind'. In spite of it, orthographic and other errors occurred, and manuscripts varied. It therefore became increasingly important to establish an authoritative version. This task was undertaken by a succession of Palestinian Jewish scholars, chiefly at Tiberias, from the seventh century onwards, and it was effectively completed by Aaron ben Asher in the tenth century. The result was what became known as the Masoretic Text.

BIBLE TRANSLATIONS

Although Hebrew ceased to be a spoken language (until it was revived in modern times), it remained the chief language of Jewish worship and scholarship. Accordingly, most of the literature surveyed in this chapter was written in Hebrew. Nevertheless,

many books were written in other languages which Jews adopted
as their vernacular. Likewise, a need was felt to translate the
Bible into these other languages, as it had previously been
translated into Greek and Aramaic. Thus Saadiah ben Joseph
(Babylonia*) translated it into Arabic, and in recent centuries
Jews (as well as non-Jews) have translated it into many other
languages.

BIBLE COMMENTARIES

Although many of the midrashic works mentioned in the preceding chapter were edited in the post-talmudic period, they
failed to satisfy the need for a more explanatory exegesis that was
still brief enough to be published alongside the scriptural text.
This need produced an ever growing number of Bible com-
mentaries, the most popular being that of Rashi (Solomon ben
Isaac, Northern France), which became a standard textbook of
Jewish education. Other commentaries of major importance are
those of Abraham ibn Ezra (1089–1164, Spain), Rashbam
(Samuel ben Meir, c. 1085–c. 1174, northern France), Radak
(David Kimchi, 1160–1235, Provence), Ramban (Moses ben
Nachman, or Nachmanides, 1195–1270, Spain), Ralbag (Levi ben
Gershon, or Gersonides, 1288–1344, Provence), Don Isaac
Abravanel (Spain and Italy) and Obadiah Sforno (c. 1470–
c. 1550, Italy). All these commentaries are concerned with the religious teachings of the Bible rather than its literary-historical
analysis in the manner of modern scholarship. Nevertheless, they
differ from each other in the extent to which they confine themselves to the elucidation of the plain sense of the text or seek to
discover in it deeper or remoter meanings, midrashic, philosophical or mystical.

COMMENTARIES ON RABBINIC LITERATURE

Many commentaries were also written on the classical works of
Rabbinic Literature, including the Midrashim. The most important commentaries on the Mishnah are those of Maimonides

* Only the *principal* country or countries in which each author lived and
wrote will be indicated.

(Moses ben Maimon, known as Rambam, Egypt) and Obadiah Bertinoro (*c.* 1450–*c.* 1515, Italy and Palestine); on the Babylonian Talmud, that of Rashi, together with the *Tosafot* (see p. 101).

RESPONSA

One of the major branches of post-talmudic Jewish literature, known as 'Question and Answers' or 'Responsa', consists of replies to enquiries on problems of Jewish law and practice submitted by individuals or communities to whomever they considered the leading contemporary authority. From the gaonic age to the present, almost every eminent halachic scholar has received such inquiries and written such replies, which were usually collected and published either by the authors themselves or by their disciples. These collections amount to thousands of volumes and deal with an extremely wide and varied range of topics. The more important respondents include: Sherira Gaon (*c.* 906–1006, Babylonia), Hai Gaon (939–1038, Babylonia), Rabbenu Gershom (Gershom ben Judah, *c.* 960–1028, Germany), Rabbenu Tam (Jacob ben Meir, 1100–71, northern France), Maimonides, Meir of Rothenburg (*c.* 1215–93, Germany), Rashba (Solomon ben Adret, 1235–1310, Spain), Rabbenu Asher (Asher ben Yechiel, *c.* 1250–1327, Germany and Spain), Ribash (Isaac ben Sheshet Barfat, 1326–1408, Spain and North Africa), Rashbatz (Simeon ben Tzemach Duran, 1361–1444, Spain and North Africa), Israel Isserlein (1390–1460, Austria), Maharik (Joseph Colon, *c.* 1420–80, Italy), Radbaz (David ben Zimra, 1479–1573, Palestine and Egypt), Yaavetz (Jacob Emden, 1697–1776, Germany), Ezekiel Landau (1713–93, Bohemia), Chatam Sofer (Moses Schreiber, 1763–1839, Slovakia), Solomon Kluger (1783–1869, Galicia), Joseph Saul Nathanson (1808–75, Ukraine), Isaac Elchanan Spektor (1817–96, Lithuania), David Hoffmann (1843–1921, Germany) and Benzion Uziel (1880–1954, Palestine–Israel).

CODES

Soon after the completion of the Talmud, the need began to be felt for a systematic presentation of Jewish law, which would both distil the definitive legislation contained in the Talmud and bring it up to date in the light of all subsequent rulings (as handed down in the Responsa or, orally, in the law courts) as well as new customs which had established themselves among the communities. Although the earliest attempts at such codification had already been made in the gaonic period, the first major achievement in this genre was a halachic epitome of the Talmud by the Rif (Isac Alfasi, 1013–1103, North Africa and Spain). This paved the way for the greatest code of all: the *Mishneh Torah*, 'Recapitulation of the Law', by Maimonides. The work was popularly known as *Yad ha-Chazakah*, 'The Mighty Hand', on account of its division into fourteen books, fourteen being the numerical value of the Hebrew letters of the word *yad*.

Ashkenazi Jews also produced a number of codes, such as the *Sefer Mitzvot Gadol*, 'Great Book of the Commandments', by Moses of Coucy (thirteenth century, northern France). Especially influential were the codes of Mordecai ben Hillel (*c.* 1240–98, Germany) and Asher ben Yechiel. The latter migrated from Germany to Spain, where his son Jacob ben Asher (*c.* 1270–1340) compiled an even more influential code, the *Arba'ah Turim*, 'Four Rows'. Its four parts are: (1) *Orach Chayyim*, 'The Path of Life', which deals with prayer and worship, sabbath and festivals; (2) *Yoreh De'ah*, 'Teacher of Knowledge', covering a variety of topics, from the dietary laws to the laws of burial and mourning; (3) *Even ha-Ezer*, 'The Stone of Help', devoted to matrimonial law; and (4) *Choshen ha-Mishpat*, 'The Breastplate of Judgement', comprising civil and criminal law.

This arrangement served as a model for what ultimately became the most authoritative of all the codes: the *Shulchan Aruch*, 'Prepared Table', by Joseph Caro (1488–1575, Turkey and Palestine). This, however, predominantly represented the Sephardi tradition and therefore did not gain universal acceptance until the balance was redressed by the glosses, soon incorporated into all editions, of the Ashkenazi Moses Isserles (*c.* 1525–1572, Poland). These glosses are popularly known as the *Mappah*, 'Tablecloth'.

COMMENTARIES ON THE CODES

The publication of the *Shulchan Aruch* marked the beginning of a new period in the history of the *halachah*: that of the *acharonim*, the 'later authorities', as distinct from their predecessors, the *rishonim*, the 'earlier authorities'. It also virtually ended the age of codification. However, the writing of commentaries on the codes, which had begun long before, continued and now concentrated increasingly on the *Shulchan Aruch*. The most important commentators on the *Mishneh Torah* include Abraham ben David of Posquières (*c.* 1125–98, Provence) and Vidal Yom-Tov of Tolosa (fourteenth century, Spain); those on the *Arba'ah Turim*, Joseph Caro and Joel Sirkes (1561–1640, Poland); those on the *Shulchan Aruch*, Joshua Falk (1555–1614, Poland), David ben Samuel ha-Levi (1586–1667, Poland), Moses Lima (*c.* 1605–58, Lithuania), Shabbetai Cohen (1622–63, Poland), Abraham Gumbiner (1637–83, Poland) and Samuel ben Uri Phoebus (seventeenth century, Poland).

LITURGY

Tradition ascribes the basic prayers of the Jewish liturgy to the men of the Great Assembly; it is more likely that they stem from the Pharisees. They are frequently alluded to, or cited in full or in part, in the Mishnah and Talmud. There is also ample evidence that the liturgy continued to grow throughout that period as well as later. But it was transmitted, in the main, orally until the ninth century, when an enquiry from a Jewish community in Spain elicited from Amram ben Sheshna, Gaon of Sura around 860, a responsum which became in effect the first Jewish prayer book, known as *Seder Rav Amram*, 'The Order of Rav Amram', and the 'ancestor' of all subsequent Jewish prayer books. However, those compiled by Saadiah and Maimonides served more directly as prototypes of the Sephardi liturgy, while the Ashkenazi liturgy derives mainly from the prayer books of Rashi and his disciple Simchah ben Samuel of Vitry, the latter's work being known as *Machzor Vitry*, 'The Cycle of Vitry'.

In the course of the Middle Ages the Jewish liturgy grew more elaborate, through the inclusion of religious poems called *piyyutim* as well as kabbalistic compositions, and ramified into a number of distinct *minhagim*, 'rites'. Since the invention of the printing press, Jewish prayer books have been published in profusion: Sephardi, Ashkenazi, Chasidic, Orthodox, Conservative and Progressive, many of them with translations into European languages.

MORALISTIC AND PIETISTIC LITERATURE

Under this heading we must survey a variety of writings which include moral codes, pious admonitions and ethical treatises. For instance, the so-called 'Minor Tractates' commonly appended to the fourth order of the Babylonian Talmud have among them a moral code entitled *Derech Eretz*, 'Good Manners' (or literally, the 'Way of the Land'). There are also some quasi-midrashic works, such as *Pirkei de-Rabbi Eliezer*, 'The Chapters of Rabbi Eliezer' (eighth century, Palestine) and *Seder Eliyahu*, 'The Order of Elijah' (tenth century, Palestine), which deserve mention here because of their ethical tone. *The Duties of the Heart* by Bachya ibn Pakuda (eleventh century, Spain) may be described as a philosophical textbook for the cultivation of piety and good character. The so-called *Chasidei Ashkenaz*, the 'pietists of Germany', also produced an impressive literature, of which the outstanding example is the code-like *Sefer Chasidim*, the 'Book of the Pious', by Judah ben Samuel of Regensburg (c. 1150–1217, Germany). Maimonides expounded his ethical theory in the 'Eight Chapters' included in his Mishnah commentary as a preface to the tractate *Avot*. There is also an extensive literature of 'ethical wills' (authentic ones, unlike the imaginary kind represented by the *Testaments of the Twelve Patriarchs* to which we have previously referred). Other works which merit a mention in this section are *The Improvement of the Moral Qualities* by Solomon ibn Gabirol (c. 1020–c. 1057, Spain); *Menorat ha-Maor*, 'The Candlestick', by Isaac Aboab (fourteenth century, probably Spain); and *Mesillat Yesharim*, 'The Path of the Upright', by Moses Chayyim Luzzatto (1707–46, Italy).

PHILOSOPHY AND THEOLOGY

Like other religions, Judaism has at various times tried to explain and justify itself philosophically. We have already noted an instance of this tendency in the writings of Philo of Alexandria, who was responding to Greek philosophy. The challenge was taken up anew in the Middle Ages, chiefly as a result of Judaism's contact with Islam. Islamic teachers studied Greek philosophy, translated it into Arabic and sought to harmonize their own religion with it. Similarly, Jewish thinkers constructed systems of philosophical theology or theological philosophy by which they sought to prove that Judaism, properly understood, is both compatible with, and superior to, the then fashionable Greek philosophy (Neo-Platonic or Aristotelian), suggesting that there is no conflict between revelation and reason, or else that revelation is an altogether more reliable source of knowledge than reason. Outstanding examples of such works are: *The Book of Beliefs and Opinions* by Saadiah; *The Fountain of Life* by Solomon ibn Gabirol; *The Book of the Kuzari* by Judah Halevi (before 1075–1141, Spain) – which takes the form of an imaginary conversation between the king of the Khazars, in search of the true faith, and a rabbi, who convinces him that it is to be found in Judaism; *The Guide for the Perplexed* by Maimonides (which aroused the fiercest controversy but also exerted the greatest influence); *The Wars of the Lord* by Gersonides; *The Light of the Lord* by Chasdai Crescas (*c.* 1340–*c.* 1410, Spain); and *The Book of Principles* by Joseph Albo (*c.* 1380–*c.* 1440, Spain).

The greatest Jewish philosopher of all was Baruch Spinoza (Holland), but his writings, though strongly influenced by Judaism, belong more to general European philosophy. The philosophical-theological writings of Moses Mendelssohn (1729–86, Germany) are in the spirit of eighteenth-century Rationalism; those of Nachman Krochmal (1785–1840, Galicia) amount to a philosophy of history showing Hegelian influence; those of Hermann Cohen (1842–1918, Germany) represent a synthesis of Judaism with neo-Kantianism. The last exerted a profound influence on Leo Baeck (1873–1956, Germany), author of *The Essence of Judaism*, Martin Buber (1878–1965, Germany and Palestine–Israel), author of *I and Thou*, and Franz Rosenzweig

(1886–1929, Germany), author of *Star of Redemption*. Buber and Rosenzweig (more so than Baeck) may be described as existentialists. The same may be said of Abraham Joshua Heschel (1907–73, USA), who was also greatly influenced by Chasidism. Perhaps the most profound Orthodox Jewish thinker of modern times was Abraham Kook (1865–1935, Palestine), whose writings belong as much to mysticism as to philosophy. At the other extreme, Mordecai Kaplan (1881–1983, USA), developed a naturalistic and sociological interpretation of Judaism called Reconstructionism.

KABBALISTIC LITERATURE

Jewish mysticism has its roots in antiquity, but until the Middle Ages it did not produce an extensive literature; it then became known as *kabbalah*, which means 'received tradition'. It is a theosophical doctrine concerning the ultimate mysteries of the universe, based on an esoteric interpretation of the Bible (especially the Creation story and Ezekiel's vision of the heavenly chariot), as well as a devotional discipline by which man may apprehend something of these mysteries and help to unite the lower, imperfect, visible world with the higher, perfect, invisible one. Its medieval efflorescence began in Provence around 1200 CE and quickly spread to Spain, where, towards the end of the thirteenth century, it produced its chief textbook, *Sefer ha-Zohar*, the 'Book of Splendour'. Pseudepigraphically attributed to the second-century Palestinian rabbi, Simeon ben Yochai, it was in fact compiled, on the basis of older sources, by Moses de Leon (*c.* 1240–1305). In large part it is a midrashic commentary on the Pentateuch, written in an artificial Aramaic.

To its devotees the *Zohar* became almost a second Bible, as sacred as the Talmud, if not more so. It exerted a profound influence on subsequent generations, especially on the Jewish mystics of Safed in Palestine, among them Moses Cordovero (1522–70), author of *Pardes Rimmonim*, 'Orchard of Pomegranates', and *Tomer Devorah*, 'The Palm Tree of Deborah', and Isaac Luria (1534–72), founder of a new ('Lurianic') school of *kabbalah*, whose teachings were given literary form by his disciple

Chayyim Vital (1543–1620) in a book entitled *Etz Chayyim*, 'The Tree of Life'. A later kabbalistic work which enjoyed great popularity is the code-like *Shenei Luchot ha-Berit*, the 'Two Tablets of the Covenant', by Isaiah Horowitz (*c.* 1565–1630, Poland, Bohemia, Germany and Palestine).

CHASIDIC LITERATURE

The *kabbalah* also exerted great influence on Chasidism, the pietist movement which had been founded by Israel ben Eliezer, known as the Baal Shem Tov, the 'Master of the Good Name', in Podolia. Although the ideas of the sect were at first transmitted orally, it began to produce its own literature towards the end of the eighteenth century. This consists mainly of sermons, letters and pamphlets, as well as anthologies of tales about, and sayings of, the founder and his successors. One of the latter was Shneur Zalman of Lyady (1745–1813, Russia) who founded the *chabad* – an abbreviation of *chochmah* (wisdom), *binah* (understanding) and *da'at* (knowledge) – movement, the teachings of which he expounded in a work entitled *Likkutei Amarim*, 'Collections of Sayings'. This is popularly known as the *Tanya*, meaning 'It has been taught'. Probably the most profound religious thinker among the chasidic masters was Nachman of Bratzlav (1772–1811, Podolia) whose works were committed to writing by his disciple Nathan Sternharz (1780–1845) under such titles as *Likkutei Moharan*, 'The Collected Teachings of Rabbi Nachman'.

POETRY

We have already referred to a type of religious poetry called *piyyut*. The earliest examples of this are found in the Jewish liturgy and seem to date from late amoraic or gaonic times; they are by poets such as Yose ben Yose, Yannai and Eleazar Kallir, about whom, however, almost nothing is known. Also included in the Jewish liturgy are *piyyutim* by various members of the Kalonymos family, who migrated from Italy to Germany around 1000 CE. It was, however, in Spain that Hebrew poetry, influenced by Arabic models but ultimately inspired by the Bible itself, flourished most brilliantly. Most of it is religious, and some found its way into the Jewish liturgy; but much of it is secular, including satirical and love poetry. The greatest Hebrew poet of the Spanish school was Judah Halevi. Other outstanding ones include: Samuel ha-Nagid (993–1055), Solomon ibn Gabirol, Moses ibn Ezra (c. 1055–c. 1135), Abraham ibn Ezra (1089–1164) and Judah al-Charizi (1170–1235).

In the ensuing centuries, Hebrew poets of quality appeared but rarely, though mention may be made of Immanuel of Rome (c. 1261–1328) and, much later, Moses Chayyim Luzzatto, who also wrote some poetic drama. But the achievements of the Spanish Hebrew poets remained unequalled until the modern revival of the Hebrew language at the end of the nineteenth century. Since then a whole galaxy of Hebrew poets has appeared, including one of genius: Chayyim Nachman Bialik (1873–1934, Russia and Palestine), who may perhaps be regarded as the greatest Hebrew poet since the Middle Ages, if not since the Bible itself. Other noteworthy representatives of the modern school are: Judah Leib Gordon (1830–92), Saul Tchernichovski (1875–1943, Russia, Germany and Palestine), David Shimoni (1886–1956, Russia and Palestine–Israel), Abraham Shlonsky (b. 1900, Russia and Palestine–Israel) and Nathan Alterman (1910–70, Poland and Palestine–Israel).

FICTION

While fictional works of various kinds have been written by Jews in most periods, it was as a result of the *haskalah* that novels and short stories became, in the nineteenth and twentieth centuries, an accepted form for the expression of Jewish thought and feeling. Major Hebrew writers, some of whom have also written in Yiddish, are: Abraham Mapu (1808–67, Lithuania), Mendele Mocher Seforim, 'Mendele the Bookseller' (Shalom Jacob Abramowitsch, 1835–1917, Russia), Peretz Smolenskin (Russia and Austria) and Samuel Joseph Agnon (1888–1970, Galicia and Palestine–Israel). Notable Yiddish writers, some of whom have also written in Hebrew, include: Isaac Leib Peretz (1852–1915, Russia and Poland), Sholem Aleichem (Shalom Rabinovitz, 1859–1916, Ukraine), Sholem Asch (1880–1957, Poland and USA) and Isaac Bashevis Singer (born 1904, Poland and USA). Among writers in English, Israel Zangwill (1864–1926, England), Saul Bellow (b. 1915, USA), Elie Wiesel (b. 1928, France and USA) and Chaim Potok (b. 1929, USA) made use of specifically Jewish themes.

MISCELLANEOUS

The most popular travel tales in the Middle Ages were those of Benjamin of Tudela (twelfth century, Spain). Autobiography is represented by Leon Modena (1571–1648, Italy), who wrote in Hebrew, and Glückel of Hameln (1646–1724) – she wrote in Yiddish. Perhaps the greatest Hebrew essayist was the Zionist philosopher who called himself Achad Ha-Am, 'One of the People' (Ukraine, England and Palestine). Others who laid the foundations of modern Zionism by their writings were Moses Hess (1812–75, Germany), author of *Rome and Jerusalem*; Judah Loeb Pinsker (1821–91, Russia), author of *Auto-Emancipation*; and Theodor Herzl (Austria), author of *The Jewish State*.

Jewish historiography has had eminent exponents in Solomon Rapaport (1790–1867, Galicia and Bohemia), Isaac Marcus Jost (1793–1860, Germany), Heinrich Graetz (Germany), Simon Dubnow (1860–1941, Russia) and Salo Wittmayer Baron (b. 1895, USA). In addition, the modern period has produced a host of scholars who have investigated various aspects of Jewish history and literature. The most important of these have included: Elijah ben Solomon, the 'Vilna Gaon' (Lithuania), Leopold Zunz (1794–1886, Germany), Zacharias Frankel (Germany), Abraham Geiger (Germany), Moritz Steinschneider (1816–1907, Germany), Solomon Schechter (before 1850–1915, Romania, England and USA), Israel Abrahams (1858–1924, England), Louis Ginzberg (1873–1953, Lithuania and USA), Ismar Elbogen (1874–1943, Germany), Menachem Kasher (b. 1895, Poland and Palestine–Israel), Louis Finkelstein (b. 1895, USA), Gershom Scholem (1897–1982, Germany and Palestine–Israel), Saul Lieberman (b. 1898, Russia, Palestine and USA) and Ephraim Elimelech Urbach (b. 1912, Germany and Palestine–Israel).

Finally, it should be mentioned that the traditional kind of halachic learning has also continued to produce figures of stature, among them Yechiel Michael Epstein (1829–1908, Russia), author of a code entitled *Aruch ha-Shulchan*, 'Prepared is the Table', and Israel Meir ha-Cohen (1838–1933), known as Chafetz Chayyim, 'He who Desires Life', after the title (cf. Psalm 34:13) of one of his books, dealing with the sins of gossip and tale-bearing. He also wrote an authoritative commentary on the first part of the *Shulchan Aruch*, called *Mishnah Berurah*, 'The Mishnah Clarified'.

'Of making many books there is no end,' said the author of Ecclesiastes (12:12). He could hardly have foreseen how true that would become of Jewish literature. If the vitality of a religion is reflected in its literary creativity, it may be said of Judaism that it has been – and remains – very much alive.

PART III

THE THEORY OF JUDAISM

CHAPTER ONE   GOD AND HIS ATTRIBUTES

Judaism has no creed in the Christian sense. It spells out what Jews must *do* rather than what they must believe. It legislates rather than dogmatizes, regulates conduct rather than thought, constructs codes rather than creeds.

The Mishnah, for instance, is a compendium of laws, not doctrines. Admittedly in it there is a statement to the effect that three classes of persons – those who deny the resurrection of the dead, those who aver that there is no divinely revealed Torah, and those who reject all moral restraint – 'have no share in the world to come' (Sanhedrin 10:1). But this is an isolated exception. It is true that this mishnaic pronouncement elicited from Maimonides, in his commentary, a lengthy excursus on the thirteen theological affirmations which he considered fundamental to Judaism, and that a brief summary of these (by a later hand) ultimately found its way into the Jewish prayer book.* Nevertheless, Maimonides' 'Thirteen Principles of the Faith' were never formally endorsed, or declared binding by any Jewish equivalent of a Church Council. On the contrary, they were criticized by other Jewish philosophers, who put forward their own formulations of the basic tenets of Judaism. Above all, the formulation of these principles did not alter the fact that in Judaism,

---

* Maimonides' Thirteen Principles, briefly, affirm that God is the Creator, that He is One, incorporeal, eternal and alone entitled to man's worship, that the teachings of the Prophets are true, that Moses was the greatest of the Prophets, that the Torah was revealed to him, that it is immutable, that God knows what human beings do and think, that He rewards the good and punishes the wicked, that the Messiah will come and the dead will be resurrected.

theory belongs to the realm of *Aggadah*, not *Halachah*. (See above p. 211.)

Halachah defines and decides; *Aggadah* explores and speculates. *Halachah* is authoritative; *Aggadah* is suggestive. Aggadic Midrash typically offers a variety of interpretations, even mutually contradictory ones, of one and the same Bible verse, without making any attempt to harmonize them. Its tacit premise seems to be that ultimate reality is complex, mysterious and often paradoxical, so that man's perception of it is at best partial, contrary opinions may each harbour an element of truth, and the search for understanding is best conducted in an atmosphere of freedom, unregimented by dogma.

Consequently there is no one, 'official', Jewish theology. The beliefs of Judaism have to be extrapolated from its literature as a whole, not recited from a catechism, and the study of Jewish theology is therefore a historical enterprise. It involves, of course, more than simply reporting what Jews have believed in the past; it is a matter of identifying trends. One has to judge what is more, and what is less, characteristic of, coherent with, and significant for, the whole. Such judgements are unavoidably subjective; one can only try to be fair to the facts.

EXISTENCE

The most basic affirmation of Judaism is the existence of God. It is this which makes it a religion. (In a wider sense, Judaism is a culture, and one which even non-believers may cherish; but it is with Judaism as a religion that we are here concerned.) In the classical sources of Judaism (Bible, Mishnah, Talmud and Midrash), God's existence is always assumed, even when not explicitly asserted, and it is regarded as the most important of all truths. To work out the implications of this belief is the chief preoccupation of Jewish writers from ancient until modern times.

According to Maimonides, there is a positive obligation to affirm God's existence, derived from the first of the Ten Commandments, which, according to Jewish tradition, consists solely of the verse, expressed in the indicative but implying an imperative: 'I am the Lord your God, who brought you out of the land of Egypt, out of the house of bondage' (Exodus 20:2; Deuteronomy 5:6). Indeed, it heads his list of the 613 commandments to be found, according to rabbinic tradition, in the Pentateuch.

Atheism, as we know it, was not a problem in ancient Israel. All believed in deities of one kind or another. The concern of the biblical writers was, rather, to assert the true God against the false ones, and to call for obedience to Him alone. The 'fool' who, according to the psalmist, says, 'There is no God' (14:1; 53:2; Christian Bibles, 53:1), is one who ignores God's will rather than one who denies His existence.

Philo and the medieval and later Jewish philosophers did indeed attempt to prove God's existence, using similar arguments as Christian and Muslim philosophers. Today it is, however, generally accepted that such reasoning can, at best, establish only a *probability* in favour of theism. Modern Jewish thinkers tend to stress the distinction between believing *that* God exists and believing *in* God, and to make the point that the latter can only be attained through some kind of personal encounter with Him rather than through philosophy. They also remind us that the pertinent Hebrew word, *emunah*, means 'trust' and hence refers to a commitment of the will rather than mere intellectual assent.

UNITY

Next to His existence, the most fundamental affirmation of Judaism is the unity of God. According to the Midrash, Abraham arrived at the conviction that there must be a single 'First Cause'. Even if one maintains that the second of the Ten Commandments only forbids the *worship* of other gods, and does not deny their existence, it is clear that in the Creation story (Genesis 1) and in Amos (5:8; 9:5 f.) God is already the Lord of the universe. More explicitly, the author of Deuteronomy declares: 'Know therefore this day, and lay it to your heart, that the Lord is God in heaven above, and on the earth beneath; there is no other' (4:39); and Deutero-Isaiah leaves no room for doubt when he says in God's name: 'I am the Lord, and there is no other, besides Me there is no God' (45:5). Indeed, the whole Bible is to a large extent the record of a long drawn-out, but ultimately successful, struggle for the allegiance of the Jewish people to the purest monotheism and their utter rejection of polytheism with its attendant idolatry.

Some time during the Second Temple period, one biblical passage, Deuteronomy 6:4–9, was singled out to be recited twice daily, morning and evening, by every Jew. Known from its opening word as the *Shema*, it begins: 'Hear, O Israel, the Lord is our God, the Lord is One.' That verse became the watchword of Judaism. By tradition, it is the first phrase to be taught to a Jewish child, and the last to be uttered by a Jew before he dies. Rabbi Akiva, the Talmud tells us, recited it while being tortured to death, and expired with the word *Echad*, 'One', on his lips (Berachot 61b).

Rabbinic literature frequently repudiates the dualistic doctrine of 'two (ultimate, cosmic) powers' and reveals a growing emphasis on the intrinsic, as well as extrinsic, unity of God. This view was further developed by the medieval Jewish philosophers – particularly on the ground that spirit, unlike matter, is by its very nature indivisible – and used as an argument against Christian Trinitarianism. However, the Jewish *kabbalah*, too, makes distinctions in its conception of God, particularly between the unknowable God-as-He-is-in-Himself, called *Ein Sof* ('without end'), and the Ten *Sefirot* ('emanations') which represent the various stages of His entry into the world as human beings experience it.

Maimonides regards the affirmation of God's unity as a positive obligation, derived from Deuteronomy 6:4, and gives it second place in his list of the 613 commandments. It is, in addition to the affirmation of God's existence, the only other exception to the general rule that belief, unlike action, belongs to *Aggadah*, not *Halachah*, and is therefore not subject to legislation. There is no question but that it is fundamental to Judaism – virtually the only dogma Judaism has – and that the Jewish liturgy is right when it characterizes the Jews as 'the people who proclaim God's unity', adding: 'Happy are we! How good is our portion, and how pleasant our lot, and how beautiful our heritage! Happy are we who, early and late, morning and evening, twice every day, declare: Hear, O Israel, the Lord is our God, the Lord is One.'

ATTRIBUTES OF GOD

Creator

The implications of monotheism are profound. From monotheism follows the view of the cosmos as a unitary whole, obeying a single set of laws; this is the root assumption of science, as well as of the conception of mankind as one family, having in God, as it were, a common Father. Moreover, as the number one has mathematical properties different from those of any other number, so the God of monotheism is different *in kind* from the gods of polytheism. He is the cause of, and the power behind, not this or that aspect of the universe, but the universe in its entirety. He is its Creator. In the words of the Psalmist, 'For all the gods of the peoples are idols; but the Lord made the heavens' (96:5). Furthermore, as the Creator of the universe, God is necessarily different from, and greater than, any of its parts. They are limited in duration: He is eternal. They are limited in extension: He is infinite. They are limited in power: He is omnipotent. They are limited in knowledge: He is omniscient.

Eternal

That God is eternal is always implied and often stated in the literature of Judaism. Whereas the pagan mythologies speak of the birth and death of the gods, the biblical Creation story assumes that God always existed. Well known are the words of the ninetieth Psalm: 'Lord, thou hast been our dwelling place in all generations. Before the mountains were brought forth, or ever thou hadst formed the earth and the world, from everlasting to everlasting thou art God . . . For a thousand years in thy sight are but as yesterday when it is past, or as a watch in the night.' Likewise, it is asserted that God will never cease to be, for all things 'will perish, but thou dost endure . . . thy years have no end' (Psalms 102:27 f.); 'The Lord will reign for ever and ever' (Exodus 15:18; Psalms 146:10). Similarly, a medieval Jewish hymn known from its opening words as *Adon Olam* asserts: 'He is the eternal Lord, who reigned before any creature had yet been fashioned; when all was made according to His will, already then His name was King. And after all has ceased to be, still will He

reign in solitary majesty; He was, He is and He shall be in glory
... without beginning, without end.'

Infinite

As God is unlimited by time, so He is unlimited by space: He is
infinite. Though there are 'holy places' where He may especially
manifest Himself, He is not restricted to any particular location.
'Great is the Lord, beyond the border of Israel' (Malachi 1:5);
'The earth is the Lord's, and the fulness thereof' (Psalms 24:1);
'The whole earth is full of His glory' (Isaiah 6:3); 'Thus says the
Lord: Heaven is My throne and the earth is My footstool; what is
the house which you would build for Me, and what is the place of
My rest?' (Isaiah 66:1); 'But will God indeed dwell on the earth?
Behold, heaven and the highest heaven cannot contain thee; how
much less this house which I have built!' (I Kings 8:27). The
Rabbis pushed this line of thought even further when they said:
'God is the place of the universe; the universe is not the place of
God' (Genesis Rabbah 68:9).

Omnipotent

God's omnipotence is also stressed in Judaism. Not only does His
power vastly exceed that of the pagan deities, which are indeed
declared impotent (Psalms 115:5 ff.), but He is in total command
of all the elements of nature (Isaiah 40:12–26; Psalms 104). Sometimes, indeed, it is asserted that His power is literally limitless,
that nothing is 'too hard' or 'too wonderful' for Him (Genesis
18:14; Numbers 11:23; Isaiah 59:1; Jeremiah 32:27). As for the
philosophical puzzle, whether God can do, not only what is for
humans *physically* impossible, but what is *logically* impossible,
the answer, already suggested by medieval Jewish philosophers
such as Saadiah and Albo, is that it is a specious problem, since a
sentence such as 'God can make a round square' simply does not
express a meaningful proposition at all.

Omniscient

The concept of God's omniscience is expressed in various w.
that He created the world with wisdom (Psalms 104:24; Prover
3:19); that He alone has a full understanding of wisdom (Job
28:23) and is its source (Proverbs 2:6; Job 12:13; Daniel 2:20 f.);
and that He is 'the all-seeing Eye and the all-hearing Ear' (Avot
2:1) who is aware of everything that takes place in the universe,
including the human heart (Jeremiah 17:10; Psalms 11:4; 33:13 f.;
Job 28:24).

Incorporeal

In all these respects God is regarded as immeasurably *greater
than* the universe or any part of it, whether it be mineral, vegetable, animal or human. 'To whom then will you liken God, or
what likeness compare with Him?' (Isaiah 40:18) is a recurring
theme in Jewish literature. Before Him the nations are 'as a
drop from a bucket', and the inhabitants of the earth 'like grass-
hoppers' (Isaiah 40:15, 22). 'For My thoughts are not your
thoughts, neither are your ways My ways, says the Lord. For
as the heavens are higher than the earth, so are My ways higher
than your ways, and My thoughts than your thoughts' (Isaiah
55:8 f.).

As its Creator, God is also *different from* His creation. He is
not physical at all: He is pure spirit, without a body. That is, of
course, a difficult notion which could not have been fully grasped
at the beginning of the monotheistic period. Certainly the Bible
frequently refers to God in human terms, and though allowance
must be made for poetic imagery, it is doubtful whether these
anthropomorphisms were always understood in a purely metaphorical sense. Nevertheless, there is a clear tendency towards a
spiritual conception of God. That must have been one reason
why idolatry was considered so objectionable even in the worship
of the One God: it encouraged those who practised it to think of
Him in physical terms. Likewise, when Moses asks to be shown
God's glory and receives the enigmatic answer, 'I will make all
My goodness pass before you ... But, He said, you cannot see
My face; for man shall not see Me and live' (Exodus 33:19 f.),

it must be assumed that the author, in spite of the anthropomorphic language, is attempting to explain that God is not a physical being.

In the Rabbinic *Aggadah*, too, anthropomorphisms abound; they provide much of its picturesqueness, charm and humour. But there is always the implicit understanding that they are metaphorical, and this is often made explicit by the disclaimer *kiveyachol*, which may be translated 'as it were' or '*per impossibile*'. Even more emphatic in their assertion of God's incorporeality are the medieval Jewish philosophers, and Maimonides stresses with particular insistence that the anthropomorphisms of the Bible are nothing but metaphors and must on no account be taken literally.

Transcendent and Immanent

Much of what we have been saying can be summed up in the word 'transcendence': God transcends the universe He has created it and all its components and inhabitants. This affirmation lies at the heart of Judaism. The Hebrew Bible is in large part the story of the weaning of the Israelites from paganism – the essence of which is that it ascribes divinity to things, animals or humans (ancestors, kings, saviours) – and their dedication to the exclusive worship of the one, invisible, supremely exalted, transcendent God.

Of course, the more God is conceived as transcendent, the wider becomes the gulf that seemingly separates Him from humanity. The advanced religions, which do stress God's transcendence, have tried to deal with this problem in various ways. One is the way of Deism, which simply accepts the gulf and, accordingly, maintains that God, having created the world, is no longer an active presence within it. This view, which flourished especially in eighteenth-century England, was notably opposed by David Nieto (1654–1728), the Italian-born rabbi of the London Sephardi community.

Another way seeks to bridge the gulf between man and God by interposing intermediaries of one kind or another (angels, demiurges, emanations, incarnations) between them. This tendency is by no means unrepresented in Judaism. Angels do play a significant if obscure role in the writings of the ancient Jewish apocalyptists and those of the medieval Jewish mystics and philosophers. But in the literature more familiar to the average Jew, such as Bible and Midrash, they are hardly more than folkloristic fancies; and in the prayer book they appear mainly as anonymous celestial choirs, corporately singing God's praise. Likewise, the kabbalistic doctrine of the *Sefirot* is too esoteric to be considered normative.

A third way, that of Pantheism, is, as it were, to bring God down to earth by identifying Him with Nature. Such, in a highly sophisticated form, is the philosophy of Spinoza. On a more popular level, there is an apparent tendency towards Pantheism in Chasidism with its emphasis on God's presence 'in' all things.

Mainstream Judaism, however, has resolved the problem by counterbalancing its emphasis on God's transcendence with an equal emphasis on His immanence – His active presence in the world as human beings experience it. This dual emphasis is a hallmark of the Jewish conception of God. It is, of course, a paradox; but then, reality is often paradoxical. Yet it is perhaps not as paradoxical as it seems, for in some respects God's immanence actually follows from His transcendence. For instance, because He transcends time, He also permeates it, and can be encountered in any moment of it. Likewise, because He transcends space, He also pervades it: He is omnipresent. In the words of the psalmist, 'Whither shall I go from thy spirit? Or whither shall I flee from thy presence? If I ascend to heaven, thou art there! If I make my bed in Sheol, thou art there! If I take the wings of the morning, and dwell in the uttermost parts of the sea, even there thy hand shall lead me, and thy right hand shall hold me' (139:7–10).

In the same vein, the Rabbis declared that 'there is no place devoid of the Divine Presence' (Exodus Rabbah 2:5), using, as they frequently did, the word *Shechinah*, from a verb meaning 'to dwell' which occurs in the key verse, Exodus 25:8 ('Let them make Me a sanctuary, that I may dwell in their midst'), and thus corresponds to the etymology of 'immanence', which comes from the Latin word *manere*, to abide. Similarly, Judah Halevi wrote:

> Lord, where shall I find You,
> Whose place is hidden and high?
> And where shall I not find You,
> Whose glory fills all space?

This tension between transcendence and immanence is one which we encounter again and again in Judaism. Deutero-Isaiah gave it classical expression: 'For thus says the high and lofty One who inhabits eternity, whose name is Holy; "I dwell in the high and holy place, and also with him who is of a contrite and humble spirit, to revive the spirit of the humble, and to revive the heart of the contrite"' (57:15). The hymn *Adon Olam*, with its dramatically abrupt change of theme from God's transcendence, awesomely proclaimed in the first three stanzas, to His immanence, confidently affirmed in the last two, most tellingly makes the point:

He is the eternal Lord, who reigned before any creature had yet been fashioned; when all was made according to His will, already then His name was King.

And after all has ceased to be, still will He reign in solitary majesty; He was, He is, and He will be in glory.

And He is One; there is no other to compare with Him, or to consort with Him; He is without beginning, without end, and His are power and dominion.

And He is *my* God, and my living Redeemer, my Rock in trouble and distress; He is my banner and my refuge, my benefactor when I call on Him.

Into His hand I entrust my spirit, both when I sleep and when I wake; and with my spirit, my body also: the Lord is with me, I will not fear.

At this point we need to ask: to what extent is it possible for human beings to apprehend God at all? According to the Kabbalists, the *Ein Sof*, as distinct from the *Sefirot*, is altogether unknowable. Maimonides is the outstanding exponent in Judaism of the *via negativa*, which maintains that the only assertions we can validly make about God are negations: we can only say what He is *not*. And yet the classical sources of Judaism do make many positive statements about Him. Are they, then, to be dismissed? Most Jews would say: no, but they must be understood metaphorically. Such metaphors are not illegitimate as long as we remember what they are: mere pointers to a mystery which must for ever transcend human understanding.

Nevertheless, metaphors can be more or less *appropriate*. Many of those found in classical Jewish literature seem to imply that God is a 'person'; and though that, too, is a metaphor, we need to ask how appropriate it is. There are indeed in contemporary Judaism, as there are in contemporary Christianity, radical theologians who try to get away from such a 'personal' conception of God. But many, probably most, Jews still feel instinctively that it is more appropriate to think of God as a 'person' rather than, for instance, a 'force', and therefore to refer to God as 'He' rather than 'it'. Their instinct is, moreover, supported by these considerations: that Creation presupposes intelligence and therefore mind; that the Creator of a universe which includes persons can hardly be less than a person but must, rather, be a 'supra-person'; and that only such an assumption can account for the nature of religious experience, and, more generally, the manifestations of God's immanence.

Righteousness

Above all, what Judaism has understood of God's self-manifestations in human history has led it to assert strongly that He is the possessor of a moral will. Jewish monotheism is *ethical* monotheism, and it is the adjective, as much as the noun, which distinguishes it from paganism. What this means is twofold: that God is moral in Himself, and therefore in His dealings with human beings; and that moral conduct is what He demands from them. 'For the Lord is righteous, He loves righteous deeds' (Psalms 11:7).

The moral qualities attributed to God in Jewish traditon fall broadly into two categories. The 'sterner' ones are referred to by such terms as *tzedek* (righteousness), *mishpat* and *din* (both meaning justice); the 'gentler' ones are expressed in words such as *tov* (good), *channun* (gracious), *chesed* (lovingkindness) and *rachamim* (compassion).

In the Hebrew Bible, taken as a whole, the two categories receive approximately equal stress and are often asserted simultaneously, as in Jeremiah: 'Let not the wise man glory in his wisdom, let not the mighty man glory in his might, let not the rich man glory in his riches; but let him who glories glory in this, that he understands and knows Me, that I am the Lord who practise steadfast love, justice and righteousness in the earth; for in these things I delight, says the Lord' (9:22 f.).

In Rabbinic literature, too, the two aspects of God's moral

243

nature are generally seen as balancing each other. A typical Midrash states the dilemma God faced in creating the world: 'If I create it with the attribute of compassion, its sins will increase; if with the attribute of justice, how will it be able to endure?' Therefore He created the world with justice *and* compassion (Genesis Rabbah 12:15).

Sometimes, however, one discerns a tendency to tilt the balance in favour of the 'gentler' attributes. Of this the outstanding example, as well as a major contributory cause, is the fact that the Rabbis singled out, for solemn recitation on the holiest days of the year, the following scriptural passage: 'The Lord, the Lord, a God merciful and gracious, slow to anger, abounding in steadfast love and faithfulness, keeping steadfast love for thousands, forgiving iniquity and transgression and sin, but who will by no means clear the guilty . . .' (Exodus 34:6 f.). Furthermore, a literal translation of the Hebrew for 'who will by no means clear' is 'and as for clearing, He will not clear'; by omitting the last part of the phrase, the rabbis transformed even that into an affirmation of God's forgiveness. It is in this form that the passage became known as *shelosh-esreh middot*, 'The Thirteen Attributes of God', and passed into the Jewish liturgy, and hence into the Jewish consciousness.

Holiness

One more divine attribute needs to be mentioned: holiness. The root meaning of the Hebrew word for 'holy', *kadosh*, is 'set apart', but in the particular sense that what is holy needs to be treated with the utmost respect because of the immense awe which it inspires in the beholder on account of its 'otherness', its greatness, power and excellence.

In its primary sense, holiness inheres only in God. 'There is none holy like the Lord, there is none besides thee' (I Samuel 2:2). But holiness communicates itself to people, places and things which have been especially exposed to the 'radiation' of God's holiness, so that they may be described as holy in a secondary sense. For instance, Moses at the burning bush feels himself commanded: 'Do not come near; put off your shoes from your

feet, for the place on which you are standing is holy ground'
(Exodus 3:5).

Applied to God, the word 'holiness' alludes to those aspects of
His nature which we have already discussed under the heading of
'transcendence', but it also has a *moral* connotation, referring to
God's perfect righteousness before which man feels unworthy,
humbled and rebuked. Thus Isaiah's mystic vision, in which the
angels proclaim, 'Holy, holy, holy is the Lord of hosts', prompts
him to confess: 'I am a man of unclean lips, and I dwell in the
midst of a people of unclean lips' (Isaiah 6:3, 5). Therefore, too,
the apprehension of God's holiness evokes from man a sense of
moral challenge. 'Who shall ascend the hill of the Lord? And who
shall stand in His holy place? He who has clean hands, and a pure
heart . . .' (Psalms 24:3 f.).

NAMES OF GOD

The way in which Jews have thought of God is reflected in the
names by which they have referred to and addressed Him, and a
few of these might usefully be considered before we conclude this
chapter. The least specific are *El, Eloah* and *Elohim*, the last of
which seems to be a plural of majesty, all of them usually translated 'God'. The first also occurs in the combination *El Shaddai*,
an appellation of the God of the Patriarchs, generally rendered as
'God Almighty', but of uncertain meaning. According to Exodus
6:2, it was superseded under Moses by the Tetragrammaton –
YHWH – possibly pronounced Yahweh, the meaning of which
is likewise uncertain, though the Bible (Exodus 3:13–15) derives
it from the verb *hayah*, 'to be', perhaps in the sense of 'He Who
Is' (the Eternal One), perhaps in the sense of 'He Who Causes To
Be' (the Creator).

Already in pre-Christian times, as the Septuagint testifies, the
tetragrammaton was considered so sacred that it had become
customary, when reading the Bible, to substitute for it the word
Adonai, meaning 'My Lord'. This explains why in English Bibles
YHWH is usually translated 'the Lord'. It also explains the
erroneous form 'Jehovah', still used in some Christian circles,
which came about through ignorance of the Jewish scribal device
whereby the consonants of the tetragrammaton (in German

transliteration, JHWH) are pointed with the vowels of *Adonai*, as a reminder that the latter is to be read.

But the substitute-word *Adonai* soon acquired its own sanctity, so that for purposes other than devotional study, prayer and worship still other names and circumlocutions were evolved. Among the most common is *Ha-Makom*, meaning 'the Place', which may have originated as a reference to the Temple – 'the place which the Lord your God shall choose' (e.g., Deuteronomy 12:5) – but was explained as an allusion to God's transcendence (see above, p. 238). Another oblique reference to God, by the mention of a 'place' with which He is especially associated, is *Shamayim*, 'Heaven'. (The true meaning of *Malchut Shamayim* is not 'Kingdom of Heaven' but 'Kingship of God'.)

Other frequently found names of God are: *Ha-Bore*, 'The Creator'; *Ribbono Shel Olam*, 'Lord of the Universe'; *Mi She-Amar V'hayah ha-Olam*, 'He Who Spoke and the World came into Being'; *Gevurah*, 'Power'; *Melech Malchei ha-Melachim*, 'The King above all kings'; *Ha-Shem*, 'The Name' (an allusion to the Tetragrammaton); *Ha-Kadosh Baruch Hu*, 'The Holy One, blessed be He'; *Shechinah*, 'The Divine Presence'; and *Ha-Rachaman*, 'The Compassionate One'.

CHAPTER TWO   GOD AND HIS WORLD

CREATION

'In the beginning God created the heavens and the earth.' That
majestic opening statement of the Bible is echoed by Maimonides,
who starts his monumental code, the Mishneh Torah, with these
words: 'The foundation of foundations, and the pillar of all
wisdom, is to know that there is a First Being, who brings into
existence whatsoever exists, so that all things in heaven and on
earth, and in between, owe their existence solely to the fact of His
existence.'

That the world is God's creation is indeed a basic affirmation
of Judaism. But it raises a number of questions. For instance, *how*
did God create the world? The Creation story in the first chapter
of Genesis gives an answer which, until relatively recent times,
was accepted as a matter of course by Jews and Christians
alike. The axiomatically held belief in the revealed character
of Holy Scripture seemed to guarantee its veracity, and there
was no strong evidence to the contrary. However, modern cosmology and biology have, to say the least, cast considerable
doubt upon it; and to that challenge Jews have reacted in various
ways.

Some have simply reasserted the traditional view and rejected
any scientific evidence or theory inconsistent with it. Others have
attempted to reconcile the biblical account with the scientific one;
for instance, by invoking the principle of Rabbinic exegesis that
the Torah does not always follow a chronological order, or by
suggesting that the six 'days' of Creation are to be understood, on
the basis of Psalm 90:4, as long ages.

Many would accept the critical view, that the biblical creation story is a myth, and even an adaptation of a still older, Meso-potamian myth. To say that is not, however, to disparage it: myths can express great truths. But mythical truth is different from historical truth; it is more akin to poetical truth. Conse-quently, to read the first chapter of Genesis as though it were history is to misunderstand its nature. To be sure, the writer would have thought of his account as factual; presumably it accorded with the best 'scientific' knowledge available to him. But the details, possibly drawn from the Babylonian creation epic, were not of primary importance to him. He used them, as a poet uses images, to convey much profounder truths; and about these there is agreement among Jews of all varieties of religious outlook.

Foremost among them is the truth *that* – never mind how – God created the world: that it is not a product of chance, or of a plurality of creative agencies, but of a single Divine Creator and consequently, as the word 'universe' implies, a unitary, orderly whole: a cosmos ruled by one, benevolent God, which does not behave capriciously but obeys His laws, and in which human beings may therefore feel secure.

Another truth is the transcendental greatness of the Creator God, who created the world out of nothing by a mere exertion of His Will. That, contrary to the Aristotelian view of eternally existent matter, seems to be implied in the biblical narrative, which portrays God as creating the world by a series of *commands*: 'Let there be light . . . Let the earth bring forth . . .' Similarly, the psalmist declares: 'By the word of the Lord the heavens were made, and all their host by the breath of His mouth . . . For He spoke, and it came to be; He commanded, and it stood forth' (Psalms 33:6, 9). And an old Jewish morning prayer begins: 'Blessed be He who spoke, and the world came into being . . . Blessed be He whose word is deed.'

It is also a striking feature of the biblical account of the origin of the world and its inhabitants that, in a manner remarkably similar to the modern scientific one, it presents the process as a well-ordered progression from lower to higher forms of existence, each fresh advance occurring only when the necessary conditions for it have been established, and all leading up to the appearance of man as the grand finale. Interestingly, too, the verb *bara*, 'to create', is used only at three points, each of which marks the crossing of a boundary of extraordinary significance: from nothing to matter, from matter to life, and from life to man (Genesis 1:1, 21, 27).

This view of man as the 'crown of Creation' is undoubtedly one of the major truths which the biblical creation story seeks to express. All the preceding stages are related as a setting of the scene for man's arrival, and he alone is declared to have been created 'in the image of God'. Whatever precisely the author may have meant by that phrase, it clearly implies that man is exalted far above all other creatures. He evidently wished to convey that, in creating the world, God had a purpose, that this was a good purpose, and that it crucially involved man. Such is the impression unmistakably conveyed by the recurring phrase, 'And God saw that it was good' (Genesis 1:4, 12, 18, 25), culminating, when the process is completed with the arrival of man, in the triumphant declaration, 'And God saw everything that He had made, and behold, it was very good' (1:31).

It is evidently to be understood that God was well pleased with His handiwork. Yet in the very expression of His satisfaction there is perhaps a hint of a suggestion that it might not have turned out so well, that it was in the nature of an experiment which could have failed. Accordingly, we do find in the Rabbinic *Aggadah* the speculative notion that God created and destroyed several worlds before creating ours (Genesis Rabbah 3:7, 9:2). However that may be, it is a fundamental affirmation of the biblical creation story that ours is a *good* world.

THE PROBLEM OF EVIL

To say that we live in a good world is, however, immediately to raise the problem of evil, and hence of theodicy: how to account for the presence of evil in a world allegedly created by a benevolent God.

What makes the problem all the more acute for Judaism is that it cannot evade it by attributing the evil to an ultimate source independent of God, for that would be a denial of monotheism. It cannot, for instance, countenance the dualistic doctrine of Zoroastrianism with its two deities, of light and darkness, from which the good and the evil respectively emanate. Indeed, the Prophet of the Exile repudiated that very doctrine when he said in God's name: 'I am the Lord, and there is no other. I form light and create darkness, I make weal (other versions: 'peace') and create woe (other versions: 'evil'), I am the Lord who do all these things' (Isaiah 45:6 f.).

What has been said holds true notwithstanding the occasional appearance of the figure of Satan in the Bible and subsequent Jewish literature. For in Job and Zechariah Satan is an accusing angel rather than an evil being; and though in later Jewish folklore he became a tempter, and was identified with Samael, the prince of the demons, and joined by various other demons, they always remained subordinate to God and never became an independent evil force.

The nearest approach in Judaism to such a dualistic notion is found in the Lurianic *kabbalah*, with its concept of the 'other side' (*sitra achra*), the dark and demonic realm which is said to be the result of God's 'self-contraction' (*tzimtzum*) and the consequent cosmic catastrophe known as the 'breaking of the vessels' (*shevirat ha-kelim*). Nevertheless, the Kabbalists have always emphatically denied that theirs is a dualistic doctrine, pointing out that it was an autonomous decision on God's part to 'withdraw into Himself' and thereby to allow the 'other side' to emerge, in order that human beings might have the opportunity of choosing between good and evil.

TRADITIONAL SOLUTIONS

The problem of theodicy would disappear if it could be demonstrated that what we humans regard as evil is not really evil but only seems so to us. Just such a theory was propounded in the Middle Ages, notably by Abraham ibn Daud (twelfth century, Spain) and Moses Maimonides, who maintained that what we call evil is merely the absence of good, as darkness is the absence of light, and therefore cannot be said in any true sense to have been 'created' at all. But this solution has had few followers, for it is, to say the least, hard to believe that, for example, an illness involving severe pain is merely the absence of health.

Another, much older, way of solving the problem of theodicy is to assert that what we call evil, though real enough, always serves a good purpose and therefore does not derogate from the goodness of the Creator. That does indeed seem to be assumed throughout the Bible. Nor is it contradicted by the Deutero-Isaiah verse quoted above, for there the Hebrew word *ra* does not mean moral evil but has, as modern translations such as the Revised Standard Version make clear, the morally neutral sense of 'woe'.

What, however, is the good purpose served by the seemingly evil? According to the usual form of the belief, it is a punitive purpose. That is to say, the adversities of human life are to be seen as manifestations of God's retributive justice; and since that is an essential aspect of His righteousness, they do not impugn, but rather confirm, His moral character.

This retribution theory, though generally taken for granted in biblical times and long after, did not, however, go unchallenged. To some, it seemed to fly in the face of the evidence of everyday experience that, all too often, the righteous suffer and the wicked prosper. This is the main point of the book of Job. Job is innocent. That is not a blindly self-righteous self-perception on the hero's part. It is a fundamental premise of the book, as the prologue makes clear. Therefore the old, conventional, simplistic reward-and-punishment doctrine, so tenaciously and unconvincingly argued by Job's friends, must be rejected as a total explanation of human suffering.

Not only can it not be assumed that those who suffer invariably deserve their suffering: it can even be argued that the good are peculiarly likely to suffer because, as champions of truth and right, they are prone to draw upon themselves the ire of the protagonists of falsehood and wrong. That seems to be the idea underlying the 'Servant Poems' in Deutero-Isaiah (42:1–4; 49:1–6; 50:4–9; 52:13–53:12) which should most probably be understood as a parable of a persecuted prophet who symbolizes the Jewish people. It may also be implied in a story the Talmud tells of how Moses, granted a vision of the mangled flesh of the martyred Rabbi Akiva, exclaimed, 'Such is the Torah, and such is its reward!' and received from God the peremptory rebuke, 'Be silent; such is My will' (Menachot 29b).

If it is a fact that in this world the good often suffer, and the bad as often prosper, maybe the injustice of it will be redressed in another world? This line of thinking must have been a powerful factor in the welcome accorded to the belief in an after life, especially in the wake of the Maccabean wars, in which so many good and brave young men died so brutally. If the scene of God's retributive justice is thus extended into the hereafter, nothing that happens on this earth can refute it; and there is no doubt that many Jews, throughout the ages, have found such a belief both credible and comforting.

But divine punishment is not necessarily retributive; it may be remedial. This thought is often expressed in the Bible; for instance, 'Know then in your heart that, as a man disciplines his son, the Lord your God disciplines you' (Deuteronomy 8:5), and, 'For the Lord reproves him whom He loves, as a father the son in whom he delights' (Proverbs 3:12).

It was such passages as these which gave rise to the quaint notion, found in the Rabbinic *Aggadah*, that the sufferings of the righteous are to be understood as 'chastisements of love' (*yissurin shel ahavah*) – and therefore as tokens of God's kindness rather than His anger – which He visits on them, not only for their own good in this world, but also in order that He may be able to reward them all the more abundantly in the world to come (Berachot 5a).

But it is not essential for Judaism to maintain that all suffering is punitive, whether in a retributive or in a remedial sense. What does go unquestioned in the classical Jewish sources is that whatever happens in this world happens by God's will. 'Does evil befall a city, unless the Lord has done it?' asks Amos (3:6), while the Talmud states the belief in its most extreme form when it quotes Rabbi Chanina to the effect that 'no man bruises his finger here below unless it has been so decreed for him above' (Chullin 7b). The divine purpose, however, is not always readily apparent, or necessarily comprehensible, to man. In the Bible, and not least in the patriarchal narratives of Genesis, we often encounter what has been called the 'two-tier' view of history: on one level, human beings act out their own motives; on another, unbeknown to them, God uses them to advance, inexorably, His own, inscrutable plan.

Thus all of Judaism's attempts to solve the riddle of theodicy must end, when pressed to the limit, with a confession of human ignorance. It is not only that we don't know the answer, but that our humanity *precludes* us from knowing it. That is the import of God's speech out of the whirlwind when He says to Job: 'Where were you when I laid the foundations of the earth . . .?' (38:4). And it is echoed by the candid admission of a second-century rabbi, 'It does not lie within our power to explain either the well-being of the wicked or the sufferings of the righteous' (Avot 4:15).

MODERN SPECULATIONS

That aphorism characterizes better than anything the approach of modern Jewish thinkers to the discussion of theodicy, which has tended to be reticent, critical of dogmatic assumptions and suspicious of neat and tidy solutions.

Two factors in particular have contributed to this stance. One is our awareness of the natural sciences and therefore the workings of natural law. The other is our consciousness of the Holocaust, which, though it may not have been objectively different in kind from all other historical episodes, has raised to new levels of sensitivity our perception of the brutality of which human beings are capable and of the agonies suffered in our world by the innocent.

Both factors have, moreover, impressed on us in a new way the need to differentiate between 'natural' and 'moral' evils. Natural evils are not caused by human action and may not even affect human beings, since they include the cruelties observable in the animal world – Tennyson's 'Nature, red in tooth and claw', though we have chiefly in mind those which do cause human suffering: flood, famine, earthquake, disease and death itself.

In the past such happenings were regarded as 'acts of God' (as they are still termed in English law); today we tend to look upon the casualties, not as individually singled out for suffering by some divine decree, but as victims of unfortunate conglomerations of circumstances within a system that operates according to general natural laws. For us, therefore, what calls for explanation is not why particular calamities happen to particular people, but why they occur at all.

Here we can speculate that there must be death, so that the generations may succeed one another; that pain is nature's way of alerting us to bodily danger; that accidents are unavoidable in any logically possible world that is governed by universal laws, and do not necessarily negate the benevolence of its Creator; that all these seeming evils serve at least the one good purpose of challenging human beings to learn to conquer or control them, and thus of stimulating progress; and that they assume a different complexion when viewed in the perspective of an evolving, rather than a static, universe. Such speculations do not, of course, resolve the problem; but they do, perhaps, reduce somewhat its enormity.

The moral or man-made evils – crime, war, oppression, persecution, torture, genocide – present a different problem. In past ages, as we have seen, these, too, were regarded as manifestations of God's retributive justice. After the 'first *churban* (destruction)', that of the First Temple in 586 BCE, and again after the 'second *churban*', that of the Second Temple in 70 CE, Jews were inclined to blame themselves and say, in the words of the prayerbook, *mipnei chata'einu*, 'It was because of our sins'. After the Holocaust, many Jews, though not all, while admiring the humility of their ancestors, find such self-castigation no longer intellectually or emotionally possible. To suggest that the six million Jewish men, women and children in any sense deserved their fate, seems to them positively sacrilegious. On the contrary, there is a tendency among Jews to refer to them by the term traditionally applied to martyrs, as *kedoshim*, 'holy ones'.

Modern Jewish thinkers have therefore tended either to abandon altogether the search for a rational solution of the problem of theodicy, on the ground that it is futile and presumptuous, or else to approach it in radically new ways.

One such way is to give up the time-hallowed belief that such happenings are to be regarded as 'acts of God'. How *can* they be, it is argued, since they are by their very nature flagrant violations of the Divine Will? God does not command, but on the contrary, forbids, the murderer to commit murder; therefore He cannot be said to *cause* either the act or the suffering that results from it. However, He has created a universe in which such things can and do happen. He allows them, and does not prevent them. It is in this and only in this sense that He can be said to be 'responsible' for 'man's inhumanity to man'.

Why then does He not prevent it? That is how contemporary

Jewish (and, of course, not only Jewish) thinkers see the problem of theodicy. Either, they say, God is unable to prevent the evil, in which case He is not all-powerful, or he is unwilling to prevent it, in which case He is not all-good.

Faced with this dilemma, some have taken the bold step of questioning God's omnipotence and proposing the concept, known as 'process theology', of a God who is *not yet* omnipotent and depends on man's cooperation to become so; who is, indeed, still in the process of becoming. Shocking as this proposal may seem, it needs to be added that, among the profusion of ideas to be found in the Rabbinic *Aggadah*, it is not impossible to find teachings from which it can draw a measure of support: for instance, that Abraham 'enthroned' the God of heaven on the earth (Sifrei Deuteronomy 313); that when Israel goes into exile, the *Shechinah* goes into exile (Megillah 29a); and that by certain actions, such as procreating and judging justly, man may be considered God's partner (*shuttaf*) in the work of creation (Kiddushin 30b; Shabbat 10a).

Other Jewish thinkers, perhaps influenced by such concepts as the kabbalistic one of *tzimtzum* (see above, page 250), have denied the dilemma by suggesting that God may have the power to prevent evil but, for some reason that does not, after all, negate His goodness, restrains Himself from exercising it. Such a reason might be the preservation of human freedom. So great, it has been suggested, is the value *sub specie aeternitatis* of the existence in the cosmos of a species capable of exercising free choice that not even the whole awesome immensity of the evils human beings do to one another in the misuse of that freedom, outweighs it in God's mind. In the words of a modern Jewish novelist,

God has given us free will . . . to choose between good and evil. Hence, for free will to exist, evil had to exist, in order that man's choice might be his own. God could not thereafter permit Himself to interfere in man's actions, for then there would be an end to free will and an end to the ascending revelation of life . . . This, and only this . . . can give us back a belief in God – in a compassionate, torn and sorrowing God who gave us free will out of love, and having forbidden Himself to interfere, must behold in agony what we do with our freedom . . . For man to become truly free, God had to put man's will beyond even divine intervention.

(Meyer Levin, *The Fanatic*)

MIRACLES

But is divine intervention really ruled out? *In extremis,* when human wickedness has burst all bounds, could and should not God then intervene, while leaving human freedom otherwise intact? Could and should He not have intervened to stop the Holocaust, for instance?

This unavoidable question leads us to consider the position of Judaism on miracles, that is to say, happenings that astound because they involve, or seem to involve, a suspension of the normal workings of nature, and which, because they seem to advance God's purpose in unexpected ways, are perceived as divine interventions in human affairs.

The Hebrew Bible records some major miracles, such as the Ten Plagues and the Crossing of the Red Sea, and a few (remarkably few, one might think) minor ones. It also asserts in principle God's power to cause such events to happen: 'Is anything too hard for the Lord?' (Genesis 18:14); 'Behold, the Lord's hand is not shortened, that it cannot save' (Isaiah 59:1).

Rabbinic literature accepts the principle, does not question the historicity of the miracles recounted in the Bible, and tells some subsequent ones. On the other hand, some of the Rabbis, apparently uncomfortable with the thought that an all-wise God should have needed to make 'contingency adjustments' to His handiwork, surmised that the events in question had been pre-ordained: already at the time of Creation God had commanded the sea to divide before Moses; the sun and moon to stand still before Joshua; the ravens to feed Elijah; the fire not to hurt Hananiah, Mishael and Azariah; the lions not to harm Daniel; the heavens to open before Ezekiel; and the fish to vomit out Jonah (Genesis Rabbah 5:5; cf. Avot 5:6).

When we come to the Middle Ages, we notice among the more rationalistically inclined of the Jewish philosophers, such as Maimonides and Albo, a tendency to play down the miraculous. According to them, the miracle stories of the Bible should in some instances be understood as parables, or as accounts of dreams or visions, rather than factual narratives; and though they believed that exceptional individuals could attain supernatural powers, they no longer expected God Himself to intervene miraculously in their historical era.

Modern Jewish thinkers, in so far as they confront the problem, tend to be even more sceptical, or at least diffident, about miracles. That is partly because modern science has disposed us to think of the laws of nature as unvariable, partly because modern Bible scholarship has shown how necessary, and yet how difficult, it is to disentangle history from legend in the ancient documents. It is also, some would say, because of the conspicuous absence of miracles in recent times, when they have been so sorely needed. A God who does not intervene to stop the Holocaust, they are inclined to think, is a God who, for whatever reason, does not act through miracles.

But against that it needs to be pointed out that the latest developments in science, especially quantum physics with its principle of indeterminacy, and perhaps also parapsychology, demand so fundamental a reconsideration of the whole concept of causation, that the distinction between the normal, the abnormal and the miraculous has become newly problematic. In addition, there is a widespread feeling about certain recent events of a momentous and redemptive kind, including the establishment of the State of Israel, that we are perhaps too close to them in time either to affirm with confidence or to dismiss out of hand the possibility that they involved an element of the miraculous. For all these reasons, one suspects that on the subject of miracles most Jews today would be inclined to endorse Hamlet's words to Horatio, that 'there are more things in heaven and earth . . .', or at least the counsel of an ancient rabbi, 'Teach your tongue to say: I do not know' (Berachot 4a).

DIVINE GUIDANCE

Whether or not miracles occur, God's activity in the universe is not to be sought primarily in the realm of the supernatural. For one thing, Judaism teaches, He is active in the *normal* phenomena of nature which, by their grandeur and beauty, reveal His power and wisdom. 'The heavens are telling the glory of God; and the firmament proclaims his handiwork' (Psalms 19:1; Christian versions, 19:2). The Rabbis said that 'the day when it rains is as great as the day on which heaven and earth were created' (Ta'anit 7b). An ancient Jewish prayer praises God for the fact that 'in His mercy He gives light to the earth and those who dwell upon it, and in His goodness He renews the work of creation continually, day by day'; and another thanks God 'for the miracles that are daily with us, and for Your wondrous kindness at all times, evening, morn and noon'.

Furthermore, as God governs nature by general physical laws, so He governs human history by general moral laws. That is a fundamental principle of Judaism, constantly affirmed by implication, when not explicitly stated, by Prophets and Rabbis alike. It may indeed be questioned whether the law of reward and punishment always applies to individuals, but it does seem to apply to societies and civilizations. At any rate, the larger the collectivity, from family to nation to mankind, and the longer the time-scale, the clearer it becomes that goodness conduces to welfare and evil to disaster; and in this fact the operation of God's justice may be seen.

God also guides human beings in ways that manifest His love: by making known to them – through revelation, inspiration and the 'still, small voice' of the conscience – something of His will; and by exerting on them a constant pressure, which yet falls short of compulsion, to act rightly.

So there *is* divine guidance both in the lives of individuals and in the history of humanity. But guidance is not governance. Man remains free to heed, ignore or defy the guidance: to choose good or evil, blessing or curse, life or death (Deuteronomy 30:15, 19). Therefore what happens to God's world depends significantly, even if not ultimately, on man.

CHAPTER THREE   MAN AND HIS
DESTINY

The Hebraic view of the world is theocentric, seeing God as the originator, sustainer and arbiter of all things. Yet it is also anthropocentric, since its chief concern is with human life, though always in its relation to the Divine Will. This perspective becomes apparent already in the opening chapter of the Bible which, as we have noted, moves swiftly through the various stages of Creation until it comes to man, who is henceforth to occupy the centre of the stage, when it continues:

Then God said, 'Let us make man in our image, after our likeness; and let them have dominion over the fish of the sea, and over the birds of the air, and over the cattle, and over all the earth, and over every creeping thing that creeps upon the earth.' So God created man in His own image, in the image of God He created him: male and female He created them. And God blessed them, and God said to them, 'Be fruitful and multiply, and fill the earth and subdue it; and have dominion over the fish of the sea and over the birds of the air and over every living thing that moves upon the earth.'

(Genesis 1:26 ff.)

This is the primary source of the Jewish understanding of man and his place in the cosmos; therefore we need to examine what Judaism has made of the passage.

DIGNITY

One thing, at least, is clear: that it confers on man a high privilege, and thereby invests him with a great dignity. Not only does it raise him above the animals, but it assigns to him a position second only to that of God Himself. Accordingly, it prompted the author of the eighth Psalm to exclaim:

> When I look at thy heavens, the work of thy fingers,
> the moon and the stars which thou hast established;
> what is man that thou art mindful of him,
> and the son of man, that thou dost care for him?

> Yet thou hast made him little less than God,
> and dost crown him with glory and honour.
> Thou hast given him dominion over the works of thy hands;
> thou hast put all things under his feet,
> all sheep and oxen,
> and also the beasts of the field,
> the birds of the air, and the fish of the sea,
> whatever passes along the paths of the sea.

The most obvious evidence of man's exalted status, emphasized in both passages, is the extent of his mastery over his environment. It is this which makes him seem 'Godlike'. This mastery is, of course, also a biological fact, attributable to man's superior intelligence and skill. What the Bible adds is that man is *divinely mandated* to exercise these powers, so that he is the bearer, not only of a high privilege, but of a corresponding responsibility. He is responsible to God for the use he makes of his powers. In a striking phrase, that recurs in Jewish literature, he is 'God's partner in the work of Creation', but in the subordinate sense of being His 'steward' on earth – so wrote Rashi, commenting on the psalm verse, 'The heavens are the Lord's heavens, but the earth he has given to the sons of men' (115:16).

FREE WILL

'Responsibility' suggests that human beings possess a measure of freedom of action. If that is so, it furnishes another instance of their 'Godlikeness'. But though it does indeed seem obvious that at least some human actions are genuinely voluntary, the result of deliberation and choice, the assertion raises intellectual difficulties. Philosophically, it is difficult to fit in with any theory of causation; theologically, it seems to detract from God's omnipotence and foreknowledge. Consequently the deterministic view, which denies man's ultimate freedom, has had its advocates among Jewish thinkers. But in the main, Judaism has not only upheld the notion of free will, but strongly emphasized it for moral purposes.

Within the Bible, the commandments of the Pentateuch, the exhortations of the Prophets and the good advice of the Wisdom writers, all imply that those to whom they are addressed are free to obey or disobey, to act rightly or wrongly, sagaciously or foolishly, and, sometimes, that freedom is dramatically affirmed: 'I call heaven and earth to witness against you this day, that I have set before you life and death, blessing and curse; therefore choose life' (Deuteronomy 30:19).

Among the earliest post-biblical Jewish writers, the author of Ecclesiasticus is particularly explicit: 'It was God who created man in the beginning, and He left him in the power of his own inclination. If you will, you can keep the commandments, and to act faithfully is a matter of your choice' (15:14 f.).

The Pharisees and Rabbis tended to affirm human freedom, but without denying divine prescience, as in Rabbi Akiva's statement of the paradox: 'Everything is foreseen, yet free will is given' (Avot 3:16). They insisted that in the most significant decisions – to do or not to do God's will – the power to choose is real. A key source of this doctrine was for them the biblical exhortation: 'And now, Israel, what does the Lord your God require of you, but to fear the Lord your God, to walk in all His ways, to love Him, to serve the Lord your God with all your heart and with all your soul, and to keep the commandments and statutes of the Lord, which I command you this day for your good?' (Deuteronomy 10:12 f.). From this they derived the principle that 'everything is in the hand of God except the fear of God' (Berachot 33b et al.), on which Rashi comments: 'Everything that happens to a man is in the hand of God, for instance whether he is tall or short, poor or rich, intelligent or unintelligent, white or black; but whether he is righteous or wicked is not in the hand of God, but He has entrusted it into the hand of man, and set before him two ways, so that he may choose the way of the fear of God.'

The same line of thought is followed by most of the Jewish philosophers, including Maimonides, who wrote:

Every human being has been given free-will. If he wishes to incline himself towards the good way and to be righteous, he is free to do so;

and if he wishes to incline himself towards the evil way and to be wicked, he is free to do that . . . Every individual is capable of being righteous like Moses or wicked like Jeroboam, wise or foolish, merciful or cruel, mean or generous, and so with all the other dispositions; and there is no power that compels him, or decrees for him, or pulls him one way or the other; but he himself, by his own volition, chooses the path he desires . . . And this is a major principle and fundamental premise of the Torah and commandments.

(*Mishneh Torah*, Laws of Repentance 5:1–3).

An impressive endorsement of Judaism's affirmation of the reality of free-will is provided by Viktor E. Frankl, a psychiatrist and concentration-camp survivor:

The experiences of camp life show that man does have a choice of action. There were enough examples, often of a heroic nature, which proved that apathy could be overcome, irritability suppressed. Man *can* preserve a vestige of spiritual freedom, of independence of mind, even in such terrible conditions of psychic and physical stress. We who lived in concentration camps can remember the men who walked through the huts comforting others, giving away their last piece of bread. They may have been few in number, but they offer sufficient proof that everything can be taken from a man but one thing: the last of the human freedoms – to choose one's attitude in any given circumstances, to choose one's own way.

(*Man's Search for Meaning*)

THE TWO INCLINATIONS

If it is true that human beings are free to choose between good and evil, it is also true that all too frequently they choose the latter. Why, granted such freedom, are they so prone to misuse it, and how can that fact be reconciled with the doctrine of the Divine Image?

The fact itself is not denied, but rather emphasized, by Judaism. 'Surely there is not a righteous man on earth who does good and never sins' (Ecclesiastes 7:20). The Bible uses a great variety of terms for wrongdoing; a modern scholar examines eighteen, pointing out that it is not a complete list. The Prophets, in particular, unsparingly denounce every kind of immorality and injustice on the part of individuals and nations, not least Israel itself. The Jewish liturgy is not lacking in confessions of the most self-condemnatory kind: one such confession, in the form of an alphabetic acrostic, runs through the whole alphabet in order to spell out the dismal catalogue of sins we are prone to commit; another pleads, 'Our Father, our King, be gracious to us and answer us, for we are bereft of good deeds; therefore treat us with charity and kindness, and save us.' And the experience of the Jewish people through the ages has been one of ever-recurring exposure to the dismal phenomenon of man's inhumanity to man. It is therefore hardly to be expected that Jews, least of all in this post-Holocaust age, would underestimate the human propensity for evil.

One possible way of explaining this propensity would be to assert that, having been created in God's image, man rebelled against his Creator and thereby fatally flawed his original right-eousness. But of this doctrine of the Fall of Man, so prominent in Christian tradition, there is barely a trace in Jewish tradition, which therefore left itself with the problem of accounting for the human propensity to sin, without impugning the unimpaired reality of the Divine Image.

It has characteristically tried to do so in terms of quite another doctrine, greatly stressed in Rabbinic literature, which says that man is impelled by two conflicting forces: the *yetzer tov*, commonly translated 'good inclination', and the *yetzer ha-ra*, the 'evil inclination'. The latter, as usually understood, in spite of its name, is not intrinsically evil. On the contrary, like the leaven in the dough to which it is sometimes likened, it serves a good purpose. What that purpose might be is best inferred from a saying of the Rabbis that, 'if it were not for the evil inclination, a man would not build a house, marry, beget children, or engage in business' (Genesis Rabbah 9:7). Evidently, *yetzer ha-ra* is a generic term for those basic human drives – for property, pleasure, power and survival – which are readily seen to be biologically necessary. It is called 'evil' only because these drives, being so powerful, are always liable, if not controlled, to lead a man into actions that harm others. But they can and should be harnessed to good ends. Hence the Rabbis could enunciate the paradox, that a man should serve God with *both* his good inclination and his evil inclination (Sifrei Deuteronomy 32).

The evil inclination, as understood in Jewish tradition, no

doubt accounts for most of the wrongs, even of a violent nature, which human beings do to one another. Yet there are also depths of depravity and brutality, reported in the criminal courts and perpetrated on a mass scale in the more barbaric episodes of history, for which such an explanation seems less than adequate. They have a demoniac quality which suggests yet other, psychopathological causes, such as sadism and mass-hysteria. Yet these very terms imply abnormality and therefore do not invalidate the belief, characteristic of Judaism, that man, in his normal condition, inclines towards righteousness. He seeks pleasure, power, wealth and the like; in the pursuit of these aims, especially if frustrated, he may become obsessive, inconsiderate of others and aggressive; but he does not, unless perverted, desire evil for evil's sake.

Moreover, he is not powerless to control his self-regarding drives. To begin with, he is born untainted by sin. An ancient Jewish prayer affirms: 'The soul which You have given me, O God, is pure. For You have created it, and formed it, and breathed it into me' (Berachot 60b). Furthermore, he has a conscience: that is, an inborn capacity to discern between right and wrong, a tendency to favour the right, and an altruistic impulse. That is what *yetzer tov*, the good inclination, means. And although, if left uncultivated, it may be too weak to overcome the forces of passion arrayed against it, it can be trained. That is precisely the purpose of the Torah. 'The Holy One, blessed be He, spoke to Israel: My children, I have created the Evil Inclination, but I have also created the Torah as an antidote to it; if you occupy yourselves with the Torah, you will not be delivered into its power' (Kiddushin 30b).

REPENTANCE

Nevertheless, the difficulties of mastering the evil inclination are formidable, especially as it grows progressively more dominating if it is not checked. In the words of Rabbi Akiva, 'At first sin appears as a spider's web, in the end it becomes like a ship's rope; at first it enters as a visitor, in the end it makes itself master of the house' (Genesis Rabbah 22:6). Therefore, man needs ever and again to make a deliberate effort to free himself from its stranglehold, to listen to his conscience, to return to the right path; in short, to repent. Such repentance is called in Hebrew *teshuvah*, which means 'returning'.

The concept is biblical. 'Let the wicked forsake his way, and the unrighteous man his thoughts; let him return to the Lord, that He may have mercy on him, and to our God, for He will abundantly pardon' (Isaiah 55:7). 'Return, O Israel, to the Lord your God, for you have stumbled because of your iniquity' (Hosea 14:2; in Christian Bibles, 14:1). 'Return to Me, and I will return to you, says the Lord of hosts' (Malachi 3:7). But it was the Pharisees and Rabbis who coined the noun *teshuvah* in the sense of repentance. They re-emphasized God's longing for man's repentance and His ready responsiveness to even the slightest effort he may make in that direction. 'The Holy One, blessed be He, says to Israel: Open for Me one gate of repentance by as little as the point of a needle, and I will open for you gates wide enough for carriages and coaches to pass through' (Canticles Rabbah 5:2). They also stressed – perhaps polemically, against the Christian salvation doctrine – that no superhuman mediator is involved. In this vein, Rabbi Akiva said: 'Happy are you, O Israel! Before whom are you made clean, and who makes you clean? Your Father in heaven, as it says [Ezekiel 36:25], I will sprinkle clean water upon you, and you shall be clean' (Yoma 8:9).

Even human intermediaries, in the form of priests, were declared unnecessary after the destruction of the Temple. That is the import of a remarkable Midrash. Wisdom, it says, was asked, 'What is the sinner's punishment?' and answered: 'Misfortune pursues sinners' (Proverbs 13:21). Then the question was put to Prophecy, which replied, 'the soul that sins shall die' (Ezekiel 18:4); then to the Torah, which responded: 'Let him bring a guilt offering, and he will be forgiven' – this in allusion to Leviticus 5:6, which says: '. . . and the priest shall make atonement for him for his sin.' Finally, God Himself is asked, and He, as it were overruling all three parts of the Bible – Torah, Prophets and Writings, simply says: 'Let him repent, and he will be forgiven.' (Jerusalem Talmud, Makkot 2:6, in interpretation of Psalms 25:8, 'therefore He instructs sinners in the way'.)

In repenting, man 'returns', not only to the 'way', but to God Himself. Sin breaches man's relationship with God: 'Your iniquities have made a separation between you and your God, and your sins have hid His face from you' (Isaiah 59:2). Repentance restores the relationship. Man's 'returning' and God's forgiving together effect atonement, that is, reconciliation; and the word *teshuvah* often connotes the whole process.

PRAYER AND REVELATION

Underlying all this is the assumption that a relationship between man and God is possible; and not only that, but that it is the kind of I–Thou relationship which is involved in direct communication. This is yet another implication of the teaching that man was created in God's image: there is enough 'affinity' between them to make communication possible.

Prayer is not necessarily verbal communication. Judaism knows of silent meditation, and Chasidism uses, devotionally, songs without words. But the human tendency to verbalize is strong, almost irresistible, and Judaism has evolved an extensive liturgy. Some of its prayers refer to God in the third person; many address Him in the second person and therefore express man's I–Thou relationship with God. (According to a modern scholar, Joseph Heinemann, the former originated in the schools, the latter in the synagogues.) They include praise, confession, supplication and thanksgiving.

Supplicatory (or petitionary) prayers raise the question, whether by reciting them the worshipper may hope to influence God. Traditionally, Judaism has not ruled out that possibility. The Talmud, for instance, has stories about men of exceptional piety who were able successfully to pray for rain in times of drought, and the synagogue liturgy includes prayers for recovery from illness. But in the main Judaism stresses the effect of prayer on man rather than on God. On that basis, it is possible to justify petitionary prayers by the supposition that the changes they produce in the volitional state of the worshipper enable God to respond without deviating from His own unchanging ways. That would accord with the teaching of Rabban Gamaliel III: 'Make God's will your will, so that He may make your will His will' (Avot 2:4).

More generally, it may be said that all prayer, whatever its verbal form, is essentially an attempt to actualize man's potential relationship with God, and so to reopen the channel of His influence upon the worshipper.

If there is, nevertheless, a large element of mystery about the way prayer 'works', the same applies to its converse: Revelation. Why, for instance, does it occur so rarely? And how is the Bible to be understood when it says that God 'spoke' to individual men and women, or to the assembled people at Mount Sinai? There have no doubt always been those who have taken such expressions literally. Others have regarded them as anthropomorphisms referring to what must have been non-verbal communications, verbally interpreted by the human beings who received them. What matters for our present purpose is only this, that traditional Judaism has consistently maintained that divine–human communication is possible and has, as a matter of fact, occurred.

RESURRECTION AND IMMORTALITY

If man was created in God's image, may it be inferred that he shares his Creator's eternity? In one form or another, such a belief has indeed been an integral part of Jewish thought for over two thousand years. But it was not always so. In the Hebrew Bible there are few references to an afterlife. The common conception of the human being, in those days, was of a body animated by the 'breath of life': 'Then the Lord God formed man of dust from the ground, and breathed into his nostrils the breath of life; and man became a living being' (Genesis 2:7). Death was the withdrawal of the animating breath: 'When thou takest away their breath, they die, and return to their dust' (Psalms 104:29); 'When his breath departs he returns to his earth; on that very day his plans perish' (Psalms 146:4).

There was also a popular belief that the dead descended into an underworld called *sheol* where they 'slept with their fathers'. But if so, might it not be possible to reawaken them? That such a notion was entertained is shown by the story of the woman of Endor, who at Saul's bidding raised the spirit of Samuel (I Samuel 28). But it was evidently discouraged by the people's religious leaders because it was too closely associated with pagan myths about humans becoming immortal by being transformed into gods, and with occult practices. Hence Adam is forbidden to eat of the tree of life, lest he 'live for ever' (Genesis 3:22); hence the condemnations of necromancy (Leviticus 19:31; Deuteronomy 18:11); hence the absence of any affirmation of the afterlife in the writings of the Prophets.

Nevertheless, these beliefs persisted, as is demonstrated, for instance, by Ezekiel's use of resurrection as a metaphor for the hoped-for national restoration after the exile (37:1–14). It was apparently during the ensuing centuries of Persian and Greek rule that such beliefs gained ground, and, as already mentioned (p. 252), in the Maccabean age that they achieved official recognition.

They also divided into two streams. On the one hand there was the belief in the bodily resurrection of the dead, which found expression, as an eschatological expectation, in the biblical book of Daniel – 'And many of those who sleep in the dust of the earth shall awake, some to everlasting life, and some to shame and everlasting contempt' (12:2), and, as a more immediate hope, in the apocryphal II Maccabees (e.g., 7:9). On the other hand there was the belief in the survival of the soul. Ecclesiastes had taught that 'the dust returns to the earth as it was: and the spirit returns to God who gave it' (12:7). Now it was asserted that the spirit would retain its individuality:

The souls of the righteous are in the hand of God, and no torment shall touch them. In the eyes of the foolish they seem to have died, and their departure is thought an affliction, and their going from us their destruction; but they are at peace, for though in the sight of men they have been punished, they have a sure hope of immortality.

(Wisdom of Solomon 3:1–4).

The Pharisees, unlike the Sadducees, accepted both doctrines, resurrection and immortality. Therefore both passed into Rabbinic Judaism and into the liturgy of the Synagogue, which asserts that God 'revives the dead' and that He has 'implanted eternal life within us'. It is, however, often far from clear how the distinction and interrelationship between the two concepts was understood, and what precise connotation was ascribed to terms such as the World to Come, Garden of Eden (paradise) and *gehinnom* (hell). Something of the flavour of rabbinic teachings about the afterlife may nevertheless be conveyed by the following examples.

This world is like a vestibule before the world to come; prepare yourself in the vestibule, that you may enter into the hall . . . One hour of repentance and good deeds in this world is better than the whole life of the world to come; yet one hour of bliss in the world to come is better than the whole life of this world . . . In the world to come there is no eating or drinking or procreation or trading or jealousy or hatred or competition, but the righteous sit with crowns on their heads, feasting on the radiance of the *Shechinah*.

(Avot 4:16, 17; Berachot 17a)

Of the Jewish philosophers, it may be said, as a generalization, that some tended to cling to the concept of resurrection, others (notably Philo, Maimonides and Mendelssohn) to emphasize that of immortality, while the kabbalists were inclined to espouse yet another doctrine, that of metempsychosis, or the transmigration of souls.

Ordinary Jews, one supposes, were generally content to believe that there is *some* kind of life after death, and to draw comfort and hope from prayers such as this, recited at the end of the sabbath grace after meals: 'May the Merciful One let us inherit the day which shall be all sabbath and rest in the life of eternity.'

In modern times, however, the spirit of enlightenment and rationalism caused many Jews to reject the belief in bodily resurrection as patently untenable, and to cling only to a vaguely conceived immortality of the soul. Such a position was, in fact, formally adopted by the Reform movement, especially in America, which amended the relevant liturgical texts accordingly. On the other hand, secularism has induced a more general scepticism about *any* kind of afterlife. Thus, contemporary Jewish attitudes to the subject vary widely. But it may nevertheless be surmised that most Jews, if they do not firmly believe, at least entertain the hope, or do not dismiss the possibility, that 'death is not the end'.

DESTINY OF MANKIND

From the destiny of the individual in a possible hereafter, we now turn to the destiny of mankind within the known world of space and time. About that, Judaism has been characteristically optimistic. This does not mean that it anticipates constant, let alone automatic, progress, but that it regards human history as having a divinely conceived purpose, which will ultimately be accomplished.

This optimism may seem surprising in view of the Jewish experience of oppression and persecution. But it rests on two respectable foundations: the conviction that God's will cannot for ever be thwarted, but must, in the end, prevail, and the belief that He created man in His image.

To these, however, a third affirmation needs to be added: that, in spite of the free will, itself an aspect of the Divine Image, which human beings possess, God nevertheless guides their collective destiny. How that paradox is to be explained is another question. As we have noted previously, it is often the way of Judaism to affirm a paradox without resolving it, accepting that reality is sometimes paradoxical. The 'two-tier' conception of history, to which reference was made in the preceding chapter (p. 252) does just that, since it affirms simultaneously human freedom and divine guidance.

Perhaps, however, a hint towards the resolution of the paradox can be found in statements such as this, by a third-century rabbi: 'Whoever wishes to pollute himself with sin will find all the gates open before him; and whoever desires to attain the highest purity will find all the forces of goodness ready to help him' (Yoma 38b). Perhaps the truth is that while God *permits* human beings to do wrong (in the sense of not preventing them), He actually *reinforces* any impulse on their part to do right; that there is a kind of cosmic moral pressure – Matthew Arnold's 'enduring power, not ourselves, which makes for righteousness' – which, without nullifying human freedom, tilts the balance in favour of the ultimate victory of good over evil.

MESSIANIC HOPE

That the triumph of good over evil will be the end result of the drama of human history, Judaism never doubts. But as to the precise nature of the dénouement – the details of the eschatology – there is diverse speculation.

Much of it relates to the figure of the Messiah. The word, from the Hebrew *mashiach*, means 'anointed' and was applied in Bible times to various individuals – kings, priests, prophets – who were regarded as having been divinely commissioned for a sacred task: even, in one instance, the Persian king, Cyrus (Isaiah 45:1). The Hebrew Bible does *not* use it in its later, eschatological sense. This is a post-biblical concept though with roots in the Bible and particularly in the hopes for a better national future – of unity, justice, glory and peace – which, after the time of King David, were vested in his dynasty. Hence the idealistic picture of the 'shoot from the stump of Jesse' (David's father), who will be wise and God-fearing and rule the people with righteousness (Isaiah 11 and many other such passages).

It was in the post-biblical period that this hoped-for future king became, under the title 'Messiah', an eschatological figure, playing the leading role in an increasingly bizarre scenario of the 'last things'. Contributory factors were the patriotic fervour aroused by the Maccabean rebellion; resentment at the Hasmonean rulers who usurped the royal title; and the Roman oppression, culminating in the destruction of the Temple, which engendered both furious anger and despair of salvation by anything other than a supernatural, divine intervention. The scenario, as depicted in the apocalyptic writings of the time, includes, besides the royal Messiah of the house of David, several other messianic figures such as Elijah redivivus, the 'Son of Man', a Moses-like prophet, a 'True Priest' and a warrior Messiah of the house of Joseph; and, as regards events, the ingathering of the exiles, the rebuilding of the Temple (this after 70 CE), the conversion of gentiles, the successful war of the forces of light against the forces of darkness under their kings, Gog and Magog, the reign of the Messiah-King, the Day of Judgement, the resurrection of the dead, and the world to come.

The Pharisees and Rabbis accepted this eschatology in general outline, with emphasis on the Davidic Messiah and Elijah as his forerunner, but on the whole discouraged too much preoccupation with it and, especially, speculation regarding its chronology. One third-century scholar taught that the messianic age would be distinguished from the present only by Israel's freedom from subjugation to foreign empires (Berachot 34b); another declared, 'All the alleged ends of the world have already come and gone; now everything depends on repentance and good deeds' (Sanhedrin 97b); and a fourth-century rabbi, unique in this respect, went so far as to say that no personal Messiah was to be expected at all, since the relevant prophecies had already been fulfilled long ago in the person of Hezekiah (Sanhedrin 99a).

During the subsequent centuries, Jewish messianic expectancy fluctuated. It naturally tended to grow in intensity at times of severe persecution and suffering; then it would sometimes give rise to messianic movements, focusing in the first instance on the return to Zion, such as those of David Alroy (twelfth century) and Shabbetai Tzevi (seventeenth century). Sometimes favourable historical developments would also encourage it, with emphasis on the redemption of mankind as a whole. Thus the Emancipation generated among many western Jews a great wave of exuberant optimism for the future. The bad old days of ignorance and strife, they believed, were finally coming to an end, and would give way to a bright new era of enlightenment and brotherhood. Such was the mood of the Reform movement in the nineteenth century, especially in America, and it contributed to the tendency, reflected in its liturgy, to play down the narrower, national aspects of the messianic hope and to re-emphasize the broader, universalistic ones.

The whirlwind of the Holocaust blew out the last flickering flames of that premature optimism, and lent a poignant timeliness to the warning of a second-century rabbi who, commenting on the Psalm verse, 'Then our mouth was filled with laughter, and our tongue with shouts of joy' (126:2), remarked: 'It is forbidden to fill one's mouth with laughter in this world' (Berachot 31a). This world remains, as it has always been, stubbornly and tragically unredeemed. And yet the knowledge that it is so has engendered among Jews a sense of realism rather than despair. In that realism there is still room for hope, even conviction, that ultimately good will triumph over evil. It will do so, Judaism teaches, either because of man or in spite of him: because of man, since he was created in God's image; in spite of him, because God's will cannot finally be thwarted. On the enigmatic phrase, 'I am the Lord; in its time I will hasten it' (Isaiah 60:22), a third-century rabbi commented: 'If you are not worthy, the redemption will come in its own time; if you are worthy, I will hasten it' (Canticles Rabbah 8:14:1).

CHAPTER FOUR   THE JEWISH PEOPLE AND THEIR TASK

History, as Judaism sees it, is a purposive process that leads from Creation to Redemption, though not in a straight line. There have been, and will be, ups and downs, and nobody knows what disasters may yet lie ahead. Indeed, one of the recurring themes of Jewish apocalyptic thinking places the worst catastrophe of all, sometimes described as the 'birth-pangs of the Messiah', in the future, as the penultimate eschatological event. Nevertheless, Judaism has never doubted that history will culminate in a messianic age or the 'kingdom of Heaven', when God's rule will become fully operative in the life of mankind. Then truth will finally prevail over falsehood, right over might, joy over sorrow, and all that is now imperfect will become perfect.

This conviction derives partly from Judaism's faith in man, as having been created in God's image and therefore endowed with a good inclination, but chiefly from its faith in God, who is the source of history's forward thrust, and who will ensure that in the end His purpose wins through.

As the basis of the belief is twofold – faith in man and faith in God – so is the redemptive process itself. It, too, involves both God and man; it is a combined operation. Often, in Jewish literature, man is referred to as God's 'partner'. But the partnership is not an equal one. Man, as we have noted, can only hasten or delay the consummation, which is ultimately guaranteed by God's invincible will.

It is also guaranteed, some would say, by explicit divine assurances contained in the Sacred Scriptures, such as God's 'covenant' with Noah, with its promise, symbolized by the rainbow, that no global destruction will in the future be allowed to supervene, to foil His redemptive plan (Genesis 9:8–17).

As for the manner of the divine guidance which, in spite of all setbacks, steers the historic process towards its messianic goal, we touched on that at the end of chapter 2 (pp. 257–8); here we need to take a closer look at its history, as Judaism sees it.

The earliest ancestors of the human race were already recipients of divine revelation in that sense. That emerges from the opening chapters of Genesis, and served the Rabbis as a basis for their doctrine of the 'commandments of the descendants of Noah' or 'Noachide laws': elementary rules of conduct which, having been revealed to the very first generations, from Adam to Noah, are said to be incumbent on all human beings. They are generally said to be seven in number, and forbid idolatry, blasphemy, incest, murder, robbery and cruelty to animals, as well as demanding the establishment of lawcourts for the dispensation of justice.

COVENANT

But the Noachide laws were only the beginning. The further unfolding of God's plan required that a whole people should be trained to play a pioneering role in the redemptive process. God chose Abraham as the progenitor of such a people-to-be.

The choice was not arbitrary. Abraham was the first human to show the requisite aptitude and responsiveness. 'He believed in the Lord; and He reckoned it to him as righteousness,' says the Bible (Genesis 15:6). The Midrash adds that God sifted ten generations as with a fine-tooth comb before He discovered this gem of a man: an interpretation derived from Nehemiah 9:8, 'And thou didst find his heart faithful before thee' (Genesis Rabbah 39:10).

With Abraham, therefore, God entered into that special relationship of solemn mutual commitment which is known as the Covenant. We have already encountered the term in a broader sense. Here it means that the people to be reared by Abraham are to be God's servants and witnesses, proclaiming His sovereignty, testifying to His unity, exemplifying His moral law, and so paving the way for the establishment of His kingdom, while He, on the condition of their continuing loyalty, will give them the instruction, the strength and the means (including a territorial base) to endure and to carry out their assignment.

This Covenant, whose outward symbol is circumcision (Genesis 17:1–14), is one of the key concepts of Judaism; and one of the major motifs of the Bible, from the twelfth chapter of Genesis, is the saga of this Covenant's precarious transmission from Abraham to Isaac, Jacob-Israel and his descendants, almost to be crushed out by the period of slavery in Egypt. But just when all seems lost, there is a dramatic new beginning. Moses hears God's call, God liberates His people, and at Sinai the great hope invested in Abraham at last comes true: an entire people reaffirms the Covenant, receives God's teaching, and pledges itself to live by its precepts, including in that pledge its future generations, yet unborn, until the end of time.

After that, the way is by no means easy. There still remains the completion of the arduous journey through the wilderness and the struggle to establish a new society in the Promised Land. There will be backsliding and rebellion. Prophet after prophet will need to recall the people to their divine vocation. The Temple will be built and destroyed. Kingdoms will rise and fall. Autonomy will be lost and regained. Long ages of dispersion and persecution, but also of dogged survival and dazzling creativity, still lie ahead. God's teaching will be interpreted and reinterpreted. A whole literature will yet be written, a whole history enacted.

Nevertheless, Sinai is the cardinal event, the supremely significant halfway point between the two poles of the historic process: Creation and Redemption. Therefore we need now to explore more fully the interrelated concepts of election, people, revelation and mission which Sinai signifies.

ELECTION

The sense of chosen-ness, as applied to the Jewish people, permeates the classical sources of Judaism, not least its liturgy, and needs to be confronted by anyone who wishes to understand the religion.

It also raises difficulties, which have at times shocked, embarrassed or perplexed not only gentiles but also, especially in this modern, secular age, Jews: so much so that one contemporary

Jewish religious movement – that of the Reconstructionists, founded by Rabbi Mordecai Kaplan in the USA – has actually repudiated the 'chosen people' idea and expunged it from its prayer books. Most Jewish theologians, however, believe that the objections to this doctrine are spurious, provided that it is correctly understood. They therefore continue to affirm it.

It would be wrong, for instance, to criticize the doctrine on the ground that it implied a limited, national deity. On the contrary, a choosing God must, in the nature of the case, be a universal God: 'Now therefore, if you will obey My voice and keep My covenant, you shall be My own possession among all peoples; *for all the earth is Mine*, and you shall be to Me a kingdom of priests and a holy nation' (Exodus 19:5 f.). (The italics are the author's own.)

A more serious objection to the concept of the election of Israel (nicely encapsulated in the Ogden Nash rhyme, 'How odd/Of God/To choose/The Jews!') is that such a choice on God's part would reflect, not on His universality, but on His impartiality or His good judgement; the implication being that it would be justified only if the Jews were superior to other peoples, which is manifestly not the case.

The concept does indeed carry with it the danger that it may induce a sense of superiority, and it would be ingenuous to pretend that Jews had never succumbed to it. But for that very reason the teachers of Judaism, since ancient times, have been at pains to warn against any such notion. The Prophets, for instance, could hardly have been more scathing in their condemnations of the people's sins, self-righteousness among them. Nor did the message go unheeded, for the very people so castigated preserved and canonized the prophetic writings!

It is precisely because national superiority has been ruled out as an explanation that the doctrine of Election has always been a source of puzzlement, not only to non-Jews, but to Jews themselves. That it was a fact, they could not very well deny. For they had, or felt themselves to have, a relationship with the One God of the universe which, so far as they knew, no other people in antiquity had. They alone, however vacillatingly, acknowledged Him. They alone, however perfunctorily, worshipped Him. The Election, therefore, was not in doubt, only the reason for it.

Why Chosen

Perhaps there is no reason, or none that human beings can understand. Perhaps God's choice must simply be accepted as a mystery, as unaccountable as love. There is such a trend, notably in Hosea: 'When Israel was a child, I loved him, and out of Egypt I called My son . . .' (11:1). But speculation persists, and particularly the endeavour to square God's choice with His justice.

We have already mentioned the belief that Abraham was especially responsive to God. This became enlarged into the doctrine of the 'merit of the fathers' (in Hebrew, *zechut avot*): that the Patriarchs, from Abraham onwards, had by their righteousness proved themselves worthy of God's favour. A further development of the same trend can be seen in the recurring theme found in the Rabbinic *Aggadah*, that God offered His Torah to all the nations of mankind but that, for one reason or another, they all refused it; all, that is, except the Israelites, who, assembled at Mount Sinai, showed such eagerness for it that they promised to obey it even before they had been apprised of its contents, this being inferred from the sequence of their affirmation, 'We will do, and we will hear' (Exodus 24:7; Mechilta Yitro 5 to Exodus 20:2).

The advantage of such theories is that they enabled subsequent generations of Jews to disclaim any special virtue for themselves by attributing their chosen-ness to that of their remote ancestors; to say, in so many words: However unworthy we may be, we are nevertheless the descendants of those spiritually sensitive souls who, in the dim and distant past, became the founding fathers of our people and, at Mount Sinai, pledged their collective loyalty to God. A daily morning prayer, dating from talmudic times, makes that very point: 'What are we? What is our life, and what our piety? What our goodness, and what our strength? . . . Yet we are Your people, the children of Your Covenant . . .'

It is the Covenant, consummated at Sinai, which confers on the Jewish people their elected status. But to say that is to raise the question whether it is permanent and unbreakable. Often, that is what the Bible seems to be saying: 'I will betroth you to Me for ever; . . . How can I give you up, O Ephraim! (Hosea 2:21 – in Christian Bibles, 2:19; 11:8). The Rabbis, too, emphasized the point, especially, one suspects, in order to sustain the morale of their people against the impact of Christian polemic, with its assertion that God had withdrawn His favour from them. (This may lie behind the controversy in the Talmud, Berachot 11b, as to whether a certain prayer should begin 'With a *great* love' or 'With *everlasting* love have You loved the House of Israel, Your people . . .') But the contrary trend, which makes the continuation of the Covenant conditional on the people's fidelity, is also well represented: '*If* you will obey My voice and keep My covenant, you shall be My own possession among all peoples' (Exodus 19:5). Likewise, on the verse, 'You shall be holy men consecrated to Me' (Exodus 22:30), the Rabbis commented: '*If* you are holy, only then are you Mine' (Mechilta Mishpatim 20 ad loc.).

There is thus, on this subject, an ambivalence in Jewish literature which conveys enough assurance to uphold the people's collective self-esteem, but also enough warning to remind them that their Election is a privilege they may never take for granted but must always strive anew to earn.

As for the question whether they have *in fact* remained faithful to the Sinaitic Covenant – or whether at any rate enough of them have done so in each generation to ensure its continuity – who is qualified to answer it? Jews can only say that they hope and believe so; others must judge for themselves whether their record of loyalty to their religious traditions, given the circumstances of their history, is or is not remarkable.

Exclusiveness?

But even if it be admitted that the doctrine of Election, as applied to the Jewish people, has retained its validity, one still needs to confront the frequently heard objection, that it is too exclusive. This, however, can mean one of two things. It may mean that, by implication, it denies a similar status to other peoples; and it must be conceded that such is the prevailing outlook one finds in the ancient Jewish writings. In those days the non-Jewish peoples (often lumped together as *ha-goyim*, 'the nations', from which the use of the word 'gentiles' in this sense derives) were, in so far as the Jews had contact with or knowledge of them, under the domination of polytheistic and idolatrous religions which tolerated all manner of immoral practices. To such paganism, ancient Judaism was irreconcilably hostile, so that the gentile peoples are rarely portrayed favourably in ancient Jewish literature, except in the context of the eschatological hope that ultimately all the families of mankind will turn to the worship of the true God.

Gradually, with the emergence of other monotheistic religions teaching a high morality, Judaism recognized that the old equation of gentile with pagan was no longer valid. In the Middle Ages it became an accepted principle that Christians and Muslims were to be regarded as worshippers of the One God and observers of the Noachide laws, and Maimonides advanced the daring thought that they actually served 'to prepare the whole world to worship God with one accord' (*Mishneh Torah*, Hilchot Melachim, chapter 11, uncensored version).

It would only be an extension of that trend to concede that other communities also have a positive role to play in the divine scheme, so that they, too, are in a sense 'chosen': an acknowledgement which, in this modern age of greater mutual knowledge and appreciation between the religions, many Jews are willing to make. Such a view would not negate the unique character and significance of the Sinaitic Covenant, but it would make the doctrine of the Election of Israel less exclusive.

In another sense, however, that doctrine, contrary to a common misapprehension, has never been exclusive: membership of the chosen people has never been confined to those born into it. It has always been possible for gentiles to become Jewish, and in every age such conversions have occurred.

Of course, the rate of the influx has varied. Sometimes, as in the Graeco-Roman period, it has been a large stream, at other times a mere trickle. That has depended on external circumstances (under Christian rule Jewish proselytism was often forbidden) as well as the attitudes of the Jewish authorities in reaction to these circumstances. Among the biblical writers, for instance, the author of the book of Ruth was, one supposes, favourably disposed towards the acceptance of gentiles into the Jewish community. So were, preponderantly, the Pharisees and Rabbis, as recent studies have demonstrated. They also formulated the rules and procedures of conversion. Just how stringently these should nowadays be applied is a matter of disagreement between the Orthodox and Progressive streams of contemporary Judaism. But the *principle* that, as the Rabbis put it, 'the gates are open at all times, and whoever wishes to enter may enter' (Exodus Rabbah 19:4), is undisputed.

Race?

The principle that 'the gates are open' is of the greatest importance for a correct understanding of the nature of the Jewish people. The issue has been much confused, in modern times, by loose talk of the Jews as a 'race'. Not only is it wrong to suppose that there is any large measure of racial homogeneity among today's Jews, but it is even doubtful whether they ever were anything approaching a 'pure race'. Already the book of Exodus relates that the Israelites, on their journey out of Egypt, were accompanied by a 'mixed multitude' (12:38), and since then both intermarriage and conversion have produced considerable further diversification.

It is true that most Jews, in most times and places, have been Jewish because they were born of Jewish parents; and though the same may hold true for the great majority of Christians, there is this significant difference, that in Jewish law and tradition a child born of Jewish parents is deemed Jewish by virtue of that fact alone, and does not become so only through a rite of initiation.

But it does not follow that Jewishness is transmitted genetically: it is, of course, transmitted culturally. The explanation of the paradox lies in the nature of the Sinaitic Covenant, which, as Judaism has always understood it, involved a collective commitment by those present on their own behalf and on behalf of their posterity: 'Nor is it with you only that I make this sworn covenant, but with him who is not here with us this day as well as with him who stands here with us this day before the Lord our God' (Deuteronomy 29:13 f.; in Christian Bibles, 29:14 f.).

Thus membership of the house of Israel passes automatically from generation to generation, but only because it is demanded and expected that each generation will transmit to the next a sense of responsibility for the continuation of the Covenant; and that is, of course, a theological convention, not a biological fact. Accordingly, the process of transmission is educational: 'He established a testimony in Jacob, and appointed a law in Israel, which He commanded our fathers to teach to their children; that the next generation might know them, the children yet unborn, and arise and tell them to their children, so that they should set their hope in God, and not forget the works of God, but keep His commandments' (Psalms 78:5 ff.).

If only *one* parent is Jewish, the transmission which is normally taken for granted becomes problematic. The Rabbis, however, ruled that in such cases the mother's status was the determining factor (Kiddushin 68b). Just why they did so, seemingly contrary to biblical precedent, is not certain. But one can see the advantage of such a clear-cut definition, which obviates the need for going into individual case histories. It has in fact remained normative down to our time. Only recently has it been proposed by some branches of Progressive Judaism that patrilineal descent should be given as much weight as matrilineal, provided that there has been effective Jewish education and identification.

Whatever one may think about that, the general principle remains unaffected: a Jew is a person who, either by reason of birth or by reason of conversion, has had conferred on him the responsibility of membership of the Covenant people. Whether, and how well, any individual will discharge that responsibility is neither predictable nor controllable. Hence there are good, bad and indifferent Jews. What unites them is the responsibility that is deemed to rest upon them. A well-known Midrash makes that point when it likens the Israelites to the 'four species' of the festival of Sukkot (see p. 359): as the fruits differ from each other in respect of fragrance and edibility, so some Jews are learned without being righteous, some are righteous without being learned, some are both and some are neither. Yet, as the four species are bound together in one bunch, so the four types of Israelites form one people, the better ones atoning for the worse (Pesikta Rabbati 51:2).

Nation?

The above passage highlights the two key dimensions of Jewish identity: the religious and the ethnic. In modern times, however, there has sometimes been a tendency to elevate one at the expense of the other. Thus Progressive Judaism, in its earlier phases, tended to regard the Jew as an individual who differed from his fellow citizens only in his private religious beliefs and observances, while some elements of Zionism have gone to the opposite extreme and declared the Jews to be a nation like other nations, with a national culture in which religion is only one element, and an optional and obsolescent one at that.

To think of the Jews as a nation is indeed more appropriate than to think of them as a race. The large role played in Jewish history, life and consciousness by the land of Israel and the Hebrew language; the emergence of secular Jews, strongly asserting their Jewish identity; the modern rebirth of the State of Israel, and the solidarity which the Diaspora communities have shown with it and with one another: all these phenomena may plausibly be regarded as indicators of nationhood. But they do not give a complete picture. The historical record shows that Jewish particularism has always been counterbalanced by universalism, and the homing impulse by a centrifugal drive. It also demonstrates a strong tendency on the part of Diaspora Jews to integrate themselves – when permitted to do so – into the political, social and cultural life of their countries of domicile, and yet to preserve their own identity.

Above all, the secular-national view fails to pay due regard to the central place which religion has hitherto held in Jewish life and self-understanding. The very survival of the Jews, in times of prosperity and adversity, must surely be attributed in large measure to the tenacity of their religious faith. Their literature (Bible, Talmud, Midrash, codes, commentaries, responsa, *Zohar*, etc.) deals predominantly with religious themes. Their characteristic institutions (temple, synagogue, school) and forms of leadership (priest, prophet, rabbi) have been religious. The very name Israel has a profound religious connotation (see Genesis 32:29; in Christian Bibles, 32:28). The liturgy defines the Jews as 'the people who proclaim God's unity'. Most significant of all, the only mode of entry into the Jewish community, other than by birth, has always been the religious process of conversion.

The Jews are, therefore, a unique blend of people and religion. The word 'people', which we have used repeatedly, is intended to convey their corporateness, which resembles that of a nation; the word 'religion', the essence of their cultural distinctiveness. They are a people bearing a corporate, religious responsibility.

MISSION

What is the nature of that responsibility? The question demands an answer, because without one, the doctrine of Election hangs in the air. 'Chosen' means chosen for a purpose. Election implies mission. The word may seem inappropriate, as it does to many Jews, because of its associations with Christian evangelism, and therefore a synonym, such as 'vocation', 'role' or 'task', may be preferable. But the concept is inescapable. The Israelites were not chosen to receive a benefit – their chosen-ness has brought them untold suffering – but to render a service.

In general terms, the purpose of that service is clear enough. It is, as we said at the beginning of this chapter, a redemptive purpose: to push history along towards its messianic goal. But how?

Clearly, a precondition of all else is that the Jewish people must survive. Survival therefore has a high priority on their agenda, especially today, when they have seen their survival so gravely threatened by anti-Semitism and anti-Zionism as well as the subtler erosions of assimilation and intermarriage. Excessive concentration on survival can, however, become self-defeating when it is pursued as an end in itself or by means that obscure the purpose beyond it.

That purpose is to influence mankind in ways which advance God's redemptive purpose: 'It is too light a thing that you should be My servant to raise up the tribes of Jacob and to restore the preserved of Israel; I will give you as a light to the nations, that My salvation may reach to the end of the earth' (Isaiah 49:6). Alluding to the Exodus verse, 'And you shall be to Me a kingdom of priests and a holy nation' (19:6), Morris Joseph once wrote: 'A kingdom of priests implies something more than a people leading a consecrated, but self-contained, life. It means a people whose holiness, travelling beyond the national confines, shall help to consecrate mankind. A priest presupposes a congregation, and a kingdom of priests a world to minister to' (*Judaism as Creed and Life*).

The most effective way of influencing others is by example.

Again and again, the Israelites are challenged to be a holy people. Holy means separate, different, but *nobly* so. Because of the Covenant, the standards of behaviour God expects of the Jews are more exacting: 'You only have I known of all the families of the earth; therefore I will punish you for all your iniquities' (Amos 3:2). The role of the Jews is therefore one of witnessing: they are required, by their example, to witness to the reality, unity, righteousness and power of God. 'You are My witnesses, says the Lord, and My servant whom I have chosen' (Isaiah 43:10). The concept is not only found in the Prophets. The Rabbis, too, affirmed it, and the traditional Jewish prayer book draws attention to it by emphasizing the final letters of the first and last words of the opening verse of the *Shema* (Deuteronomy 6:4), and so making them spell the Hebrew word, *ed*, for 'witness'.

The ultimate act of witness is that of the martyr, who demonstrates his loyalty to his faith by surrendering his very life for it. Given certain extreme circumstances of religious persecution (but only then), such self-sacrifice is indeed incumbent on all Jews, and the historical record shows that very many have risen to that supreme challenge and died, as the tradition puts it, *al kiddush ha-Shem*, 'for the sanctification of the divine Name'.

But is not a witness required to testify by word as well as by deed, to teach by precept as well as example, and is there not therefore an obligation upon Jews to commend the beliefs they hold true to their fellow men – in other words, to proselytize? Such an inference could be drawn from the 'Servant Poems' in the book of Isaiah, inasmuch as the individual they portray, in illustration of the collective task of Israel, is essentially a *prophet* – 'The Lord God has given me the tongue of those who are taught' (50:4) – who proclaims God's truth, and is made to suffer for it. There is also, as has been mentioned, ample evidence of Jewish proselytism in the Graeco-Roman period; and in modern times such a policy has been advocated by no less a Jew than Rabbi Leo Baeck, the revered leader of German Jewry during the Nazi period.

Mostly, however, contemporary Jews tend to recoil from such an idea, because it smacks of 'soul snatching', or else on the grounds that there is no need for it, since gentiles are only required to observe the noachide laws and therefore one doesn't have to be Jewish to be 'saved'.

This generally held view is not incompatible, however, with the unquestioned principle that a non-Jew who of his own volition seeks conversion to Judaism should be sympathetically received. Such an applicant may indeed find that the conditions which have to be satisfied are exacting, but only by way of testing his sincerity and ensuring that he is fully equipped to lead a Jewish life.

It could nevertheless be cogently argued that the Jewish task is not primarily to influence minds but to improve conditions; not so much to teach Judaism as to apply it, by contributing to the amelioration of society on the basis of Jewish values, such as justice, compassion and peace. Whether or not they would put it that way or see it in that light, it is a striking characteristic of many Jews, both religious and secular, that they tend to display an urge to improve the world. (Part of the evidence is their tendency to become involved in radical political movements and voluntary social service.) Of course, there are many explanations for this phenomenon; but it is perhaps not too fanciful to detect in it a conscious or unconscious response to the challenge of the Covenant, a holy impatience that stems ultimately from Sinai.

SINAI

What happened at Sinai was so tremendous that the impact of it has not yet spent itself, but reverberates still. Jewish tradition refers to the event as *mattan torah*, the 'giving of the Torah'.

The word Torah means 'teaching', but always in the specific sense of that which is taught by, or in the name of, God, and hence is revealed. Such revelations are never about God's essence, which is beyond human understanding, a point the Bible makes by saying that no man can see His face (Exodus 33:17–23); only rarely (e.g., Exodus 34:6 f.) are they about His attributes, but almost invariably about His *will*. They communicate the demands He makes upon His devotees and are therefore characteristically expressed in the imperative: in precepts and exhortations. Hence the common translation of Torah as 'law'.

In the Bible itself, the word 'Torah' is variously used. Sometimes it refers (in the plural) to individual injunctions (e.g., Exodus 18:16), sometimes to a group of regulations dealing with a limited subject (Numbers 6:21), sometimes to a prophetic oracle spoken on a particular occasion (Isaiah 1:10), sometimes, collectively, to the message of the prophets (Jeremiah 26:4 f.) or the instruction of the priests (Malachi 2:7). Finally, it comes to denote the entire corpus of divine legislation, especially as mediated by Moses (Deuteronomy 4:44 f.; 33:4; Malachi 3:22, in Christian Bibles, 4:4).

This last sense became the prevalent one in post-biblical Judaism, which also elaborated and extended it in various ways. One was to emphasize the uniqueness of Sinai by telescoping the entire revelational process into that single event, all previous revelations (e.g., to the Patriarchs) being regarded as merely anticipatory of the Sinaitic theophany, and all subsequent ones as somehow already contained in it. Thus we are told that everything the prophets prophesied in subsequent generations, and everything the sages taught in still later ages, was already revealed at Sinai (Exodus Rabbah 28:6), and certain phrases occurring in the biblical account of the Sinaitic revelation are interpreted to yield forward allusions to Mishnah and Talmud, *Halachah* and *Aggadah* (Berachot 5a; Exodus Rabbah 46:1; 47:1).

The extraordinary, cataclysmic character of the event was further accentuated. The biblical narrative speaks of 'thunders and lightnings, and a thick cloud upon the mountain, and a very loud trumpet blast' (Exodus 19:16), and the Midrash adds that 'when God revealed the Torah no bird chirped, no fowl beat its wings, no ox bellowed, . . . the sea did not stir, no creature uttered a sound, the world was silent and still, and the Divine Voice spoke' (Exodus Rabbah 29:9).

With this went increased stress on the role of Moses as the principal human agent in the Sinaitic event. Not that one can go much further than the Deuteronomic epitaph, that 'there has not arisen a prophet since in Israel like Moses, whom the Lord knew face to face' (34:10). But the Rabbinic *Aggadah*, without denying his mortality, delights in extolling his extraordinary wisdom, noble virtues and miraculous powers, and Maimonides made his pre-eminence over all other prophets an article of faith.

WRITTEN TORAH AND ORAL TORAH

Moses also came to be regarded as the author of the Pentateuch. Strictly speaking, the 'Five Books of Moses', as they have come to be known, are an anonymous work; but so many sections of it are explicitly stated to contain the very words which 'the Lord spoke to Moses, saying, Speak to the children of Israel . . .', that it was a natural step to credit him with having written all of it. Already some late biblical passages attest to such an attribution (Nehemiah 8:1; II Chronicles 34:14), while in rabbinic literature it is always taken for granted and occasionally asserted (Bava Batra 15a).

Regarded as the work of Moses and the record of the Sinaitic Revelation, and indeed containing practically all there is of legislation in the Bible, as well as the early history of the Jewish people, the Pentateuch was elevated and venerated above all other books.

However, the sanctity of the other books of Scripture was also maintained. They, too, it was affirmed, were written 'by the holy spirit', that is, under the guidance of prophetic inspiration, which was, indeed, the proof of their canonicity. They, too, therefore, were revelational literature; and sometimes, especially in polemic against the Samaritans, who denied it, it was emphatically asserted that 'the Prophets and Hagiographa are also Torah' (Tanchuma, Re'eh 1, referring to Psalms 78:1, Proverbs 4:2 and Daniel 9:10).

Occasionally, therefore, the term Torah is applied to the entire Hebrew Bible, although its use is more commonly restricted to the Pentateuch. On the other hand its connotation was enormously enlarged by the concept of the 'Oral Torah', which interprets and supplements the 'Written Torah' of the Pentateuch, and which, it was taught, had likewise been revealed by God to Moses on Mount Sinai, but then handed down by word of mouth to Joshua, the Elders, the Prophets and the men of the Great Assembly (Avot 1:1), finally to become the subject-matter of rabbinic literature.

Moreover, since the process of interpretation still continues, the Oral Torah, unlike the Written, is unfinished. As the Rabbis put it, 'the words of Torah are fruitful and multiply' (Chagigah 3b).

This ongoing process does not depend on any fresh divine

communications. Revelation in the fullest sense did not, according to the Rabbis, occur again after Sinai, and even prophecy is said to have ceased after Haggai, Zechariah and Malachi, or after the destruction of the Temple. This does not mean that God ceased to manifest Himself to human beings – the Talmud relates many instances in which the *Shechinah* was experienced, or a *bat kol* ('Heavenly Voice') heard. It means that the elucidation of God's will was now to be carried forward in another way: by the application of human intelligence to the data already supplied by God, and the clues already contained, in the Scriptures and the ancient oral traditions, and even, if necessary, by democratic majority decision on the part of the accredited teachers.

The point is graphically made in an amusing but pertinent talmudic story about two second-century rabbis, Eliezer and Joshua, who disputed a point of ritual law. When Eliezer invokes a *bat kol* in support of his opinion, Joshua rejects it as inadmissible evidence on the ground that the Torah 'is not in heaven' (Deuteronomy 30:12); and a later comment portrays God as well pleased with the maturity thus shown by His children (Bava Metzia 59a–b).

The Rabbis were well aware that the process of interpretation often led a long way from the plain or literal meaning of the text. For instance, they tell a story in which Moses returns to earth and listens to Rabbi Akiva expounding a supposedly Sinaitic law, but cannot understand what he is saying (Menachot 29b); and they concede that certain sections of their legislation, including the laws of the sabbath, are 'like mountains suspended by a hair, in that they rest on a slender scriptural basis and a multitude of oral traditions' (Chagigah 1:8). Nevertheless, the Rabbis remain firm in their conviction that the entire edifice of the twofold Torah, Written and Oral, is sound, and they do not weary in their praises of its excellence and the benefits it bestows on those who study and practise it.

Such eulogies are even found in the Bible itself, notably in Psalm 19 ('The Torah of the Lord is perfect . . .') and Psalm 119, which is one long litany on that very theme. But the Rabbis go even further. They identify Torah with the Wisdom so strikingly hypostasized and rhapsodized in books such as Proverbs. They aver that God created the Torah before the world, and the world by its model and for its sake. It is, they say, God's choicest gift. 'Turn it over and over,' commends one rabbi, 'for everything is contained in it; contemplate it, grow old and spend yourself in the study of it, and never stir from it, for you can have no better rule than that' (Avot 5:22).

This veneration of the Torah remained characteristic of Jewish piety all through the Middle Ages and beyond, and is still to be found among devoutly Orthodox, or 'Torah-true', Jews. It accounts for their staunch self-submission, in the absence of any external coercion, to the all-embracing, complex and exacting discipline of the Torah way of life, and their unflinching acceptance of whatever sacrifice and inconvenience it may entail.

MODERN VIEWS

Since the Emancipation, however, such unquestioning obedience has ceased to prevail among the majority of Jews. That is mainly owing to the impact of secularism, which has eroded religious faith, and of scepticism, which has made it respectable to doubt what former generations took on trust. But it is also because of the challenge to the traditional conception of the Torah from modern Bible scholarship, with its theories about the multiple authorship of the Pentateuch and the interaction between Judaism and other ancient Near Eastern cultures, and from the apparent conflict between particular laws of the Torah and contemporary ethical attitudes towards, for instance, the status of women.

Some Jewish thinkers, anxious both to perpetuate Judaism and to do justice to these modern perceptions, have therefore tried to evolve a conception of Revelation somewhat different from the traditional one, seeing it as a gradual process in which divine message and human interpretation intermingle, and cultural factors play a large part, so that the literature resulting from it is not inerrant, and there is correspondingly greater scope for development and change.

Such an approach underlies the Progressive movement in modern Judaism in its various forms. It has its own difficulties and dangers – such as excessive rationalism, subjectivism and relativism – as the neo-traditionalists in its own ranks have not failed to warn. Orthodox Jews, for their part, are alarmed by any questioning of the authority of the tradition they regard as sacred, and have sometimes reacted with a fundamentalist dogmatism uncharacteristic of historic Judaism.

Thus there is controversy. But it should not be allowed to obscure the common ground that unites religious Jews of all tendencies. Whatever precisely happened at Sinai, they know that it generated a powerful spiritual impulse which set in motion a distinctive and continuing tradition, and that they have a solemn obligation to cherish and exemplify the essential values of that tradition, and to inject them into the life-stream of humanity as their contribution to its redemption.

PART IV

THE PRACTICE OF JUDAISM

CHAPTER ONE   THE ETHICAL DIMENSION

The dominant preoccupation of Judaism has always been the question, 'And now, Israel, what does the Lord your God require of you?' (Deuteronomy 10:12). The answer, in all its multiformity, is to be found throughout the Torah literature, from the first chapter of Genesis to the latest volume of responsa. Included in it are general exhortations, such as abound in the books of the Prophets; but its characteristic mode of expression is the *mitzvah*. The word means 'commandment' but has acquired a richer connotation. A *mitzvah* (plural, *mitzvot*) is a rule of conduct or ritual which is seen as an obligation one owes, not to any human authority, but to God Himself, so that in carrying it out one is bringing one's own life, and in some small measure the world, into closer harmony with His will.

To a large extent, Judaism is a system of *mitzvot*. Admittedly, that sounds tantamount to equating it with *Halachah* and omitting its other side, *Aggadah* (see above, pp. 211 and 234). But the two are symbiotically interrelated, action leading to contemplation, and contemplation to action. As the modern Hebrew poet Bialik wrote in a celebrated essay, 'The *Halachah* is the crystallization ... of the *Aggadah* ... As a dream yearns for its interpretation, the will to become deed, the thought to become word, the blossom to become fruit, so *Aggadah* finds its fulfilment in *Halachah*' (the essay is entitled '*Halachah* and *Aggadah*').

As well as stimulating the will to observe the *mitzvot*, the *Aggadah* nourishes the inwardness necessary if they are to be observed, as Judaism desires, not behaviouristically, but in a spirit of sincere devotion (*kavvanah*) and religious joy (*simchah shel mitzvah*).

The total number of *mitzvot* is said to be 613, comprising 248 of a positive nature and 365 prohibitions. But not too much should be made of these figures, which the Rabbis obtained by simply counting the number of discrete laws and commandments in the Pentateuch, including many applicable only to particular categories of persons, or in particular circumstances. Besides, a large proportion of the 613 are no longer operative because the conditions or institutions to which they relate ceased to exist after the biblical period, while, on the other hand, these figures convey nothing of the vast amount of elaboration and amplification which every item of Pentateuchal legislation received in the development of the Oral Torah. In any case, it is the content rather than the quantity of the *mitzvot* that concerns us.

Of the various ways in which they have been classified, the most illuminating, for our present purpose, divides them into those which pertain to man's relationship with his fellow human being (*beyn adam la-chavero*) and those which pertain to his relationship with God (*beyn adam la-Makom*). The distinction corresponds broadly to that between moral law and ritual law, but with the important qualification that in the first category civil law must be included as well. For that, too, regulates human relations, and what matters about these from a Jewish point of view is that they should be conducted in accordance with the demands of justice, compassion and peace. In other words, the ethical motive is implicit, not only in the dos and don'ts of personal moral behaviour, but also in those large tracts of pentateuchal and talmudic legislation which deal with commerce, labour, crime, government and social policy.

Although Jewish civil law is largely inoperative today, since Diaspora Jews are ruled in these matters by the legal systems of the countries in which they live, while the State of Israel, having inherited a legal system going back to the British mandate and Ottoman times, maintains talmudic law only through the limited jurisdiction of the rabbinic courts, nevertheless, the ethical values embodied in that tradition remain important both for an understanding of historic Judaism and for the guidance that can still be drawn from them in tackling contemporary social problems.

ETHICAL EMPHASIS

The paramountcy of ethics is a major theme in the teaching of the
prophets, especially those of the eighth century BCE.

I hate, I despise your feasts,
and I take no delight in your solemn assemblies.
Even though you offer Me your burnt offerings and cereal offerings,
I will not accept them,
and the peace offerings of your fatted beasts
I will not look upon.
Take away from Me the noise of your songs:
to the melody of your harps I will not listen.
But let justice roll down like waters,
and righteousness like an ever-flowing stream.   Amos 5:21–24

For I desire steadfast love and not sacrifice,
the knowledge of God rather than burnt offerings.   Hosea 6:6

What to Me is the multitude of your sacrifices?
    says the Lord;
I have had enough of burnt offerings of rams
    and the fat of fed beasts;
I do not delight in the blood of bulls,
    or of lambs, or of he-goats.
When you come to appear before Me,
    who requires of you
    this trampling of My courts?
Bring no more vain offerings;
    incense is an abomination to Me.
New moon and sabbath and the calling of assemblies –
    I cannot endure iniquity and solemn assembly.
Your new moons and your appointed feasts
    my soul hates; they have become a burden to Me,
    I am weary of bearing them.
When you spread forth your hands,
    I will hide My eyes from you;
even though you make many prayers,
    I will not listen;
    your hands are full of blood.
Wash yourselves; make yourselves clean;
    remove the evil of your doings
    from before My eyes;
cease to do evil,

learn to do good;
seek justice,
correct oppression;
defend the fatherless,
plead for the widow.   Isaiah 1:11–17

With what shall I come before the Lord,
and bow myself before God on high?
Shall I come before Him with burnt offerings, with calves a year old?
Will the Lord be pleased with thousands of rams,
with ten thousands of rivers of oil?
Shall I give my first-born for my transgression,
the fruit of my body for the sin of my soul?
He has showed you, O man, what is good;
and what does the Lord require of you
but to do justice, and to love kindness,
and to walk humbly with your God?   Micah 6:6 ff.

The import of such passages is not that cultic worship, sacrificial or otherwise, is a bad thing, or even that it is unimportant,
but that it is not of the same *order* of importance as right conduct,
which alone God categorically demands of those who would serve
Him, and by which alone He ultimately judges them.

The distinction, it is true, was not so sharply maintained by the
Rabbis, who saw it as their task to inculcate loyalty to the Torah
way of life *in its totality* and, indeed, considered it equally obligatory (which is not to say equally important) in all its parts.
Thus Judah the Prince, editor of the Mishnah, urged: 'Be as
meticulous in observing a minor precept as a major one' (Avot
2:1). Yet it was the Rabbis who translated the lofty moral idealism
of the Prophets into legislative measures designed to give them
practical effect; and whenever it came to defining the *quintessence*
of the Torah, they did not fail to do so in ethical terms. Thus
Rabbi Simlai (third century) taught that 613 commandments had
been revealed to Moses, and that they were successively summarized in eleven by David (Psalm 15), in six by Isaiah (33:15),
in three by Micah (6:8) and in one by Amos (5:4), all the quoted
passages being of moral import (Makkot 23b–24a).

Even more striking is a Midrash which asks why the generation
of the Flood was destroyed (except for Noah and his family)
whereas the generation of the Tower of Babel was merely scattered,

and answers: because the former, though they defied God, loved one another, that being inferred from the statement (Genesis 11:1) that 'the whole earth was of one language, and of one speech' (Genesis Rabbah 38:6).

Noteworthy also is the lengthy confession traditionally recited on the Day of Atonement, which lists only transgressions of a moral, not a ritual kind. Judaism's answer to the question, 'What does the Lord require of you?' has always been largely ethical in intent and content.

IMITATION OF GOD

Of the general principles involved, the most general is the 'imitation of God', namely that in all one's conduct one should model oneself on the Divine Attributes. This principle is indeed one of the 613 *mitzvot* according to Maimonides (*Sefer ha-Mitzvot*, Mitzvot Aseh 8), who derives it from the injunction, that you shall 'walk in His ways' (Deuteronomy 28:9; cf. 10:12; 13:5). It is also expressed in other scriptural verses, such as 'Walk before Me, and be blameless' (Genesis 17:1), 'You shall be holy; for I the Lord your God am holy' (Leviticus 19:2), and 'He executes justice for the fatherless and the widow, and loves the stranger, giving him food and clothing. Love the stranger, therefore' (Deuteronomy 10:18 ff.). And the Rabbis reaffirmed and enlarged on the doctrine: 'As God is called merciful, so you should be merciful; as He is called gracious, so you should be gracious; as He is called righteous, so you should be righteous; as He is called faithful, so you should be faithful' (Sifrei 49 to Deuteronomy 11:22). Similarly: 'As God clothes the naked, visits the sick, comforts the mourners and buries the dead, so should you' (Sotah 14a).

GOLDEN RULE

Another principle of great generality is the commandment, 'You shall love your neighbour as yourself' (Leviticus 19:18), which Rabbi Akiva (around 100 CE) declared to be the greatest principle of the Torah (Sifra 89b ad loc.). In thus highlighting the 'golden rule', Rabbi Akiva only clinched a trend which can be traced back to pre-Christian times. There is, for instance, a negative formulation of it in the apocryphal book of Tobit, which may date from the fourth century BCE: 'What you hate, do not do to any one' (4:15). Likewise, there is the well-known story of the Pharisaic teacher Hillel (first century BCE), who, when asked by a would-be convert to teach him the whole Torah while he stood on one foot, replied: 'What is hateful to you, do not do to your fellow man; that is the essence of the Torah, the rest is commentary: go and learn' (Shabbat 31a).

Rabbi Akiva's opinion was, however, challenged by his colleague ben Azzai, who maintained that an even greater principle than 'Love your neighbour as yourself' was contained in the Genesis verse (5:1): 'This is the book of the generations of Adam. When God created man, he made him in the likeness of God' (Genesis Rabbah 24:7; Sifra 89b). The point he wished to make seems to be twofold: first, that the golden rule is based on the essential equality of all human beings, so that 'neighbour' must be understood in that all-inclusive sense; secondly, that the principle of equality, in its turn, derives from the perception of man as created in God's image, which means that human beings are not merely equal, but of equal worth in the most exalted sense.

Negative Implications

So understood, the golden rule has both negative and positive implications. Negatively, it means that it is wrong to harm a fellow human being deliberately, in any way at all.

Murder, the extreme case of such harm, is regarded with particular horror precisely because it is the destruction of a being created in God's image. 'Whoever sheds the blood of man, by man shall his blood be shed: for God made man in His own image' (Genesis 9:6). Hence, too, the prominence of the prohibition of murder in the Ten Commandments (Exodus 20; Deuteronomy 5).

The Rabbis, too, were very conscious of the sanctity of human life, as can be seen, for instance, in the extraordinarily stringent precautions they demanded to prevent any possibility of a wrongful conviction in a capital case. A solemn warning was to be addressed to the witnesses to testify truthfully, since 'he who destroys a single human life is considered by Scripture as if he had destroyed an entire world, and he who saves a single human life as if he had saved an entire world' (Sanhedrin 4:5). Accordingly, the Rabbis included 'the shedding of blood', along with idolatry and incest, among the three unconditionally forbidden sins which a man may not commit even to save his own life (Sanhedrin 74a; Pesachim 25b).

Other violations of the golden rule are condemned in the nineteenth chapter of Leviticus:

You shall not steal, nor deal falsely, nor lie to one another . . . You shall not oppress your neighbour or rob him . . . You shall not curse the deaf or put a stumbling block before the blind . . . You shall not go up and down as a slanderer among your people, and you shall not stand forth against the life of your neighbour . . . You shall not hate your brother in your heart, but you shall reason with your neighbour, lest you bear sin because of him. You shall not take vengeance or bear any grudge against the sons of your own people, but you shall love your neighbour as yourself (19:11–18).

Sometimes the traditional interpretation is illuminating or surprising. For instance, 'you shall not curse the deaf' is expounded to mean not *even* the deaf, who cannot hear the curse, how much less those who can hear. You shall not 'put a stumbling block before the blind' is understood to refer to any action by which one may become the indirect cause of a fellow man's transgressing the law. 'You shall not steal', taken literally in the above passage, is interpreted in the Ten Commandments as alluding to the even graver crime of kidnapping. Any kind of verbal deception is described as a 'theft of the mind' (*genevat da'at*) (Chullin 44a), and the injunction, 'Keep far from a false charge' (Exodus 23:7), is applied to a whole host of situations in which seemingly innocent deviations from the highest standards of truthfulness are nevertheless condemned (Shevu'ot 30b–31a).

Great sensitivity is shown by Jewish tradition when it warns against any action which may damage another person's good name or self-esteem. Just as the Rabbis taught, 'Let your neighbour's property be as dear to you as your own' (Avot 2:12), so they demanded, 'Let your neighbour's honour be as dear to you as your own' (Avot 2:10). Especially strongly did they deprecate the sin of 'wronging with words', which they deduced from Leviticus

25:17, and regarded as prohibiting any verbal humiliation of a fellow man, such as taunting him with the sins of his past, showing up his ignorance, or calling him by a disparaging nickname. 'He who publicly shames his neighbour,' they said with exaggeration for emphasis, 'is as though he shed blood' (Bava Metzia 58b).

More generally, all malicious talk (*lashon ha-ra*) was strongly condemned, one of the key passages being: 'What man is there who desires life, and covets many days, that he may enjoy good? Keep your tongue from evil, and your lips from speaking deceit' (Psalms 34:13 f.; in Christian Bibles, 34:12 f.).

Positive Implications

These, then, are some of the negative implications of the golden rule. It also requires positive action. Psalm thirty-four continues: 'Depart from evil, and do good,' echoing Isaiah's 'Cease to do evil, learn to do good' (1:16 f.); and Hillel, whose negative formulation of the golden rule has been cited, is equally famous for his dictum, 'Be of the disciples of Aaron, loving peace and pursuing peace, loving your fellow human beings, and drawing them near to the Torah' (Avot 1:12).

The positive fulfilment of the golden rule is known in Jewish tradition as *gemilut chasadim*, 'the performance of deeds of loving-kindness'. The great importance attached to it can be gauged from the motto of Simeon the Just, who was a high priest in the time of Alexander the Great, that 'the world is sustained by three things: by the [study of the] Torah, by the worship [of the Temple] and by *gemilut chasadim*' (Avot 1:2). The term occurs also in a Mishnah paragraph (Pe'ah 1:1) particularly familiar to observant Jews because of its place in the daily morning liturgy, which includes it among those commandments that have no 'fixed measure', that is, which the Torah does not quantify. The passage, in the slightly elaborated version of the prayer book, goes on to specify some of the ways of discharging the obligation: giving hospitality to strangers, visiting the sick, dowering a (poor or orphaned) bride, and accompanying the dead to the grave. Similarly, Maimonides states in his great law code: 'It is a positive commandment of the Oral Torah to visit the sick, to comfort the mourners, to accompany the dead, to dower the bride, to escort one's guests, to attend to all the needs of burial . . . and to enhance the happiness of the bride and bridegroom . . . These acts are what is meant by *gemilut chasadim* . . . and they are included in the principle of "You shall love your neighbour yourself"' (Hilchot Avel 14:1).

CHARITY

A related concept is that of *tzedakah*, a word which in the Bible means justice or righteousness but later came to signify charity, in the sense of almsgiving. The connecting link between the two connotations is perhaps to be sought in the characteristic Jewish emphasis that the rich, in giving to the poor, are not doing them a favour but discharging an obligation they owe as a matter of justice. By the same token, any assumption of superiority on the part of the giver is unwarranted, and it is perhaps in order to make this point that the Bible goes out of its way to refer to the beneficiary as 'your brother'. 'If your brother becomes poor, and cannot maintain himself with you, you shall maintain him . . . that your brother may live beside you' (Leviticus 25:35 f.). 'If there is among you a poor man . . . you shall not harden your heart or shut your hand against your poor brother, but you shall open your hand to him, and lend him sufficient for his need, whatever it may be . . . You shall give him freely, and your heart shall not be grudging when you give to him . . . You shall open wide your hand to your brother, to the needy and to the poor in the land' (Deuteronomy 15:7–11).

Accordingly, it is strongly stressed in Rabbinic Judaism that almsgiving should be done *secretly*, so that the recipient may not be humiliated (Chagigah 5a), and even that charity should be dispensed *with due deliberation*, since the psalmist does not say 'Blessed is he who *gives* to the poor' but 'Blessed is he who *considers* the poor' (Psalms 41:1), that is, who ponders how best to help the person concerned (Jerusalem Talmud Pe'ah 8:9). Both purposes were served by an institution which is said to have already existed in the Temple (Shekalim 5:6) and which subsequently became standard in all Jewish communities: a publicly administered charity chest that preserved the anonymity of donors and recipients alike.

Maimonides clinched many rabbinic teachings with his list of the eight 'degrees' of charity in descending order of praise-worthiness: (1) to help one who has become impoverished to re-habilitate himself by making him a gift or loan, or entering into a partnership with him, or finding him a job; (2) to give anony-mously by contributing to the community chest; (3) to give in such a way that the donor knows the identity of the recipient but the recipient does not know the identity of the donor; (4) con-versely; (5) to give before being asked; (6) to give only when asked; (7) to give cheerfully but less than one should; (8) to give grudgingly (Mishneh Torah, Hilchot Mattenot Aniyyim 10:7–14).

Charity is praised in Jewish tradition almost to excess. It is said to weigh as much as all the other commandments put together (Bava Batra 9a), to deliver from death (Proverbs 10:2; Tobit 12:9; Shabbat 156b) and to hasten the time of redemption (Bava Batra 10a). Nevertheless, the practice of charity to the point of self-destitution was frowned upon, and it was enacted that no man should give away more than a fifth of his possessions (Jerusalem Talmud, Pe'ah 1:1). It was not forgotten that *gemilut chasadim* is ethically superior to *tzedakah* inasmuch as it involves personal service rather than mere 'chequebook charity' and is done for poor and rich alike, indeed, for the dead as well as the living (Sukkah 49b). At any rate, both have always been strongly urged. The Day of Atonement liturgy, which affirms that 'repentance, prayer and *tzedakah* mitigate the severity of God's judgement', also gives prominence to the prophetic lesson which proclaims:

> Is not this the fast that I choose:
> to loose the bonds of wickedness,
> to undo the thongs of the yoke,
> to let the oppressed go free,
> and to break every yoke?
> Is it not to share your bread with the hungry,
> and bring the homeless poor into your house;
> when you see the naked, to cover him,
> and not to hide yourself from your own flesh?
>
> Isaiah 58:6 f.

FORGIVENESS

Since the golden rule is grounded in the equal worth of all human beings as bearers of God's image, which is an objective principle, it does not depend on how one *feels* towards any given individual, and may not be set aside if he happens to be one's enemy. 'If you meet your enemy's ox or his ass going astray, you shall bring it back to him. If you see the ass of one who hates you lying under its burden, you shall refrain from leaving him with it, you shall help to lift it up' (Exodus 23:4 f.). 'If your enemy is hungry, give him bread to eat; if he is thirsty, give him water to drink' (Proverbs 25:21).

Vindictiveness is disapproved of. The principle of 'eye for eye' (Exodus 21:23 ff.; Leviticus 24:20; Deuteronomy 19:21) has no relevance here, since it deals with the punishment of crime by the law-courts, not inter-personal behaviour. On the contrary, it was probably intended to *prevent* private revenge, as well as to humanize the law by excluding excessively severe sentences: not *more* than an eye for an eye. Furthermore, although the *lex talionis* does indeed embody the concept of retribution, it must be noted that in Judaism it was early reinterpreted, if it was not always understood, *metaphorically*, as requiring monetary compensation commensurate with the bodily harm inflicted.

In private life, vengefulness is condemned. 'You shall not take vengeance or bear any grudge against the sons of your own people' (Leviticus 19:18). 'Do not say, I will do to him as he has done to me; I will pay the man back for what he has done' (Proverbs 24:29). This does not mean that one should not seek the prosecution of criminals, or that one should forgive wrongdoers in the absence of any remorse on their part. But it does mean that any retribution must be left to the due process of law, that one should respect the human rights and needs even of those by whom one has been wronged, and that one ought to be quick and generous in forgiveness when remorse has been shown. Once again, Maimonides may summarize for us the gist of Jewish teaching: 'It is forbidden for a man to be harsh and irreconcilable, but he should be easy to placate and hard to provoke. If the offender apologizes, he should forgive him with a whole heart and a willing spirit. Even if he has vexed and sinned against him greatly, he should not take vengeance or bear a grudge' (*Mishneh Torah*, Hilchot Teshuvah 2:10).

INDIVIDUAL AND SOCIETY

So far we have explored the ethical obligations of any individual towards any other, simply as a human being. It remains to consider those which arise in the more specific and complex relationships of human beings as members of society.

A community has a life of its own, over and above that of its members, which, like the life of the individual, is subject to God's judgement and must be brought into harmony with His moral will. Judaism is neither a world-negating nor a world-affirming religion, but one that is world-transforming. One of the most important prayers of the Jewish liturgy contains the significant phrase *le-takken olam be-malchut Shaddai*, 'to perfect the world through the kingship of the Almighty'. In such contexts 'world' means, or includes, the social order.

Organized society is also a means by which individuals can discharge their obligations towards, and help and benefit, one another, by providing mutual protection, goods and services, as well as opportunities for self-fulfilment and combined achievement through cooperative activity.

For all these reasons, Judaism is positively concerned with the social dimension of human life. 'If I am not for myself,' said Hillel, 'who will be for me? But if I am only for myself, what am I? And if not now, when?' (Avot 1:14). Another of his aphorisms was: 'Do not separate yourself from the community' (Avot 2:4).

The smallest community, and the prototype of every other, is the family, a subject we shall reserve for another context, in the last chapter of this section. For our present purpose we should keep in mind that society, as Judaism sees it, is a family of families, so that the problem of social ethics is essentially how to transpose the mutual, caring characteristics of family-life at its best into the larger contexts of city, state, and ultimately, humanity as a whole.

Law and Order

Judaism affirms and emphasizes that the obligation of the individual as a citizen of a state is to obey its laws, since the state cannot otherwise function. It is not, indeed, an unconditional obligation. If a government were to enact legislation violating a fundamental moral principle, or abrogating an essential religious freedom, there would be a duty to offer passive or even active resistance. But with that proviso, Jews are positively required by their own tradition to observe the principle, formulated by the Babylonian *amora*, Samuel, in the third century, that 'the law of the state is the law' (Gittin 10b). (See above, p.89.)

More generally, Jews are enjoined to identify themselves with the society in which they live, and to contribute to its welfare. Already Jeremiah wrote to his fellow Jews in Babylonia: 'Seek the peace [or 'welfare'; the Hebrew *shalom* has both meanings] of the city where I have sent you into exile, and pray to the Lord on its behalf, for in its peace you will find your peace' (29:7). More cynically, an ancient Palestinian rabbi taught: 'Pray for the peace of the government, for if it were not for the fear of it men would devour each other!' (Avot 3:2). Accordingly, it has long been customary in the Synagogue to recite a prayer for the government or the royal family at a solemn point in the sabbath and festival morning services.

The most obvious function of the state is to maintain law and order. This includes the prevention and, when it nevertheless occurs, punishment of crime. Rabbinic jurisprudence includes an extensive code of criminal law which is remarkable for its humaneness. We have already seen that it interpreted the biblical *lex talionis* as calling for monetary compensation. There was, it is true, one exception: 'a life for a life' was understood literally, since the Pentateuch expressly states, 'You shall accept no ransom for the life of a murderer' (Numbers 35:31), and, indeed, stipulates the death penalty for a number of the gravest offences. (These, however, do *not* include offences against property.) In theory, therefore, capital punishment was maintained. But in practice it was all but abolished. For the rules of evidence in capital cases were made so stringent (Sanhedrin 4–5) as to make conviction virtually impossible. Thus the Mishnah says that a court which carries out one death sentence in seven years is considered brutal, then quotes three of the most eminent rabbis of the first and second centuries, Eleazar saying, 'one in seventy years', Tarfon and Akiva declaring, 'If we had been in the Sanhedrin, no one would ever have been put to death' (Makkot 1:10).

More generally, it is the duty of society to ensure that justice is administered impartially. 'You shall do no injustice in judgement; you shall not be partial to the poor or defer to the great, but in righteousness shall you judge your neighbour' (Leviticus 19:15). 'You shall have one law for the sojourner and for the native' (Leviticus 24:22). Such exhortations abound in the Scriptures.

Responsibility of Government

But justice and humaneness are qualities which are not only essential in the law-courts: they must characterize the life of society in all its aspects, and this imperative must therefore be the guiding principle of all who exercise leadership and authority. The government, in particular, is charged with the responsibility of implementing God's moral will, and is subject to His judgement. Hence the frequent and fearless denunciations of the king – who *was* the government in ancient monarchies – on the part of the Prophets whenever, in their divinely inspired judgement, he flagrantly violated that principle. (Particularly dramatic instances are Nathan's rebuke of David in II Samuel 12, and Elijah's of Ahab in I Kings 21.) Hence, too, the Deuteronomic prescriptions for the monarch must be understood to apply to *any* form of government:

When he sits on the throne of his kingdom, he shall write for himself in a book a copy of this law . . . and it shall be with him, and he shall read in it all the days of his life, that he may learn to fear the Lord his God, by keeping all the words of this law and these statutes, and doing them; that his heart may not be lifted up above his brethren, and that he may not turn aside from the commandment, either to the right hand or to the left.

(17:18 ff.)

This last passage is one of many in the Bible indicating an ambivalence towards the institution of kingship. On the one hand the kings, at least of the Davidic line, were regarded as divinely appointed; on the other hand bitter experience all too often showed that they could not be trusted to act accordingly. All the more resolutely did the Israelites reject the deification of the king so prevalent in the ancient world, and resist the absolutism that went with it.

One can indeed discern in the history of Judaism a marked tendency towards democracy. The evidence includes the council of elders occasionally mentioned in the Bible (Exodus 3:16; 24:1; Numbers 11:16 f.; Ezra 10:8) as well as the democratic character of the synagogue and of the self-governing Jewish communities in the Middle Ages; and in modern times this predilection has been strengthened by the fact that the Jews have owed their emancipation to the rise of political liberalism, and that they have generally fared well in democratic countries and badly in totalitarian ones, both of the right and of the left.

Of course the *ultimate* Jewish ideal is theocracy, not in the sense of priestly rule but of Gideon's response to the offer of kingship: 'I will not rule over you, and my son will not rule over you; the Lord will rule over you' (Judges 8:23). It is humanity's voluntary self-submission to the rule of God. But democracy, most Jews would say, is the only safe road towards that distant goal.

Socio-economic Ideals

On the economic side, it is a citizen's obligation to contribute by his work to the material prosperity of his country, so that there may be enough to satisfy the needs of all. There is in Jewish tradition considerable emphasis on the value of work. Even the fourth Commandment, which stresses the importance of rest, begins: 'Six days you shall labour, and do all your work ...' The Rabbis, who considered the study of Torah man's highest activity, nevertheless preferred that it should be combined with a worldly occupation (Avot 2:2), an ideal which they themselves exemplified, since they earned their living in all sorts of trades and crafts. (The professionalization of the rabbinate is a post-medieval development.) Likewise, they ruled that it is a father's duty to teach his son a craft (*Tosefta*, Kiddushin 1:11).

Among the reasons for the high estimation of work, apart from its economic necessity, is the psychological fact that earning one's own living makes for self-respect, as well as the satisfaction obtainable from creative – or at least useful – activity. 'Great is work, for it confers dignity on those who do it' (Nedarim 49b), was a slogan of some rabbis, while others emphasized the psalm verse (Psalms 128:2), 'You shall eat the fruit of the labour of your hands; you shall be happy, and it shall be well with you' (Berachot 8a).

Rabbinic law also spells out in detail the obligations an employee has to his employer. These include the right to withhold his labour if he has a serious grievance and cannot obtain redress by other means; but otherwise he is duty-bound to do his work conscientiously. 'Four things,' said the rabbis, 'require exertion: the study of Torah, the performance of *gemilut chasadim*, prayer and one's worldly occupation' (Berachot 32b; Rashi's interpretation).

Conversely, Judaism greatly stresses the responsibility of the employer to treat his employees justly and considerately. A case in point is the biblical commandment, 'The wages of a hired servant shall not remain with you all night until the morning' (Leviticus 19:13), which gave rise to much legislation for the protection of the employee in Rabbinic times. And though it is true that ancient Judaism tolerated slavery, it sought in various ways, unparalleled in antiquity, to humanize it. For instance, it made sabbath rest mandatory for slaves as well as others (Deuteronomy 5:14) and, in the case of Hebrew slaves, limited the period of service to six years (Exodus 21:2). These biblical precedents, and the spirit they express, contributed to the eventual abolition of slavery in Europe and America.

Commerce must be conducted honestly and justly. 'You shall have just balances, just weights, a just ephah, and a just hin' (Leviticus 19:36). 'And if you sell to your neighbour, or buy from your neighbour, you shall not wrong one another' (Leviticus 25:14). Several tractates of the Talmud are devoted to the implications of these, and related, laws.

Society has a special responsibility towards its weakest members: the orphaned, the widowed, the old, the handicapped, the poor and the stranger, all of whom are frequently singled out, both in the laws of the Pentateuch and in the exhortations of the

Prophets, as particularly in need of protection, concern and help. This is not a matter only for private charity, which we have already discussed, but for public policy through social legislation. Such is the clear implication of several legal institutions, mentioned in the Bible and elaborated in the Talmud, including the sabbatical year (Leviticus 25:1–7), the jubilee year (Leviticus 25:8–12), the poor-tithe (Deuteronomy 14:28 f.) and the law requiring the farmer to leave the corners of his fields unharvested so that the poor may help themselves (Leviticus 19:9 f.).

It may therefore be said that the modern concept of the Welfare State is in line with biblical tradition, and that the individual citizen's payment of his taxes, in so far as they provide social security and welfare services, is one way of fulfilling his obligation of *tzedakah* towards his fellow citizens.

Another biblical law relevant to the economic dimension of social justice is the one forbidding interest on loans to the poor (Exodus 22:24; Leviticus 25:35 ff.; Deuteronomy 23:20 f.). How far it was or could be enforced in the simple agrarian society for which it was intended, is not certain. With the development of more complex economies based on industry, trade and banking, it became an impracticable ideal, and ways were found by interpretation and legal fiction to avoid its application. This was especially necessary in the Middle Ages, when the exclusion of Jews from most other livelihoods drove many of them into moneylending as an occupation. But the moral principle underlying the biblical law, that the poor must be protected from economic exploitation, remains valid.

The question therefore poses itself, what sort of an economic system is needed to implement Jewish ethical teachings? About that there is no unanimity or even consensus, as evidenced by the fact that Jews are to be found in all major political parties. All that can be safely said is that from the point of view of Judaism any economic theory must be judged by the moral quality of the society it produces, and by the kind of human relations it fosters. Freedom, justice, brotherhood, compassion: these are the essentials. Whether a welfare-capitalist, a liberal-socialist or some intermediate system is most conducive to the achievement of these ideals, has yet to be conclusively demonstrated.

ATTITUDE TO NATURE

There is yet another criterion by which a society – today more than ever – must be judged: its attitude to nature. Judaism teaches respect for nature as God's creation: 'The earth is the Lord's and the fulness thereof; the world, and those who dwell therein' (Psalms 24:1). Man, because of the great power he is able to exercise over his environment, has a responsibility to treat it with respect. He is God's *steward* on earth, said Rashi in a comment on the psalm verse, 'The heavens are the Lord's heavens, but the earth He has given to the sons of men' (115:16).

Particular emphasis is found in Jewish tradition on the need to avoid inflicting any unnecessary suffering on animals, even though the killing of animals for food, by a method designed to meet this requirement, is permitted. (Although there are Jewish vegetarians, Judaism does not *demand* vegetarianism.) Already in the Bible there is much humane legislation on this subject. It includes prohibitions against taking the mother bird away from her young (Deuteronomy 22:6 f.), ploughing with an ox and ass yoked together (Deuteronomy 22:10) and muzzling an ox when it is threshing the corn (Deuteronomy 25:4) and, in the fourth Commandment, the stipulation that domestic animals are to share with their human owners the respite of sabbath rest.

Further laws were enacted by the Rabbis, for instance that one may not buy an animal if one is not able to look after it properly (Jerusalem Talmud, Yevamot 15:3) and that one should always feed one's animals before sitting down to one's own meal (Berachot 40a). They also told a charming legend about Moses: how he once went to great lengths to rescue a kid that had run away from the flock and by this act of compassion proved himself worthy in the eyes of God to become the shepherd of His people, Israel (Exodus Rabbah 2:2).

Such a tradition would not look favourably upon hunting as a sport, which, indeed, was strongly condemned by the eminent eighteenth-century rabbi, Ezekiel Landau, in one of his Responsa. 'It is not the way of the children of Abraham, Isaac and Jacob,' he wrote (Solomon B. Freehof, *A Treasury of Responsa*, p. 218).

But respect for nature extends beyond animals. That it may not be exploited without some restraint, is suggested by the biblical law requiring the farmer to let his land lie fallow every seventh year (Leviticus 25:3 ff.); and another law, forbidding an army to cut down the fruit trees when besieging a city (Deuteronomy 20:19), was generalized by later Jewish interpretation into a prohibition against *any* wanton destruction (Maimonides, *Sefer ha-Mitzvot*, prohibition 57).

So understood, this commandment, which is, of course, one of the 613, has become particularly relevant in recent times, as humanity has woken up to the potential danger to its very survival from the reckless spoliation of the natural environment. It, too, is a *mitzvah* 'between man and his fellow man', but in the special sense that it relates to the responsibility which every generation of human beings bears towards posterity. It is therefore the negative counterpart of a story in the Rabbinic *Aggadah* of an old man who, when asked why he was taking the trouble to plant a new tree even though he could not expect to live long enough to enjoy its fruit, replied: 'As my ancestors laboured for me, so I labour for my children' (Leviticus Rabbah 25:5).

WAR AND PEACE

The ancient Israelites engaged in warfare, especially in the conquest and defence of the land which they believed God had promised them, and they therefore thought of themselves as acting out His will in so doing. It is also true that the Rabbis, interpreting the biblical record, developed a theory of obligatory and permissible wars (Sotah 44b). Furthermore, Jewish armies, both in ancient and in modern times, have fought with great bravery and skill, and individual Jews have served in the armies of many countries. Nevertheless, abhorrence for war, because of the sanctity of human life, which it destroys, and the suffering and devastation it causes, and a corresponding yearning for peace, are a persistent theme in Jewish literature.

The classic expression of it is in Isaiah: 'They shall beat their swords into ploughshares, and their spears into pruning hooks: nation shall not lift up sword against nation, neither shall they learn war any more' (Isaiah 2:4), a prophecy found also in Micah, who adds: 'But they shall sit every man under his vine and under his fig tree; and none shall make them afraid' (4:4). Highly significant, too, is the reason given for the fact that King David was not allowed the privilege of building the Temple, God saying to him: 'You may not build a house for My name, for you are a warrior and have shed blood' (I Chronicles 28:3). It is, moreover, emphasized that peace is not merely the absence of war but a state of harmony resulting from a society's ethical soundness: 'Then justice will dwell in the wilderness, and righteousness abide in the fruitful field. And the effect of righteousness will be peace, and the result of righteousness, quietness and trust for ever' (Isaiah 32:15 f.). Ultimately, therefore, harmony depends on humanity's perception of God and His will: 'They shall not hurt or destroy in all My holy mountain: for the earth shall be full of the knowledge of the Lord, as the waters cover the sea' (Isaiah 11:9).

Rabban Simeon ben Gamaliel, the father of Judah the Prince, taught: 'By three things is the world sustained: by justice, by truth and by peace' (Avot 1:18). Rabbinic literature abounds in the praises of peace. It includes whole litanies with the refrain 'great is peace', or, 'beloved is peace', quoting countless proof-texts to validate the point (e.g. Leviticus Rabbah 9:9; Deuteronomy Rabbah 5:15), and even the statement that 'the whole Torah exists only for the sake of peace, as it says [Proverbs 3:17], Her ways are ways of pleasantness, and all her paths are peace' (Gittin 59b).

In the Jewish liturgy, especially, the word *shalom* is ubiquitous, and few passages evoke a more fervent response from the congregation than the Priestly Benediction, 'The Lord bless you and keep you; the Lord make His face to shine upon you, and be gracious to you; the Lord lift up His countenance upon you, and give you peace' (Numbers 6:24 ff.); or the psalm verse, 'May the Lord give strength to His people! May the Lord bless His people with peace!' (29:11)

In spite of all that, Judaism has never espoused pacifism, though naturally there have been Jewish pacifists. It has always held that resort to military force may in some extreme circumstances be necessary in order to prevent an even greater evil. Of course there can be no greater evil than the annihilation of humanity which would result from all-out nuclear war, and this fact has created a new situation to which some previously valid judgements may no longer apply. Certainly, it lays on Jews an obligation to press with the utmost urgency for the cessation of the nuclear-arms race and the abolition of nuclear weaponry throughout the world, by whatever means are most likely to lead to that result. Whether the process would be furthered by unilateral disarmament on the part of one country or another, is not a question which can be answered by reference to Jewish ethical teachings alone, since it involves complex political calculations. All one can say is that the possible moral impact of a good example should not be lightly dismissed by the heirs of a tradition that teaches, 'Not by might, nor by power, but by My spirit, says the Lord of hosts' (Zechariah 4:6).

CHAPTER TWO   THE DEVOTIONAL DISCIPLINE

Judaism's goal is the implementation of God's moral law in all aspects of human life, individual and collective, private and public. In order that it may be attained, we must *know* what God requires of us, and we must have the *will* to do it. Accordingly, for all its emphasis on deeds, it should not be thought that Judaism cares only about overt conduct. It also concerns itself with man's inner state: the furnishing of his mind and the orientation of his heart. It is about being as well as doing.

IDEAL TYPES

One way of appreciating this aspect of Judaism is to consider the sort of person it aims to create. Four ideal types receive particular praise in Jewish tradition. One is the *talmid chacham*, literally 'disciple of the wise'. He is the scholar, steeped in Jewish law and lore. Thus the quality here singled out is a cognitive one; but not exclusively so: it is always implied and often stressed that the *talmid chacham* is nobly intentioned and exerts a positive influence. 'The disciples of the wise increase peace in the world,' says an ancient rabbinic motto (Berachot 64a), and a panegyric in 'The Ethics of the Fathers' declares:

He who studies the Torah in order to learn and do God's will acquires many merits; and not only that, but the whole world is indebted to him. He is cherished as a friend, a lover of God and of his fellow men. It clothes him with humility and reverence; it helps him to become upright and saintly, righteous and faithful; it keeps him far from sin and brings

314

him near to virtue; he benefits mankind with counsel and knowledge, wisdom and strength. He becomes like a never-failing fountain, and like a river that grows ever mightier as it flows. He is modest, slow to anger and forgiving of insults; and it magnifies and exalts him above all things.

(Avot 6:1)

Another model is the *chasid*, i.e., the 'pious' or 'faithful' one. The term has been appropriated by Jewish pietistic movements in ancient, medieval and modern times to designate their adherents, but it has also retained its general significance. The quality stressed here is a volitional one. The *chasid* is a person motivated by a constant love of God and desire to do His will, so that he responds to the biblical exhortation, 'In all your ways acknowledge Him, and He will direct your paths' (Proverbs 3:6), and the rabbinic injunction, 'Let all your actions be for the sake of Heaven' (Avot 1:12), and he is able to say, with the psalmist: 'I have set the Lord always before me' (16:8).

A more comprehensive ideal is that of the *tzaddik*, or 'righteous one'. He represents the nearest humanly possible approach to perfection, in respect of both inner motivation and overt conduct. This accolade is commonly applied in the Rabbinic *Aggadah* to Abraham (cf. Genesis 15:6) and the other Patriarchs and Matriarchs, whose human shortcomings are overlooked for this purpose. It also features in the legend of the 'thirty-six righteous ones' by whose merit, in every generation, the world endures. Less discriminatingly, it served in eighteenth- and nineteenth-century Chasidism as a title conferred on the heads of the dynasties of that movement. (See part I, chapter 10.)

The highest exemplar is the *kadosh*, the 'holy one' or 'saint', whose relationship with God is so intimate that his whole being is irradiated by exposure to the primary, divine source of holiness (see above pp. 244 f.). The term is used sparingly in Jewish tradition. Only exceptionally revered teachers (Yehudah ha-Nasi, Isaac Luria) are sometimes so referred to by their disciples. Traditionally, however, the epithet *kedoshim*, 'holy ones', is also given to Jewish martyrs, their death being regarded as the ultimate fulfilment of the obligation of *kiddush ha-Shem*, the 'sanctification of the divine Name', i.e., that a Jew should so conduct himself as to enhance respect for the God to whom he witnesses. (The concept was derived from Leviticus 22:32, 'And you shall not profane

My holy name; but I will be hallowed among the people of Israel.')

While these qualities of learning, piety, righteousness and holiness indicate the nature of the ideal, it is not anticipated that all Jews will attain it, or come equally close to it. But all Jews are expected to observe a devotional discipline which, if sincerely practised, should help them to move along that path.

That discipline is, in fact, a remarkably intensive one, comparable to the kind of strenuous regimen of spiritual exercises that is imposed in other religions only on priests and members of monastic orders. But then the Rabbis took very seriously the biblical challenge, 'You shall be to Me a kingdom of priests and a holy nation' (Exodus 19:6), and therefore saw it as their task to bring about, on the part of ordinary people leading ordinary lives, a level of spirituality that is elsewhere aspired to only by the mystic recluse.

RELIGIOUS EDUCATION

The means Judaism has devised for the cultivation of spirituality are those *mitzvot* which tradition designates *beyn adam la-Makom*, as pertaining to the relationship between the individual and God. Chief among these is *talmud torah*, a term which is perhaps best translated 'Jewish religious education', since the obligation involved is both to learn and to teach. It is an obligation repeatedly enjoined in the Bible itself: 'And these words which I command you this day shall be upon your heart; and you shall teach them diligently to your children' (Deuteronomy 6:6); 'This book of the law shall not depart out of your mouth, but you shall meditate on it day and night' (Joshua 1:8); 'All your sons shall be taught by the Lord, and great shall be the prosperity of your sons' (Isaiah 54:13). In the literature of Rabbinic Judaism, the obligation is constantly emphasized, and raised to the highest status. A few sample passages from the 'Ethics of the Fathers' will illustrate the general tenor.

Get yourself a teacher and a friend to study with . . . Make your study of Torah a fixed habit . . . Do not say 'When I have leisure I will study'; perhaps you will have no leisure . . . If you have learned much Torah, do not claim credit for yourself; it is the purpose for which you were created . . . Turn it [the Torah] over and over, for everything is contained in it; contemplate it, grow old and spend yourself in the study of it, and never stir from it, for you can have no better rule than that.

(Avot 1:6, 15; 2:4, 8; 5:22)

The study of Torah occupies a unique position among the obligations of a Jew because, as the Rabbis stressed, it leads to the fulfilment of all the other obligations, both those of an ethical and those of a devotional nature. That is how one must understand a famous Mishnah passage, cited and elaborated in the Jewish prayer book, which speaks of honouring father and mother, acts of kindness, regular study, hospitality, visiting the sick, dowering the bride, attending the burial of the dead, devotion in prayer, and making peace between man and man, and then delivers the punch line: 'But the study of Torah is equal to them all' (Pe'ah 5:1; prayer books – see Bibliography, p. 386).

At the same time, the study of Torah is itself a devotional act, as sacred as prayer, even marginally more so, for to engage in it is to be in touch with the mind of God as the Author or Inspirer of the sacred text. Thus we read that if ten people study Torah together, or even if one person does so on his own, the *Shechinah* abides there (Avot 3:2, 6); that the study of Torah is greater than the rebuilding of the Temple (Megillah 16b); and that, while a house of prayer may be converted into a house of study, a house of study (being the more sacred) may not be converted into a house of prayer (Megillah 27a).

Two further reasons help to explain the huge emphasis given to religious education in Jewish tradition. One is the plain fact that the transmission of Judaism, and the survival of the Jewish community, which has so often found itself in the position of an oppressed minority, depend on it. The other is the concept, fundamental to Pharisaism, of a religious democracy in which the status of the laity is 'levelled up' to that of the priesthood (again one recalls that key verse about 'a kingdom of priests and a holy nation'), an aim that could be accomplished only through popular education.

It is a remarkable fact that already in Pharisaic times the first steps were taken in Palestine towards the establishment of a network of schools for the religious instruction of all, the poor and orphans being educated at the expense of the community. In subsequent times Judaism evolved a variety of educational institutions, such as the *talmud torah* or *cheder* for elementary tuition, the *beit ha-midrash* ('house of study') and the *yeshivah* for higher learning. The synagogue itself, it should be added, is to a large extent an educational institution, not only because it has often housed the school, but because its worship, as we shall see, combines prayer with study.

Fundamentally, of course, the religious education of children is their parents' responsibility, although one which was formerly considered incumbent only on fathers in relation to their sons. That is because the Rabbis of the talmudic period, apparently fearful that literacy might expose Jewish girls to the licentiousness of the Graeco-Roman culture, inclined to the view that education was not obligatory for them. Since the nineteenth century, however, that imbalance has been redressed in Progressive Judaism, and more recently, to some extent in Orthodox Judaism also. The chief textbook of Jewish education is the Bible, particularly the Pentateuch, but as interpreted in subsequent Jewish tradition, so that the syllabus is potentially vast. At the advanced level, the focus shifts to the Talmud and its commentaries, and in the more modern schools and seminaries Jewish history, philosophy etc., are taught as independent subjects. There is no 'school-leaving age', for when the formal educational process ceases (as in the past it tended to do for boys after their bar-mitzvah, at the age of thirteen), it remains the individual's obligation to study the weekly Torah portion and to deepen his Jewish knowledge. As Maimonides summed up the tradition, 'Every Jew is obligated to study Torah, whether he is rich or poor, well or sick, young or old' (*Mishneh Torah*, Hilchot Talmud Torah 1:8).

TEMPLE WORSHIP

For the rest, Judaism's devotional discipline may be subsumed under the general heading of worship, if we use that term to include all the various acts by which human beings may express towards God those feelings which the contemplation of His Being arouses in them: awe or love, praise or gratitude, humility or contrition, longing for His favour, protection, help and guidance, or merely to experience His presence. Such acts may be individual or corporate, spontaneous or prescribed, inward or outward.

In ancient times, Jewish corporate worship was centred in the Temple in Jerusalem and, in common with other religions of antiquity, sacrificial in nature. It differed from them, however, in that it was directed to the One God of heaven and earth, and that idolatrous and immoral practices were excluded. Twice daily, morning and afternoon, with additional services on sabbaths and festivals, the priests would offer the prescribed sacrifices, while the Levites chanted psalms and the people watched the spectacle in silent awe. A high point, at which the people prostrated themselves, was the pronouncement of the Priestly Benediction: 'The Lord bless you and keep you; the Lord make His face to shine upon you, and be gracious to you; the Lord lift up His countenance upon you, and give you peace' (Numbers 6:24–26). At some stage, on the testimony of the Mishnah (Tamid 5:1), it became customary to include in the Temple service several other prayers along with the recitation of the Ten Commandments and the *Shema* (Deuteronomy 6:4–9; 11: 13–21; Numbers 15:37–41).

The destruction of the Temple in 70 CE was for the Jews a devastating blow, since it removed what had been to them the proud symbol of their monotheistic faith, the dwelling-place of the *Shechinah* and, as such, the holiest place on earth. Their reaction to this calamity was twofold. On the one hand they bewailed the ruined edifice, cherished its memory, prayed for its restoration, and continued to study the laws that governed its cult, considering it not superseded but only in abeyance – an attitude maintained to this day in Orthodox, though not in Progressive, Judaism. On the other hand, they consoled themselves with the reassurances of their Pharisaic teachers, that the practice of prayer, repentance and charity was still open to them, and that this was as acceptable to God as sacrifice – and even more so.

In this comforting thought they derived encouragement from the teachings of the Prophets and, as regards prayer, especially from the prophecy of Hosea, 'We will render instead of bullocks the offering of our lips' (14:3; in Christian Bibles, 14:2). Similarly, scriptural phrases calling on the Israelites to 'serve' the Lord their God, and to do so 'with all their hearts' (Exodus 23:25; Deuteronomy 11:13) were understood as alluding to prayer. 'What is this "service with the heart" (or "worship with the mind")? You must say: it is prayer' (Ta'anit 2a).

THE JEWISH HOME

With the destruction of the Temple, the scene of Jewish worship shifted not only to the synagogue but also to the home. The latter, like the former, became a 'little sanctuary' or 'miniature temple' (Ezekiel 11:16) in which the dining-table represented the altar and quasi-priestly acts of prayer and ritual were daily conducted by the master of the house (*baal ha-bayit*) as well as his wife and other members of the family. It is one of the lasting positive achievements of the Pharisees that they made the home a place of religious activity by introducing into it such ceremonies as the kindling of the sabbath lights. Ever since, it has been a major feature of Judaism that it is not only in the synagogue, but in the home, that daily prayer and study take place, the sabbath and festivals are celebrated, and the life-cycle events, from birth to death, are ritually observed.

To enter an observant Jewish home is therefore to enter a place hallowed by 'the practice of the presence of God', a fact visually manifested by the ritual objects and sacred books to be found within it, and by the so-called *mezuzah* ('doorpost'), a cylinder containing a tiny parchment scroll inscribed with the scriptural passages (Deuteronomy 6:4–9 and 11:13–21) including the injunction that God's words be written 'on the doorposts of your house and on your gates', which is affixed to the right-hand post of the main entrance and of the living-room doors.

THE SYNAGOGUE

The synagogue (*beit ha-k'neset*, 'house of assembly'), which had coexisted with the Temple for some centuries, differed from it in the following crucial respects. First, its worship involved no offering of sacrifices, but consisted solely of prayer, together with the public reading and expounding of the Scriptures. Secondly, it did not require priests, but any sufficiently knowledgeable member of the community could act as precentor (he was known as *sheliach tzibbur*, the 'representative of the community') or preacher. Here it should be mentioned that the rabbi had no prerogative role in the synagogue; he was and is, as his title implies, a teacher, not a priest (though it should be added that nowadays he is commonly expected to perform liturgical and pastoral functions as well). Thirdly, synagogue worship was congregational, enabling the common people to be active participants rather than, as they had been in the Temple, essentially passive spectators. Fourthly, synagogues, unlike the Temple, were not confined to a single place. They could be established anywhere, in Jerusalem and the provinces, in Palestine and the Diaspora, and thus brought corporate worship within the reach of every Jew. Indeed, it was ruled that in any location where at least ten Jewish householders lived, there was a positive obligation to establish a synagogue. Finally, because synagogue worship employed *language* (spoken and chanted) rather than sacrificial ritual, it necessitated the composition of a far more extensive and elaborate liturgy than had previously existed; to this subject we shall return presently.

Over the centuries, synagogues have been built in many styles, shapes and sizes, varying from simple huts to imposing edifices. In fact, they need not be purpose-built at all. Any house or room can be made into a synagogue by being so designated and used. It needs, however, to be equipped with a few essential appurtenances.

Appurtenances

The most important of these is the Scroll of the Law (*sefer torah*) containing the unvocalized Hebrew text of the Pentateuch, ornamentally handwritten by a trained scribe (*sofer*) on a series of sheets of parchment which are stitched end to end and then fastened to a pair of wooden rollers. Each of the latter is known as a 'tree of life' (*etz chayyim*) in allusion to Proverbs 3:18, where the 'Wisdom' of the context is traditionally identified with Torah. Rolled up for storage, the scroll is, among Ashkenazi Jews, secured by a silk or velvet band, then clothed in an embroidered mantle; among Sephardi Jews it is placed in an ornamented wooden case. Suspended by a chain from the protruding top ends of the rollers is a silver pointer, its end shaped like a miniature hand with extended index finger, which is known as the *yad* ('hand'), and is used in the reading of the Torah, to avoid touching the parchment. Similarly suspended, according to Ashkenazi custom, is a silver shield or 'breastplate' (reminiscent of the High Priest's breastplate, see Exodus 28:15–30) which originally served to label a particular scroll as regards the occasion for which it had been set, but which has now became purely decorative. Finally, the rollers are surmounted by a pair of silver finials known from their usual shape as *rimmonim* ('pomegranates'), incorporating tiny silver bells. Over the *rimmonim* there may be placed, additionally, a large silver crown (*keter*), so called in allusion to a passage in the 'Ethics of the Fathers' which speaks of the 'crown of the Torah' (Avot 4:13).

A synagogue will usually possess several scrolls, to allow for those occasions, as when a sabbath coincides with a festival, on which more than one passage, perhaps from different books of the Pentateuch, is read; also because it enhances the pageantry if several scrolls can be paraded in procession, as is done on the festival of *Simchat Torah* (see p. 361).

When not being read, the scrolls are housed in a cupboard or other enclosure known in English as the ark. The ancient name for it was *tevah* ('chest'). In Ashkenazi tradition it is known as *aron ha-kodesh* ('the holy ark'), in Sephardi tradition as *heichal* ('sanctuary'). The ark is usually located against the wall that faces Jerusalem, and is fronted by a curtain (*parochet*), reminiscent of the veil that screened the holy of holies in the Temple (Exodus 27:21); the curtain is ceremonially drawn open when the scroll or scrolls are taken out.

Inscribed on the ark is likely to be an appropriate quotation from the Bible or Talmud, and in front of it is hung an oil lamp known as *ner tamid* (the 'perpetual light') which derives its name from the candelabrum of the Temple (Exodus 27:20) and symbolizes the spiritual light which it is the task of the House of Israel, through the Torah ('For the commandment is a lamp and the teaching is light', Proverbs 6:23), to diffuse throughout the world (Exodus Rabbah 36:1; cf. Isaiah 42:6).

The public Scripture-reading is conducted from a raised platform, known as a *bimah* (a word of Greek origin), or *almemar* (of Arabic origin), reminiscent of the wooden platform used by

Ezra for a similar purpose (Nehemiah 8:4). This is traditionally located in the middle of the synagogue, but in many modern synagogues it has been moved forward towards the ark, in order to use the intervening space for seating accommodation. During the prayers the *sheliach tzibbur* traditionally stands at a desk facing the ark while another desk or pulpit, facing the congregation, is generally provided for the preacher. In a synagogue where the *bimah* occupies the forward position, in front of the ark, both desks will be located on it.

SYNAGOGUE WORSHIP

The *sheliach tzibbur* may be any member of the congregation invited to step forward and lead the prayers. Alternatively, he may be the rabbi or another, musically trained, professional functionary known as the cantor or *chazzan*. Large synagogues are likely to have both a rabbi and a cantor.

In Orthodox, but not Progressive, synagogues the women are segregated from the men by a partition (*mechitzah*), or accommodated in a gallery, and do not play an active part in the service, as men do. Whether this was always so is not certain, for though there were separate courts for men and women in the Temple, there is no conclusive evidence that synagogues provided separate accommodation for women prior to the Middle Ages, and the statement of the Talmud (Megillah 23a) that, in principle though not in practice, women may be called up to read from the Torah, leaves room for doubt.

Traditionally, both the Scripture portions and, for the most part, the prayers, are chanted, and there is a rich heritage of Jewish liturgical music, varying in mode from occasion to occasion as well as differing between the Ashkenazi and Sephardi traditions. It is largely *vocal* music, for the playing of instruments is traditionally disallowed since the destruction of the Temple (in which instrumental music featured largely), also because of the risk of an accidental violation of the sabbath through the need to repair a musical instrument. In Progressive synagogues, however, these compunctions are generally disregarded and organ-accompanied choral singing is the norm. On the other hand, much of the service is, in Progressive synagogues, read rather than sung.

Although the medieval Jewish law codes, based on the Talmud, are almost unreservedly permissive as regards the language of prayer, Jewish worship is traditionally conducted in Hebrew. In Orthodox Judaism that remains the practice, on the grounds of the antiquity, universality and sanctity of the 'holy tongue' (*leshon ha-kodesh*), as well as the impossibility of translating the ancient Hebrew texts into modern tongues without loss of nuance. Progressive Jews, however, influenced by the same considerations, yet wishing to make their services comprehensible even to those with little knowledge of Hebrew, conduct them partly in Hebrew and partly in the vernacular, the proportion varying from congregation to congregation.

The classical sources of Jewish law do not require men to cover their heads, and it seems that they did not generally do so in ancient times or, except in Sephardi communities, until the late Middle Ages. Nevertheless, traditionalist Jews have long regarded the covering of the head as a way of expressing reverence towards God and it is therefore obligatory, at least in synagogue and when praying, studying sacred texts, and eating. In Progressive synagogues, too, male worshippers are generally expected to cover their heads, except in the United States of America, where the Reform movement made the contrary practice the norm in the nineteenth century, and a few synagogues in other English-speaking countries which follow the American Reform tradition to the extent of leaving the matter optional. The form of head-covering generally worn by traditionally observant Jewish men is a skull-cap, known as a *yarmulka* (a word of Slavonic origin), a *kappel* (Yiddish) or a *kippah* (Hebrew).

As far as women are concerned, there is a strong insistence in Orthodox tradition that, at least when married, they should always have their hair covered in public, and wear a headscarf or a wig (known in Yiddish as a *sheitel*). There is also a general feeling in most sections of the Jewish community that it is appropriate for women to wear some sort of head-covering in synagogue.

Tallit

Many Jewish observances have the express purpose of serving as *reminders*, either of particular historical events or, more generally, of the religious responsibilities involved in being a member of the

Jewish people. An example of the latter is the scriptural injunction that the Israelites were to attach a tassel (*tzitzit*) to each of the four corners of their garments, 'that you may look upon it, and remember all the commandments of the Lord . . .' (Numbers 15:37–41). Literally applied in ancient times, until the Jews abandoned the oriental, rectangular mantle for the more varied styles of European dress, the intention of this commandment came to be expressed through the *tallit* ('mantle'), or prayer-shawl, usually made of white wool, cotton or silk, with blue or black stripes, fringed hems and a tassel at each corner. This is traditionally worn, by men only, during the morning service, but on the Day of Atonement it is worn at all services, on the fast of Av at the afternoon service only, and by the *sheliach tzibbur* at most services. As regards women, although the Talmud (Menachot 43a) debates whether the practice is obligatory or optional for them, the custom is that they do not wear the *tallit*. Even in Progressive synagogues that differentiation still generally persists, though in some congregations attempts are being made to discontinue it.

There is also a smaller version, called the *tallit katan* ('little tallit'), which the most rigorously observant, Orthodox Jewish males wear all day (except on sabbaths and festivals) as an undergarment, but with the tassels showing, in order to fulfil the scriptural commandment, 'and it shall be to you a tassel to look upon and to remember all the commandments of the Lord' (Numbers 15:39).

Tefillin

Another observance of the 'reminder' kind derives from the phrase, 'You shall bind them [God's commandments] as a sign upon your hand, and they shall be as frontlets between your eyes,' which occurs in the Shema (Deuteronomy 6:4–9) and, with variations, in three other scriptural passages (Exodus 13:1–10; 11–16; Deuteronomy 11:13–21). Although originally intended metaphorically, this injunction was at some stage, perhaps in the Pharisaic period, given physical expression in the form of the so-called *tefillin* ('prayer accessories', sometimes mistranslated 'phylacteries', with the incorrect implication that they are amulets). These are a pair of cubical leather boxes, with straps attached, containing the above-mentioned four scriptural passages, hand-written on tiny strips of parchment. One of the boxes is tied on the left upper arm, opposite the heart, and its strap wound seven times round the forearm, then round the middle finger and the palm of the hand. The other box is placed on the forehead, with its two straps knotted together above the nape of the neck, then brought forward to hang over the shoulders. Thus they are worn by traditional observant male Jews, from the age of religious majority, during morning prayers, every day except sabbaths and festivals.

These and the other outward symbols which feature in Jewish religious practice are not 'sacraments'. Their purpose is to aid remembrance, to express religious thoughts and feelings and, by their cumulative effect, to nurture the consciousness of the presence of God, and thus to hallow human life. They are therefore no less 'inward' in intent than the act of prayer itself, to which we now return.

Daily Services

To the two daily services of the Temple, the Synagogue added a third, in the evening. These three are known respectively as *shacharit* (from *shachar*, 'dawn'), *minchah* ('afternoon offering') and *arvit* or *ma'ariv* (both terms deriving from *erev*, 'evening', the latter alluding more specifically to a phrase in the liturgy of that service which praises God who 'brings on the evening twilight'). On sabbaths, new moons and festivals the morning service is followed by an additional service (*musaf*), and the Day of Atonement concludes with yet another service (*ne'ilah*, 'closing').

Any individuals who are unable to worship with the congregation in the synagogue are expected to do so at home, preferably at the same time, thus associating themselves mentally with their fellow Jews. Many Jews do, in fact, pray at home on weekdays; but others practise the more rigorous discipline of joining their fellow congregants at early-morning service in the synagogue before going to work (ideally, the morning prayers should be recited at sunrise) and again at dusk, when the afternoon prayers may be followed immediately by the evening prayers.

This daily gathering of the faithful for prayer is sometimes referred to as a *minyan*, in allusion to the rule that a complete service, including those elements which involve the public proclamation of God's holiness, may only be conducted in the presence of a congregation (*edah*), which is technically defined as constituted by a quorum (*minyan*) of at least ten male adults (Megillah 23b on the basis of Leviticus 22:32 and Numbers 14:27), a rule strictly adhered to in Orthodox Judaism but relaxed in Progressive and Conservative Judaism, at least to the extent of women being included in the quorum.

Here again we see the great emphasis on *community* which characterizes Jewish worship, also evidenced by the ubiquitous use of the first person plural in the prayers. There is indeed provision for purely private prayer and meditation, but mostly the individual is expected to identify himself with the congregation and, even beyond that, with the Jewish people, which the congregation represents in miniature. This concept is further reinforced by the tradition that a Jew, whether at home or in a synagogue, should always face towards Jerusalem when reciting the principal prayers. It could indeed be said that Jewish worship is, in large part, a corporate act by the world-wide House of Israel, rededicating itself to its responsibility under the Covenant.

JEWISH LITURGY

As regards the history of the Jewish liturgy, three major stages may be identified. First, the formative period of the Pharisaic-Rabbinic age. In this period scriptural passages were selected for liturgical use and the so-called *Stammgebete* (German: 'basic prayers') formulated. These are mostly of the *berachah* ('benediction') type, which means that they address God in the second person, as 'Lord' and 'King', and that their framework is one of praise, even though their content may be one of thanksgiving, supplication or otherwise. There are two kinds of benediction, short and long. A short benediction is a single-sentence prayer praising God as the Creator of the food or other good things about to be enjoyed, or else as the author of the *mitzvah* about to be performed. A long benediction is a longer prayer, with a concluding eulogy (*chatimah*) which 'clinches' the benediction with a phrase succinctly summarizing its main theme.

The second stage was in the Middle Ages. During this period the liturgy was greatly elaborated and enriched, particularly by new compositions of a poetical kind, known as *piyyutim*, which originated mainly in Babylonia, Palestine, Germany and Spain, as well as some other countries. Furthermore, because the increasingly dispersed Jewish communities tended to make different selections from this new material, and to develop local customs, there occurred a diversification of liturgical traditions or 'rites' (*minhagim*) falling broadly into two types: the Sephardi or Spanish rite with its variants (Persian, Yemenite, Roman, etc.) and the Ashkenazi or German rite with its variants (French, Polish, Lithuanian, etc.). In addition, from the Middle Ages we have the earliest manuscript prayer books, beginning with the *Seder Rav Amram* in the ninth century (see above, p. 222), the Jewish liturgy having been previously transmitted orally.

The third and modern period in the history of the Jewish liturgy dates from the invention of printing in the fifteenth century. This led to a proliferation of prayer-book editions, some of them complete with translations into European languages. A weekday and sabbath prayer book now became known as a *siddur*, which means 'arrangement', and a festival prayer book as a *machzor*, which means 'cycle'; previously these and other terms had been used without such a distinction. While recent centuries have seen a tendency to standardize the traditional liturgy, resulting in such widely used prayer books as Singer's (see Bibliography, p. 386), there has also been further diversification, first with the emergence of a distinctive Chasidic liturgical tradition, deriving from the sixteenth-century Kabbalist Isaac Luria, then, beginning in 1819, with the appearance of a great variety of Reform and other non-Orthodox prayer books, which partly modify the traditional texts and partly supplement them with novel selections from Jewish literature and newly written prayers seeking to express contemporary Jewish concerns and aspirations.

The Tefillah

Turning from the history of the Jewish liturgy to its contents, let us conclude this chapter with a brief survey of the principal elements.

The kernel of every statutory service is the so-called *tefillah*, which simply means 'prayer'. About the etymology of the word there has been much speculation, but little agreement. It is clear, however, that it refers to the worship of the synagogue rather than that of the Temple, for which the word *avodah* ('cult') is more commonly used, and that, unlike the English word 'prayer', it does not etymologically imply petition.

In the narrower sense which concerns us here, the *tefillah* is a particular sequence of benedictions (of the long kind) which in the days of the Mishnah numbered eighteen and, though a nineteenth was subsequently added, are still commonly known as the *shemoneh-esreh*, 'the eighteen (benedictions)'. Yet another name for this prayer is *amidah* ('standing'), because traditionally one stands to recite it.

The benedictions it comprises fall into three groups. The first three are in the nature of praise. Thus, the first benediction, which tradition particularly stresses must be recited with *kavvanah* (concentration of the mind), begins, 'Blessed are You, Lord our God and God of our fathers, God of Abraham, God of Isaac and God of Jacob, great, mighty and awesome God . . .' and goes on to speak of God's redemptive guidance in the history and destiny of the Jewish people. The second benediction is about God's power as revealed both in nature and in the resurrection of the dead, the latter being reinterpreted or reformulated in Progressive liturgies to refer to the immortality of the soul or the gift of life. The third benediction celebrates God's holiness and, when recited publicly, is elaborated into a doxology called *kedushah* ('holiness') based on Isaiah's 'Holy, holy, holy, is the Lord of hosts; the whole earth is full of His glory' (6:3).

The second group of benedictions is variable, in the sense that on weekdays it comprises thirteen of a petitionary kind whereas, on sabbaths and festivals, these are omitted and replaced by one (or, on one occasion, three) specific to the day. Something of the character of the intermediate benedictions (as they are called) recited on weekdays may be gauged from their concluding eulogies, which respectively praise God as the gracious giver of knowledge, who delights in repentance, abundantly forgives, redeems Israel, heals the sick, blesses the years, gathers the dispersed, loves righteousness and justice, humbles the arrogant, supports the righteous, will rebuild Jerusalem, and cause the horn of salvation to flourish, and hearkens to prayer. (In some of these benedictions the individual may insert personal petitions.)

In the last group, the accent is on thanksgiving. However, the first of the group was originally a supplication for God's acceptance of Israel's sacrificial cult in the Temple, and subsequently became a plea for its restoration. (In some Progressive liturgies it has been reformulated as a prayer for God's acceptance of the worship offered to Him in the synagogue.) The penultimate benediction begins: 'We gratefully acknowledge that You are the Lord our God and God of our fathers, the God of all generations. You are the Rock of our life, the Shield of our salvation in every age. We thank and praise You for our lives, which are in Your hand; for our souls, which are ever in Your keeping; for the miracles that are daily with us; and for Your wondrous kindness at all times, morning, noon and night . . .' The final benediction is a prayer for peace, based on the Priestly Benediction ('The Lord bless you and keep you . . .,' see above, p. 319), which is incorporated in the benediction when it is recited publicly and, in Orthodox synagogues, on the festivals, pronounced in a solemn ceremony (usually referred to as *duchaning*, after the Hebrew word for the dais from which it was conducted in the Temple) by the Kohanim, i.e., those presumptively descended from the ancient priests.

At certain points in the *tefillah* the worshipper traditionally bends his knees and bows his head. The whole *tefillah* has a 'prologue', taken from the fifty-first Psalm: 'O Lord, open thou my lips, and my mouth shall show forth thy praise' (verse 17). It also has an 'epilogue' incorporating the verse, 'Let the words of my mouth and the meditation of my heart be acceptable in thy sight, O Lord, my Rock and my redeemer' (Psalms 19:15).

In ancient times the *tefillah* was followed by a silent period in which the worshippers prostrated themselves and offered their personal prayers for God's favour and mercy. The 'epilogue' just mentioned was, in fact, originally such an individual prayer, by a Babylonian rabbi of the fourth to fifth centuries (Berachot 17a). But in the course of the Middle Ages and after, this practice developed into a set liturgy of prayers and Scripture passages in a penitential vein, recited after the *tefillah* on weekday mornings and afternoons. These prayers, known as *tachanun* ('supplication') or *nefilat appayim* ('prostration'), used to be recited prostrate; since gaonic times the posture has been modified into a forward inclination, with the forehead resting on the left arm.

Recitation of the Shema

The *tefillah* is preceded in the morning and evening services, but not in the afternoon service, by the recitation of the *Shema*. The kernel of this section of the liturgy is the *Shema* itself (see above, p. 236), that is, the scriptural passage Deuteronomy 6:4–9, followed by Deuteronomy 11:13–21 and Numbers 15:37–41. The first of these passages begins with the solemn proclamation of God's unity, 'Hear, O Israel, the Lord is our God, the Lord is One,' to which Jewish tradition attaches supreme importance – to recite it is to take upon oneself 'the yoke of the kingdom of Heaven' and it is therefore essential that it be said with *kavvanah* (see above, p. 329). This is followed by the non-scriptural response, 'Blessed be His name, whose glorious kingdom is for ever and ever,' and then the rest of the passage: 'And you shall love the Lord your God with all your heart, and with all your soul, and with all your might . . .'

In the morning service the recitation of the Scripture passages is preceded by two benedictions and followed by one. Of these three, the first praises God as the 'Maker of light and Creator of darkness'; the second emphasizes the love God has shown in revealing the Torah to His people, Israel; the third reaffirms the truth proclaimed in the *Shema* and goes on to speak of God's redemptive guidance as epitomized in the Exodus from Egypt. Thus the sequence highlights the three major phases of God's activity: Creation, Revelation, Redemption.

In the evening service the Scripture passages are preceded by two benedictions and followed by two. Of these four, the first three are similar to those of the morning service, while the additional one is a prayer for God's protection as darkness descends which begins: 'Grant, O Lord our God, that we may lie down in peace, and that we may rise up, O our King, unto life . . .'

The whole liturgical section is introduced by the *sheliach tzibbur's* call to worship, 'Bless (*barechu*) the Lord, who is to be blessed,' to which the congregation responds, 'Blessed be the Lord, who is to be blessed for ever and ever.'

Other Prayers

That is not, however, where the entire service begins. For the Mishnah records that the ancient *chasidim* (see above, p. 65) 'used to wait a whole hour before praying, the better to concentrate their minds on God' (Berachot 5:1), a precedent which gave rise to the concept of a period of preparatory meditation, so that the individual's mind may be attuned to worship before the service reaches, with the *barechu*, its more formal and public phase. This concept, which was applied mainly to the morning service, yielded in course of time an extensive liturgy, divided into three sections: the *birchot ha-shachar* ('morning benedictions') consisting mainly of prayers appropriate to the beginning of a new day; the *korbanot* ('sacrifices') recalling in extracts from the Pentateuch and rabbinic literature the ancient Temple cult; and the *pesukei de-zimra* ('verses of song') comprising psalms and compilations of Scripture verses having as their theme the praise of God, with an introductory benediction ('Blessed be He who spoke, and the world existed . . .') and a closing benediction ('Praised be Your name for ever, O our King . . .').

There is also a prayer to be recited on entering the synagogue, incorporating a verse from the book of Numbers (24:5) which the ancient rabbis interpreted homiletically to refer to synagogues and schools: 'How fair are your tents, O Jacob, your encampments, O Israel!'

On sabbath and festival mornings, and certain other occasions, the service reaches its climax, after the completion of the *tefillah*, with the reading of the Torah. This includes some colourful rituals, such as the ceremonial opening and closing of the ark, the taking out (*hotza'ah*), undressing and dressing (*gelilah*, 'wrapping'), elevation (*hagbahah*), circumambulation (*hakkafah*) and

332

returning (*hachnasah*) of the Torah scroll, as well as prayers for the congregation, the government of the country, nowadays also for the State of Israel, and above all, of course, the Scripture readings themselves (of which more will be said in the next chapter).

The closing of the ark is usually followed by a sermon (*derashah*) expounding the Scripture readings and drawing from them a moral for contemporary life. After that and (in Orthodox synagogues) the additional service there remain only the concluding prayers and hymns, the latter including the *Adon Olam* which we mentioned in connection with the Divine Attributes (see above, pp. 237 and 242). Of the prayers, two might be mentioned here, both illustrating the two most prominent themes of the Jewish liturgy: exultant praise of God, and fervent longing for the coming of His kingdom.

One is the *kaddish* ('holy'), an Aramaic doxology dating from before the destruction of the Temple. There are several versions of this, according to whether it concludes an entire service, or a section of the service, or a study-session, or serves as a mourner's prayer, so that, especially in an Orthodox service, it is likely to be heard repeatedly. It begins in all versions:

Extolled and hallowed be God's great name in the world He has created according to His will. May He soon establish His kingdom, in your lifetime, and let us say Amen. May His great name be praised to all eternity. Lauded and praised, glorified, exalted and adored, honoured, extolled and acclaimed be the name of the Holy One, who is to be blessed, though He is above all the blessings and hymns, praises and consolations that are uttered in the world, and let us say Amen . . .

The other is the *aleinu*, so called from the opening word of its first sentence: '*It is our duty* to praise the Lord of all, to proclaim the greatness of Him who formed the world in the beginning . . .' The first part of this prayer is believed to date from Temple times. The second part, attributed to the third-century Babylonian teacher Rav, begins:

Trusting in You, O Lord our God, we hope soon to behold the glory of Your might, when false gods shall cease to take Your place in the hearts of men, and the world will be perfected under Your unchallenged rule; when all mankind will call upon Your name and, forsaking evil, turn to

You alone. Let all who dwell on earth understand that unto You every knee must bend, and every tongue swear loyalty. Before You, O Lord our God, let them humble themselves, and to Your glorious name let them give honour. Let all accept the yoke of Your kingdom, so that You may rule over them soon and for ever . . .

The prayer ends on a triumphant note by quoting from the book of the prophet Zechariah (14:9): 'On that day the Lord will be one and His name one.'

CHAPTER THREE   FROM WEEK TO WEEK

'A man should make himself strong as a lion to rise in the morning for the service of his Creator, so that he may awake the dawn.' So begins the *Shulchan Aruch*, alluding to a passage in the 'Ethics of the Fathers' which exhorts, 'Be strong as a leopard, swift as an eagle, fleet as a gazelle and brave as a lion to do the will of your Father in heaven' (5:20), as well as a psalm verse, 'Awake, my soul! Awake, O harp and lyre! I will awake the dawn!' (57:8). This gave rise to the legend that every midnight King David would be roused by the wind playing on his harp, whereupon he would get up and study Torah (Lamentations Rabbah 2:22), which in turn contributed to a tendency in Jewish tradition to recommend the habit of early rising.

Taking that moment as our starting point, let us follow the waking life of a traditionally observant Jew and notice how the devotional discipline of Judaism impinges on it continually.

THE SANCTIFICATION OF DAILY LIFE

Even the most mundane actions and experiences are invested with spiritual significance by being regulated in the name of a religious law, and in many instances sanctified by a benediction. Thus the act of washing upon rising and before meals is accompanied by a benediction praising God for having 'sanctified us by His commandments, and enjoined us concerning the washing of hands' and so made reminiscent of the ritual purifications of the priests in Temple times.

The act of dressing, too, has its religious connotation, not only because it involves the covering of the head and the donning of the *tallit* (see above, pp. 324 f.) but on account of a biblical law forbidding clothes made of a material called *sha'atnez* (Leviticus 19:19), defined as a mixture of wool and linen (Deuteronomy 22:11). The reason for this prohibition is obscure; but that does not invalidate it in the eyes of the rabbinic tradition. Accordingly, Orthodox Judaism (though not Progressive Judaism) regards it as still obligatory.

The cultivation of everyday God-consciousness is chiefly effected through acts of prayer. We have already referred to the three daily services (above, p. 326) which our observant Jew will attend at the synagogue; otherwise he will pray (or *davven*, as an Ashkenazi Jew may well say, using a Yiddish word) at home. On Monday and Thursday mornings he may make a special effort to get to the synagogue, for on those days the morning service includes a prolonged *tachanun* (see above, p. 331) as well as the reading of the first section of the week's portion from the Torah scroll. This custom, which according to the Talmud was instituted by Ezra, originated in the fact that in ancient Palestine, Mondays and Thursdays were market and assize days, when the villagers would gather in the towns. The practice has been carried on ever since, so strong is the conservative tendency in Jewish tradition.

Besides the three statutory services, the day affords other occasions for prayer, including mealtimes. On the principle that 'man is forbidden to taste anything without first blessing God' (Berachot 35a), every meal is preceded by a short benediction. This, if the meal includes bread, praises God, in allusion to Psalm 104:14, for 'bringing forth bread from the earth'. Likewise, on the basis of a verse in Deuteronomy, 'And you shall eat and be full, and you shall bless the Lord your God for the good land He has given you' (8:10), Jewish tradition ordains a lengthy grace after meals (*birkat ha-mazon*, 'benediction for food'). The full version of this (there are shorter versions for recitation after a snack) consists of four long benedictions, of which the first reads:

Blessed are You, O Lord our God, King of the universe, by whose goodness the whole world is sustained. With grace, love and mercy You give food to all flesh, for Your love is unending. Through Your great goodness, we have never lacked our daily bread; may we never do so, for Your great name's sake. For You feed and nourish all, You are good to all, and provide food for all Your creatures. Blessed are You, O Lord, Sustainer of all.

DIETARY LAWS

Mealtime has a religious dimension also on account of the extensive legislation found in the Bible and its subsequent interpretation concerning permitted and forbidden foods. This is known generically as *kashrut*, an abstract noun derived from the adjective *kasher* (kosher according to the Ashkenazi pronunciation) which means 'fit' in the sense of 'fit to be eaten'. Whatever is not *kasher* is said to be *trefah*, a word which originally denoted the carcass of an animal that had been 'torn' by a predator (Exodus 22:30; Christian Bibles, 22:31).

While there are a few restrictions relating to vegetable food (see, for example, Leviticus 19:19, 23 ff.; 23:9–14; Deuteronomy 22:9), it is with *animal* food that the legislation chiefly concerns itself.

That eating animal flesh is permitted at all, is presented in the Bible as a divine concession, made only after the Flood and immediately qualified (Genesis 1:29; 9:3 f.). There was evidently a diffidence about it, prompted, one supposes, both by humanitarian sentiment and by a desire to distance Judaism from the pagan sacrificial cults, and, on both counts, an urge to circumscribe the practice with the most stringent safeguards.

What, more precisely, lies behind the laws in question, is a matter for historical and anthropological speculation; and since the legislation is complex, it is likely that a multiplicity of causes will have contributed to it. Among those that have been suggested are ancient taboos as well as instinctive feelings of revulsion towards some species of animals on account of their abhorrent appearance or cruel ways. Even hygienic considerations may have played a part, although there is no explicit mention of any such motivation in the scriptural sources. The sole purpose stated there is the 'holiness' becoming the Covenant people (Leviticus 11:44 f.), that is, its differentiation from the surrounding paganism.

From an Orthodox point of view, these laws have been divinely ordained, and that is their validation. Those who share that conviction are naturally conscience-bound to observe them. Those who do not, may nevertheless adhere to them, to a greater or lesser extent, from other motives, e.g. for their supposed hygienic value, as an exercise in self-discipline, as a gesture of identification or simply by way of carrying on a family tradition. But there are also many Jews who, without questioning the religious significance which the dietary laws undoubtedly have for others, see in them neither divine imperative nor contemporary relevance, and pay little or no attention to them.

What is involved in these laws, as stated in the Bible and elaborated in the subsequent literature, may be briefly summarized as follows. First, certain species are forbidden: all, in fact, except quadrupeds which both have a divided hoof and chew the cud, birds expressly permitted, and fish that have both fins and scales (Leviticus 11:1–47; Deuteronomy 14:3–20). Secondly, the animal (not including fish) must be slaughtered by a licensed slaughterer (*shochet*) according to a method (*shechitah*) designed both to allow maximum blood drainage and to cause minimum pain. This method, often attacked on humanitarian grounds, is believed by its defenders, who are able to quote expert scientific opinion, to be at least as humane as any other. Thirdly, the carcass must be inspected for defects; if such are found, it is declared *trefah*. If the carcass is passed, some prohibited organs are removed; these include certain fats (Leviticus 7:23) as well as the ischiatic nerve (Genesis 32:33); and because of the difficulty of removing the latter from the surrounding flesh, it is the custom of some communities to exclude the hindquarters altogether.

In order to drain off still more of the blood, the meat is next submitted to a process called *melichah* ('salting') or, more popularly, *koshering* ('making fit'), by which it is soaked in water for half an hour, then covered with salt for one hour, then rinsed, before being cooked. This process is carried out at home if it has not already been done, as is usually the case nowadays, in the butcher's shop.

Even then further restrictions have to be heeded. For there is a biblical law that forbids the boiling of a kid in its mother's milk (Exodus 23:19; 34:26; Deuteronomy 14:21), which may have been originally directed against a particular pagan fertility rite, as Maimonides conjectured and recent archaeology seems to have confirmed, but which the Rabbis interpreted so as to prohibit any mixing of meat with milk or milk products, even stipulating a waiting period (of between one and six hours, depending on the strictness of the community's established custom) after a meat meal, before milk, butter or cheese may be consumed. For the same reason, great care must be taken to keep separate utensils for the two kinds of food.

This multitude of rules and regulations may seem burdensome to the outsider. But in a devoutly Orthodox household its observance is taken for granted, and the effort involved has positive religious significance for those who make it, and adds to their feeling that their home is a sanctuary.

VARIOUS BENEDICTIONS

More directly relevant to the sanctification of daily life are acts of prayer. The Jewish liturgy offers a whole miscellany of benedictions to be recited on various occasions, for instance, on seeing a startling sight, such as a flash of lightning, a falling star, a lofty mountain, a great ocean, a fruit tree in blossom, a beautiful animal, a giant or a dwarf; likewise when tasting any fruit for the first time in the year, or entering a new home, or putting on a new garment, the benediction in these latter cases being: 'Blessed are You, O Lord our God, King of the universe, who have kept us alive, sustained us and enabled us to reach this season.'

There are also prayers for the end of the day, before going to bed, when the observant Jew will once more recite the *Shema*, and conclude appropriately with the last verse of the *Adon Olam*, based on Psalm 31:6 (Christian Bibles, verse 5), 'Into His hand I entrust my spirit: both when I sleep and when I wake; and with my spirit, my body also: the Lord is with me, I will not fear.'

THE SABBATH

'There was evening and there was morning,' is the recurring phrase in the Creation story. Accordingly, the Jewish day runs from dusk to dusk, Sunday being the first day, Monday the second and so forth. With the seventh day the Jewish week reaches its high point, the sabbath; and because one may 'add from the profane to the holy' but not vice versa, it is reckoned to last from a little before dusk on Friday until a little after dusk on Saturday.

Basically, the sabbath is a day of rest from work. It expresses the idea that, however noble work may be, man also needs leisure to fulfil himself. From the first, that principle was applied to all classes of society, including the most oppressed, namely slaves, and extended even to domestic animals: 'Six days you shall do your work, but on the seventh day you shall rest; that your ox and your ass may have rest, and the son of your bondmaid, and the alien, may be refreshed' (Exodus 23:12). The same compassionate motive is present in the Deuteronomic version of the fourth Commandment, and reinforced by the invocation of Israel's own historic experience of slavery in Egypt. On the seventh day, it says,

You shall not do any work, you, or your son, or your daughter, or your manservant or your maidservant, or your ox, or your ass, or any of your cattle, or the sojourner who is within your gates, that your manservant and your maidservant may rest as well as you. You shall remember that you were a servant in the land of Egypt, and the Lord your God brought you out thence with a mighty hand and an outstretched arm; therefore the Lord your God commanded you to keep the sabbath day.

(5:14 f.)

On this level the sabbath is a great liberating, humanizing and equalizing social institution which belongs to the ethical side of Judaism and represents one of its enduring contributions to civilization. But at an early stage there entered into the understanding of the sabbath a second, mystical element which the Exodus version of the fourth Commandment expresses in allusion to the Creation story (Genesis 2:1–3) by declaring the sabbath to be a divine as well as a human rest day: 'For in six days the Lord made heaven and earth, the sea, and all that is in them, and rested on the seventh day; therefore the Lord blessed the sabbath day and hallowed it' (Exodus 20:11).

So understood, the sabbath becomes, more than a social institution, a contemplation of nature and its divine Creator, a listening to the heartbeat of the cosmos, a devotional exercise and a spiritual experience. Both elements, the social and the mystical, have shaped the Jewish sabbath; they are respectively referred to in its liturgy as *zecher litzi'at mitzrayim*, a 'reminder of the Exodus from Egypt', and *zikkaron le-ma'aseh ve-reshit*, a 'commemoration of the creation of the world'.

Both, moreover, made it imperative to define with the greatest precision what constitutes work. From the biblical account of the construction of the Tabernacle, and from its interruption by a solemn warning that on the sabbath all work must cease (Exodus 31:12–17), the Rabbis deduced thirty-nine basic categories of work (Shabbat 7:2), and from these, in turn, innumerable sub-categories. Their purpose was not to make life difficult, but to hallow it, and to protect the holiness of the sabbath from any likely or unlikely encroachment, by acting on the counsel of the 'men of the Great Assembly', to 'make a fence round the Torah' (Avot 1:1). They particularly emphasized that if the sabbath laws (or any other laws except the three cardinal prohibitions against idolatry, incest and murder) should ever conflict with the saving of life (*pikkuach nefesh*), then that takes priority and the laws in question not only may but *must* be violated, for 'the sabbath has been committed to you, not you to the sabbath' (Mechilta Va-Yak'hel to Exodus 32:14).

In recent times, strict, traditional sabbath observance has been facilitated by the five-day week as well as the availability of electronic gadgets (such as automatic time-switches) to replace human action. On the other hand, the social conditions and economic pressures of modern life – with its mobility and mech-anization and, above all, the fact that it is regulated by the clock rather than the sun – have made such observance more difficult than it was for our ancestors. Orthodox Judaism is undeterred by these difficulties and demands that they be resisted. Progressive Judaism makes what it deems necessary or reasonable concessions to them. Among many Jews, whether synagogue-affiliated or not, the sabbath is nowadays largely neglected. Whatever the causes of this neglect, it cannot be viewed with equanimity, for there is in Jewish tradition a deep-rooted intuition that the very survival of Judaism is bound up with the sabbath. 'The people of Israel shall keep the sabbath, observing the sabbath throughout their gener-ations, as a perpetual covenant. It is a sign for ever between Me and the people of Israel' (Exodus 31:16 f.). 'More than Israel has kept the sabbath,' said Achad Ha-Am, 'the sabbath has kept Israel.'

So far we have spoken of the sabbath as a day of rest. But it is more than that. The space created by the rest is to be put to good use. There is to be, not only contemplative passivity, but devotional activity. That, according to the traditional interpretation, is the import of the word 'remember' in the Exodus version of the fourth Commandment, as distinct from the word 'observe' in the Deuteronomy version. Similarly, the words of the prophet, 'If you . . . call the sabbath a delight . . . and honour it' (Isaiah 58:13), were taken to mean that one should positively strive to make the sabbath a day of joy and dignity, when, for instance, the home should be made to look festive, the best clothes worn, the best crockery used, the best food eaten.

The sabbath is ushered in at home by the lighting of candles, usually two in number. This was a daring innovation of the Pharisees, inspired by the concept of the sabbath as a joyful day, against the opposition of the Sadducees, who supposed that the biblical prohibition against kindling fires on the sabbath (Exodus 35:3) made it necessary to spend Friday night in darkness. The mother, whose privilege it is to perform this ceremony, even recites a benediction declaring that God has 'commanded' us to kindle the sabbath lights.

The sabbath eve service, attended in synagogue if possible, begins with a special liturgy called *kabbalat shabbat* ('welcoming the sabbath') which includes a sequence of psalms celebrating God's rule over nature as well as a lovely hymn by the sixteenth-century Safed mystic Solomon Alkabetz with the refrain: 'Come, my friend (*lechah dodi*), to greet the bride; let us welcome the sabbath day.' In all the sabbath services, the intermediate benediction of the *tefillah* is about the sabbath, beginning: 'Our God and God of our fathers, may our rest on this day be pleasing in Your sight . . .' The service ends with the *yigdal* ('magnified'), a fourteenth-century hymn based on Maimonides' 'Thirteen Principles of the Faith'.

Back at home, the father by tradition asks God's blessing on the children, praying that the boys may become 'like Ephraim and Manasseh', the girls 'like Sarah, Rebekah, Rachel and Leah', and reciting the Priestly Benediction (Numbers 6:24 ff.). He may also recite, in honour of his wife, the praise of the 'woman of worth' from the thirty-first chapter of the book of Proverbs. Then he makes *kiddush*: over a cup of wine, symbolic of the joy of the sabbath, he praises God who 'creates the fruit of the vine' and chants a longer benediction in thanksgiving for the holiness of the sabbath. Then all drink a little wine and, before sitting down to the first of the three festive meals traditionally taken during the sabbath, recite the standard benediction over bread (see above, p. 336). The sabbath bread, however, is of a special, twisted kind called *challah* ('dough'), and there are two loaves of it, covered by an embroidered cloth. The meal may be interspersed with the singing of table hymns called *zemirot* and concludes with the sabbath version of the grace after meals (see p. 336).

The sabbath morning service is more elaborate than the weekday one, and its highlight is the reading of the Torah. For this purpose the Pentateuch is divided into a sufficient number of portions so that on every sabbath of the year one such portion (*sidrah* or *parashah*) may be read; occasionally, two are combined. That is according to the now universal one-year cycle which originated in Babylonia and, in the course of the Middle Ages, displaced the triennial cycle of Palestinian Jewry. The portion is further subdivided, so that seven members of the congregation may be called up to read one section each, or at least (as is more usual nowadays) to recite the benedictions before and after it while the cantor or another qualified person chants the portion. An eighth person is called up to read the *haftarah* ('dismissal'), a passage from the Prophets that in some way complements the Torah portion. Whereas the Torah portion is cantillated from the scroll, the *haftarah* is cantillated from a folio book containing both the Pentateuch and the Prophetic portions; this is commonly referred to as a *chummash* ('fifth'), because in former times it was usual to have separate volumes for each of the books of the Pentateuch.

In Progressive synagogues the whole procedure is much abridged. Generally, only a selected part of the Torah portion is read (rather than cantillated) and translated, fewer congregants are called up, and a degree of latitude is exercised in the choice of the *haftarah*, which is usually but not always the traditionally appointed one.

Back at home after the service, *kiddush* is again recited. Following the midday meal, the afternoon is a time for resting or walking, and also for religious study. During the summer months, for instance, it is customary, every sabbath afternoon, to study a chapter from the 'Ethics of the Fathers'. The afternoon service again includes a Torah reading, but a shorter one, taken from the beginning of the next week's portion. The evening service follows the weekday liturgy, with an insertion alluding to the conclusion of the sabbath. After the 'third meal' (*se'udah shelishit*), which in Chasidic circles is often an extended festivity, so that the duration of the sabbath may be prolonged, the day ends with a colourful ritual called *havdalah* ('distinction'). This involves three symbols – a cup of wine, a box of spices and a twisted candle – and a prayer praising God for 'making a distinction between holy and profane'. The ceremony expresses nostalgic regret that the sabbath is ending as well as wistful longing that the new week may bring the time of redemption nearer.

The nostalgia is a measure of the feeling of spiritual elation which the observant Jew experiences on the sabbath: the sense of being transported from the flawed world of everyday struggle into a realm of transcendental perfection. Jewish literature tries to convey something of this mysterious power and beauty of the sabbath by describing it as the choicest of days, a royal bride, a garland of glory, a crown of salvation, a divine gift, conferring peace and tranquillity, quietness and safety, light and rejoicing, endowing those who faithfully observe it with an 'extra soul' (*neshamah yeterah*; according to one interpretation of the *havdalah* spices, their fragrance is a fond farewell-gift offered to this extra soul as it takes its leave) and giving them a 'foretaste of the world to come'.

CHAPTER FOUR   FROM YEAR TO YEAR

'From new moon to new moon, and from sabbath to sabbath, all flesh shall come to worship before Me, says the Lord' (Isaiah 66:23). That verse is one of several indications in the Bible that in those days the new moon was a popular festival. Later it declined in importance, but under the name of *Rosh Chodesh* ('head of the month') it still plays a significant role in traditional Jewish religious life. On the day itself an appropriate insertion is made in the *tefillah*, a short *hallel* (see below, p. 350) is recited, the Torah is read, and there is an additional service (*musaf*); on the preceding sabbath its coming is announced, and a prayer offered that the new month may bring the house of Israel 'life and peace, joy and happiness, salvation and consolation'.

THE JEWISH CALENDAR

The Jewish calendar is a lunar one, so that a normal year consists of twelve months, each running from new moon to new moon. Of these months, some always have twenty-nine days, some thirty, some may have twenty-nine or thirty, the number being varied from year to year according to certain fixed formulas. However, in order that the Jewish year may keep in step with the solar year – which is essential if the seasonal festivals are always to fall in their seasons – the yearly shortfall of about eleven days is made good by the intercalation of an extra month in the third, sixth, eighth, eleventh, seventeenth and nineteenth year of every nineteen-year cycle.

The present system was permanently established under Hillel II, Patriarch of Palestinian Jewry, about 360 CE. Prior to that, the beginning of each month was determined by the Sanhedrin in

Jerusalem on the evidence of witnesses reporting that they had sighted the new moon. Since it was therefore impossible to know in advance whether the current month would have twenty-nine or thirty days, a problem arose concerning the observance of the festival of Rosh Hashanah ('head of the year') which, alone among the festivals, falls on the first day of the month. Hence it was decided always to observe it for *two* days, beginning after the twenty-ninth day of the preceding month. (Similarly, *Rosh Chodesh* is traditionally observed for two days when it follows a thirty-day month.) In the communities of the Diaspora, however, the same calendrical uncertainty could persist into the middle of the month, since they depended on notification by messenger from Jerusalem. Accordingly, they added an extra day to *all* the major festivals, with the exception of the Day of Atonement, because it was not thought reasonable to extend the strict fast which it required.

The observance of these extra days has continued ever since, except in the land of Israel, where it has always applied to Rosh Hashanah only and, in modern times, in Progressive Judaism, which has generally reverted to the biblically prescribed duration for *all* the festivals.

The reckoning of the years takes as its starting point the creation of the world, which medieval Jewish scholars, on the basis of biblical data, calculated to have occurred in the year 3760 BCE. While such a dating is hardly in accord with modern cosmology, it is nevertheless a strikingly universalistic feature of Judaism that its calendar should base itself on an event of *cosmic* rather than only Jewish significance.

Let us now travel through the year, pausing at those dates which Jewish tradition has invested with special significance. The question is, where shall we begin our journey?

Two divergent traditions are discernible in the Bible: a nomadic-pastoral one, which says of the spring month, 'This month shall be for you the beginning of months' (Exodus 12:2), and a settled-agricultural one, which refers to the autumn harvest as 'the end of the year' (Exodus 23:16). Ultimately, the latter became the more influential; hence the autumn new year festival of Rosh Hashanah. But the former still underlies the sacred calendar as stated in the twenty-third chapter of Leviticus; and on that basis the Mishnah, which mentions no less than *four* new-year days for different purposes, declares that for the purpose of the sequence of festivals, the first day of the spring month is to be considered the beginning of the year (Rosh Hashanah 1:1).

PESACH

That month is called Nisan. Like all the months, it is known by its Babylonian name, although in this case the Bible also preserves an older, Hebrew name, Aviv, which means 'spring' (Exodus 13:4). The month of Nisan is dominated by the first of the 'three pilgrimage festivals' (*shalosh regalim*) during which, in ancient times, male Israelites were expected to bring offerings to the Temple in Jerusalem (Exodus 23:14; Deuteronomy 16:16 f.). It is the festival of *Pesach* ('Passover'), also referred to as *Chag ha-Matzot* ('feast of unleavened bread').

These two names reflect the pastoral-agricultural duality we have already noted. The name *Pesach* comes from a verb meaning 'to limp' or 'to skip' which might have been used to describe the first unsteady steps of a new-born lamb; it seems that the noun originally denoted such a lamb (the paschal lamb), which then gave its name to the pastoral festival of the lambing season. The feast of unleavened bread, on the other hand, was an agricultural festival, celebrating the first grain harvest, which likewise began in the spring.

With the establishment of a unified national life in the land of Israel, comprising farmers and shepherds alike, the two festivals, occurring at the same season, coalesced; but what really welded them together was the new significance, transcending them both, that was infused into the combined festival when it became the great annual commemoration of the Exodus from Egypt, which had also taken place in spring time (Exodus 13:4).

To achieve this, the name *Pesach* was reinterpreted to allude to the last of the Ten Plagues, when God destroyed the firstborn of the Egyptians but 'spared' (another possible meaning of the word) or 'passed over' (hence 'Passover') the houses of the Israelites (Exodus 12:13), and the unleavened bread was reinterpreted to recall the haste of their flight from Egypt, which did not permit them to leaven their dough (Exodus 12:39).

Such reinterpretations mark a general tendency on the part of ancient Judaism to play down (without suppressing) the celebration of nature, with its pagan associations, in favour of the commemoration of historical events, manifesting God's guidance, which would fortify the people's sense of distinctiveness and responsibility.

Among these historical events, the Exodus from Egypt occupied a unique position, for it was seen as the supreme demonstration of God's love for His people, fulfilling His promises to their ancestors and setting the scene for the consummation of His Covenant with them at Sinai. It marked, in effect, the beginning of their history as a self-conscious people with a sense of common purpose and destiny. Furthermore, because the event was a liberation from slavery, the celebration of it became a celebration of freedom; and because it was the chief paradigm of God's redemptive intervention in human affairs, its commemoration – particularly in times of oppression, as under the Romans – engendered a fervent longing for the culmination of that redemptive process in the messianic age.

Biblically, it lasts seven days, from 15 to 21 Nisan. The first day, and again the last, is a *yom tov* or 'holy day' (literally, 'good day'), while the intermediate days are known as *chol ha-moed* ('the everyday part of the season'). However, among Orthodox Jews in the Diaspora, for the calendrical reason explained above, it is an eight-day festival, and the first two and the last two days are observed as 'holy days'.

A 'holy day' is a full festival, requiring both the holding of a 'sacred assembly' (*mikra kodesh*) for public worship, and abstention from work, the definition of work being the same as for the sabbath, except for certain leniencies derived from a qualifying clause in the biblical legislation concerning 'what every man must eat' (Exodus 12:16). The intermediate days are 'half-festivals' on which services are held (with features similar to the *Rosh Chodesh* services, see above, p. 345), when only essential work is permitted.

The observance of the festival has both negative and positive aspects. On the negative side, its chief feature, as traditionally practised, is the strictest abstention, on the basis of a repeated biblical prohibition (Exodus 12:15, 19, 20; 13:3, 7), from any leaven (*chametz*) or food containing an admixture of leaven. Related to this is an elaborate ritual, much enjoyed by children, whereby, prior to the festival, the house is thoroughly spring-cleaned, after which a few breadcrumbs are strategically placed in nooks and crannies and ceremonially searched out. Then, on the morning of the day before the festival, they are burned.

On the positive side, the most colourful feature of the festival is the celebratory meal which takes place in the home on the first eve and, among Orthodox Jews in the Diaspora, again on the second. This is called *Seder*, which is short for *Seder Haggadah*, 'order of narration', because its principal purpose is the re-counting of the Exodus story, as enjoined in the Bible: 'You shall tell your son on that day . . .' (Exodus 13:8).

In ancient times the meal consisted mainly of the paschal lamb, which was eaten, together with unleavened bread and bitter herbs, by families or family groups (Numbers 9:11). After the cessation of sacrifices, the lamb was omitted, and represented instead by a symbolic bone; but the unleavened bread (*matzah*) and bitter herbs (*maror*) were retained and, together with other statutory dishes, were allegorically interpreted so as to illustrate the Exodus story.

The celebration proceeds according to a unique liturgical and educational text known as the *Haggadah*, of which there are many illuminated and illustrated editions. The kernel of this is a phrase-by-phrase midrashic commentary on the succinct account of the Exodus contained in the biblical passage beginning 'A wander-ing Aramean was my father . . .' (Deuteronomy 26:5–8). This is recited by the leader, along with other explanatory passages, in response to the 'four questions' which, by tradition, the youngest child asks, beginning: 'How does this night differ from all other nights?'

There is also a well ordered sequence of prayers, psalms and songs, as well as plenty of spontaneous conversation and discus-sion, before, during and after the meal. The whole ritual is conducted with a quaint blend of solemnity and jollity and is designed, through sight and sound and taste, to make the greatest impact on the participants, particularly children, so that in their imagination they may relive the liberation of their ancestors; for that is the purpose of the exercise. As the *Haggadah* puts it, 'In every generation the individual should regard himself as if he personally had come out of Egypt.'

Some aspects of the ceremonial are reminiscent of the ancient Greek symposium or Roman banquet. For instance, four cups of wine are drunk in the course of the evening 'in the manner of freemen'. These are said, among other explanations, to represent the four divine promises, 'I will bring you out . . . I will deliver you . . . I will redeem you . . . I will take you for My people' (Exodus 6:6 f.).

The celebration reaches its climax when the door is opened for the prophet Elijah, who is in Jewish folklore forerunner of the Messiah (Malachi 3:23; Christian Bibles, 4:5); he is invited to enter and announce the advent of the messianic age. A fifth cup of wine has been poured out in readiness for him, but it remains undrunk. In this twofold affirmation lies the essence of the Jewish understanding of the historic process: that the time of redemption will come, and that it has not come yet.

The synagogue services also have special features, such as poetic embellishments of the liturgy and appropriately chosen readings from the Scriptures. Specific to *Pesach* is the reading of the Song of Songs, which is interpreted in Jewish tradition as an allegory about the love between God and Israel. It also evokes the seasonal mood with its lovely lines,

> Arise, my love, my fair one,
>> and come away;
> For lo, the winter is past,
>> the rain is over and gone.
> The flowers appear on the earth,
>> the time of singing has come,
> and the voice of the turtledove is heard in our land.

(2:10 f.)

As on other joyful festivals, the *hallel* is recited in the morning service. (It is also included in the Seder.) The term *hallel*, meaning 'praise', denotes a group of psalms, comprising numbers 113–18, but shortened on the last six days of *Pesach* by the omission of most of Psalms 115 and 116. One reason found in the tradition for this shortening is that the recollection of the drowning of the Egyptians in the Red Sea should prompt us to restrain our jubilation, since we are enjoined: 'Do not rejoice when your enemy falls' (Proverbs 24:17; Pesikta de-Rav Kahana, ed. Mandelbaum, II, 458).

SHAVUOT

For all its emphasis on the historical, Exodus motif, Judaism did not entirely discard the agricultural aspect of the spring festival. As long as the Temple stood, every pilgrim was required to bring a sheaf (*omer*) of the newly harvested barley, which the priest was to offer 'on the morrow after the sabbath' (Leviticus 23:11); and from that day, which the Pharisees, against the opposition of the Sadducees, understood as the second day of the festival, every day was to be counted for the next seven weeks, culminating in the second of the three pilgrimage festivals, that of *Shavuot* ('weeks'), sometimes referred to by its Greek name 'Pentecost' which signifies that it is the feast of the fiftieth day (Leviticus 23:15–21).

After the destruction of the Temple, the ceremonial counting of the days was continued, as it is still, with an appropriate announcement in the evening service, and the whole period became known as the *sefirah* ('counting'), or *omer*, season. It also came to be observed as a time of austerity during most of which it was considered improper to celebrate marriages, to cut one's hair or to wear new clothes. This custom probably originated in anxiety over the as yet uncertain outcome of the harvest, which may account for similar practices in other cultures, including the Christian Lent. In Jewish tradition, various explanations of it have been proposed, chief among them a story in the Talmud to the effect that thousands of Rabbi Akiva's disciples died of a plague during this period (Yevamot 62b).

The period also recalls other tragedies of Jewish history, such as the Rhineland massacres during the Crusades and, most recently, the Holocaust. That is because 27 Nisan, which is the anniversary of the Warsaw Ghetto rising (see above pp. 175 ff.), has been declared by Israel's Parliament a day of memorial for the victims of the Nazi period. It is known as *Yom ha-Sho'ah* ('Day of the Holocaust').

Three days, however, are allowed to interrupt the sombreness of the *sefirah* season. One is the anniversary of the establishment

351

of the State of Israel, which falls on 5 Iyyar, the second month of the Jewish calendar, and has established itself as a minor festival under the name of *Yom ha-Atzma'ut* ('Independence Day'). Another is *Lag ba-Omer* ('33 Omer'), on which the restrictions of the season are suspended: for instance, weddings are allowed, and in Israel children light bonfires and shoot arrows. These celebrations, reminiscent of May Day and perhaps of similar origin, have been variously interpreted. It has been suggested, for example, that on this day the plague among Rabbi Akiva's students ceased, or that it recalls the day on which Rabbi Simeon ben Yochai, traditionally regarded as the founder of Jewish mysticism, died blissfully after revealing his secret doctrine to his followers. The third exception is 28 Iyyar, which has lately come to be observed as *Yom Yerushalayim* ('Jerusalem Day'), commemorating the reunification of the Holy City in the Six Day War of 1967.

The festival of *Shavuot* (Exodus 23:14–17, 34:22; Leviticus 28:26; Deuteronomy 16:9–12), which concludes the *sefirah* period, falls, according to the Pharisaic calendar, on 6 Sivan, the third month of the Jewish calendar, and is observed for two days by Orthodox Jews outside the land of Israel. In biblical times it was purely an agricultural festival, marking the end of the barley harvest and the beginning of the wheat harvest. Only in post-biblical times was a historical interpretation superimposed on it, when, on the basis of the scriptural information that the Israelites entered the wilderness of Sinai *in the third month* after their departure from Egypt (Exodus 19:1), it came to be regarded as a commemoration of the Sinaitic theophany. Just as the liturgy refers to Pesach as *zeman cherutenu*, 'the season of our freedom', so it refers to *Shavuot* as *zeman mattan toratenu*, 'the season of the giving of our Torah'.

In rabbinic literature it is generally called *atzeret*, a word of uncertain meaning which may have signified 'concluding feast'. If so, it would emphasize the interrelationship of the two festivals, since *Shavuot* would mark in two senses the conclusion of a process begun at *Pesach*: agriculturally, the barley harvest; historically, the journey from Egypt to Sinai. It is a recurring theme of rabbinic theology that the Revelation of the Torah was the consummation of the liberation from slavery that preceded it. Thus, a rabbinic play on words has it that the freedom (*cherut*) attained by the Exodus finds its fulfilment in submission to the divine commandments engraved (*charut*) on the stone tablets (Avot 6:2).

The celebration of the festival includes the public reading of the Decalogue, in reminiscence and re-enactment of the Sinaitic Revelation. It also includes the reading of the book of Ruth, perhaps on account of the parallel between Ruth's individual acceptance of the Jewish faith and the Israelites' collective affirmation of the Torah at Sinai, perhaps because of the seasonal topicality of the harvest scene in the second chapter of the book. The nature aspect of the festival is further evoked by the practice of decorating the synagogue with flowers and greenery. An ancient custom, of obscure origin, is to eat dairy dishes during the festival. Another, which began among kabbalistic circles in the Middle Ages, is to spend the entire night of 6 Sivan in the study of a little volume called *Tikkun Leil Shavuot* ('Shavuot Night Ritual') which is a compilation of passages from the Pentateuch, Mishnah and *Zohar*. This custom has recently been revived and adapted in some communities in an effort to give a fresh impetus to the observance of a festival which has never enjoyed the same popularity as Judaism's other, more colourful seasonal festivals, and is nowadays much neglected.

FAST DAYS

Less surprising is the general neglect, except among the most pious, of the fast days of the Jewish calendar (other than *Yom Kippur*). These, four in number, are mentioned already in the Bible (Zechariah 8:19), having been instituted after the Babylonian exile to commemorate the various stages of the great débâcle which preceded that historical episode.

The one that concerns us at this point of our journey through the Jewish year is 17 Tammuz (the fourth month) which recalls the breaching of the walls of Jerusalem by the Babylonians and again, centuries later, by the Romans. It also inaugurates another period of austerity during which, as during the *sefirah* period, joyful celebrations such as weddings are traditionally disallowed.

That period, which becomes more sombre with the onset of the fifth month, Av, lasts for three weeks and culminates in *Tish'ah* be-Av ('9 Av'). The most mournful day of the year, it commemorates the destruction both of the first Temple in 586 BCE and of the second Temple in 70 CE. It has additionally become associated with other disasters which, by coincidence, occurred at the same time of the year, such as the expulsion of the Jews from Spain in 1492 and even the outbreak of the First World War.

Unlike the other three, which are only dawn-to-dusk fasts, 9 Av calls for abstention from food from sunset to sunset. The chief feature of its observance is the reading of the book of Lamentations, during which the worshippers traditionally sit on the floor or on low stools as a sign of mourning. Likewise, leather shoes are removed before entering the synagogue, and the *tallit* is not worn.

Having plumbed the depths of sorrow, the ever-changing mood of the Jewish year now turns to hope. The next sabbath, with its prophetical reading taken from the fortieth chapter of Isaiah – 'Comfort, comfort My people . . .', sounds a new note of consolation, which is sustained on the ensuing six sabbaths. These seven weeks also evoke a mounting expectancy as they lead up to the 'high season' of the Jewish calendar: that of the autumn festivals.

ROSH HASHANAH

In earliest times, it would seem, the festivities of this season amounted only to a prolonged celebration of the final ingathering of the year's harvest. But as the people's religious consciousness deepened, the ending of the agricultural year also inspired more solemn thoughts. Then it came to be felt that the religious year ought to begin with a period of individual and national introspection and rededication, and the autumnal observance divided into a penitential, then a celebratory phase. A critical analysis of the scriptural evidence suggests that this process culminated after the Babylonian exile.

The penitential season begins on the first day of the seventh month, Tishri, and lasts for ten days, known as *Aseret Yemey Teshuvah*, 'the ten days of repentance'. During this time, the daily liturgy is subtly modified to express the seasonal theme, and special supplications for divine forgiveness, called *selichot*, are recited every morning. The pious anticipate the season by reciting *selichot* throughout the preceding month of Elul. Many communities hold a midnight *selichot* service on the Saturday night immediately preceding 1 Tishri or, if the latter falls on or before the Tuesday of the week, a week earlier.

The first day of Tishri is referred to in the Bible as the 'day of trumpet blowing' (Numbers 29:1) or the 'memorial of trumpet blowing' (Leviticus 23:24). Evidently, the blowing of a *shofar*, which characterizes the festival to this day, is one of its oldest features. But it was only in post-exilic times that it came to be understood both as a call to repentance and as the annunciation of a new year, and it is only in post-biblical Jewish literature, beginning with the Mishnah, that the day is designated Rosh Hashanah.

In that literature, too, the significance of the penitential season is at once universalized and internalized. 1 Tishri is declared to be the anniversary of the day on which the world was created (Rosh Hashanah 11a) as well as the Day of Judgement, when all human beings are arraigned before the heavenly throne to have their fate decreed according to their past conduct, although the sentence is not sealed until 10 Tishri, so that the intervening days of grace may be used, through repentance, to secure a mitigated verdict (Rosh Hashanah 16a).

This mythology – the term is not meant disparagingly – found expression in the recurring phrase of the penitential liturgy, 'Remember us unto life, for You, O King, delight in life; inscribe us in the Book of Life, for Your sake, O God of life,' and in the greeting exchanged among Jews at this season, 'May you be inscribed and sealed for a good year.' It reinforced the spiritual impact of these days by making the individual feel as though involved in a cosmic drama, so that the most strenuous effort was required of him to recognize and confess his sins and to seek his Creator's pardon.

In the home, by a custom dating from the Middle Ages, apples and honey are eaten in token of the hope that the new year may be 'good and sweet'. In the synagogue there is an atmosphere of uncommon solemnity. For one thing, the synagogue itself is crowded, for none but the housebound and the indifferent fail at this time to heed Hillel's exhortation, 'Do not separate yourself

355

from the community' (Avot 2:4). But more than that, it is the *message* of Rosh Hashanah, and its powerful expression in the words and melodies of the liturgy, that create the mood.

The highlight of the liturgy is the blowing of the *shofar*, according to a well-defined series of notes, interspersed with scriptural verses celebrating God's kingship, His remembrance of the Covenant, and His guidance of the historic process from the Revelation at Mount Sinai to the future day when the 'great *shofar*' (Isaiah 27:13) of universal redemption will resound.

The *shofar* requires little explanation. Given the significance of the season, the plaintive, pleading and challenging sound of its notes speaks for itself. Nevertheless, more specific meanings have also been found in it; among them, an allusion to the 'ram caught in a thicket by his horns' (Genesis 22:13) in the story of the binding of Isaac which supplies the most dramatic scripture lesson of the festival.

As explained at the beginning of this chapter, Rosh Hashanah is traditionally observed for two days, not only in the Diaspora, but also in the land of Israel. In synagogues following that tradition the story of the binding of Isaac is read on the second day.

A custom of late-medieval origin, still practised by the most observant among Orthodox Jews, is to go to the bank of a river, lake or sea on the afternoon of the first day of the festival (or, if that falls on a sabbath, the second) and there to recite such verses as Micah's, 'Thou wilt cast all their sins into the depths of the sea' (7:19). From the Hebrew for 'Thou wilt cast', the ceremony is called *tashlich*.

The second day of Rosh Hashanah is followed, on 3 Tishri, by one of Judaism's minor fast days, recalling the assassination of Gedaliah, governor of Judah (II Kings 25:22–26). The following sabbath derives its special significance from the penitential season in which it falls, and its name, *Shabbat Shuvah*, from the *haftarah* which is by tradition read on that day, from the fourteenth chapter of Hosea, beginning 'Return (*shuvah*), O Israel, to the Lord your God.'

YOM KIPPUR

The tenth and culminating day of the penitential season is Yom Kippur, the Day of Atonement. It concludes the spiritual journey begun on Rosh Hashanah. Both days are known as 'high holy days' and 'days of awe' (*yamim nora'im*); but Yom Kippur is the *more* awesome. It is, quite simply, the holiest day of Judaism's sacred calendar, when the sense of the numinous becomes almost tangible.

On the eve of the day all synagogues are filled to capacity as on no other evening of the year. In many, the worshippers, or at least the officiants, wear a white robe called a *kittel* (Yiddish for smock). The ritual begins with a solemn declaration annulling all unfulfillable vows, which is sung to so haunting a melody that the whole service has come to be called, after the opening words of the declaration, *Kol Nidrei*, 'All vows'.

It is a long service. There is no need to hurry home, for the entire day has but a single purpose: the attainment of the supreme blessing of at-one-ment – reconciliation with God. Beside this, eating, drinking and all other mundane activities are irrelevancies which the spiritually sensitive would eschew even if it were not an ancient rule that the day is to be observed as a complete fast. The rule, derived from the Torah's injunction 'You shall afflict yourselves' (Leviticus 16:29; 23:27), is taken very seriously and set aside only for those whose health might be dangerously affected by its observance.

In the morning the day's worship is resumed and continues without pause until nightfall. Not all congregants remain throughout the day. Some go out for a breath of fresh air, or absent themselves during the afternoon. But in the morning, and again in the evening, there are few empty seats.

A recurring feature of the liturgy is a long confession listing all the sins an individual may have committed during the past year. But the worshipper knows that it is not enough to acknowledge them, however sincerely, before God, and to resolve not to repeat them. There is a precondition: that beforehand forgiveness be sought, and restitution made, as far as possible, at the human level. Few Jews are not familiar with the teaching of the Mishnah: 'For transgressions between man and God, the Day of Atonement atones; but for transgressions between a man and his fellow man, the Day of Atonement does not atone unless he has first reconciled his fellow man' (Yoma 8:9).

This ethical motif, which runs through the entire liturgy, becomes especially emphatic in the *haftarah* of the morning service (Isaiah 57:14–58:14) in which the prophet of the Exile declares that mere fasting counts for nothing compared with right conduct:

> Is such the fast that I choose?
>   a day for a man to humble himself? . . .
> Is not *this* the fast that I choose:
>   to loose the bonds of wickedness,
>   to undo the thongs of the yoke,
> to let the oppressed go free,
>   and to break every yoke?
> Is it not to share your bread with the hungry,
>   and bring the homeless poor into your house;
> when you see the naked, to cover him,
>   and not to hide yourself from your own flesh?
>
> (Isaiah 58:5–7)

The *haftarah* of the afternoon service is the whole book of Jonah, which has a dual relevance. On the one hand it proclaims God's longing for repentance, not only on the part of Jews but, since He is the universal God, of *all* human beings, represented in this prophetic short story by the Ninevites. On the other hand, it delivers a wholesome reminder that *change of conduct*, rather than mere remorse, is the hallmark of repentance. For, as the Mishnah points out (Ta'anit 2:1), it does not say that 'God saw their sackcloth and their fasting' but that He 'saw what they did, how they had turned from their evil way' (Jonah 3:10).

The day's worship concludes when the ark is opened for the last time and the standing congregation proclaims, 'The Lord, He is God' (I Kings 18:39). Then the ark is closed and the worshippers, physically exhausted but spiritually elated, go home to break their fast.

SUKKOT

Within five days the mood changes dramatically from repentance to rejoicing, for with the full moon the second, celebratory phase of the autumn festival season begins, described in the liturgy as *zeman simchatenu*, the 'season of our gladness'. It is the third of the three pilgrimage festivals, generally known as the feast of Sukkot, that is, of 'tabernacles' or 'booths' (Leviticus 23:34; Deuteronomy 16:13), but also referred to in the Bible as the feast of ingathering (Exodus 23:16), the feast of the Lord (Leviticus 23:39) and, simply, the feast (Ezekiel 45:23; II Chronicles 7:8). It is a seven-day festival, immediately followed by the so-called *Shemini Atzeret*, which means 'eighth day of assembly' or, possibly, 'eighth day of conclusion'. Of these eight days, only the first and the last, i.e., 15 and 22 Tishri, are biblical 'holy days', but to each of them another was added by the Diaspora communities in post-biblical times.

Sukkot, more than *Pesach* and *Shavuot*, has noticeably retained its original character as a harvest festival. During this holiday, the Jew turns from penitential introspection to the natural world around him, and gives thanks for it. He even brings nature into his home and into his synagogue, in two ways. First, by the custom of 'dwelling in booths' (Leviticus 23:42) from which the festival derives its name, a *sukkah* being a makeshift hut with a roof made of foliage. Observant Jewish families will build their own *sukkah* and, weather permitting, take their meals or even sleep in it during the festival, while others will at least visit the communal *sukkah* – lavishly decorated with fruit and flowers that exude a sweet fragrance – after the synagogue services. Secondly, by ritual use of the 'four species' alluded to in the Torah (Leviticus 23:40), which comprise a palm branch, called a *lulav*, tied together with two willow and three myrtle twigs, and a citron, called an *etrog*. These are ceremonially held, and waved in all directions, as well as being carried in procession (*hakkafah*) during the *hallel*.

Nevertheless, the characteristic Jewish emphasis on morality and history has influenced the understanding even of this nature festival. Already in the Bible the point is made that gratitude for the harvest should express itself in the generous sharing of God's gifts: 'You shall rejoice in your feast, you and your son and your daughter, your manservant and your maidservant, the Levite, the sojourner, the fatherless, and the widow . . .' (Deuteronomy 16:14). The four species are said, in one rabbinic interpretation, to represent four parts of the body (spine, eye, mouth and heart), all of which must be dedicated to the service of God, and in another, four types of Jew, the ideal being the one who, like the *etrog* which both gives forth fragrance and bears fruit, combines religious knowledge with good deeds. Above all, the *sukkah* itself is already linked in the Pentateuch with the historical episode of the journey through the wilderness: 'You shall dwell in booths for seven days; . . . that your generations may know that I made the people of Israel dwell in booths when I brought them out of the land of Egypt' (Leviticus 23:42 f.).

This passage raises the obvious difficulty that the materials for making booths would not have been readily available in the Sinai desert. Accordingly, historians have conjectured that the real origin of the *sukkah* might be found in temporary shelters which Israelite farmers of a later period erected in the field at harvest time. Within Jewish tradition itself the view is well represented that the 'booths of the wilderness' are not to be understood literally, but as an allusion to the 'clouds of glory' which accompanied the Israelites on their journey, and hence, to God's protection.

Thus to 'dwell in booths' is indeed to relive the wilderness experience; but the purpose of doing so at this particular season is so that, instead of succumbing to a proud sense of security and self-satisfaction at harvest-time, we should humbly remember our ultimate dependence on nature and its divine Creator. That is the essential meaning and message of the festival. It is reinforced by the traditional custom of reading on the sabbath in *Sukkot* the book of Kohelet (Ecclesiastes).

The seventh day of *Sukkot* has a special name, *Hoshana Rabbah*, the 'great hosanna'. This alludes to a custom which harks back to remote antiquity, when a major concern of the autumn festival was the hope for abundant rain to ensure the next year's harvest. The custom, as it has survived in Orthodox Judaism, is to make a seven-circuit procession with the Torah scrolls as well as the *lulav* and *etrog*, then to recite penitential litanies with the refrain *hosha-na* ('save now') while holding bunches of willow twigs; these are subsequently struck against the floor or chairs.

On this day the penitential mood of the high holy days resurfaces; it is even customary for the *sheliach tzibbur* again to wear a white *kittel*. The same applies to the eighth day, *Shemini Atzeret*, suggesting that only now is the period of repentance, begun at Rosh Hashanah, fully concluded, and reinforcing the connection between the two phases of the autumnal festive season.

The second day of *Shemini Atzeret*, observed by Orthodox Jews in the Diaspora, has since the Middle Ages acquired a distinctive character of its own under the name of *Simchat Torah*, 'rejoicing in the Law'. For on this day the annual cycle of Torah readings is completed and immediately recommenced, and the Torah scrolls are carried round the synagogue in numerous *hakkafot*, with much joyful singing and even dancing, children in particular being encouraged to join in. The reader of the last portion of Deuteronomy is called *chatan torah*, the 'bridegroom of the law', and the reader of the first portion of the first book of the Torah, *chatan bereshit*, the 'bridegroom of Genesis', and these two show their appreciation of their privilege by inviting the congregation to a celebratory *kiddush* after the service.

The spirit of these festivities – which Progressive Jews, and Orthodox Jews in Israel, perform on *Shemini Atzeret* itself – is summed up in the words of the *Simchat Torah* liturgy: 'Happy are you, O Israel' (this is said three times), 'whom God has chosen to make the Torah your heritage.'

MINOR FESTIVALS

After this long season of autumn festivals, the *sukkah* is dismantled and life finally resumes its normal rhythm. Not until the advent of winter is there another festival, the 'minor' one (in the sense that it involves no abstention from work) of *Chanukkah* ('dedication'), which begins on 25 Kislev and lasts eight days. It commemorates the re-dedication of the Temple following the victory of the Maccabees (see above, pp. 65 f). The values which the festival highlights are loyalty and courage under oppression, the importance of religious freedom, and the power of right to conquer might. Aptly, the key verse of the *haftarah* traditionally read on the sabbath of the festival is: 'Not by might, nor by power, but by My spirit, saith the Lord' (Zechariah 4:6).

From the apocryphal II Maccabees one surmises that the first *Chanukkah* was a delayed celebration of *Sukkot*, and that is why it was observed for eight days (10:6); but a more popular explanation of the festival's duration is a legend, first found in the Talmud (Shabbat 21b), which says that a single cruse of undefiled oil, found by the victorious Maccabees on entering the Temple, miraculously lasted for eight days.

The principal feature of the observance of the festival is the progressive kindling of the eight lights of an eight-branched candelabrum (*menorah* or *chanukkiyyah*): one on the first night, two on the second and so forth. This is done not only in the synagogue but in every home, and the candelabrum is placed near a front door or window in order, in the rabbinic phrase, to 'publicize the miracle'.

A week after the conclusion of *Chanukkah* we come to the last of the four minor fasts mentioned above (p. 353); it falls on 10 Tevet and commemorates the beginning of the siege of Jerusalem by the Babylonians in 586 BCE.

A minor feast occurs some five weeks later, and is known by its calendrical date as *Chamishah-Asar bi-Shevat* or *Tu bi-Shevat*, '15 Shevat'. It is first mentioned in the Mishnah (Rosh Hashanah 1:1), where it is designated the 'new year of the trees', and is nowadays celebrated in Israel by the ceremonial planting of sapling trees, especially by school-children, and in the Diaspora by eating fruit grown in the land of Israel.

The annual cycle of special days and seasons ends on a light-hearted note with the minor feast of *Purim* ('lots'), which commemorates the events recounted in the biblical book of Esther, and derives its name from the lots cast by its villain, Haman, to determine the most propitious day for the extermination of Persia's Jews (3:7; 9:24). The plot is foiled by the timely intervention of the eponymous heroine, prompted by her cousin Mordecai, who thereupon enjoins his fellow Jews:

that they should keep the fourteenth day of the month Adar and also the fifteenth day of the same, year by year, as the days on which the Jews got relief from their enemies, and as the month that had been turned for them from sorrow into gladness and from mourning into a holiday; that they should make them days of feasting and gladness, days for sending portions to one another and gifts to the poor.

(Esther 9:21 f.)

By tradition, *Purim* is preceded by a day of fasting and celebrated on the fourteenth day of the twelfth month (Adar), except that in Jerusalem and certain other ancient walled cities it is celebrated on the fifteenth day, which is called *Shushan Purim*, in allusion to the ancient Persian capital of Susa (see 9:18 f.). However, in a leap year (see p. 345) the celebrations are held on the corresponding days of the thirteenth month, *Adar Sheni*.

The chief observance of the festival is the reading of the book of Esther from a parchment scroll which is commonly referred to simply as 'the *megillah*' ('scroll'). This is done with a measure of levity, in keeping with the tongue-in-cheek humour of the book, with stampings of feet and twirlings of a rattle at every mention of Haman's name. Other customs include children's fancy-dress parties, performances of specially written humorous plays (*Purimspiel* in the singular), and the festive meals featuring three-cornered, poppy-seed filled cakes called *hamantaschen*, or 'Haman's Ears', and intoxicating drinks, which are permitted beyond normal limits. Among the pious, the ancient practice of 'sending portions one to another, and gifts to the poor' is also maintained.

Modern scholarship is inclined to regard the book of Esther as a fictional short story, perhaps with a kernel of historical truth, composed in Hasmonean times to bolster Jewish patriotism and possibly to replace both a pagan spring carnival and Nicanor Day, which commemorated a victory in the Maccabean War. Jews tend to regard such speculations as having little bearing on the validity of the festival, since the Esther story is undoubtedly true in the typological sense that its pattern of events has occurred and recurred many times in the course of Jewish history.

That heritage of persecution weighs heavily on the folk-memory of the Jew. The feast of *Purim*, by its very jollity, helps to lighten the burden for him. It also provides relief from the religious solemnity which, in varying degrees, characterizes the rest of the year. On a deeper level it offers reassurance that, in spite of all contrary evidence, oppressors will not have the last word, and so points toward the festival of redemption (Passover), with which, only four weeks later, the cycle of the Jewish sacred calendar will begin again.

THE MONTHS OF THE JEWISH YEAR
with the Festivals and Fast Days occurring in them

1 NISAN	30 days	15	PESACH day 1
		16	PESACH day 2
		17 *to* 20	Chol ha-Mo'ed
		21	PESACH day 7
		22	PESACH day 8
		27	Yom ha-Sho'ah
2 IYYAR	29 days	5	Yom ha-Atzma'ut
		18	Lag ba-Omer
		28	Yom Yerushalayim
3 SIVAN	30 days	6	SHAVUOT day 1
		7	SHAVUOT day 2
4 TAMMUZ	29 days	17	Fast of Tammuz
5 AV	30 days	9	Tish'ah be'Av
6 ELUL	29 days		
7 TISHRI	30 days	1	ROSH HASHANAH day 1
		2	ROSH HASHANAH day 2
		3	Fast of Gedaliah
		10	YOM KIPPUR
		15	SUKKOT day 1
		16	SUKKOT day 2
		17 *to* 21	Chol ha-Mo'ed
		21	Hoshana Rabbah
		22	SHEMINI ATZERET
		23	SIMCHAT TORAH
8 CHESHVAN	29/30 days		
9 KISLEV	29/30 days	25 *to* 29/30	Chanukkah days 1 to 5/6
10 TEVET	29 days	1 *to* 3/2	Chanukkah days 6/7 *to* 8
		10	Fast of Tevet
11 SHEVAT	30 days	15	Tu bi-Shevat
12 ADAR	29 days	14	Purim
ADAR RISHON	*30 days*		
13 *ADAR SHENI*	*29 days*	*14*	*Purim*

The second and eighth days of Pesach, the second day of Shavuot and the second and ninth days of Sukkot are not observed as Holy Days in Israel, where Simchat Torah is observed on Shemini Atzeret. The same applies to Progressive Jews, who do not generally observe the second day of Rosh Hashanah either.

There are thirteen months in the third, sixth, eighth, eleventh, seventeenth and nineteenth years of every nineteen-year cycle; then the twelfth month is called Adar Rishon (First Adar) and has thirty days. See page 345.

Cheshvan is also called Marcheshvan.

CHAPTER FIVE   FROM BIRTH TO DEATH

The flow of time, seen in the succession of days and seasons, assumes even greater significance for human life in the journey of the individual from the cradle to the grave. Like other religions, Judaism celebrates the various phases of that journey with 'rites of passage' that harness for spiritual ends the emotions they arouse.

BIRTH

The birth of a child represents for its parents and the community the hope of continuity, and is thus a cause for rejoicing. Among Jews it promises, more particularly, the survival of the 'Covenant people' which, having so often hung in the balance, is held all the more precious.

Chief among the symbols of continuity is the rite of circumcision. Common to many societies, both ancient and modern, though of uncertain origin, in Judaism it has always been associated with the Covenant and is indeed termed *b'rit milah*, the 'Covenant of circumcision'. According to the biblical tradition it was instituted by Abraham (Genesis 17) but subsequently neglected and revived (Joshua 5:2–8). There is evidence that it received increased emphasis when Jews lived among uncircumcised peoples, as in Canaan and Babylonia, and especially in times of persecution, when the practice was proscribed or ridiculed by their enemies, as happened more than once in the Graeco-Roman period.

Circumcision does not actually confer Jewish status, since that is, except in the case of converts, a matter of birth; but it is nevertheless traditionally regarded as an initiation into the Covenant, and hence as having a quasi-sacramental significance.

366

Although in modern times some individual Jews have expressed reservations about the great emphasis traditionally given to circumcision, the practice itself is maintained as a matter of course among virtually all Jews. The commonly held belief that it has hygienic value has also helped to perpetuate it.

Unless there is a medical reason for postponing it, it is done on the eighth day of the boy's life, even if that should be a sabbath or a festival. In the Middle Ages it usually took place in the synagogue; nowadays it is carried out in the home or in the hospital. The operation is performed by a trained circumciser, the *mohel*, who recites an appropriate benediction, as does the father. A third person, called *sandek* from the Greek for 'godfather', has the honour of holding the baby during the operation. Prior to that, it is momentarily placed on a special chair known as the 'chair of Elijah', Elijah being the 'messenger of the Covenant' (Malachi 3:1; cf. I Kings 19:10). Afterwards a prayer is recited in which a Jewish name is conferred on the child, and the hope expressed that 'as he has entered into the Covenant, so may he enter into (the knowledge of) the Torah, the wedding canopy, and (the doing of) good deeds'. Then a cup of wine is drunk, and a family celebration follows.

Naming

While a boy is thus named at his circumcision, the naming of a girl takes place at the synagogue on the first (or, according to a variant tradition, the fourth) sabbath after her birth, when the father is 'called up' to the reading of the Torah. Another custom, known since the Middle Ages, is to have the naming at a special thanksgiving ceremony, four or more weeks after the birth, when both parents bring the child, boy or girl, to the synagogue.

The practice of giving a Jewish child a Jewish (generally Hebrew) name, over and above the 'secular' one, is still generally observed, but in regard to the choice of the name custom varies. Ashkenazi Jews commonly name the child after a deceased relative, Sephardi Jews after a living one. Alternatively, a Hebrew name may be chosen which corresponds to the secular one in meaning or sound; or the secular name may merely be transliterated from the vernacular into Hebrew characters.

Redemption of the Firstborn

In many cultures special status is accorded to the firstborn. There are several traces of this in the Hebrew Bible, for instance in the Esau–Jacob story (Genesis 25, 27) and the law of inheritance (Deuteronomy 21:17). In particular, there was a widespread belief that the firstborn 'belonged' to the deity. In pagan religions this gave rise to the practice of child-sacrifice (cf. Micah 6:7). In Judaism it yielded the notion, reinforced by the story of the deliverance of Israel's firstborn in Egypt, that they should be consecrated to the service of God (Exodus 13:1–16; 22:28; Christian Bibles, 22:29). At one time, perhaps, they actually served in the sanctuary. Ultimately, that privilege was restricted to the Aaronides (Kohanim) and Levites, and it then became established practice to 'redeem' the firstborn by the payment of a ransom (Numbers 3:12 ff.; 18:16).

Such a ceremony, known as *pidyon ha-ben* or 'redemption of the firstborn', has persisted to this day among Orthodox Jews. It is applicable only if the child is the mother's firstborn and male, and if the father is not a Kohen or a Levi (a presumed descendant of the ancient priests or Levites) nor the mother a daughter of such a father. The ceremony is performed when the child is thirty days old. Then, on his thirty-first day – or, if that is a sabbath or festival, the day after – the father presents him to a Kohen and proceeds to redeem him by the payment of the notional equivalent in silver coins of the five shekels stipulated in the Bible (Numbers 18:16). Thereupon the Kohen blesses the child with the Priestly Benediction (Numbers 6:24 ff.).

According to early Rabbinic sources, it is the duty of the father, not only to circumcise his son and, if he is the firstborn, to redeem him, but also to teach him Torah as well as a trade. Some add, to teach him to swim; others, also civic responsibility (Tosefta Kiddushin 1:11; Mechilta, Bo to Exodus 13:13; Kiddushin 29a–31b).

The teaching of Torah, that is, religious education, has received the greatest stress in Judaism, especially since Pharisaic times. The obligation begins as soon as the child is able to speak; there is a tradition that the first words he should be taught to say are those of the *Shema*, 'Hear, O Israel, the Lord is our God, the Lord is One' (Deuteronomy 6:4; Jerusalem Talmud, Chagigah

1:2). In a more formal sense, religious education begins at the age of five or six and continues at least until the attainment of majority, though the duty to go on learning never ceases. (See above, pp. 316 ff.)

COMING OF AGE

The age of majority was fixed by the Rabbis, in relation to the onset of puberty, at thirteen for boys and twelve for girls. Surprisingly, however, there is no mention of a coming-of-age ceremony in the ancient Jewish sources. Indeed, apart from a passing reference in an early medieval tractate to a Jerusalem custom of parents taking their thirteen-year-old sons to the elders of the city, to be blessed and exhorted by them (Soferim 18:5), it is not until the late Middle Ages that we have evidence of a generally accepted coming-of-age ceremony, called bar-mitzvah. (The term itself is talmudic and simply denotes a boy who, having attained the age of majority, is 'subject to the commandments'.)

The essence of the custom, as it has become established, is that the boy, having become subject to the commandments and instructed in the performance of them, exercises his newly acquired status as an 'adult' member of the community by taking a prominent part in the synagogue service, and especially in the public reading of the Torah, on the sabbath (or the Monday or Thursday) coinciding with or following his thirteenth birthday. Special prayers are said by him and on his behalf, and the preacher will appropriately congratulate and exhort him. Afterwards, there will be a family celebration during which the boy may give a talmudic discourse or just make a little speech thanking his parents and teachers for their instruction, and his guests for their gifts.

The Progressive movement in Judaism, beginning in the nineteenth century, took exception to the traditional bar-mitzvah on three counts: that it was confined to boys; that it came at too young an age; and that it tended to foreshorten the formal educational process. It therefore developed another coming-of-age ceremony, collective rather than individual, for boys and girls alike, at the age of sixteen or thereabouts. The first such ceremony was held in Berlin in 1817; subsequently it became very popular in the Progressive Jewish communities of the English-speaking world, especially in North America, where it became known as confirmation and was generally held on the festival of *Shavuot*. More recently it has come to be called by Hebrew names such as *kabbalat torah* ('acceptance of Torah'). At the same time the traditional bar-mitzvah ceremony has been revived as well and supplemented by a corresponding ceremony for girls called bat mitzvah (*bar* is Aramaic for 'son', *bat* is Hebrew for 'daughter', but both are used in the sense of 'subject to'), so that in Progressive communities the coming-of-age process is celebrated at *two* stages.

In Orthodox and Conservative communities, too, the case for a greater involvement of girls has come to be widely conceded, and individual or group coming-of-age ceremonies have been instituted for them under such as names as bat-mitzvah, *bat-torah* and *bat-chayil* (*chayil* meaning 'virtue' and alluding to such verses as Proverbs 31:10, 29), the age of the girls varying from twelve or thirteen to fifteen or sixteen.

MARRIAGE

An ancient rabbinic formulation of the 'ages of man' has it that 'five is the age for the study of Scripture, ten for the study of Mishnah, thirteen for the observance of the commandments, fifteen for the study of Talmud, eighteen for marriage . . .' (Avot 5:21/24), indicating that relatively early marriage was both normal and commended.

Marriage is highly regarded in Jewish tradition: so much so that it was declared to be an obligation, and celibacy, far from being extolled as superior, was considered allowable only in exceptional circumstances. (The practice of celibacy among the Essenes did not commend itself to mainstream Judaism.) It is also noteworthy that in ancient Judaism the priests were not expected to be celibate and that, on the contrary, the High Priest was positively required to marry (Leviticus 21:13 f.).

Marriage, as understood in Judaism, serves three interrelated purposes. First, the propagation of the human species, in fulfilment of the commandment, 'Be fruitful, and multiply' (Genesis 1:28). According to talmudic law, this requirement is deemed to have been satisfied when a man has begotten at least one son and

one daughter, just as God created 'male and female' (Genesis
1:27). Even then, contraception is traditionally viewed with dis-
favour, except when there is reason to suppose that it might avert
a life-threatening consequence. Progressive and Conservative
Judaism are, however, more permissive in this matter than
Orthodox Judaism.

Secondly, the companionship which marriage affords, for, 'It
is not good that man should be alone ... Therefore a man
leaves his father and his mother, and cleaves to his wife, and they
become one flesh' (Genesis 2:18, 24). Marriage, in other words,
makes for happiness. As the Rabbis said, with exaggeration for
emphasis, 'a man without a wife lives without blessing, life, joy,
help, good and peace' (Yevamot 62b). It is, ideally, a lifelong
relationship, just as God's Covenant with Israel, to which it is
often likened by the Prophets, is eternal (e.g., Hosea 2:21 f.;
Christian Bibles, 2:19 f.). It is, indeed, a sacred relationship,
which requires mutual fidelity, respect, consideration and love. A
typical rabbinic teaching praises the man 'who loves his wife as
himself, and honours her even more than himself' (Yevamot
62b).

Thirdly, marriage is highly valued in Jewish tradition because
it establishes the family as the basic social unit and the home as
the 'little sanctuary' (Ezekiel 11:16) in which the father is like a
priest, the mother like a priestess, and the dining-room table like
an altar (Berachot 55a), where children can enjoy their childhood
and grow to maturity under the loving protection and guidance of
their parents, and where the Jewish religion can be practised,
experienced and transmitted from generation to generation.

Impediments

In former times Jewish marriages were commonly arranged by
the parents, sometimes with the help of a matchmaker, called a
shadchan. Nowadays, in most Jewish communities, young people
choose their own partners – to the pleasure or displeasure of their
parents! The choice is subject to a number of restrictions on the
part of Judaism.

First, Jewish marriage is monogamous. It was not always so. In
biblical and talmudic times male (but not female) polygamy was

theoretically permitted and occasionally, though increasingly rarely, practised. However, in the Middle Ages it was prohibited. The decree in question, now accepted by practically all Jewish communities, is traditionally attributed to Rabbi Gershom ben Judah of Mayence, but recent scholarship has shown that it probably dates from the twelfth century (Z. W. Falk, *Jewish Matrimonial Law in the Middle Ages*).

Secondly, a Jewish marriage is only possible if both parties are Jewish. Judaism has opposed mixed marriages since ancient times, when it was feared that they would subvert the nation's religious life with paganizing influences (Deuteronomy 7:3 f., Ezra 10:10 f., Nehemiah 13:23–27). With the dispersion, even when Jews found themselves living in monotheistic (Christian or Muslim) environments, the opposition persisted because of the threat to their survival, as a minority group, which such marriages were thought to pose. That consideration has not ceased to be applicable, except in the State of Israel. For in most other countries the number of marriages out of the faith has risen to what many regard as demographically disastrous proportions: between 25 and 50 per cent. In addition, there is the more general case against mixed marriages, that they are likely to create difficulties for the marriage relationship itself and for the religious upbringing of any children.

It goes without saying that a gentile who converts to Judaism is a Jew and may marry a Jew. But conversion to Judaism is not easy. Although the principle is that 'the gates are open at all times' (see above, p. 280), there are stringent conditions, primarily of total sincerity and substantial knowledge, gained during a lengthy course of instruction. The actual process of admission involves, by tradition, circumcision in the case of a male proselyte, immersion in a ritual bath, and a declaration of loyalty to the Jewish faith and community. Orthodox Judaism is more rigorous in its insistence on these conditions and procedures than Progressive Judaism, and tends to withhold recognition as Jews from those admitted under non-Orthodox auspices.

A third restriction is represented by the 'forbidden degrees' of consanguinity and affinity as stated in the Bible (principally in Leviticus 18) and elaborated in subsequent Jewish law. As these are broadly in accord with the legislation of most countries, it might be thought that violations of them would rarely occur. There are, however, two complications. One is that if a husband disappears without trace, whereas the civil authorities may in certain cases declare the putative widow free to remarry, rabbinic law, in the absence of what it considers indubitable evidence of his death, would not permit her to do so. The other complication may arise in divorce cases.

Judaism, as already mentioned, regards marriage as ideally permanent, but not as indissoluble. It discourages divorce, and regrets it when it occurs. 'The very altar weeps,' said an ancient Rabbi, 'when a man divorces the wife of his youth' (Gittin 90b, alluding to Malachi 2:14 ff.). But it allows divorce, both on the ground of a serious matrimonial offence and, when all attempts at reconciliation have failed, by mutual consent. The procedure, based on Deuteronomy 24:1–4, takes place before a rabbinic court and involves the writing of a writ of divorce called *get* on behalf of the husband and its delivery to the wife, whose consent has been mandatory since the Middle Ages. Since the Emancipation, however, Jews have generally come under the jurisdiction of their lands of domicile, so that they need to obtain a civil dissolution of marriage before a Jewish divorce can be transacted; and it sometimes happens that they fail to take that second step, either because one party refuses to cooperate or for some other reason.

In either of these cases, that of the 'deserted wife' and that of a civil divorce without a *get*, the woman is considered in rabbinic law an *agunah*, i.e., still 'tied' to her former husband, with the result that if she were to remarry in these circumstances, her subsequent marriage would be technically adulterous and in violation of the 'forbidden degrees'. (The same would not apply to the former husband because the medieval decree mentioned above, while *prohibiting* male polygamy, could not and did not render it null and void.)

Such cases, when they occur, are all the more serious because, according to the rabbinic interpretation of another biblical law (Deuteronomy 23:3; Christian Bibles, 23:2), the offspring of a union in contravention of the 'forbidden degrees' is a *mamzer*. This term, of uncertain etymology, is generally translated 'bastard', but is defined only as has just been stated and does not refer to the offspring of unwedded unions generally. The chief disability entailed is that a *mamzer* may not marry an 'untainted' Jew. This problem is a very difficult one for Orthodox Judaism, and causes its exponents grave anxiety. Progressive Judaism disregards the law of the *mamzer* and, in those cases in which it seems to its rabbinic authorities ethically right to do so, allows an *agunah* to remarry without satisfying all the legal requirements on which Orthodox rabbis feel duty-bound to insist. (Some branches of Progressive Judaism execute their own divorce documents, some take the view that a civil divorce alone effectively dissolves a Jewish marriage.)

Yet another complication which needs to be mentioned is the relatively rare case of a widow whose husband has died childless. Biblically, such a woman is subject to the law of the levirate; i.e., her late husband's brother is obliged to marry her, 'that his name may not be blotted out of Israel', but he may obtain exemption from that obligation by a ceremony called *chalitzah* ('taking off the shoe', Deuteronomy 25:5–10). For many centuries now the exemption ceremony has been preferred, or even required, with the result that, until it has been performed, a widow in such a position may not remarry according to Orthodox Judaism. Progressive Judaism discountenances both the law of the levirate and the exemption ceremony.

A fourth restriction derives from a biblical law forbidding priests to marry certain categories of women (Leviticus 21:7) which was so interpreted as to preclude a Kohen from marrying a divorcee, a *chalitzah*-widow or a proselyte. This is another prohibition upheld in Orthodox Judaism but disregarded in Progressive Judaism.

These, then, are the principal possible impediments (there are a few more, too technical to be gone into here) of which the young Jew needs to be aware in choosing a marriage partner.

Marriage Rites

If there are no impediments, the couple may become engaged. This is an oral agreement, which has no legally binding force but is regarded as demanded by propriety, that the marriage will take place at a future date. In Hebrew it is called *shidduchin* ('matchmaking') or *tena'im* ('conditions').

The date of the marriage needs to be chosen with due regard to the Jewish religious calendar. It may not take place on a sabbath or a holy day, and there are other days on which marriages are traditionally disallowed, principally the intermediate days of Passover and Tabernacles, the feast of *Purim*, the various fast days, the period of the counting of the Omer (with certain exceptions, see above, pp. 351 f.) and the three weeks culminating in *Tish'ah be-Av* (see above, p. 353). These are the restrictions applicable in Orthodox Judaism. Progressive Judaism is more permissive in these matters, but disallows marriages on sabbaths, holy days and *Tish'ah be-Av*, with the addition, in some communities, of the Ten Days of Repentance.

The marriage service comprises two ceremonies, formerly separate, which since the late Middle Ages have been combined and generally held in a synagogue or in the open air, particularly in the synagogue courtyard, less frequently in the home of the bride's or bridegroom's parents or in a hotel, under a canopy called a *chuppah*.

Of the two ceremonies, the first is called *erusin* ('betrothal') or *kiddushin* ('consecration') and consists of the bridegroom, in the presence of witnesses, giving the bride a ring while saying to her: 'Behold, you are consecrated to me by this ring according to the law of Moses and Israel.' In Progressive Judaism this declaration is repeated by the bride, and there may be an exchange of rings. This act is preceded by two benedictions: over a cup of wine, and the 'blessing of betrothal' which praises God, 'who hallows His people Israel by the rites of the *chuppah* and *kiddushin*'.

While this act establishes the legal bond of marriage, until the late Middle Ages bride and bridegroom generally went on living in their respective homes for another year. Only then would the marriage be consummated. In ancient times *chuppah* was the name given to the hut or chamber in which the consummation took place; today the term refers to the canopy, supported by four poles, under which the combined service is celebrated and which therefore serves as a *symbol* of the new home about to be established. There used to follow a prolonged feast during which the 'seven wedding benedictions' would be recited. They are still recited today and, together with the *chuppah*, represent the second stage of the marriage process, known as *nissu'in* ('nuptials'). These benedictions are again recited over a cup of wine and praise God as the 'Creator of man' who 'causes the bridegroom to rejoice with the bride'. As after the 'blessing of betrothal', bride and groom each take a sip from the cup of wine, a symbol of the fact that they will henceforth share all things.

Between the two parts of the ceremony it is customary for the officiant (usually the rabbi) to read out the *ketubbah*. This is a marriage contract, said to date from the first century BCE, originally intended to discourage divorce, and to give the wife a measure of security, by stipulating a sum of money payable to her by the husband if he should divorce her, or out of his estate if he should predecease her. Nowadays it serves more as a marriage certificate, recording the agreement of the parties to marry one another and their acceptance of the consequent obligations, particularly the bridegroom's pledge to 'honour, support and maintain' his wife 'after the manner of Jewish husbands'. It is traditionally written in Aramaic and often colourfully decorated. Progressive synagogues tend to use an abridged version, in Hebrew and with a translation.

At the end of the service the bridegroom breaks a glass in remembrance of the ancient destruction of Jerusalem, itself a symbol of the fact that the world is as yet unredeemed, and that therefore life is not all happiness: a fact Jews are bidden to remember even on the most joyful occasions, in fulfilment of the Psalmist's pledge,

> If I forget you, O Jerusalem,
>   let my right hand wither!
> Let my tongue cleave to the roof of my mouth,
>   if I do not remember you,
> if I do not set Jerusalem
>   above my highest joy!
>
> (Psalm 137:5 f.)

The wedding is followed by a feast at which the 'seven benedictions', or at least the last of them, are again recited, in conjunction with the grace after meals. Then the couple depart for their honeymoon, a custom which may be said to have a basis in Jewish tradition in that Rabbinic law requires the bridegroom to 'rejoice with the bride' for seven days (Ketubbot 7a–b). On return, they take up residence in their marital home. This is dedicated by a ceremony called *chanukkat ha-bayit*, 'consecration of the house', which includes the affixing of the *mezuzah* (see above, p. 320). (There is an allusion to such a dedication ceremony already in the Bible, Deuteronomy 20:5.) Then they settle down to the rhythm of domestic life, including all its daily, weekly, yearly and life-cycle religious observances.

Purification

The word 'rhythm' is also applicable to the most intimate aspect of marital life, the sexual. Towards this Judaism has generally taken what modern psychology would regard as a healthy attitude: modest rather than prudish; positive and even reverential. One of the most explicit statements of that attitude occurs in a thirteenth-century kabbalistic work, the *Iggeret ha-Kodesh* ('Epistle on Holiness'), erroneously attributed to Nachmanides. 'The act of sexual union,' it says, 'is holy and pure ... For the Lord created all things in accordance with His wisdom, and did not create anything shameful or ugly ... When a man cohabits with his wife in holiness, the *Shechinah* is with them' (*Kitvey Rabbenu Mosheh ben Nachman*, Mosad ha-Rav Kook, Vol. I I, p. 323). In particular, there is considerable insistence in Rabbinic law on the husband's conjugal duties towards his wife. However, the Torah emphatically forbids marital intercourse during the wife's menstrual period (Leviticus 18:19, 20:18), and this restriction was greatly elaborated in Rabbinic law, requiring the wife to anticipate the onset of her period and to prolong the time of abstinence by seven 'clean' days, then to purify herself by immersion in a ritual bath (*mikveh*). Such purification is also required of the bride before her wedding day. These laws are commonly referred to by the generic term, *tohorat ha-mishpachah*, 'purity of the family'. They are considered very important in Orthodox Judaism, and often praised for their psychological value. Progressive Judaism tends to question the concept of ritual purity, as distinct from hygiene, and leaves these matters to the discretion of the individual.

AGING AND DYING

The previously quoted Rabbinic aphorism about the 'ages of man' continues, not without a touch of humour: 'Twenty is the age for pursuing [a livelihood], thirty for full vigour, forty for understanding, fifty for counsel, sixty for elderliness, seventy for old age, eighty for special strength (cf. Psalms 90:10), ninety for being bent with age, and at a hundred a man is as if he were already dead and had passed away from the world.'

Judaism teaches its adherents to accept the aging process and the fact of mortality with resignation and trust, knowing that it is the condition of the succession of the generations and the unfolding of God's redemptive purpose. 'A generation goes, and a generation comes, but the earth remains for ever ... For everything there is a season, and a time for every matter under heaven: A time to be born, and a time to die . . .' (Ecclesiastes 1:4, 3:1 f.). 'Do not fear the summons of death; remember those who have gone before you and those who will come after you. It is the Lord's decree for all flesh' (Ecclesiasticus 41:3 f.).

Judaism also emphasizes that those who have lived long are entitled to respect and may need help. 'You shall rise before the hoary head,' says the Torah, 'and honour the face of an old man' (Leviticus 19:32). More particularly, Judaism has always stressed the obligation of children to look after their parents in old age, and seen it as one of the chief implications of the Fifth Commandment, 'Honour your father and your mother' (Exodus 20:12, Deuteronomy 5:16). It should perhaps be pointed out that this obligation applies *equally* towards both parents, an inference which the Rabbis drew from the fact that in another statement of it (Leviticus 19:3) the order is reversed (Sifra ad loc.).

It is considered a particularly important *mitzvah* to visit the sick (*bikkur cholim*) and to pray for their recovery. If the patient is seriously ill he should be encouraged, according to Jewish tradition, not to abandon hope but nevertheless to recite the last prayers, including a confession of sins and the *Shema*, concluding with the word *echad*, 'One' (see p. 236).

Burial

When death has occurred, the 'last rites' are performed. They are minutely regulated by Jewish tradition and generally carried out by a group of volunteers known as *chevrah kaddisha* ('holy society'). The eyes of the deceased are closed, the body is arranged in the prescribed posture and covered with a sheet, and a lighted candle is placed near the head. As the patient is not left unattended while dying, so too his body is guarded from the time of death until the funeral, the 'watcher' being known as *wacher* (Yiddish) or *shomer* (Hebrew). The body is prepared for the funeral by being washed according to a ritual called *tohorah* ('purification'), then wrapped in shrouds (*tachrichim*). However, Progressive Jews are generally prepared to leave these matters to the nurses to carry out in accordance with established procedures. Then the body is placed in a coffin. In the case of a man, his *tallit* may be placed in it with him. By tradition, the coffin is simple and unornamented, so that there may be no distinction between rich and poor.

From a biblical law relating to the body of an executed criminal (Deuteronomy 21:23) it was inferred that the funeral should take place on the day of the death, or as soon as possible thereafter, but it is accepted that there may need to be a delay in order to comply with the civil law (e.g., if an inquest is ordered) or to notify the relatives. Orthodox Judaism (but not Progressive Judaism) disallows cremation, considering it disrespectful to the deceased and at variance with Jewish tradition, which, it is said, positively requires that the dead be buried. The traditional Jewish belief in the resurrection of the dead (see above, pp. 267–9) has also contributed to this reluctance to accept cremation.

Before the funeral a short service may be held in the home of the bereaved family. The cemetery is known euphemistically as *beit olam*, the 'house of eternity', or *beit chayyim*, the 'house of the living'. Before the burial it is customary for the deceased's next-of-kin to make a small tear in their outer garment as a mark of grief. This ritual, called *keri'ah* ('rending'), is very ancient and well attested in the Bible (e.g., II Samuel 1:11). It is not generally observed among Progressive Jews. The funeral service is called *tzidduk ha-din*, which may be translated 'reaffirmation of

God's justice'. Its key phrase, 'Blessed be the true Judge,' derives from the rabbinic doctrine that 'a man is obligated to praise God for the evil that befalls him as well as the good' (Berachot 9:5), as Job did when he said, 'The Lord gave, and the Lord has taken away; blessed be the name of the Lord' (Job 1:21). That very verse is, in fact, recited during the funeral service. The coffin is lowered into the grave with the words, 'May he [or she] come to his [or her] resting-place in peace.' Then the mourners take turns in throwing a little earth into the grave, by way of participating in the act of burial. The practice of covering the coffin with flowers, or of planting flowers over the grave, is contrary to Jewish custom and generally disallowed in Orthodox cemeteries.

Whereas in other religions the burial of the dead was a particular prerogative and preoccupation of the priesthood, in Judaism the reverse was the case, and the Jewish priests were actually forbidden to 'defile themselves' through contact with the dead, except when mourning for their immediate next-of-kin (Leviticus 21:1 ff.). In Orthodox Judaism (but not Progressive) it therefore remains the rule to this day that anyone who is a Kohen, if attending the funeral of one not closely related to him, keeps some distance away from the coffin.

MOURNING

Mourning is considered a religious obligation if the deceased is a near relative – father or mother, husband or wife, brother or sister, son or daughter – and consists of several well-defined stages. Between the death and the burial the mourner (called *onen*) is exempt from normal religious observances, such as daily prayer, and required (except on a sabbath) to abstain from meat and wine. Once the burial has taken place, the mourner, now called an *avel*, observes an intensive phase of mourning which lasts for seven days from the day of the funeral and is therefore called *shiv'ah* ('seven'), but this is suspended on a sabbath and terminated by the intervention of a festival, for on such days private sorrow gives way to communal rejoicing. During the *shiv'ah* period, the mourners stay at home, sit on low stools and refrain from wearing leather shoes. To enable them to recite *kaddish*, which requires the presence of a quorum of ten men, relatives and friends gather in the mourners' home, where a memorial candle is kept burning throughout this period, to hold daily services with them, especially in the evening.

After the seven days, the laws of mourning are relaxed, but the mourners still practise a degree of restraint, by keeping away from places of amusement and the like, until thirty days have elapsed from the day of the funeral, so that this phase is known as *sheloshim* ('thirty'), though again, it may be shortened if a festival intervenes. One who is mourning for a parent is expected to observe the same restrictions for a whole year, as well as to recite the mourner's *kaddish* in the synagogue during the first eleven months. A tombstone (*matzevah*) is usually erected and dedicated after a year, though custom varies in that regard. The inscription on it commonly includes a Hebrew acronym which stands for the words, 'May his [or her] soul be bound up in the bond of eternal life.'

The anniversary of a parent's death is known, from the Yiddish, as *yahrzeit*. On this day, traditionally calculated according to the Jewish calendar, the children light a memorial candle, visit the grave and recite *kaddish*. If they cannot attend a synagogue service on the actual day, they do so, and recite *kaddish*, on the preceding sabbath. This remembrance of parents plays an important role in Judaism, binding the generations to one another in a continuum of time.

These Jewish laws and customs of mourning may seem strange and complicated to those unfamiliar with them, and it must not be thought that all Jews observe them with equal meticulousness. Progressive Judaism, in particular, has relaxed them in several regards. Nevertheless, as the psychology of bereavement has come to be better understood, it is increasingly appreciated that these rites play a therapeutic role in helping the mourners, with the support of their community, to cope with their grief and gradually to surmount it.

The journey of the individual from birth to death traverses many sorrows and many joys. What does Judaism do for Jews responsive to their heritage? It gives them strength to endure the sorrows, and reverence to sanctify the joys, to see meaning in them, and eternity beyond them. It helps them live with dignity and decency, poise and purpose, whatever each day brings. It offers them the inspiration of a noble past, the fellowship of a living community, the pageantry of a colourful cycle of rituals, and the hope of a resplendent future. It teaches them that they are engaged in yet another journey, the journey of all humanity towards redemption, and that they are privileged to be God's partners in the struggle to reach that goal. In some mysterious way, the ancient voice of Sinai still resonates in their souls, lending a sacred urgency to all their activities. They are held in thrall by the promise of a day which, like Moses on Mount Nebo, they know they will never see, but which nevertheless suffuses all their ordinary days with significance, and saves them from the wilderness of meaninglessness: the day when the human family will finally acknowledge its Divine Father, and live together in justice, love and peace. 'On that day,' they know, 'the Lord will be one, and His name one' (Zechariah 14:9).

GLOSSARY

of the more important Hebrew terms – for other terms and fuller definitions see Index

AGGADAH: Rabbinic lore (as distinct from law)

ALIYAH: 'Going up' to take part in a service; immigration to Israel

AMORA'IM: Rabbis of 200–500 CE

ARON (HA-KODESH): (Holy) Ark

ASHKENAZIM: Jews of German and Eastern European origin

BAR MITZVAH: Boy's coming-of-age ceremony

BAT KOL: Heavenly voice

BERACHAH: Benediction

BIMAH: Platform (in synagogue)

BIRKAT HA-MAZON: Thanksgiving for food (grace)

(B'RIT) MILAH: (Covenant of) Circumcision

CHALLAH: Sabbath bread

CHAMETZ: Leaven

CHANUKKAH: Festival commemorating the Maccabees' rededication of the Temple

CHASID: Member of a pietistic sect

CHAZZAN: Synagogue cantor

CHEDER: Religion school

CHUMASH: Pentateuch

CHUPPAH: Wedding canopy

DERECH ERETZ: Good manners; secular learning or occupation

EIN SOF: In *Kabbalah*, the transcendent, unknowable God

EL, ELOAH, ELOHIM: God

EL SHADDAI: 'God Almighty', the God of the Patriarchs

EMUNAH: Faith, trust

ETROG: Citron (used at Sukkot)

GAON: 'Excellency', title of heads of the academies of Sura and Pumbedita

GEMARA: Amoraic stratum of Talmud

GEMILUT CHASADIM: Practical kindness

HAFTARAH: Prophetic lesson

HAGGADAH: Book containing the Passover eve ritual

HALACHAH: Rabbinic law (as distinct from lore)

HALLEL: 'Praise'. Psalms 113–18

HASKALAH: The Enlightenment

HAVDALAH: Ceremony ushering out the sabbath

KABBALAH: Jewish mysticism

KADDISH: Doxology used as concluding and mourner's prayer

KASHER: (Ashkenazi pronunciation: kosher) Fit (to be eaten)

KASHRUT: Dietary laws

KAVVANAH: Concentration, devotion in prayer

KEHILLAH: Community

KIBBUTZ: Commune

KIDDUSH: Prayer and ritual ushering in a sabbath or festival

KIDDUSH HA-SHEM: Sanctification of God's Name

KIDDUSHIN: Betrothal

LAG BA-OMER: 33rd day of the Sefirah, minor festival

LULAV: Palm branch used at Sukkot

GLOSSARY

MA'ARIV: Evening service

MACHZOR: Festival prayer book

MAROR: Bitter herbs used in the Passover eve ritual

MASHIACH: Anointed One, Messiah

MATZAH: Unleavened bread eaten during Passover

MEGILLAH: Scroll (especially of Esther)

MENORAH: (Chanukkah) candlestick

MEZUZAH: Case containing Scripture passages affixed to doorpost

MIDRASH: Bible interpretation

MIKVEH: Ritual bath

MINCHAH: Afternoon service

MINHAG: Custom

MINYAN: Quorum (for worship)

MISHNAH: Earliest compendium of the Oral Torah

MITZVAH: Commandment, duty

NER TAMID: Perpetual light

NISSU'IN: Nuptials

OMER: Sheaf of corn

PARASHAH: Section of the Torah

PESACH: Passover

PIDYON HA-BEN: Redemption of the firstborn

PIKKUACH NEFESH: Saving of life

PIYYUT: Liturgical poetry

PURIM: Feast of lots, based on the book of Esther

RABBI: Teacher, especially of Jewish law

ROSH CHODESH: New Moon

ROSH HASHANAH: New Year

SEDER: Passover eve ritual

SEFER: Book or scroll

SEFER TORAH: Scroll of the law

SEPHARDIM: Jews of Spanish and North African origin

SHACHARIT: Morning service

SHALOM: Peace, a greeting

SHALOSH REGALIM: The three pilgrimage festivals

SHAVUOT: Feast of Weeks, Pentecost

SHECHINAH: Presence of God

SHECHITAH: Slaughter of animals for food

SHEMA: Scripture passages (Deuteronomy 6 : 4–9, 11 : 13–21, Numbers 15 : 37–41) recited daily as a declaration of loyalty to Judaism

SHOCHET: Slaughterer

SHOFAR: Ram's horn

SIDDUR: Daily and sabbath prayer book

SIDRA: Weekly Torah portion

SOFER: Scribe

SUKKAH: Booth, used at Sukkot

SUKKOT: Feast of Booths or Tabernacles

TALLIT: Prayer shawl

TALMUD: Literature amplifying the Mishnah

TALMUD TORAH: Study of Torah; Jewish religious education

TANACH: Hebrew Bible (Torah, Prophets, Hagiographa)

TANNA'IM: Rabbis of 70–200 CE

TARGUM: Aramaic translation of the Bible

TEFILLAH: Prayer, especially the series of benedictions also known as Amidah and Shemoneh Esreh

TEFILLIN: Leather boxes containing Scripture verses tied to forehead and forearm during prayer

TESHUVAH: Repentance

TISH'AH B'AV: Ninth of Av, fast day recalling fall of Temple

TORAH: Teaching, especially Pentateuch and the oral tradition

TREFAH: 'Torn'; unfit to be eaten

TZADDIK: Righteous; Chasidic leader

TZEDAKAH: Charity

YAD: Hand; pointer

YAMIM NORA'IM: Days of awe

YESHIVAH: Talmudic academy

YOM HA-ATZMA'UT: Day of (Israel's) Independence

YOM KIPPUR: Day of Atonement

YOM TOV: Holy day

SELECT BIBLIOGRAPHY

PRIMARY SOURCES AND MODES OF CITATION

Hebrew Bible, Masoretic Text
Standard editions. Also Kittel, Rud. (ed.), *Biblia Hebraica*,
Stuttgart, Privileg. Württ. Bibelanstalt, 1949. Book, chapter, verse.
Hebrew Bible with Classic Jewish Commentaries ('*Rabbinic Bible*'),
Mikra'ot Gedolot, Standard editions, e.g., 5 volumes, Tel Aviv,
Schocken Books, 1958. Commentator, book, chapter, verse.
Hebrew Bible in English Translation
The Holy Bible, Revised Standard Version, Old Testament, New York,
Glasgow and Toronto, William Collins Sons, 1952. Book, chapter,
verse.
Apocrypha in English Translation
The Apocrypha of the Old Testament, Revised Standard Version, New
York, Toronto and Edinburgh, Thomas Nelson and Sons, 1957.
Book, chapter, verse.
Josephus
Josephus, Flavius, *The Jewish War*, translated by G. A. Williamson,
London, Penguin Books, 1970. Book, chapter, paragraph.
Mishnah
Standard editions. Also Albeck, Chanoch (ed.), *Shishah Sidrei
Mishnah*, 6 volumes, Jerusalem and Tel Aviv, Bialik Institute and
Dvir Co., 1958–9. Tractate, chapter, paragraph.
Tosefta
Zuckermandel, M. S. (ed.), *Tosefta*, Jerusalem, Wahrmann Books,
1963. Tractate, chapter, paragraph.
Mechilta
Horovitz, H. S. and Rabin, I. A. (eds.), *Mechilta de-Rabbi Yishma'el*,
Jerusalem, Bamberger and Wahrman, 1960. Tractate, chapter, bib-
lical verse.
Sifra
Standard editions, e.g. *Torat Kohanim*, Jerusalem, Sifra, 5719 (1958–
9). Folio, page, biblical verse.

Sifrei to Deuteronomy
    Finkelstein, Louis (ed.), *Sifrei Al Sefer Devarim*, New York, Jewish Theological Seminary of America, 1969. Chapter, biblical verse.

'Jerusalem' Talmud
    Standard editions (Krotoshin, 1866 or Zhitomir, 1865–6), e.g. *Talmud Yerushalmi* (Zhitomir edition, reprinted in Israel, n.d.). Tractate, chapter, paragraph.

Babylonian Talmud
    Standard editions, e.g., *Talmud Bavli*, 12 volumes, Jerusalem, Torah La-am, 5717 (1956–7). Tractate, folio, page. (All such citations refer to the Babylonian Talmud, even when that is not specified.)

Midrash Rabbah
    Standard editions. Also Mirkin, Mosheh Aryeh (ed.), *Midrash Rabbah*, 11 volumes, Tel Aviv, Yavneh, third edition, 1977. Biblical book followed by 'Rabbah', chapter, paragraph.

Tanchuma
    Standard editions, e.g. *Midrash Tanchuma*, Jerusalem, Lewin-Epstein Bros., 5720 (1959–60). Pericope, chapter.

Pesikta Rabbati
    Ish-Shalom (Friedmann), Meir (ed.), *Midrash Pesikta Rabbati*, 1880, reprinted Tel Aviv, 5723 (1972–3). Chapter, paragraph.

Maimonides
    Sefer ha-Mitzvot, Jerusalem, Mossad Harav Kook, fifth impression, 5739 (1978–9). Positive or negative commandments, number.
    Mishneh Torah, standard editions, e.g., 8 volumes, Jerusalem, 'El Hamekoroth', 5714 (1953–4). Section ('laws of . . .'), chapter, paragraph.

Prayer Book
    There are so many different editions of the Jewish prayer book that we have thought it best not to give page references. Our citations will be found easily enough by those at all familiar with the Jewish liturgy, e.g., in S. Singer (translator): *The Authorized Daily Prayer Book of the United Hebrew Congregations of the British Commonwealth of Nations*, new edition, London, Eyre and Spottiswoode, 1962. (Our translations have been taken or adapted from *Service of the Heart*, London, Union of Liberal and Progressive Synagogues, 1967.)

Tractates (of the Mishnah, Tosefta, 'Jerusalem' Talmud and Babylonian Talmud) cited are: Berachot, Pe'ah, Shabbat, Pesachim, Shekalim, Yoma, Sukkah, Rosh Hashanah, Ta'anit, Megillah, Chagigah, Yevamot, Ketubbot, Nedarim, Sotah, Gittin, Kiddushin, Bava Metzia, Bava Batra, Sanhedrin, Makkot, Shevu'ot, Avot, Menachot, Chullin, Tamid.

SELECT BIBLIOGRAPHY

MAJOR SECONDARY SOURCES USED

Reference Works

Encyclopaedia Judaica, Roth, Cecil, and Geoffrey Wigoder (eds.), 16 volumes, Jerusalem, Keter Publishing House, 1972.

The Jewish Encyclopaedia, 12 volumes, New York, Funk and Wagnalls, 1901–1907.

The History of Judaism

General Surveys

Graetz, Heinrich, *History of the Jews* (first published in German in 1891), 6 volumes, Philadelphia, Jewish Publication Society of America, 1949.

Baron, Salo Wittmayer, *A Social and Religious History of the Jews*, 18 volumes, New York, Columbia University Press, 1952–83.

Dubnow, Simon, *History of the Jews*, tr. Moshe Spiegel, 5 volumes, fourth edition, New Jersey, Thomas Yoseloff, 1969.

Finkelstein, Louis (ed.), *The Jews: Their History, Culture and Religion*, 2 volumes, New York, Schocken Books, 1970.

Rivkin, Ellis, *The Shaping of Jewish History*, New York, Charles Scribner's Sons, 1971.

Seltzer, Robert M., *Jewish People, Jewish Thought*, New York, Macmillan, 1980.

Biblical Period

Albright, William Foxwell, *From the Stone Age to Christianity*, second edition, New York, Doubleday and Company, Inc., 1959.

De Vaux, Roland, *Ancient Israel*, 2 volumes, New York, McGraw Hill, 1961.

Noth, Martin, *The History of Israel*, tr. P. R. Ackroyd, New York, Harper and Row, 1960.

Bright, John, *A History of Israel*, second edition, Philadelphia, Westminster Press, 1972.

From the Babylonian Exile to the Bar Kochba Revolt

Zeitlin, Solomon, *The Rise and Fall of the Jewish State*, 3 volumes, Philadelphia, Jewish Publication Society of America, 1962–78.

Hengel, Martin, *Judaism and Hellenism*, tr. John Bowden, 2 volumes, Philadelphia, Fortress Press, 1974.

Tcherikover, Victor, *Hellenistic Civilization and the Jews,* tr. S. Apelbaum, Philadelphia, Jewish Publication Society of America, 1959.

Schürer, Emil, *The History of the Jewish People in the Age of Christ*; Volume I, revised by Geza Vermes and Fergus Millar, 1973;

Volume II, revised by Geza Vermes, Fergus Millar and Matthew
Black, Edinburgh, T. and T. Clark, 1979.

From Bar Kochba to Medieval Times
Sharf, Andrew, *Byzantine Jewry: From Justinian to the Fourth Crusade,*
Littman Library of Jewish Civilization, London, Routledge and
Kegan Paul, 1971.
Abrahams, Israel, *Jewish Life in the Middle Ages* (first published 1896),
New York, Atheneum Publishers, 1969.
Katz, Jacob, *Exclusiveness and Tolerance*, New York, Schocken Books,
1962.
Baer, Yitzhak, *A History of the Jews of Christian Spain: Their Social,
Political and Cultural Life*, 2 volumes, Philadelphia, Jewish Pub-
lication Society of America, 1942.

From the Middle Ages to the Emancipation
Roth, Cecil, *A History of the Marranos*, Philadelphia, Jewish Publication
Society of America, 1932.
The Jews in the Renaissance, Philadelphia, Jewish Publication Society
of America, 1950.
History of the Jews of Venice, New York, Schocken Books, 1975.
Stern, Selma, *The Court Jew*, Philadelphia, Jewish Publication Society
of America, 1950.
Lewis, Bernard, *The Jews of Islam*, New Jersey, Princeton University
Press, 1984.

Modern Period
Sachar, Howard Morley, *The Course of Modern Jewish History*, New
York, Dell, 1977.
Katz, Jacob, *Out of the Ghetto: The Social Background of Jewish
Emancipation, 1770–1870*, Cambridge, Mass., Harvard University
Press, 1973.
Dubnow, Simon, *History of the Jews in Russia and Poland* (first pub-
lished 1916–18), New York, Ktav Publishing House, 1973.
Plaut, W. Gunther, *The Rise of Reform Judaism*, New York, World
Union for Progressive Judaism, 1963.
The Growth of Reform Judaism, New York, World Union for Pro-
gressive Judaism, 1965.
Gilbert, Martin, *The Holocaust, The Jewish Tragedy*, London, Collins,
1986.
Laqueur, Walter, *A History of Zionism*, New York, Holt, Rinehart and
Winston, 1972.
Eban, Abba, *My Country*, London, Weidenfeld and Nicolson, 1972.
Lucas, Noah, *A Modern History of Israel*, London, Weidenfeld and
Nicolson, 1974.

SELECT BIBLIOGRAPHY

The Literature of Judaism

General Surveys

Waxman, Meyer, *A History of Jewish Literature* (first published 1938 *et seq.*), second edition, 5 volumes, New York, Bloch Publishing Company, 1960.

Holtz, Barry W. (ed.), *Back to the Sources*, New York, Summit Books, 1984.

Bible

Eissfeldt, Otto, *The Old Testament: An Introduction* (first published in German in 1934), tr. Peter R. Ackroyd, New York and Evanston, Harper and Row, 1965.

Fohrer, Georg, *Introduction to the Old Testament* (first published in German in 1965), tr. David Green, London, S.P.C.K., 1984.

Sandmel, Samuel, *The Hebrew Scriptures*, New York, Alfred A. Knopf, 1963.

Post-biblical

Nickelsburg, George W. E., *Jewish Literature between the Bible and the Mishnah*, London, S.C.M. Press, 1981.

Strack, Hermann L., *Introduction to the Talmud and the Midrash* (first published 1887), Philadelphia, Jewish Publication Society of America, 1945.

Freehof, Solomon B., *The Responsa Literature*, Philadelphia, Jewish Publication Society of America, 1955.

The Theory of Judaism

General Surveys

Jacobs, Louis, *A Jewish Theology*, London, Darton, Longman and Todd, 1973.

Kohler, Kaufmann, *Jewish Theology, Systematically and Historically Considered*, Cincinnati, Riverdale Press, 1943.

Guttman, Julius, *Philosophies of Judaism, The History of Jewish Philosophy from Biblical Times to Franz Rosenzweig* (first published in German in 1933), Introduction by R. J. Zwi Werblowsky, tr. David W. Silverman, London, Routledge and Kegan Paul, 1964.

Particular Periods

Von Rad, Gerhard, *Old Testament Theology* (first published in German in 1957), translated by D. M. G. Stalker, 2 volumes, London, S.C.M. Press, 1975.

Moore, George Foot, *Judaism in the First Centuries of the Christian Era*, 3 volumes, Cambridge, Mass., Harvard University Press, 1927–30.

SELECT BIBLIOGRAPHY

Husik, Isaac, *A History of Mediaeval Jewish Philosophy*, Philadelphia, Jewish Publication Society of America, 1946.

Scholem, Gershom G., *Major Trends in Jewish Mysticism* (first published in 1941), New York, Schocken Books, 1961.

Kaufman, William E., *Contemporary Jewish Philosophies*, New York, Behrman House, 1976.

The Practice of Judaism

General Surveys

Bloch, Abraham P., *The Biblical and Historical Background of Jewish Customs and Ceremonies*, New York, Ktav Publishing House, 1980.

Klein, Isaac, *A Guide to Jewish Religious Practice*, New York, Jewish Theological Seminary of America, 1979.

Freehof, Solomon B., *Reform Jewish Practice and its Rabbinic Background*, New York, Union of American Hebrew Congregations, 1963.

Particular Aspects

Mattuck, Israel I., *Jewish Ethics*, London, Hutchinson's University Library, 1953.

Idelsohn, A. Z., *Jewish Liturgy and its Development* (first published 1932), New York, Schocken Books, 1967.

Schauss, Hayyim, *The Jewish Festivals* (first published 1938), London, Jewish Chronicle Publications, 1986.

The Lifetime of a Jew, Cincinnati, Union of American Hebrew Congregations, 1950.

Epstein, Louis M., *Marriage Laws in the Bible and Talmud*, Cambridge, Mass., Harvard University Press, 1942.

Lamm, Maurice, *The Jewish Way in Love and Marriage*, San Francisco, Harper and Row, 1980.

The Jewish Way in Death and Mourning, New York, Jonathan David Publishers, 1969.

A SELECTION OF BOOKS RECOMMENDED FOR FURTHER READING

Reference

Werblowsky, R. J. Zwi, and Geoffrey Wigoder, *The Encyclopedia of the Jewish Religion* (first published 1966), London, Phoenix House, 1967.

Jewish History, General Surveys

Bamberger, Bernard J. *The Story of Judaism*, New York, Union of American Hebrew Congregations, 1957.

SELECT BIBLIOGRAPHY

Kedourie, Eli (ed.), *The Jewish World: Revelation, Prophecy, History*, London, Thames and Hudson, 1979.

Eban, Abba, *Heritage: Civilization and the Jews*, London, Weidenfeld and Nicolson, 1984.

De Lange, Nicholas, *Atlas of the Jewish World*, London, Phaidon, 1984.

Jewish History, Particular Periods and Aspects

Alt, Albrecht, *Essays on Old Testament History and Religion*, tr. R. A. Wilson, New York, Doubleday and Company, 1967.

Avi-Yonah, M., *The Jews of Palestine: A Political History from the Bar Kochba War to the Arab Conquest*, New York, Schocken Books, 1976.

Lowenthal, Marvin, *The Jews of Germany: A History of Sixteen Centuries*, Philadelphia, Jewish Publication Society of America, 1938.

Goitein, S. D., *Jews and Arabs: Their Contacts through the Ages* (first published 1964), third revised edition, New York, Schocken Books, 1974.

Weinryb, Bernard D., *The Jews of Poland: A Social and Economic History . . . from 1100 to 1800*, Philadelphia, Jewish Publication Society of America, 1973.

Hertzberg, Arthur, *The French Enlightenment and the Jews*, New York, Columbia University Press, 1968.

Poliakov, Léon, *The History of Anti-Semitism*, Littman Library of Jewish Civilization, tr. Richard Howard, Natalie Gerardi and Miriam Kochan; 3 volumes, London, Routledge and Kegan Paul, 1974–5.

Dawidowicz, Lucy S. (ed.), *The Golden Tradition: Jewish Life and Thought in Eastern Europe*, New York, Holt, Rinehart and Winston, 1966.

Bach, H. I., *The German Jew: A Synthesis of Judaism and Western Civilization 1730–1930*, Littman Library of Jewish Civilization, Oxford, Oxford University Press, 1984.

Mosse, George L., *Germans and Jews*, New York, Grosset and Dunlap, 1970.

Wilson, Stephen, *Ideology and Experience: Anti-Semitism in France at the Time of the Dreyfus Affair*, Littman Library of Jewish Civilization, New Jersey, Associated University Presses, 1982.

Philipson, David, *The Reform Movement in Judaism* (first published 1907), revised edition, New York, Ktav Publishing House, 1967.

Howe, Irving, *The Immigrant Jews of New York: 1881 to the Present*, Littman Library of Jewish Civilization, Oxford, Oxford University Press, 1976.

Dawidowicz, Lucy S., *The War against the Jews, 1933–1945*, New York, Holt, Rinehart and Winston, 1975.

SELECT BIBLIOGRAPHY

Levin, Nora, *The Holocaust: The Destruction of European Jewry, 1933–1945*, New York, Schocken Books, 1973.

Vital, David, *The Origins of Zionism*, Oxford, Oxford University Press, 1975.

Gilbert, Martin, *Exile and Return: The Emergence of Jewish Statehood*, London, Weidenfeld and Nicolson, 1978.

Jewish Literature: Anthologies

Browne, Lewis, *The Wisdom of Israel* (first published 1948), revised edition, London, Michael Joseph, 1955.

Kravitz, Nathaniel, *Three Thousand Years of Hebrew Literature: from the earliest time through the twentieth century*, Chicago, Swallow Press, 1972.

Leviant, Kurt (ed.), *Masterpieces of Hebrew Literature: A Treasury of Two Thousand Years of Jewish Creativity*, New York, Ktav Publishing House, 1969.

Cohen, A., *Everyman's Talmud* (first published 1932), New York, Schocken Books, 1975.

Montefiore, Claude G. and Herbert Loewe, *A Rabbinic Anthology* (first published 1938), New York, Schocken Books, 1974.

Goldstein, David (ed. and tr.), *The Jewish Poets of Spain, 900–1250* (first published 1965), Penguin Books, 1971.

Carmi, T. (ed.), *The Penguin Book of Hebrew Verse*, Penguin Books, 1981.

Kobler, Franz (ed.), *Letters of Jews through the Ages*, 2 volumes, London, Ararat Publishing Society with East and West Library, 1952.

Freehof, Solomon B., *A Treasury of Responsa*, Philadelphia, Jewish Publication Society of America, 1963.

Twersky, Isadore (ed.), *A Maimonides Reader*, New York, Behrman House, 1972.

Newman, Louis I., with Samuel Spitz (trs. and eds.), *The Hasidic Anthology*, New York, Bloch Publishing Company, 1944.

Friedlander, Albert H. (ed.), *Out of the Whirlwind, A Reader of Holocaust Literature* (first published 1968), New York, Schocken Books, 1976.

The Theory of Judaism

Baeck, Leo, *The Essence of Judaism* (first published in German in 1905), revised edition, rendition by Irving Howe based on translation by Victor Grubenwieser and Leonard Pearl, New York, Schocken Paperbacks, 1961.

Schechter, Solomon, *Aspects of Rabbinic Theology* (first published 1909), New York, Schocken Books, 1961.

Baab, Otto J., *The Theology of the Old Testament*, New York and Nashville, Abingdon Press, 1949.

Mattuck, Israel I., *The Thought of the Prophets*, London, George Allen and Unwin, 1953.

Heschel, Abraham Joshua, *Man is Not Alone: A Philosophy of Religion*, New York, Farrar, Straus and Giroux, 1951.

God in Search of Man: A Philosophy of Judaism, New York, Farrar, Straus and Giroux, 1955.

Epstein, Isidore, *The Faith of Judaism* (first published 1954), London, Soncino Press, 1968.

Herberg, Will (ed.), *The Writings of Martin Buber*, New York, Meridian Press, 1956.

Silver, Abba Hillel, *Where Judaism Differed, An Inquiry into the Distinctiveness of Judaism*, New York, Macmillan Company, 1956.

Jacobs, Louis, *Principles of the Jewish Faith*, London, Vallentine Mitchell, 1964.

Glatzer, Nahum N., *Franz Rosenzweig: His Life and Thought*, New York, Schocken Books, 1961.

Friedlander, Albert H., *Leo Baeck, Teacher of Theresienstadt*, Littman Library of Jewish Civilization, London, Routledge and Kegan Paul, 1968.

Glatzer, Nahum N., *Modern Jewish Thought, A Source Reader*, New York, Schocken Books, 1977.

Berkovits, Eliezer, *Major Themes in Modern Philosophies of Judaism*, New York, Ktav Publishing House, 1974.

Borowitz, Eugene B., *Liberal Judaism*, New York, Union of American Hebrew Congregations, 1984.

The Practice of Judaism

Kellner, Menachem Marc (ed.), *Contemporary Jewish Ethics*, New York, Sanhedrin Press, 1978.

Spero, Shubert, *Morality, Halakha and the Jewish Tradition*, New York, Ktav Publishing House and Yeshiva University Press, 1983.

Jakobovits, Immanuel, *Jewish Medical Ethics* (first published 1959), New York, Bloch Publishing Company, 1975.

Rosner, Fred, and J. David Bleich, *Jewish Bioethics*, New York, Hebrew Publishing Company, 1979.

Gaster, Theodor H., *Festivals of the Jewish Year*, New York, William Sloane Associates, 1952.

The Holy and the Profane, New York, William Sloane Associates, 1955.

Grunfeld, Isidore, *The Jewish Dietary Laws*, 2 volumes, London, Jerusalem and New York, Soncino Press, 1972.

Eichhorn, David Max (ed.), *Conversion to Judaism: A History and Analysis*, New York, Ktav Publishing House, 1965.

Feldman, David M., *Birth Control in Jewish Law*, New York University Press and University of London Press Limited, 1968.

INDEX